Germany
1848–1991

Derrick Murphy ■ **Terry Morris** ■ **Mary Fulbrook**

pg 40 - 50

pg 46 - 56

Unification of Germany by 1871 was the
result of foresight and careful planning
by Bismarck? How far do you agree?

Collins

Published by Collins
An imprint of
HarperCollinsPublishers
77–85 Fulham Palace Road
Hammersmith
London
W6 8JB

Browse the complete Collins
catalogue at
www.collinseducation.com

ISBN-13 978 0 00 726866 5

British Library Cataloguing in
Publication Data
A Catalogue record for this
publication is available from the
British Library

Edited by Graham Bradbury
Commissioned by Michael
Upchurch
Design and typesetting by Derek Lee
Cover design by Joerg
Hartmannsgruber, White-card
Map Artwork by Tony Richardson
Picture research by Celia Dearing
and Michael Upchurch
Production by Simon Moore
Indexed by Christine Bernstein
Printed and bound by Printing
Express Ltd, Hong Kong

ACKNOWLEDGEMENTS
Every effort had been made to
contact the holders of copyright
material, but if any have been
inadvertently overlooked the
publishers will be pleased to make
the necessary arrangements at the
first opportunity.

Berg Publishers for extract from *The
German Empire 1871–1918* by Hans-
Ulrich Wehler (1985).
HarperCollins Publishers Ltd for an
extract from *The Fontana History of
Germany 1780–1918: The Long 19th
Century* by David Blackbourn
(1997). Hodder Headline for extract
from *Imperial Germany, 1867–1918:
Politics, Culture and Society in an
Authoritarian State* by Wolfgang
Mommsen (1995); *History of
Germany, 1815–1985* (Hodder
Arnold, 1987). Extracts from *The
War Against the Jews* by Lucy
Davidowicz (Weidenfeld &
Nicholson, 1975) and from *The
German Dictatorship* by Karl Bracher
(Weidenfeld & Nicholson, 1978) by
permission of the Orion Publishing
Group. Oxford University Press for
an extract from *Germany 1866–1945*
by Gordon Craig (1978). Pearson
Education for extracts from
Bismarck and Germany, 1862–90 by
D.G. Williamson (1986); *The Hitler
State* by Martin Broszat (1981); *The
1848 Revolutions* by Peter Jones
(1981); *Imperial Germany,
1890–1918* by Ian Porter and Ian
Armour (1991); *The Weimar
Republic* by John Hiden (Seminar
Studies, 1974); Mark Allinson in
*Contemporary Germany: Essays and
Texts on Politics, Economics and
Society* (Longman Contemporary
Europe Series, 2000). The following
extracts all reproduced by
permission of Penguin Books Ltd:
*The Sword and the Sceptre: The
Problem of Militarism in Germany
Vol. 2* by Gerhard Ritter (Allen Lane,
1972) © Gerhard Ritter 1972; *The
Origins of the Second World War* by
A.J.P. Taylor (Penguin Books, 1961);
*The Course of German History, A
Survey of the Development of
Germany since 1815* by A.J.P. Taylor

(1945); *Bismarck the Man and
Statesman* by A.J.P. Taylor (1968);
Bismarck and the German Empire by
Erich Eyck (1968). Routledge for
extracts from 'Bismarckian Germany'
by Geoff Eley and 'Wilhelmine
Germany' by James Retallack in
*Modern Germany Reconsidered
1879–1945* (1992); *German Foreign
Policy, 1871–1914* by Imanuel Geiss
(1976).

The publishers would like to thank
the following for permission to
reproduce pictures on these pages.
T=Top, B=Bottom, L=Left, R=Right,
C=Centre

akg-images 27, 54, 80, 88, 135, 138,
143, 154, 160, 163, 164, 176, 200,
204, 214, 222; akg-images/ullstein
bild 166, 186, 216, 223;
© Bildarchiv Preussischer
Kulturbesitz, Berlin; © DACS/ The
Bridgeman Art Library 136;
Unknown 118.

Contents

Study and examination skills

This section of the book is designed to aid Sixth Form students in their preparation for public examinations in History.

- Differences between GCSE and Sixth Form History
- Extended writing: the structured question and the essay
- How to handle sources in Sixth Form History
- Historical interpretation
- Progression in Sixth Form History
- Examination technique

Differences between GCSE and Sixth Form History

- The amount of factual knowledge required for answers to Sixth Form History questions is more detailed than at GCSE. Factual knowledge in the Sixth Form is used as supporting evidence to help answer historical questions. Knowing the facts is important, but not as important as knowing that factual knowledge supports historical analysis.

- Extended writing is more important in Sixth Form History. Students will be expected to answer either structured questions or essays.

Structured questions require students to answer more than one question on a given topic. They usually involve studying information from sources.

The first sub-question (a) requires you to engage in source analysis.

This may involve comparing two sources or assessing the value of two sources from a set of four or five sources.

The second sub-question (b) requires you to integrate information from the sources and your own knowledge to answer a specific question.

Each part of the structured question demands a different approach.

An example of this type of question from OCR Specification 'A' AS Paper F964 Option B Study Topic 4 Dictatorship and Democracy in Germany 1933–1963:

a) Compare the information about the Berlin Blockade crisis as mentioned in Source A and Source B.

b) Using your own knowledge, assess the view in the sources that the division of Germany into two states from 1949 was due mainly to the actions of the USSR.

Essay questions require students to produce one answer to a given question.

> *An example from Edexcel AS Unit 1, Option 5 Germany Divided and Reunited 1945–1991:*
>
> 'The main reason for the fall of Honecker in 1989 was the emergence of Gorbachev in the USSR.'
>
> How far do you agree with the statement?

Similarities with GCSE

● **Source analysis and evaluation**
The skills in handling historical sources, which were acquired at GCSE, are developed in Sixth Form History. In the Sixth Form, sources have to be analysed in their historical context, so a good factual knowledge of the subject is important.

● **Historical interpretations**
Skills in historical interpretation at GCSE are also developed in Sixth Form History. The ability to put forward different historical interpretations is important. Students will also be expected to explain why different historical interpretations have occurred.

Extended writing: the structured question and the essay

When faced with extended writing in Sixth Form History students can improve their performance by following a simple routine that attempts to ensure they achieve their best performance.

Answering the question

What are the command instructions?
Different questions require different types of response. For instance, 'In what ways' requires students to point out the various ways something took place in History; 'Why' questions expect students to deal with the causes or consequences of an historical event.

'How far' or 'To what extent' questions require students to produce a balanced, analytical answer. Usually, this will take the form of the case for and the case against an historical question.

Are there key words or phrases that require definition or explanation?
It is important for students to show that they understand the meaning of the question. To do this, certain historical terms or words require explanation. For instance, if a question asked 'how far' a politician was an 'innovator', an explanation of the word 'innovator' would be required.

Does the question have specific dates or issues that require coverage?
If the question mentions specific dates, these must be adhered to. For instance, if you are asked to answer a question on Bismarck it may give specific time limits such as 1871 to 1890. Also questions may mention a specific aspect such as 'domestic policy' or 'foreign affairs'.

Planning your answer

Once you have decided on what the question requires, write a brief plan. For structured questions this may be brief. This is a useful procedure to make sure that you have ordered the information you require for your answer in the most effective way. For instance, in a balanced, analytical answer this may take the form of jotting down the main points for and against an historical issue raised in the question.

Writing the answer

Communication skills

The quality of written English is important in Sixth Form History. The way you present your ideas on paper can affect the quality of your answer. Therefore, punctuation, spelling and grammar, which were awarded marks at GCSE, require close attention. Use a dictionary if you are unsure of a word's meaning or spelling. Use the glossary of terms you will find in this book to help you.

The quality of your written English will not determine the Level of Response you receive for your answer. It may well determine what mark you may receive within a level. To help you understand this point ask your teacher to see a mark scheme published by your examination board. For instance, you may be awarded Level 2 (10–15 marks) by an examiner. The quality of written English may be a factor in deciding which mark you receive in that level. Will it be 10 or 15 or a mark in between?

The introduction

For structured questions you may wish to dispense with an introduction altogether and begin writing reasons to support an answer straight away. However, essay answers should begin with an introduction. These should be both concise and precise. Introductions help 'concentrate the mind' on the question you are about to answer. Remember, do not try to write a conclusion as your opening sentence. Instead, outline briefly the areas you intend to discuss in your answer.

Balancing analysis with factual evidence

It is important to remember that factual knowledge should be used to support analysis. Merely 'telling the story' of an historical event is not enough. A structured question or essay should contain separate paragraphs, each addressing an analytical point that helps to answer the question. If, for example, the question asks for reasons why Hitler became Chancellor each paragraph should provide a reason for Hitler's rise to power in January 1933. In order to support and sustain the analysis evidence is required. Therefore, your factual knowledge should be used to substantiate analysis. Good structured question and essay answers integrate analysis and factual knowledge.

Seeing connections between reasons

In dealing with 'why'-type questions it is important to remember that the reasons for an historical event might be interconnected. Therefore, it is important to mention the connections between reasons. Also, it might be important to identify a hierarchy of reasons – that is, are some reasons more important than others in explaining an historical event?

Using quotations and statistical data

One aspect of supporting evidence that sustains analysis is the use of quotations. These can be from either a historian or a contemporary. However, unless these quotations are linked with analysis and supporting evidence, they tend to be of little value.

It can also be useful to support analysis with statistical data. In questions that deal with social and economic change, precise statistics that support your argument can be very persuasive.

The conclusion

All structured questions and essays require conclusions. If, for example, a question requires a discussion of 'how far' you agree with a question, you should offer a judgement in your conclusion. Don't be afraid of this – say what you think. If you write an analytical answer, ably supported by factual evidence, you may under-perform because you have not provided a conclusion that deals directly with the question.

Source analysis

Source analysis forms an integral part of the study of History.

In dealing with sources you should be aware that historical sources must be used 'in historical context' in Sixth Form History. This means you must understand the historical topic to which the source refers. Therefore, in this book sources are used with the factual information in each chapter. Also, specific source analysis questions are included at the end of most chapters.

How to handle sources in Sixth Form History

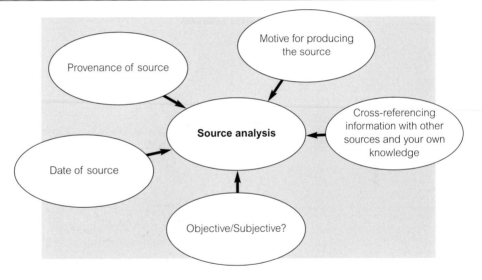

In dealing with sources, a number of basic hints will allow you to deal effectively with source-based questions and to build on your knowledge and skill in using sources at GCSE.

Written sources

Attribution or Provenance and date

It is important to identify who has written the source and when it was written. This information can be very important. If, for instance, a source was written by Otto von Bismarck, this information will be of considerable importance if you are asked about the usefulness (utility) or reliability of the source as evidence of Prussian/German government views at the time.

It is important to note that just because a source is a primary source does not mean it is more useful or less reliable than a secondary source. Both primary and secondary sources need to be analysed to decide how useful and reliable they are. This can be determined by studying other issues.

Is the content factual or opinionated?

Once you have identified the author and date of the source, it is important to study its content. The content may be factual, stating what has happened or what may happen. On the other hand, it may contain opinions that should be handled with caution. These may contain bias. Even if a source is mainly factual, there might be important and deliberate gaps in factual evidence that can make a source biased and unreliable. Usually, written sources contain elements of both opinion and factual evidence. It is important to judge the balance between these two parts.

Has the source been written for a particular audience?

To determine the reliability of a source it is important to know to whom it is directed. For instance, a public speech may be made to achieve a particular purpose and may not contain the author's true beliefs or feelings. In contrast, a private diary entry may be much more reliable in this respect.

Corroborative evidence

To test whether or not a source is reliable, the use of other evidence to support or corroborate the information it contains is important. Cross-referencing with other sources is a way of achieving this; so is cross-referencing with historical information contained within a chapter.

Visual sources

Cartoons

Cartoons are a popular form of source used at both GCSE and in Sixth Form History. However, analysing cartoons can be a demanding exercise. Not only will you be expected to understand the content of the cartoon, you may also have to explain a written caption – which appears usually at the bottom of the cartoon. In addition, cartoons will need placing in historical context. Therefore, a good knowledge of the subject matter of the topic of the cartoon will be important.

Photographs

'The camera never lies'! This phrase is not always true. When analysing photographs, study the attribution/provenance and date. Photographs can be changed so they are not always an accurate visual representation of events. Also, to test whether or not a photograph is a good representation of events you will need corroborative evidence.

Maps

Maps which appear in Sixth Form History are predominantly secondary sources. These are used to support factual coverage in the text by providing information in a different medium. Therefore, to assess whether or not information contained in maps is accurate or useful, reference should be made to other information. It is also important with written sources to check the attribution and date. These could be significant.

Statistical data and graphs

It is important when dealing with this type of source to check carefully the nature of the information contained in data or in a graph. It might state that the information is in tons (tonnes) or another measurement. Be careful to check if the information is in index numbers. These are a statistical device where a base year is chosen and given the figure 100. All other figures are based on a percentage difference from that base year.

An important point to remember when dealing with data and graphs over a period of time is to identify trends and patterns in the information. Merely describing the information in written form is not enough.

Historical interpretation

An important feature of both GCSE and Sixth Form History is the issue of historical interpretation. In Sixth Form History it is important for students to be able to explain why historians differ, or have differed, in their interpretation of the past.

Availability of evidence

An important reason is the availability of evidence on which to base historical judgements. As new evidence comes to light, an historian today may have more information on which to base judgements than historians in the past.

'A philosophy of history?'

Many historians have a specific view of history that will affect the way they make their historical judgements. For instance, Marxist historians – who take the view from the writings of Karl Marx the founder of modern socialism – believe that society has been made up of competing economic and social classes. They also place considerable importance on economic reasons in human decision making. Therefore, a Marxist historian of Bismarck's Germany may take a completely different viewpoint to a non-Marxist historian.

The role of the individual

Some historians have seen past history as being moulded by the acts of specific individuals who have changed history. Bismarck, William II and Hitler are seen as individuals whose personality and beliefs changed the course of 19th-20th century German history. Other historians have tended to 'downplay' the role of individuals; instead, they highlight the importance of more general social, economic and political change.

Placing different emphasis on the same historical evidence

Even if historians do not possess different philosophies of history or place different emphasis on the role of the individual, it is still possible for them to disagree because they place different emphases on aspects of the same factual evidence. As a result, Sixth Form History should be seen as a subject that encourages debate about the past based on historical evidence.

Progression in Sixth Form History

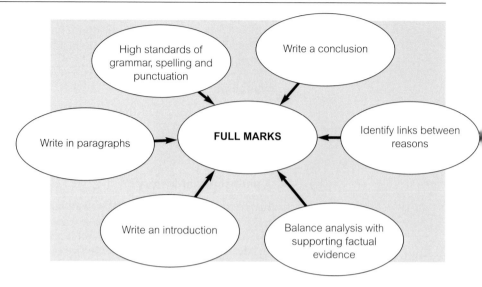

The ability to achieve high standards in Sixth Form History involves the acquisition of a number of skills:

● Good written communication skills

● Acquiring a sound factual knowledge

● Evaluating factual evidence and making historical conclusions based on that evidence

● Source analysis

● Understanding the nature of historical interpretation

● Understanding the causes and consequences of historical events

● Understanding themes in history which will involve a study of a specific topic over a long period of time

● Understanding the ideas of change and continuity associated with themes.

Students should be aware that the acquisition of these skills will take place gradually over the time spent in the Sixth Form. At the beginning of the course, the main emphasis may be on the acquisition of factual knowledge, particularly when the body of knowledge studied at GCSE was different.

When dealing with causation, students will have to build on their skills from GCSE. They will not only be expected to identify reasons for an historical event but also to provide a hierarchy of causes. They should identify the main causes and less important causes. They may also identify that causes may be interconnected and linked. Progression in Sixth Form History will come with answering the questions at the end of each sub-section in this book and practising the skills outlined through the use of the factual knowledge contained in the book.

Examination technique

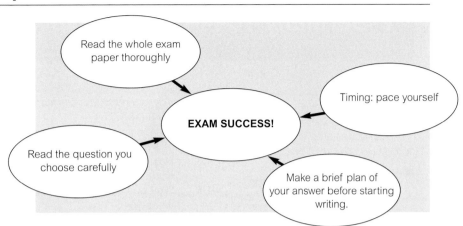

The ultimate challenge for any Sixth Form historian is the ability to produce quality work under examination conditions. Examinations will take the form of either modular examinations taken in January and June or an 'end of course' set of examinations.

Here is some advice on how to improve your performance in an examination.

- Read the whole examination paper thoroughly
  Make sure that the questions you choose are those for which you can produce a good answer. Don't rush – allow time to decide which questions to choose. It is probably too late to change your mind half way through answering a question.

- Read the question very carefully
  Once you have made the decision to answer a specific question, read it very carefully. Make sure you understand the precise demands of the question. Think about what is required in your answer. It is much better to think about this before you start writing, rather than trying to steer your essay in a different direction half way through.

- Make a brief plan
  Sketch out what you intend to include in your answer. Order the points you want to make. Examiners are not impressed with additional information included at the end of the essay, with indicators such as arrows or asterisks.

- Pace yourself as you write
  Success in examinations has a lot to do with successful time management. If, for instance, you have to answer an essay question in approximately 45 minutes, then you should be one-third of the way through after 15 minutes. With 30 minutes gone, you should start writing the last third of your answer.

Where a question is divided into sub-questions, make sure you look at the mark tariff for each question. If in a 20-mark question a sub-question is worth a maximum of 5 marks, then you should spend approximately one-quarter of the time allocated for the whole question on this sub-question.

Revision tips

Even before the examination begins make sure that you have revised thoroughly. Revision tips on the main topics in this book appear on the Collins website:

www.collinseducation.com

1 Germany 1848–1991: A synoptic overview

Key Issues

- Did Germany follow a special path (*Sonderweg*) in its political development between 1848 and 1991?

- How significant were individual leaders in the development of Germany from 1848–1991?

- How did German nationalism change in the period 1848 to 1991?

1.1 How and why was Germany unified in the period 1848–1871?

1.2 What impact did the German Empire have on European affairs between 1871 and 1918?

1.3 How and why did Germany change from democracy to dictatorship in the years 1918–1945?

1.4 Why was Germany divided and then later reunified in the years 1945–1991?

Great Powers: Name given to the most powerful military states in Europe. Between 1815 and 1914 there were five Great Powers: Britain, France, Russia, Austria, and Prussia/Germany.

Confederation: A loose political grouping of states. The German states were independent but they sent representatives to a 'Diet' in Frankfurt.

Kaiser: Emperor, especially the German emperor; a ruler superior to kings.

BETWEEN 1848 and 1991 Germany was an area central to the development of European history. In the early part of this period, from 1848 to 1871, Germany was unified into one state, the German Empire. This was achieved under the leadership of the German state, Prussia, through three wars between 1864 and 1871. In the process, Prussia defeated two of Europe's **Great Powers**, Austria and France.

By 1871 Germany had been transformed from a loose **confederation** of thirty-nine states into the greatest continental power. From 1871 to 1945, German affairs dominated European history. From 1871 to 1914, Germany developed rapidly as an economic power. By 1914 it was able to rival Britain and the USA as one of the world's great economies. The German Empire was also Europe's greatest military power. Under the Chancellorship of Otto von Bismarck (1871–1890) Germany did not exploit to the full its enormous military and economic potential. However, from the mid-1890s, under the influence of **Kaiser** William II, Germany embarked on a programme which aimed to make the German Empire a world power. This policy, *Weltpolitik*, launched Germany into a period of growing conflict with other Great Powers, most notably Britain.

By 1912 Germany, instead of reaching world power status, was faced by the opposition of France, Russia and Britain, which had formed an alliance (the Franco-Russian Alliance) and made general agreements, known as ententes, between themselves.

Much historical controversy surrounds the outbreak of world war in July/August 1914. However, many historians, several of them German, believe that Germany was willing to risk a major war in order to achieve its aims under *Weltpolitik*. Germany twice came close to winning the subsequent war – in 1914, and again in 1918. However, instead of achieving *Weltpolitik*, the German Empire collapsed into revolution in October/November 1918. The Kaiser was overthrown and a democratic republic was declared.

The German experiment with democracy lasted from 1918 to 1933. Unfortunately, it was closely associated with the Treaty of Versailles, the humiliating peace treaty that ended the First World War. Also, many political groups on the right of German politics never accepted fully the belief that Germany had been defeated militarily in the war. When the world was plunged into a major economic depression from 1929, German democracy collapsed into extremism, attacked from the left by communists and from the right by the Nazi Party.

In January 1933 the beginning of the end of German democracy occurred when the Nazi leader, Adolf Hitler, was asked to lead a right-wing coalition government. Within 18 months of taking power Hitler had created a Nazi **dictatorship**.

Dictatorship: A form of government where the ruler has complete power.

To some historians Hitler's dictatorship, from 1933 to 1945, was a unique period of German history. Hitler's decisions to launch a war of European conquest – and the Holocaust against Jews and Gypsies – plunged the world into another major war which resulted in the deaths of approximately 60 million people. However, other historians see Hitler following similar foreign policy objectives to the German Empire's *Weltpolitik*. To these historians, the whole 1914 to 1945 period was characterised by the 'German wars', when Germany attempted to achieve European domination through military means.

By 1945, German military and economic power was in ruins. In place of Germany, Europe was dominated by two superpowers, the USSR and USA. From 1945 to 1991 these two superpowers decided Germany's destiny.

And as a cold war developed between the superpowers, from 1945, Germany became the centre of their conflict. As a result, in 1949 two German states, one communist and one non-communist, were created. From 1949 to 1989 these two states followed completely different paths of development. The Federal Republic of Germany (FRG) became a prosperous non-communist state. The German Democratic Republic (GDR) was closely modelled on the Soviet Union. When Soviet power began to collapse across eastern Europe in 1989 the GDR began to crumble. In 1989 the communist regime was overthrown. By the end of 1990 the former GDR was absorbed into a federal German state.

1. Produce a timeline of the history of Germany from 1848 to 1991. Include what you regard as the ten most important events in German history.

1.1 How and why was Germany unified in the period 1848–1871?

Perhaps the most significant development in European history between the defeat of Napoleon in 1815 and the outbreak of the First World War in 1914 was the unification of Germany. In January 1848 the German area was a loose confederation of thirty-nine states. These ranged from lesser states no bigger than a small English county to two Great Powers, Prussia and the Austrian Empire. To complicate matters further, parts of both Prussia and Austria were outside the German Confederation.

In European history, 1848 was the year of revolutions. Beginning in France in February, most of central Europe was engulfed in revolutions. These revolutions aimed to replace the autocratic rule of monarchs with government where political power was shared with the liberal middle class – the businessmen, lawyers, doctors and teachers. In March, both Austria and Germany faced '**liberal**' revolutions. From March 1848 until early 1849 the two German Great Powers were paralysed by revolution. In this climate a group of liberals met in Frankfurt in an attempt to unite

Liberal: Wanting political power to be shared between a ruler and an elected parliament.

Frankfurt Parliament: The liberal assembly which contained representatives from across Germany. It met from 1848 to 1849.

Germany by consent. The **Frankfurt Parliament** lasted only as long as it took Austria and Prussia to return to political stability. Once this had occurred, in 1849, the Frankfurt Parliament was dissolved. The attempt to unite Germany by liberals had failed.

Unification was achieved, instead, because of the rivalry between Austria and Prussia about which state should dominate Germany. The two states had been political rivals since 1740, and in the 1860s this rivalry came to a head. Prussian Minister-President, Bismarck, attempted to make Prussia co-equal in power with Austria within the German Confederation. When Austria refused, a war took place, which lasted seven weeks in 1866. Prussia was victorious and dissolved the German Confederation, creating, in its place, a 'North German Confederation' under Prussian leadership.

Balance of power: Idea that no one Great Power should become so powerful that it could dominate Europe.

This development altered fundamentally the **balance of power** in central Europe. In an attempt to rectify this change, France, under Napoleon III, went to war with Prussia in 1870. The Franco-Prussian War was another spectacular success for the Prussian army. As the war came to a close, the 'German Empire' was declared in January 1871. It comprised all the German states, except Austria.

To some historians, the unification of Germany was more to do with Prussian domination over the rest of Germany than a genuine unification of the German nation. In this process Bismarck was seen as a master politician who was the architect of unification. To other historians, Bismarck was only one part of the process. Prussian success was due more to its rapid industrial growth and the prowess of the Prussian army. Also, the process of unification saw a genuine outpouring of German national feeling. In the new German Empire Bismarck's biggest supporter was the National Liberal Party.

1. Why did the 1848 revolutions in Germany fail?

2. How important was Bismarck in the unification of Germany?

1.2 What impact did the German Empire have on European affairs between 1871 and 1918?

Federal: A political arrangement where responsibility for government is split between a central government and the states. In Germany after 1871 states had responsibility for internal law and order, education and welfare. Bavaria also controlled its own railways, issued its own stamps and controlled its own army in peacetime.

The German Empire, created in 1871, was dominated by Prussia, which comprised two-thirds of the new empire. The Prussian king was German emperor. The centres of economic power, the Ruhr and Upper Silesia were also in Prussia. However, the empire had a **federal** structure, and individual states such as Bavaria retained considerable political power.

The German Empire had become the greatest of the European powers. From 1871 to 1890, under Bismarck, Germany dominated European affairs. However, the German Empire also faced major problems. Germany was ruled by an economic class of large landowners from eastern Prussia, who dominated both the government and the army. This group ruled a country which was going through a process of rapid industrialization This made Germany's development different from other industrialising states in Europe and North America. In this sense, Germany followed its own special way (*Sonderweg*) of political development. As a result, huge cities were created, containing a large industrial working class. Although ruled by landowners, the German national parliament – the Reichstag – had a democratic **franchise**. From 1875 to 1914 the industrial working class increasingly voted for the Social Democrat Party (SPD), the German Socialist Party, which wanted fundamental political, social and economic change.

Franchise: The right to vote.

The German Empire was also a state which had the potential to dominate Europe. Under Bismarck, from 1870 to 1890, Germany never exploited this potential. However, under Kaiser Wilhelm II (1888–1918) Germany embarked on a course which aimed to make Germany a world power, like Britain. By 1914 Germany's aggressive foreign policy had so alarmed other

European Great Powers that three of them, France, Britain and Russia formed agreements to support each other. Only Austria–Hungary remained a German ally amongst the Great Powers.

By 1914 the German Empire seemed to be facing two crises. One was domestic – the fear of the SDP – and in foreign affairs Germany wanted to be a world power. Both these problems helped propel Germany into world war in 1914. The 1914–1918 war was a German attempt to solve these problems. When Germany faced defeat, in the autumn of 1918, the Empire collapsed amid demonstrations within Germany. The Kaiser fled to Holland and a democratic republic was declared.

1. What impact did the reign of Kaiser Wilhelm II have on the German Empire?

1.3 How and why did Germany change from democracy to dictatorship in the years 1918–1945?

Weimar: The city in central Germany where the democratic constitution was produced.

The creation of German democracy, in the **Weimar** Republic, was born out of military defeat and the national humiliation of the Treaty of Versailles in 1919. In the treaty Germany was forced to accept responsibility for starting the war and had to pay enormous war reparations.

From 1919 to 1924 the Weimar Republic faced attempts from communists and extreme nationalists to overthrow it. It also faced massive economic problems. However, from 1924 to 1929 German democracy seemed to have survived its baptism of fire. Yet, following the **Wall Street** Crash in the USA, Germany plunged into a period of political and economic crisis, which led to its collapse by January 1933.

Wall Street: The home of the New York Stock Exchange in the USA.

Throughout the short life of the Weimar Republic it had support from the Social Democrat Party (SDP), the Catholic Centre Party and the Liberals (FDP). However, it also faced immense opposition – the armed forces were never reconciled to democracy, nor were the civil service or judiciary. It was also openly opposed by several large political groups such as the communists, the Nazis and the DNVP (right-wing nationalists). By 1933, after four years of political and economic turmoil, contemporaries expected the Republic to be replaced by some form of **authoritarian** government, either extreme left or extreme right. In the end, just when his electoral success seemed to be declining, Adolf Hitler was invited by President Hindenburg to lead a right-wing coalition government in which the Nazis were a minority. It was Hitler's genius to turn this precarious position into one of personal dictatorship within 18 months.

Authoritarian: Dictatorial, undemocratic.

Nazi rule, from 1933 to 1945, launched Germany into a disaster. At home, a totalitarian dictatorship was established. Hitler's aggressive foreign policy led to world war. At the height of the war the German state launched one of the greatest human rights crimes in world history – the Holocaust. Hitler had once declared that 'Germany would be a world power or there would be no Germany.' By the time of his suicide in April 1945 the German state had all but ceased to exist, and the country lay in ruins.

1. Give two reasons why the Weimar Republic lasted such a short time.

2. How important was Hitler's rule for Germany?

Was Hitler's rule a freak accident of history, created by the abnormal circumstances of 1929–1933? Or was he merely following traditional German foreign policy aims? Since the 1960s many German historians have come to the conclusion that Hitler's rule was the result of Germany's special path (*Sonderweg*) of development.

1.4 Why was Germany divided and then later reunified in the years 1945–1991?

The history of post-war Germany, up to 1991, was the history of the Cold War in Europe. From 1945 to the 1990s Germany was militarily occupied by the wartime allies, the USSR, the USA, Britain and France. Once the USSR and USA began to disagree about post-war Europe, Germany became their 'battleground'. The Berlin Blockade crisis of 1948–1949 was the first serious post-war confrontation between the USSR and the USA. It led directly to the creation in 1949 of two separate German states: the Federal Republic of Germany (FRG)in the west, and the German Democratic Republic (GDR) in the east. The two states had political and economic systems which mirrored the Cold War confrontation of East versus West. The GDR became a communist state on the Soviet model. The FRG became non-communist and democratic.

From 1949 to 1989 the FRG developed a highly successful economy with strong democratic institutions. In its achievement of this status two

Reunited Germany in 1991.

German politicians stand out. Konrad Adenauer was Chancellor of the FRG from 1949 to 1963, and created the political foundations of the state. Ludwig Erhard was Adenauer's Economics Minister and then his successor (1963–1966). He was responsible for the FRG's rapid economic recovery in the 1950s, the so-called German 'economic miracle'.

Two politicians also dominated the GDR's history. Walter Ulbricht was leader from 1949 to 1971 and Erich Honecker from 1971 to 1989. Both ensured that the GDR would be a model communist state.

When the GDR collapsed, in 1989, it was part of a wider process of the collapse of Soviet control over eastern Europe. In the second half of 1989 communist regimes fell in Hungary, Poland, Romania, Bulgaria and Czechoslovakia, as well as the GDR.

By the end of 1989, communist rule in Europe was coming to an end. 'Would there be two democratic German states or one?' was the main issue of debate at the beginning of 1990. The person who drove the two German states towards reunification was FRG Chancellor Helmut Kohl. Kohl worked hard to persuade the citizens of the GDR to accept reunification in early 1990. He also worked hard to persuade the four wartime allies to accept a united Germany. By October 1990 Kohl had achieved the reunification of Germany, peacefully, through negotiation and international agreement. In reality, the FRG absorbed the GDR into a federal German state.

1. In what ways did the Cold War in Europe affect German history from 1945 to 1991?

Thematic questions

1. How important were Bismarck, Wilhelm II, Hitler and Adenauer to the development of Germany? Of these four, who do you think was the most important in German history from 1848 to 1991?

2. Why do you think some historians regard Germany's political development as following a special path (*Sonderweg*) in this period?

Further Reading

The Fontana History of Germany 1780–1918; the Long Nineteenth Century by David Blackbourn (Fontana, Harper Collins, 1997) provides an excellent introduction to recent work on German history in this period.
Germany 1866–1945 by Gordon Craig (Oxford University Press, 1978)

2 The revolutions of 1848 and 1849 in Germany

Key Issues

- What were the short-term causes of the revolutions?

- What projects for political and social reform were put forward inGermany?

- Why did the revolutions collapse so suddenly in the course of 1848–49?

2.1 What role was played by economic factors in making 1848 a 'year of revolutions'?

2.2 Why did the movement for liberal reform achieve such success in Germany, and then collapse so rapidly?

2.3 In what respects was the crisis in the Austrian Empire more dangerous than in other parts of Europe?

2.4 How was the Austrian government able to re-establish its authority?

Framework of Events

1848	January: Revolt in Palermo, Sicily
	February: Abdication of Louis Philippe and proclamation of the Second Republic in France
	March: Resignation of Metternich. Violence in Berlin. War between Piedmont and Austria.
	May: First meeting of the Frankfurt Parliament
	June: Meeting of Pan-Slav Congress in Prague. Cavaignac suppresses insurrection in Paris. Windischgrätz bombards Prague
	July: Meeting of Constituent Assembly in Vienna
	October: Windischgrätz occupies Vienna
1849	March: Dissolution of the Austrian Constituent Assembly. Defeat of Piedmontese at Novara
	April: Friedrich Wilhelm IV refuses the offer of the German Crown
	August: Hungarian rebels surrender to Austrian and Russian troops.

Overview

Socio-economic crisis: A state of unrest that is caused by social and economic factors (such as unemployment and high bread prices), rather than by political events or ideas.

In the mid-1840s, the political tensions that beset the governments of Europe were compounded by a complex **socio-economic crisis**. In many parts of Europe these strains, caused by unemployment and high food prices, provoked angry urban demonstrations that added to the intellectual discontent of the middle classes. A combination of various crises led to a temporary conjunction of opposition interests, united in hostility to the governing classes of these states, but for many different reasons. Faced with a groundswell of revolt apparently as broadly based as the one that had brought down the French monarchy in 1789–92, many European governors saw flight, surrender or compromise as the safest course.

In the early months of 1848, it appeared that the politics of western Europe had been transformed by an upheaval that had no precedent in terms of extent or impact. Within a year, however, it was becoming clear that the liberal and radical movements of 1848 had brought about relatively little lasting change. In part, this was due to the incoherence of the 'revolutionary' groups. The political interests of middle-class liberals rarely coincided with the more fundamental, material requirements of unemployed workers. It had often been possible for liberals in one state to establish common ground with those in neighbouring states in terms of their constitutional demands. Yet, in 1848, this community of political interests was often cancelled out by conflicts between the nationalist demands that often accompanied progressive constitutional ideas. The most important element of all in the failure of the revolutions lay in the enduring strength of the governmental systems that they appeared to have overthrown. The economic crises affected the populations of Europe far more seriously than they affected the regimes. These retained the resources, and in particular the military strength, to survive. Above all, while individuals such as Metternich abandoned their posts, the governing classes, in general, still had the will to survive. In such men as Franz Josef in Austria, they found new leaders, who were largely willing to preserve the political bases of the pre-1848 regimes.

The revolutions did leave behind certain achievements. Prussia retained its constitutions that its rulers could not easily ignore. Feudal obligations were abolished in parts of eastern Europe, never to return. It is tempting to conclude, however, that the main beneficiaries of the 1848 revolutions were, in fact, the governing conservatives. After many years of living in fear of liberal revolt, they had now confronted it and survived. It was they, rather than the liberals, who emerged strengthened by the 'Year of Revolutions'. The next 60 years of German history were to be dominated by conservative governments, confident in their own power, and confident in their ability to harness and control the forces that once seemed such a threat to them.

It is just possible, however, that the confidence of the conservatives was misplaced in the long term. There can be little doubt that the events of 1848–49 brought profound disappointment for liberals and nationalists across Europe, yet their causes did not perish. Within 20 years, the ambitions of moderate nationalists in Germany had been realised. Conservative leaders – forced to adopt and to adapt the programmes of groups whose ideologies were too popular, and who had too great an economic impetus behind them to be resisted – had unified both states. Hungarian nationalists, also, proved too influential to be ignored by an Imperial regime that had learned few lessons from the events of 1848. In terms of purely political power, European liberals had less cause for satisfaction 20 or 30 years on. Their economic agenda, however, had proved less easy to ignore. Bismarck's Germany, in the 1870s and the 1880s, provides a prime example of a state embracing many of the economic priorities of the industrial middle classes, even as it strove to exclude them from direct political power. There can be little serious doubt, therefore, that the would-be revolutionaries of 1848 acted prematurely and sought to exploit a 'revolutionary situation' that did not really exist. The events of this 'year of revolutions', on the other hand, provided a clear indication of the evolutionary direction that European politics were following.

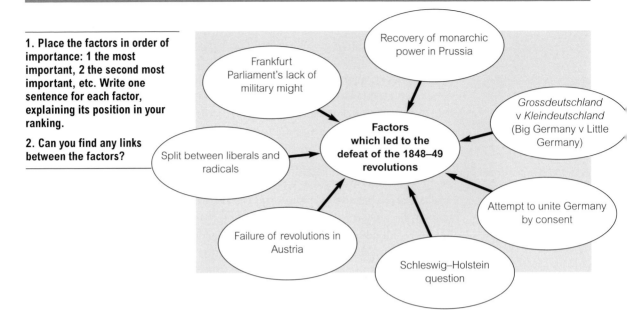

1. Place the factors in order of importance: 1 the most important, 2 the second most important, etc. Write one sentence for each factor, explaining its position in your ranking.

2. Can you find any links between the factors?

2.1 What role was played by economic factors in making 1848 a 'year of revolutions'?

The traditional forms of European society had been under pressure from economic and demographic changes for some time before 1840. The years between 1845 and 1847, however, formed a particularly severe phase of this crisis. The revolts resulted not from one crisis, but from a conjunction of several. A particularly acute agricultural crisis coincided with a newer kind of crisis, an industrial slump. The infant industrial economies of Europe had less experience of this and it gave special urgency to the political problems of the individual European states.

Agricultural crisis

European agriculture entered an acute crisis in 1845. The potato blight of that year had its most dramatic impact in Ireland, where it eventually accounted for the loss of up to a million human lives. The failure of the crop also cut a swathe of hunger and suffering across Germany. The following year, the unusually hot, dry weather caused the failure of the grain harvest. As the failures continued, it became impossible to make good the shortfall from the surplus of the previous harvest. Throughout Europe, there were sudden, steep price rises. In Hamburg the price of wheat rose 51.8% between 1841 and 1847, 70% of that increase occurring in the period 1845–47. In Switzerland, the price of rye doubled in the same two years, and bread prices doubled in the single year 1846/47. Even when imports of foreign grain were feasible, the incomplete state of most European railway systems made its passage to many parts of the continent impossible.

Industrial crisis

The years 1845–47 also saw the most severe of the industrial crises that had hit Europe at intervals of roughly ten years since the end of the Napoleonic wars. Partly, this was a crisis of overproduction, in which manufacturers, finding that they had saturated the markets available to them, cut back production and thus created unemployment or wage reductions. In Germany, the amount of spun yarn exported by the member states of the *Zollverein* fell by 40% in 1844–47. The crisis was aggravated by the impact of factory production, in some parts of Europe, upon older forms of production in other areas. The hostility shown by skilled craftsmen and artisans to factories, mills, railways and their owners, in 1848, clearly indicated what they thought to be the origins of their suffering.

The industrial crisis was closely linked to the agricultural crisis for, in many localities, the need to use government and bankers' funds to buy large quantities of foreign corn left little or nothing for investment in industry. Bankruptcies multiplied, and business confidence reached a low ebb. The impact of all this upon living conditions was naturally most severe. The coincidence of high food prices with declining wages caused widespread hardship, especially in the towns. Here, three elements of discontent came together: the unemployed and hungry artisans, the peasants fleeing from the rural ills of land-hunger and semi-feudal oppression, and the middle classes with their liberal and nationalist opposition to the existing regimes.

The relationship between crisis and revolt

1. What kinds of economic crises occurred in Europe in the years leading up to 1848?

2. Why did the agricultural crisis that affected Europe in 1846–48 have a more serious impact on Germany?

3. What evidence is there to support the claim that 'social and economic factors, rather than political ones, were responsible for the outbreak of revolution in Germany in 1848'?

The violence of 1848 did not occur at the height of the European crisis, but during the steady improvement that followed it. It resulted from the steady accumulation of frustration during the previous two and a half years of hardship. Historian Ernest Labrousse wrote that 'the wave of high prices had spread over the country like a flood, and, like a receding tide, it left behind it a ruined population.' Nevertheless, the increasing prosperity of 1848–49 goes a long way to explain the withering of rebellion in most European states after such promising beginnings. The sparks that set off the outburst of March 1848 must therefore be sought in the political circumstances and disputes of the various European states. In describing these, it is important not to generalise, for the resemblance between the affairs of one state and those of its neighbour was superficial. The views of the revolutionary leaders were usually much more diverse than the common distress that, briefly, provided them with a rank-and-file following.

2.2 Why did the movement for liberal reform achieve such success in Germany, and then collapse so rapidly?

The combination of crises in Germany

The sensational political events in France, in early 1848, impacted upon German states whose economic and political problems were subtly different. The economic crisis in the German towns displayed two distinct characteristics. The first was the material distress that had resulted from the failure of the harvest in the countryside. In 1847, there were bread riots in Stuttgart and in Ulm, and violence in Berlin triggered by the shortage of potatoes. Secondly, German urban revolt was fuelled by the distress of traditional artisans, already under pressure from the growth of mechanised production before the depression of 1846–47 hit them. The early months of 1848 witnessed such acts of '**Luddism**' as the burning of mills in Dusseldorf, demonstrations by weavers in Chemnitz, and assaults by wagoners in Nassau upon the newly constructed railways. Factory production, too,

'**Luddism**': A form of political protest, specifically against industrial mechanisation and its effect upon employment, which took the form of attacks upon factories and machinery.

experienced severe difficulties as investment and demand declined, and there were strikes for higher pay and shorter hours in Berlin, Leipzig and Dresden. The combination of all these economic factors was, in some cases, catastrophic.

Much remained to be done in the German states that had been achieved in France a generation earlier, and historians have delivered some damning verdicts. Agatha Ramm wrote, in *Germany 1789–1919: a Political History* (1968), that Germany before 1848 'was a country where to have a political opinion was difficult, to express it almost impossible, and to join with others to promote it, conspiracy punishable by the heaviest prison sentences'. A.J.P. Taylor's view (*The Course of German History*, 1945) of the personal unfitness of the rulers of many of the German principalities is only slightly exaggerated: 'Ceaseless inbreeding, power territorially circumscribed, but within those limits limitless, produced mad princes as a normal event; and of the utterly petty princes hardly one was sane.'

In Prussia, in particular, the solidarity of the governing classes appeared to be weakened by an unusual development. The mainstay of Prussian conservatism, the landowning Junker class, found itself in an unaccustomed position in the years immediately before 1848. Their desire for the construction of an eastern railway (*Ostbahn*), linking their agricultural estates in East Prussia with markets in the major cities, had temporarily placed them in the unusual position of supporting the decision to summon an assembly which alone could grant the necessary funds. Strange and perturbed as the political scene in Prussia seemed in 1846–47, and real as the economic distress was it must be stressed that no genuine governmental crisis existed. The administration was soundly organised and in many cases, in economic matters for instance, it was pursuing far-sighted and logical policies. The finances of the state were sound, far sounder than those of the Austrian Empire. The army was well trained, well equipped and loyal. In the context of the improving harvests and falling food prices in 1848, it was likely to take more than a temporary loss of nerve on the part of the government to achieve any permanent revolution in Prussia.

The first wave of reforms

In the German states, as in much of central Europe, the news of the February revolution in Paris was the trigger that turned long-term resentment into political confrontation. 'It is impossible,' declared a leading Berlin newspaper, 'to describe the amazement, the terror, the confusion aroused here by the latest reports from Paris crowding on each other almost hourly.' And if the political society of Prussia's capital seemed shaken, what hope was there for such minor entities as Mecklenburg-Strelitz?

By the second week of March, the leaders of most German states had despaired of surviving where the King of the French had perished. Instead, they began the wholesale granting of constitutional demands. In Bavaria, King Ludwig abdicated and his successor, Maximilian II, accepted the principles of a constitutional assembly, as well as ministerial responsibility, a jury system and a free press (9 March). In Baden, all feudal obligations were abolished (10 March) and, in Würtemberg, the king renounced his hunting rights. Even Prussia could not escape. At first, Friedrich Wilhelm seemed to preserve his political position by ordering his troops not to fire upon demonstrating crowds, and by putting his name to the usual list of concessions. An outbreak of street fighting on 18 March broke his nerve and he sought to save himself by ordering the withdrawal of the army from Berlin. As a virtual prisoner of his people, he then appointed a liberal ministry led by Rhineland businessmen, Ludolf Camphausen and David Hansemann.

The Frankfurt Parliament

Liberal reforms were only one of the elements in what seemed a remark-able victory for the insurgents. On the face of it, the most spectacular concession of the rulers of Prussia, Bavaria, Baden and Württemberg was their agreement to participate in the organisation of a German national parliament, a vehicle for the unification of the nation. At the height of the liberal success, the first steps towards such a body were already being taken. A group of enthusiasts, mainly academics and predominantly from the southern states, resolved at a meeting in Heidelberg (5 March) to summon a preliminary parliament (*Vorparlament*) which would, in turn, supervise elections to a German representative assembly. Thus this assembly had its origins, not in the exercise of any state's power, but in the absence of power, in a vacuum characteristic of March 1848. The *Vorparlament*, in its five-day session, decided that elections should be by universal male suffrage and **proportional representation**, with one dele-gate for every 50,000 Germans.

Proportional representation: A system of voting in elections. Each political party is represented in parliament in proportion to the number of people who vote for it.

The assembly that finally gathered in St Paul's Church in Frankfurt (18 May) was predominantly elected by those middle classes preoccupied with constitutions and parliaments. It was a classic illustration of Lewis Namier's description of 1848 as 'the revolution of the intellectuals'. Of 830 delegates who sat there at one time or another, 275 were state officials, 66 were lawyers, 50 were university professors and another 50 were school-masters. Only one came from a truly peasant background, and only four from the artisan classes. Relatively united in social origins and in their view of the Germany that they did not want, they were to discover, like most revolutionaries, that the construction of a new state and society is a much more difficult process.

The failure of the Frankfurt Parliament

Historians have dealt more harshly with the German liberals who domi-nated the Frankfurt Parliament than with any comparable group in the 19th century. Historians of the Left have followed Karl Marx and Friedrich Engels in condemning them for not taking violent action to overthrow existing power structures. In the decades immediately following unifica-tion, such 'Prussian' historians as Treitschke blamed them for their opposition to Germany's 'best hope', the Prussian monarchy. Foreign commentators, such as Lewis Namier and A.J.P. Taylor, have seen them as ideological frauds, pretending to favour democratic reform, but ultimately interested only in German power. Indeed, the failure of the Frankfurt Parliament was almost total, not because it failed to use its opportunities, but because the opportunities of 1848 were illusory.

The first set of difficulties faced by the Frankfurt delegates concerned the eventual nature of the state that they hoped to create. What would be the constitutional framework of the united Germany? The majority of deputies felt it was of great importance to recruit the princes as supporters of a monarchical Germany, rather than risk the radical politics that accom-panied republicanism. Two other issues followed from this.

● Which of Germany's royal houses should predominate?

● What should be the relationship of the Parliament with the older authorities within Germany?

Conservatives preferred to see the constitutional decisions of the Parliament implemented by the princes in their individual states, while more radical spirits wished to see princely authority overridden by that of the Parliament.

In June, under the influence of its president, Heinrich von Gagern, the Parliament took the decision to claim executive power, superior to that of any state or to that of the Federal Diet. They also decided to entrust the leadership of Germany to the greatest of the German families, the Habsburgs, in the person of the Archduke John. The Parliament was thus moving towards a 'Greater Germany' (*Grossdeutschland*), which included all German speakers, rather than a 'Lesser Germany' (*Kleindeutschland*), which excluded the Germans of the Habsburg territories. That ambition was to be thwarted by the recovery of Habsburg authority in the Austrian Empire, in October and November 1848.

The challenge of non-German nationalism

A second set of problems arose from the fundamental weakness of the Frankfurt Parliament, its total lack of material power. Lacking an army of its own, it was bound to depend upon the goodwill of the major German princes for the most basic functions of government, such as the collection of taxes. Like other constitutional bodies set up in 1848, this assembly was only, ultimately, able to survive if the regimes that it sought to replace voluntarily handed over their power.

> **František Palacky (1798–1876)**
> Czech nationalist, and author of *History of Bohemia*. President of the Pan-Slav Congress (1848). Opponent of the Dual Monarchy in Austro-Hungary after 1867.

In particular, the Parliament faced two challenges that it was powerless to resolve. Firstly, various nationalities had laid claim to territories seen by the Parliament as part of the Fatherland. In March 1848, Denmark occupied Schleswig and Holstein. This was closely followed by František Palacky's declaration that Bohemia belonged to the Czech nation, and by a rising by Polish nationalists in Posen. The initial sympathy of the assembly for the aspirations of other nationalists evaporated when those aspirations seemed to threaten German power. Seeing no other alternative to the diminution of Germany, the assembly applauded many of the selfish acts of their erstwhile enemies. The victory of the Austrian army in Prague, and the suppression of the Poles by the Prussian army both received widespread approval. When foreign pressure forced the Prussian army, in action against the Danes, to accept a disadvantageous armistice (August 1848), the assembly, for all its harsh words, could only confirm its impotence by accepting the settlement.

The challenge of working-class radicalism

The other challenge came from the undeveloped and incoherent working-class movement. In the last months of 1848, German workers' organisations were beginning to react to the failure of the Frankfurt Parliament to solve working-class problems. While the Frankfurt liberals devoted themselves to the abstract task of drawing up a constitution, separate and independent workers' assemblies met in Hamburg and in Frankfurt itself, making economic demands against the middle-class interests of the delegates in St Paul's Church. They requested the limitation of factory production, restrictions upon free economic and industrial growth, and the protection of the privileges of the old artisan guilds. When barricades went up in Frankfurt (18 September) and disturbances followed in Baden, Hesse-Cassel and Saxony, the Parliament's only recourse was to use Prussian and Austrian troops once more.

The recovery of Prussia

The emergence of the national issue and the growing fear of working-class violence were two of the factors that paved the way for the triumph of conservatism in Germany. The third factor was the steady recovery of nerve by the King of Prussia. By August, Prussia's own parliament had demonstrated its radicalism by seeking to abolish the feudal, legal and financial privileges of the Junker class. This had brought the Junkers into open opposition to the liberals. Encouraged by their support and by increasing evidence of the reliability of the army, Friedrich Wilhelm dismissed his liberal ministers and ordered his troops back into Berlin. In December, he first banished and then dissolved the Prussian parliament. The anti-nationalist stance of the Austrian Habsburgs in March 1849 gave the Frankfurt assembly little alternative but to offer the crown of Germany to the only other German powerful enough to wear it. Friedrich Wilhelm's refusal to 'pick up a crown from the gutter' sealed Frankfurt's failure.

Much has been written about the Prussian king's motives. Certainly, his distaste for constitutional monarchy was genuine, but there is also evidence that he harboured a deeply traditional belief in Austria's divinely ordained leadership of Germany and its princes. With the withdrawal of Prussian and Austrian delegates from Frankfurt, the Parliament was already a shell when it moved to Stuttgart to await its dispersal by Prussian troops (June 1849). Although permanent agrarian reforms survived from the events of 1848–49, the liberal, constitutional revolution had achieved nothing. Indeed, we may even accept the judgement of A.J.P. Taylor that there was, in no realistic sense, a political revolution of any kind in Germany in 1848. 'There was merely a vacuum in which the liberals postured until the vacuum was filled.'

1. What were the main aims of German liberals in 1848?

2. To what extent would you agree with the judgement that German liberals failed in 1848 because their aims were unrealistic, and because the existing German governments were strong and healthy?

2.3 In what respects was the crisis in the Austrian Empire more dangerous than in other parts of Europe?

Political and economic weaknesses within the Empire

Nowhere was the conjunction of different economic and political crises so dangerous as in the Austrian Empire. In 1848–49, the Empire was threatened not merely with radical constitutional change, but with the very collapse of its complex, multinational structure. Historian Hans Kohn has described the period of Austrian history between 1815 and 1848 as 'an era of stagnation'. Those years had witnessed some half-hearted attempts by Metternich at political and fiscal reform, thwarted by the conservatism of the Emperor. Latterly, the political scene had been dominated by rivalry and jealousy, notably between Metternich and his rival, Count Kolowrat. The accession, in 1835, of the Emperor Ferdinand, physically sick and mentally abnormal, merely ensured that the political malaise spread to the pinnacle of the state system.

Economically, the Austrian Empire had produced nothing to rival Prussia's policy of tariff reform and industrial modernisation. Austria and Hungary together produced 710,000 tons of coal in 1845, compared with the 5.6 million tons produced by the member states of the *Zollverein*. They made only modest and halting progress in railway construction. Although Austrian cities were, as yet, spared the horrors of industrialisation, they had little to offer those peasants driven from the countryside by **agrarian depression**. Urban unrest in Vienna or Budapest owed more to the lack of industrial employment than to the hardships that such employment entailed. Also, the government imposed, or attempted to impose, an intellectual straitjacket upon the Empire. 'I do not need scholars,' an earlier Emperor had informed his schoolteachers in 1821, 'but obedient citizens. Whosoever serves me must teach what I command.'

Agrarian depression: Economic depression (unemployment and falling wages) affecting agricultural production in the countryside.

The challenge of nationalism within the Empire

The rise of nationalism gave the Austrian crisis a distinctive flavour of its own for, in a state with so much racial diversity, such doctrines were always likely to be explosive. Although Germans dominated the politics and commerce of the Empire, they constituted only a little less than a quarter of its population. Of the total, nearly 20% were Hungarians, about 7% were Italians, 6% Romanians, and 45% Slavs. This last section then subdivided into a bewildering variety that included Czechs, Slovaks, Serbs, Ruthenes, Poles and Croats.

The question of national identity and the awareness of national cultures had come to prominence only relatively recently. At the beginning of the century, vernacular languages were largely confined to the peasant populations, with the business of the provincial assemblies, or Diets, conducted in Latin. In 1840, Hungarian nationalists succeeded in replacing Latin by **Magyar** as the official language of their Diet. Over the next four years, Magyar also became established in legal and educational usage. Other languages made headway in literary contexts, as in the publication of Jungmann's Czech dictionary, Palacky's history of the Czechs and Preseren's Slovene poetry. Otherwise, the aims of these national minorities varied. Some, such as the Czechs, aimed for improved status within the Empire. Others, such as the Italian nationalists, hoped to secede from the Empire to form part of a larger, independent nation. In Hungary, there was a significant increase in political tension in the late 1830s and early 1840s with the rise of a radical, nationalist journalist, Lajos Kossuth. Where moderate nationalism, under Count Széchenyi, had previously aimed at cultural and economic advance within the Empire, Kossuth demanded far more. His aims were administrative autonomy and parliamentary rule for Hungary. His method was to win the support of the Hungarian gentry for the revival of the old Hungarian state by appealing to their anti-Slav interests and prejudices.

Magyar: Official language of the Hungarians.

The fall of Metternich

As had been the case in Germany, the news of the February revolution in Paris triggered political revolt in Austria. Middle-class liberals, student radicals and elements of the Viennese working class joined together in street demonstrations and in the presentation of petitions to the Emperor in the first weeks of March. On 13 March, clashes with regular troops led to loss of life. The Emperor, who had already lost his wits, now lost his nerve. Later that day, the 1848 revolutionaries gained their most notable 'scalp', with the resignation of the Imperial Chancellor, Klemens von Metternich. Two elements seem to have combined in the fall of the great champion of European conservatism. Some historians, such as the Frenchman M. Pouthas, saw fear as the main motive within the Austrian court. They portray Metternich, like Guizot in Paris, as a victim sacrificed to save the rest of the establishment. For the Austrian, G. von Poelnitz, the personal antipathy of such rivals as Kolowrat played a greater role, and the popular disturbances provided an opportunity for the pursuit of personal vendettas. The difference in interpretation is important, for what could be seen as the most sensational event of early 1848, takes on far less significance if it was merely the result of temporary divisions within the governing elite of the Empire.

With the departure of Metternich into exile, Ferdinand, like Friedrich Wilhelm, preferred concessions to flight. In April, he conceded freedom of the press, and gave permission for a constitution for the German-speaking areas of the Empire. The following month, he promised a constituent assembly based upon universal manhood suffrage and accepted the arming of a volunteer National Guard in Vienna.

Confrontation across a barricade in the streets of Vienna in May 1848

Reform in Hungary

It was inevitable that the collapse of Imperial willpower would encourage opposition in the provinces of the Empire. Indeed, the Hungarian Diet meeting at Pressburg (Bratislava) had begun the formulation of its demands ten days before the fall of Metternich. These demands crystallised into the so-called March Laws, a mixture of classic liberal demands with more specifically nationalist ones. Freedom of the press, equality of taxation, equality before the law, and freedom of religion stood alongside the demand for the removal of all non-Hungarian troops from Hungarian territory. In the countryside, all remnants of serfdom were to be abolished, as was the practice of *robot*, the compulsory labour owed by many peasants to their landlords. Further, it must be understood that when Kossuth and his supporters spoke of 'Hungary' they envisaged, not merely a state embracing those areas where Magyar was spoken, but all those territories that had been part of the medieval Kingdom of Hungary. Transylvania, Croatia and Ruthenia could thus expect no Hungarian sympathy for their own cultural or national aspirations. On 11 April, Ferdinand conceded all the demands of the Hungarian Diet and effectively accepted the establishment of an independent Hungarian state.

Bohemia and Austro-Slavism

In Prague, the second great centre of nationalist unrest, confidence in national strength was less pronounced. The Pan-Slav Congress which assembled there (2 June) chose, not the path of national independence, but that which became known as 'Austro-Slavism'. This centred upon the view that the best course for the Slav peoples of the Empire lay within a reformed, yet intact, Habsburg Empire. Outside, they would merely fall prey to the selfish desires of the Germans and the Russians. Indeed, Palacky's refusal to accept a seat at the **Pan-German** Frankfurt Parliament was a landmark in the Czechs' claim for the recognition of their own national identity. 'If the Austrian Empire did not exist', he concluded, 'it would be necessary to create it' for the safety of the minor Slav nationalities.

Thus the demands from Prague were that the Czech language should have equal status with German, that the *robot* should be abolished, and that there should be what Palacky called the 'peace, the liberty and the right of my nation'. They did not include the demand for an independent Czech state. Austro-Slavism represented an impossible paradox. It depended upon the weakness of the Viennese government for its success, and upon the voluntary dismantling of absolutism by the Habsburgs. Yet it trusted in Habsburg strength for protection against German or Russian domination. While it illustrates the high hopes of 1848, it also provides a classic example of the chronically weak foundations upon which these hopes rested.

Pan-German: The policy which dictates that all those of German racial origin should be united in a single German state. This naturally involved the union of Germany with those parts of the Austro-Hungarian Empire whose population was ethnically German.

1. Which areas of the Austrian Empire were most affected by the demands of local nationalists?

2. In what ways did the demands and expectations of the revolutionaries in the Austrian Empire differ from one another?

2.4 How was the Austrian government able to re-establish its authority?

Radical defeat in Prague and Vienna

Alfred von Windischgrätz (1787–1862)
Entered Austrian army in 1804. Military commander of Bohemia (1840–48). Successful against insurgents in Prague and Vienna (1848). Captured Budapest (1849) but was unable to crush the Hungarian rising, and was recalled to Vienna in disgrace.

The first major success of the counter-revolution in 1848 occurred in Prague. As even the Czechs seemed convinced of their own weakness it is scarcely surprising that those commanding the undefeated Austrian forces in the north moved towards the same conclusion. In reaction to renewed radical and student violence in the city (13 June), General Windischgrätz took the decision to bombard Prague. Within three days, the city was in his hands. Not only was the resistance of the insurgents ineffectual, but they found themselves largely without sympathy in the outside world. The events in Prague serve well to illustrate the fatal isolation of each of the 1848 risings from all of the others.

The revolution in Vienna suffered from a steady decline rather than from a sudden collapse. By the time of Windischgrätz's triumph, the Viennese radicals had achieved some notable triumphs of their own. They had formed a constituent assembly and a National Guard, and in September the assembly struck at the social basis of rural Austria by abolishing the *robot* and the hereditary rights of the nobility in local administration. These should perhaps be seen as the major lasting changes wrought by the 'Year of Revolutions' in the Empire. The end of the practice of *robot* had a ruinous effect on the lesser gentry, who lost a valuable source of cheap labour. This breaking of the power of the local landlords, although it was not the direct aim of the assembly, was to confirm the subsequent dominance of the central authority of the Imperial government.

Fatal weaknesses were already becoming evident in the position of the revolutionaries. The dynasty remained in power and continued to be served by ministers of the 'old school'. The Imperial army was not only undefeated, but actually victorious in the provinces. Worse, divisions

**Johann Radetzky
(1766–1858)**
Austrian military commander.
Commander-in-Chief in
Lombardy (1831). Defeated
Piedmontese at Custoza and
recaptured Milan (1848). Victor
at Novara (1849). Military
Governor of Lombardy and
Venetia (1849–57).

**Count Josef Jellacic
(1801–1859)**
Croat soldier and politician. An
enthusiastic supporter of
Habsburg authority, he played
a major role, as Governor of
Croatia, in the suppression of
the 1848 risings.

**Count Felix von
Schwarzenberg (1800–1852)**
Austrian statesman.
Ambassador to Naples
(1846–48), and active in the re-
establishment of Austrian
authority in Italy in 1848–49.
Appointed chief minister of the
Emperor (November 1848), he
was active in disbanding the
Constituent Assembly and
restoring imperial authority.
Also active in negotiating
Russian intervention against
the Hungarian uprising in 1849.

began to appear in the ranks of the revolutionaries themselves. Some elements among the German-speaking radicals favoured the cutting of links with the non-German provinces of the Empire. They aimed at a form of *grossdeutsch* unity with the other states represented at the Frankfurt Parliament. Others wished to see the territorial preservation of the Empire and applauded the victories of von Windischgrätz and Radetzky.

The discussion of a constitutional settlement aggravated the divisions. Many liberals remained content with a constitutional monarchy of the sort recently overthrown in Paris, while stricter radicals sought a republic. The emergence of workers' organisations in Vienna revived memories of the 'June Days' in Paris, and in August demonstrations were broken up by the middle-class National Guard. The government's decision (3 October) to declare war on the Hungarian rebels brought matters to a head. Radical demonstrations in favour of Hungary, in which the Minister of War was lynched, emboldened the conservatives to treat Vienna as Prague had been treated. The task was harder and bloodier, but by the end of the month and at a cost of 3,000 to 5,000 lives, Generals Windischgrätz and Jellacic had reconquered Austria's capital.

The re-establishment of Imperial government

The regeneration of conservative government was steadily consolidated. In November, a new government, under Count Schwarzenberg, took office. In December, as the living symbol of regeneration, the 18-year-old Franz Josef ascended the Imperial throne upon his uncle's abdication. The new administration was firmly based upon realism and upon power politics for, in A.J.P. Taylor's words, 'Schwarzenberg was too clever to have principles, Franz Josef too blinkered to understand them.' The fate of the constituent assembly well illustrates the methods of Austria's new masters. Since October, it had lingered in exile in the Moravian town of Kremsier deliberating over an Austrian constitution. By the completion of its task (1 March 1849), Schwarzenberg felt strong enough to do without an assembly, but not without a constitution. Within three days of the formulation of the 'Kremsier Constitution' he had dissolved the assembly and allowed the Minister of the Interior, Count Stadion, to introduce an Imperial constitution of a different kind. While it permitted a parliament based upon universal manhood suffrage, it stressed the indivisible nature of the Empire. Although Hungary received recognition of its linguistic separatism, it, and all other regions of the Empire, could now expect only direct government from Vienna.

Schwarzenberg's reaction to the events of 1848–49 has significance for the history of the Habsburg Empire in the later 19th century. It suggests that he had learned much about the weaknesses of the nationalist movements, but little from the weaknesses of his own state. Therefore, while the 1850s were a decade of economic modernisation and reform in France, in Prussia and Piedmont-Sardinia, they witnessed only the consolidation of political conservatism in Austria. There was to be no Austrian Cavour, and not even an Austrian equivalent of Louis Napoleon. By the end of the century, as historian Peter Jones suggests in *The 1848 Revolutions* (1981), Austria would have paid a heavy price for that fact. 'Austria's revival was illusory. The survival of the Habsburg monarchy owed more to individuals – Radetzky, Windischgrätz, Schwarzenberg, Franz Josef – than to any revitalisation of the system of government.'

The reconquest of Hungary

The most important factor leading the government to grant constitutional concessions was the need to maintain a degree of general support while

1. What, if anything, had revolutionaries within the Austrian Empire achieved by the end of 1849?

2. Why did the Austrian Empire survive the revolutions of 1848–1849?

3. To what extent was the survival of the Austrian Empire in 1848–1850 due to the weakness of the revolutionaries?

Hungary remained undefeated. From October 1848, the policy of the Imperial government towards Hungarian autonomy had been one of open hostility. Three methods of attack suggested themselves. Firstly, tacit support for the Slav minorities alienated by Kossuth's 'March Laws' became active and overt. The advance of the Croat General Jellacic into southern Hungary was, however, short-lived (September 1848) and unsuccessful. Secondly, the hope that Windischgrätz might win a third counter-revolutionary success with Austrian troops proved ill-founded. He moved slowly against a divided Hungarian leadership and was eventually defeated at Isaszeg, in early April 1849. A week later, in response to Schwarzenberg's constitution, a Hungarian republic was proclaimed, and the Viennese government was forced into the extreme measure of appealing for foreign aid. Russia's response to the Austrian appeal owed as much to fears that the Hungarian example would be imitated in Poland as it did to conservative principles, but it proved decisive. The three-pronged attack of Jellacic, Windischgrätz and 140,000 Russians ended the life of the Hungarian republic at Vilagos (13 August 1849) and opened a period of bloody repression and retribution. The official annulment of the Hungarian constitution, in 1851, put the final touch to the conservative triumph in the Austrian Empire.

Further Reading

The 1848 Revolutions by Peter Jones (Longman, Seminar Studies series, 1981)

3 The unification of Germany, 1850–1871

Key Issues

- Why was Germany unified under Prussian rather than Austrian leadership?

- How important was the role of Bismarck in the establishment of German unity?

- What were the main motives of the Prussian leadership in bringing about this form of unification?

3.1 Why was Prussia not able to extend its political influence within Germany in the aftermath of the 1848 Revolutions?

3.2 In what ways did the balance of power between Prussia and Austria change in the years 1850–1862?

3.3 In what respects did Prussia's economy provide a basis for its dominance within Germany?

3.4 Why was there a constitutional crisis within Prussia in 1860–1862, and why did it bring Otto von Bismarck to power?

3.5 What were the bases of Bismarck's political beliefs and foreign policy?

3.6 By what means, and by what stages, was Austria excluded from German politics between 1863–1866?

3.7 What had Bismarck achieved by 1866?

3.8 What factors forced Bismarck to go beyond the settlement achieved in 1866?

3.9 Why, and with what consequences, did Prussia go to war with France in 1870?

3.10 Historical interpretation: Was German unification primarily the result of successful Bismarckian diplomacy?

Framework of Events

1850	March: Union of Erfurt
	November: Capitulation of Olmütz
1853	Commercial treaty between Prussia and Austria. Oldenburg and Hanover join *Zollverein*
1854–56	Crimean War
1858	Prince Wilhelm becomes regent of Prussia
1859	Formation of the *Nationalverein*
1860	Death of Friedrich Wilhelm IV; succession of Wilhelm I
1862	Bismarck is appointed Minister President of Prussia
1863	Polish Revolt. Prussia offers Alvensleben Convention to Russia. Schleswig incorporated into Denmark
1864	Prussia and Austria go to war with Denmark over Schleswig-Holstein
1865	Convention of Gastein. Conclusion of a new *Zollverein* treaty, from which Austria was excluded. Meetings between Bismarck and Napoleon III at Biarritz
1866	June: Outbreak of war between Prussia and Austria
	July: Prussian victory at Sadowa
	August: Peace of Prague
1867	Formation of North German Confederation. London Conference guarantees neutrality of Luxembourg
1868	Overthrow of Spanish monarchy
1870	July: Crisis over Hohenzollern candidature to the Spanish throne. Outbreak of Franco-Prussian War
	September: Defeat of French forces at Sedan
1871	Proclamation of the German Empire (Reich).

Overview

THE main forces working for and against the political unification of the German states were evident for several decades before Otto von Bismarck was called to power. Theories of German nationhood had flourished in intellectual circles throughout this period, and had occasionally been translated into action, most notably in the establishment of a German parliament in Frankfurt in 1848. As the events of 1848–49 indicated, however, such theories faced formidable opposition from several influential forces. They clashed directly with the specific political interests of the individual rulers of the German states, whose priority was invariably to resist any reduction of their own powers and prerogatives. Yet they were sometimes distracted from such preoccupations by other considerations. The experience of the Napoleonic Wars, and of the disruption of the 1840s, made it clear to them that their positions were vulnerable. They were under threat, equally, from the ambitions of a foreign power such as France, and from the radical demands of their own subjects. The desire for security jockeyed with political conservatism at the head of their agenda.

In addition to this desire for security, important economic forces worked in favour of some form of unity. German manufacturers and merchants had appreciated, for some time, the benefits to be gained from the relaxation of customs duties and the other restrictions that were involved in transporting goods and materials from one German state to another. Crucially, of course, this was a benefit that might also be enjoyed by the larger, and more economically advanced, of the German states. In particular Prussia, with territories to the west and north-east of Germany after the 1815 settlement, had a powerful vested interest in easier economic intercourse. In northern Germany, such considerations had produced a degree of economic unity as early as the 1830s, in the form of the *Zollverein*. This 'customs union' had flourished for more than two decades before Bismarck came to office.

The events of 1848 illustrated some important truths about the prospects of German unity. They made it clear, for instance, that the middle-class nationalists assembled in Frankfurt lacked the political means to impose their vision of Germany's future upon the more powerful German princes. The initiative lay with such rulers as the King of Prussia or the Emperor of Austria. For the time being, Austria remained the stronger of these two powers, with military resources and diplomatic connections that Prussia could not afford to challenge. Nor was either power greatly interested in the 'national question'. Austria was clearly preoccupied with the maintenance of its multinational Empire, while Prussia's primary concern was for its freedom of action in northern Germany, and for the maintenance of the political and economic interests of its Junker governing class. Their attitude was mirrored in neighbouring states, in France and in Russia, for instance, where the prospect of a powerful neighbour, where once there had been more than 30 lesser states, was extremely unattractive. Whatever forces worked towards German unity, they would have some thorny diplomatic or military problems to solve in this respect.

It was the following decade that transformed the prospects of German unity. In the course of the 1850s, the European context was altered in several important respects. Austria's credibility as a leader and defender of the German princes was reduced dramatically. Its decision to remain neutral in the Crimean War ruptured the conservative alliance with Russia that had served it so well in 1848–50. Its failure to resist French forces in Italy, in 1859, not only called into question its ability to defend the German princes, but also brought home to princes and to German patriots alike the potential threat posed to them by a new Napoleon Bonaparte. At the opening of the 1860s, there was not only a **power vacuum** in the politics of German leadership, but an urgent and widespread desire that it should be filled.

Power vacuum: A term used to describe a region in which no state exercises effective control. Such areas are always liable to be occupied by expansionist forces.

Such were the circumstances that prevailed when Bismarck was appointed Minister President of Prussia in 1862. The priorities that he brought to that office have been the subject of considerable debate, but few historians today would doubt that they were primarily Prussian and conservative. Above all, he sought to defend the Prussian state, as well as the interests of his Junker class, against two major threats. These were, firstly, the domestic, political ambitions of the middle classes, with their liberal, constitutional claims, and, secondly, the continued claims of Austria to be regarded as the major political authority within the German Confederation. As a primary instrument of Austrian authority, Bismarck viewed the Confederation itself as a threat to Prussian integrity, and to its freedom of political action. In political terms, it was not hard to outmanoeuvre the liberals, and by 1867 Bismarck appeared to have done so. In part, he had achieved this by taking measures to increase the size and power of the Prussian army, the key to political power, without bothering about the approval of the parliamentary deputies. It may have been illegal, but it worked. In part, however, he achieved a working relationship with the liberals by appearing to work with them on the project closest to their hearts, the promotion of political unity within Germany.

There is a strong case for claiming that, by 1866, Bismarck had achieved all that he really wished to achieve. Austrian influence had been banished from northern Germany, where Prussia now exercised the decisive influence over the **North German Confederation**. In domestic politics, the prestige of the Prussian crown and of the Prussian army was such that it could not be challenged in the foreseeable future. In the process, Bismarck had firmly established his own political position. Yet other forces drove him further. Some of these forces were diplomatic, for he could not ignore the possibility of an Austrian recovery, and of the re-establishment of its influence over the loose confederation of states that existed in southern Germany.

North German Confederation: A revised version of the German Confederation, established as a result of Prussia's victory over Austria in 1866. It comprised those German states north of the river Main, with Prussia the dominant political influence within the confederation.

More serious, and more immediate, was the French reaction to the events of 1866. Desiring compensation and security from the new Prussian 'super state', France made demands that Bismarck hoped initially to satisfy, in order to maintain his new creation. When it proved impossible to do so, he too sought security, in military alliances with the south German states, in diplomatic intrigues with Spain, and by a pretended community of interest with the nationalists in various German states.

Otto Edouard Leopold von Bismarck-Schönhausen (1815–1898) Bismarck studied law and agriculture before becoming a member of the Prussian parliament in 1847. He was Minister	President of Prussia (1862–90) and Chancellor of the German Empire (1871–90). He became Prince von Bismarck in 1871. After successfully waging war with Denmark (1863–64), he went to war with Austria and its allies	(the Seven Weeks' War, 1866). His victory forced the unification of the north German states under his own chancellorship (1867). He was then victorious against France, under the leadership of Napoleon III, in the Franco–Prussian War	(1870–71), proclaiming the German Empire and annexing Alsace-Lorraine. He tried to preserve Prussian leadership within Germany, and to guarantee German security through alliances with Russia and Austria.

1. Divide the factors mentioned in the mind map into long-term reasons and short-term reasons.

2. Which of the factors do you regard as the most important in explaining Prussia's success in uniting Germany? Give reasons for your answer.

3. Which of the factors are linked? (For instance, 'Prussian industrial power' and 'the strength of the Prussian army' aided 'Bismarck's diplomacy'.)

Can you find any other linked factors?

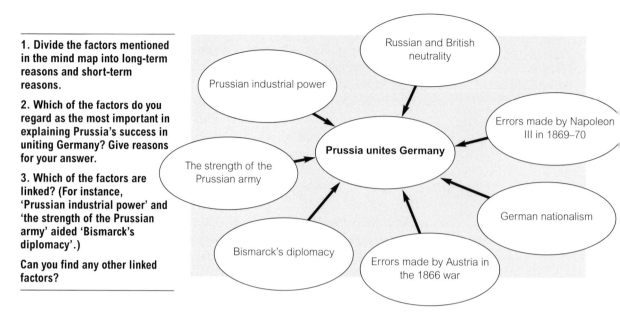

3.1 Why was Prussia not able to extend its political influence within Germany in the aftermath of the 1848 Revolutions?

The Union of Erfurt

In the short term, the revolutionary events of 1848–49 appeared to have prepared the ground for much greater Prussian influence over German politics. Following its active role in defence of German interests in Schleswig-Holstein, and against the radicalism of the Frankfurt Parliament, the prestige of the Prussian state was higher than it had been for many years in conservative circles. Austria, meanwhile, was still largely preoccupied with the affairs of its empire. The German Confederation, too, had played little part in the recent constitutional chaos, and could be regarded as obsolete. How could the vacuum in princely German politics be filled without risking the revival of radical, nationalist ideas?

This was the question that Baron Josef von Radowitz, adviser to the King of Prussia on federal reform for more than 20 years, tried to answer in a set of proposals put to a representative assembly of the German states at Erfurt in March 1850. These proposals included a union of the north German states under the presidency of the King of Prussia, and under the protection of the victorious Prussian army. For Friedrich Wilhelm, the great advantage of such a plan was that Prussian influence would be based upon sound monarchical principles and not, as the offer of the German crown had been in 1849, upon any principles of **popular sovereignty**. In general, Austria would be excluded from this 'Erfurt Union'. Radowitz proposed a compromise by which Austria might be linked to the Union by a second, wider union, based upon **free trade** and, perhaps, upon a common foreign policy.

The 'Capitulation of Olmütz'

In effect, Radowitz was moving too far, too fast. The only real basis for the Erfurt Union was the fear of the German princes at the prospect of a renewed liberal onslaught. He and Friedrich Wilhelm, as historian A.J.P. Taylor put it in *Bismarck the Man and the Statesman* (1968), 'thought

Josef von Radowitz (1797–1858)
Chief of Artillery Staff in the Prussian army (1830). Adviser to Friedrich Wilhelm IV, and enthusiastic advocate of Prussian leadership of the German princes.

Popular sovereignty: The principle or belief that the people are the true rulers of the state, and that government should serve their interests.

Free trade: A system by which trading partners accept the products of the other without taxing them, confident that both would benefit from the arrangement. The benefits of free trade were felt to be considerable: wider markets for domestic products, cheaper goods from abroad, and possible stimulation of domestic industries through competition with strong foreign industries.

Kleindeutsch ('**Little German**'):
Term used to describe the concept of a united Germany (favoured by Prussia) from which Austria is excluded.

Capitulation: Surrender (i.e. the events at Olmütz in 1850 indicated that Prussia was surrendering to the interests of Austria).

1. What factors brought about the creation of the Erfurt Union?

2. Why did it seem, in 1848–49, that Prussia might take the leading role in German politics, and why did this not turn out to be the case?

the princes converted [to the idea of a *kleindeutsch* union] when they were merely frightened'. In fact, it was already evident that many of the 'middling' German states feared Prussian hegemony as much as, if not more than, liberal revolt. Hence the refusal of 11 states – including Hanover, Bavaria, Saxony and Württemberg – to send representatives to Erfurt. The weakness of the proposals was that they arose from an Austrian withdrawal from German affairs that was only temporary. By late 1850, with the Hungarian and Italian revolts under control, the Austrian premier, Felix von Schwarzenberg, was able to declare that 'we shall not let ourselves be thrown out of Germany'. He began to insist upon the reconstruction of the Confederation as it had existed before 1848.

A constitutional conflict in the small duchy of Hesse-Cassel, which formed the vital link between the two blocks of Prussian territory (see map on page 43), provided the test of nerves between the two German powers. With the alternatives of seeking aid either from the Erfurt Union or from the Confederation, Hesse-Cassel turned to the latter. For a while, Prussia seemed prepared to fight to defend its new-found prestige, but Russian support for Austria proved to be the decisive factor. 'Only the Tsar is sovereign,' wrote Karl Marx at the time. 'In the end rebellious Prussia will bow to his command.'

So, in a meeting at Olmütz (November 1850), Friedrich Wilhelm gave in once more to his doubts, and to the doubts of many Prussian conservatives, and agreed to abandon the Erfurt Union in favour of the revival of the German Confederation under Austrian presidency. By the so-called '**Capitulation** of Olmütz', Prussia abandoned the leadership of Germany for a decade and a half. Prussian reactions ranged from conservative satisfaction at the abandonment of a dangerous innovation, to patriotic humiliation. All were aware that German leadership lay beyond Prussia's reach until there was a change in the military balance of Germany, and in the European system of alliances.

3.2 In what ways did the balance of power between Prussia and Austria change in the years 1850–1862?

Alexander, Count von Bach (1813–1893)
Austrian politician: Minister of Justice (1848); Minister of the Interior (1849–59); Chief Minister (1852–59). Negotiated Concordat with the Papacy (1855) and served as ambassador to the Holy See (1859–67).

Karl, Count von Bruck (1798–1860)
Austrian politician: delegate to the Frankfurt Parliament (1848); Minister of Commerce (1848–51); Minister of Finance (1855–60). His projected economic and financial reforms were largely thwarted by the war in Italy (1859) and he committed suicide.

The attempted extension of Austrian hegemony

Between 1851 and 1853, Austrian statesmen attempted to consolidate and to exploit the position of supremacy in German affairs manifested at Olmütz. Firstly, Schwarzenberg proposed the extension of the Confederation to include Austria's non-German territories, thus forming an 'Empire of 70 millions'. When this was rejected by the German princes assembled at Dresden in mid-1851, Austrian proposals switched to an economic tack. Alexander von Bach, Minister of the Interior, and the Baron von Bruck, the former Rhineland liberal then in charge of Austrian finances, proposed the linking of the Prussian-dominated *Zollverein* with the Empire, to produce a vast central European (*Mitteleuropa* – 'Middle Europe') economic union.

The Austrians, however, were overplaying their hand. Olmütz had restored the balance between Austrian military power and Prussian economic power upon which the independence of the lesser princes depended. These princes now had no intention of seeing Austria upset that balance, and their independence, again. Austria had to be content, therefore, with a commercial treaty with Prussia, acting as spokesman for the *Zollverein*, which was signed in February 1853.

The impact of foreign affairs: the Crimea

Karl Ferdinand, Count von Buol (1797–1865)
Austrian diplomat, serving as ambassador to Piedmont (1844), Russia (1848) and Britain (1851). As Foreign Minister (1852–59), he was unsuccessful in persuading the Emperor to join the Crimean War against Russia.

In Germany, as in most of Europe, the Crimean War acted as a great stimulant of political change. Despite the debt that his state owed to the Russians since 1849, the Austrian Foreign Minister, Count von Buol, believed that Austria should conclude an alliance with the western powers, as a safeguard against nationalist action in Italy. He also had no desire to see Russia in control of Moldavia, Wallachia and the mouth of the river Danube. This policy required an understanding with Prussia, to ensure that it would not seek to benefit in Germany from Austria's preoccupation, as it had done in 1850. Prussian opinion, however, was bitterly divided, with conservatives following a pro-Russian policy, while the liberals favoured France and Britain.

In the end, Friedrich Wilhelm followed the least controversial line, that of neutrality. Thus, neither of the German powers played any military role in the war, although Austria maintained a kindly attitude towards the allies. The events of the Crimea, nevertheless, resulted in a number of subtle changes in the political situation within German. Firstly, Austria's concerns had been shown to be purely imperial, rather than German. Its diplomacy had been dominated by thoughts of Moldavia, the Danube and Italy, and Bismarck had ridiculed these aims as being 'to procure a few stinking Wallachians'. Secondly, Austria's failure to repay its debt to Russia had ruptured forever the 'Holy Alliance' between the two great legitimist powers, leaving Austria isolated in European diplomacy. Prussia, although also neutral, owed Russia no such debt, and its neutrality had at least guaranteed Russia security on its Polish borders. In German terms, the Crimean War was a depressing episode, proving its remoteness from the great decisions of European politics and confirming its insignificance in international affairs. German historian Helmut Böhme (1966) preferred to view the war in Prussian terms, as a period of great advance in its prestige within Germany as, proportionately, Austria's national and international prestige declined.

The impact of foreign affairs: Italy

The Italian war of 1859 continued the process of Austrian humiliation. In Helmut Böhme's words, 'Austria now buried her plans for a customs union, her German policy and her economic policy on the battlefields of northern Italy.' As a legitimist, the Prussian regent, Prince Wilhelm, inclined towards aid for Austria, but Austria's isolation from all the other European powers made this a dangerous course to take. In the event, Prussia delayed the mobilisation of its forces until Austria's defeat was virtually assured (July 1859). It then mobilised in concert with the South German princes, with a view to protecting the Rhine frontier against any further French expansionism. Thus, Prussia appeared to be making a gesture for the protection of Germany at a time when it was becoming increasingly difficult to believe in Austrian protection.

The year 1860, with Napoleon III's annexation of Nice and Savoy, brought further cause for the princes to seek protection against French aggression. When Napoleon visited Baden-Baden in an attempt to dispel this anxiety (June 1860) he found himself faced with an array of German rulers, from Bavaria, Hanover, Saxony and Württemberg, united in their apprehension. In general, the European events of 1859–60 marked the beginning of German confidence in Prussia's military capacity, in addition to its undoubted economic capacity.

The reshaping of the Prussian army

In 1850, the prospects of far-ranging conquests by the Prussian army seemed remote. That army still rested very heavily upon the tactics and traditions of the Napoleonic wars and, as historian W. McElwee has stated, 'to the outward eye the Prussian army in 1859 was as clumsy and antiquated an instrument as any of the others'. The mobilisation, that year, seemed to confirm such reservations. In fact, at that very point, the Prussian military establishment was in the midst of a process of transformation.

The key date in this process was, perhaps, 1857, the year in which Helmut von Moltke was appointed as Chief of Staff. Moltke was an unusually cultured and humane man to lead a great national army. 'Every war,' he wrote later in his life, 'even one which is victorious, represents a great national misfortune.' Politically, his brand of romantic patriotism was closer to that of King Wilhelm than to the realism of Bismarck. He was not primarily, however, a political animal. 'For Moltke,' wrote Gerhard Ritter in *The Sword and the Sceptre* (1972), 'politics was an acquired interest rather than a congenial preoccupation and he was deeply concerned with it only when it directly touched the military sphere.'

In terms of numerical strength, the reforms proposed by Moltke in 1862 put the Prussian army squarely on terms with that of Austria. Sixty-three thousand men were called up each year, for a total period of seven years (three of them in the standing army and four in the front-line reserve), liable to instant recall in an emergency. This gave a standing army of 180,000, with a fully-trained reserve of 175,000. In 1866, therefore, Prussia could mobilise 370,000 men, including some **Landwehr** units. As they had fewer security commitments on other frontiers, they were able to outnumber their enemy on the Bohemian front by 278,000 to 271,000. The superior organisation of the Prussian army was equally important. The Prussian General Staff had its origins in the War Academy founded by the great military theorist Karl von Clausewitz, in the Napoleonic era. Not only did it produce officers of great expertise and professionalism, but it guaranteed a uniformity of practice and doctrine in all branches of the army. At Moltke's insistence, for example, all senior officers devoted much attention to the adaptation of modern transport and industrial methods to military needs.

By comparison, the Austrian army remained dominated by senior commanders such as Franz Gyulai and Felix von Wimpffen, who owed their rank more to influence at Court than to proven ability. At lower levels, too, the Austrian army was riddled with inefficiency. Out of a theoretical force of 600,000 men in 1866, bad reserve training and the practice of allowing the wealthy to buy themselves out of military service reduced the fighting force to about 350,000. Furthermore, basic training in the standing army was so bad that it was estimated that two troopers out of three, at the start of the Italian campaign in 1859, were unable to load and fire their muskets.

The army and technology

Finally, the Prussian army undoubtedly led Europe in the application of industrial developments to military purposes. Not only were Prussian railways specifically planned for the swift transit of troops from one frontier to another, but the General Staff operated a special department dedicated to the study of transport by rail. In both 1866 and 1870, this swift concentration of troops was a vital factor. In 1866, Prussia's five railway lines assembled its troops on Austria's northern frontiers in five days, against 45 days taken by the Austrians. In 1870, it proved possible to transport some troops from East Prussia to Lorraine in only 36 hours.

Helmut von Moltke (1800–1891)
Joined the Prussian army in 1821 and its General Staff in 1832. Influential as *aide de camp* to the Crown Prince Friedrich (1855). As Chief of General Staff in the Prussian and German army (1857–88), he undertook significant reforms that recognised the importance of advances in technology and communications. Architect of the Prussian victories over Denmark (1863–64), Austria (1866) and France (1870).

Landwehr: The part-time military force, consisting largely of middle-class recruits, which provided support for the regular army in times of crisis. The Prussian liberals regarded the *Landwehr* very favourably because it seemed to limit the overall power and authority of the aristocratic Prussian army.

Karl von Clausewitz (1780–1831)
Entered the Prussian military college in 1801, and subsequently fought in the Napoleonic Wars in the Russian army and at Waterloo (1815). Director of the Prussian Military College from 1818. In his influential book *On War*, he concentrated upon the links between war and politics, and established that the aim of war was the defeat of the enemy state as well as of the army.

Franz Gyulai (1798–1868)
Hungarian soldier in service of the Austrian Empire. As commander of the garrison at Trieste (1846) he was active against Italian rebels. Commander-in-Chief of Austrian forces during the war in Italy (1859).

In terms of armament, the Prussian infantry was synonymous for some years with the Dreyse 'needle gun'. First issued in 1848 and in general use by 1864, it fired at five times the rate of the old **muzzle-loader**, and its effect, at Sadowa, caused the correspondent of *The Times* to declare that 'the needle gun is king'. Nevertheless, it had its limitations in range and in accuracy, and the victory of 1870 owed more to the Prussian artillery. Equipped by the mid-1860s with a new **Krupp breech-loader**, with cooled steel barrel and a breech sealed against escaping gases, this branch of the army perfected its techniques in the new School of Gunnery founded in swift response to the superior performance of the Austrian gunners at Sadowa.

Muzzle-loader/Krupp breech-loader: Terms describing two firearms or cannons it was usual to insert the bullet or shell into the opening of the barrel ('muzzle') and to ram it down into place before firing. In more modern weapons, the bullet is inserted into the 'breech', an opening at the other end of the barrel, immediately above the trigger. Breech-loading enables the rifleman to load, fire and eject bullets much more rapidly.

1. What evidence is there to suggest that Prussia occupied a stronger position in German politics in 1860 than it had held in 1850?

2. Why could Austria not build, in the 1850s, upon the position of strength that it had occupied in German politics at the beginning of the decade?

3. 'It is more accurate to say that Austria got weaker in the 1850s than that Prussia became stronger.' Do you agree with this statement?

3.3 In what respects did Prussia's economy provide a basis for its dominance within Germany?

Prussian resources and government policy

Two main factors coincided to ensure that Prussia's economy would become predominant among the economies of the German states. Firstly, Prussia was blessed with remarkable natural resources, supplemented in 1814–15, by the acquisition of the richly endowed territories of the Rhineland. Through the Ruhr valley and west and south-west across the Rhine lay substantial deposits of coal and iron ore. Rich coal resources were also available in the Saar valley, in Prussian Silesia and in Upper Silesia, where zinc and iron deposits were also worked.

Secondly, although private and foreign capital was prominent in the early promotion of these industries, Prussia was remarkable for the degree of government interest and involvement in their subsequent development. The contribution of Friedrich von Motz, Finance Minister between 1825 and 1830, included tax reforms and a road building programme. P. Beuth, head of the Department of Trade and Industry (1815–45), did much to foster technical education. Meanwhile, the Prussian banking system owed much to Rother's reorganisation of the Bank of Prussia, in 1846.

The greatest monument to the economic initiative of the Prussian government was the establishment of the German Customs Union (*Zollverein*), in 1834. With an area of 415,000 square kilometres and a population of 23.5 million, the *Zollverein* was the culmination of the creation of smaller unions throughout the 1820s. Prussia benefited by securing effective links between its eastern and western territories, and by establishing its economic influence above that of Austria in German affairs. Prussia's leading position in the *Zollverein* was recognised by those clauses in the establishing treaty which accepted its tariffs as the norm for all, and which recognised the right of the Prussian government to negotiate on behalf of the union as a whole. A dramatic rise in customs revenue bore witness to the effectiveness of this leadership, from 14.4 million thalers (Prussian currency) in 1834, to 27.4 million in 1845. In addition, a string of treaties won favourable trading terms for the *Zollverein* with Piedmont-Sardinia and Holland (both 1851), Belgium (1852) and France (1862).

The development of Prussian heavy industry

Prussia also took the leading role, within Germany, in the development of those branches of heavy industry vital to a modern and militarised state. Its iron and coal industries benefited greatly from the introduction of new technology. The number of steam engines operative in Prussian industry rose from 419 (1837) to 1,444 (1848), at a time when the next best figure was Saxony's 197 (1846). Twenty-four new, deep-level mines were opened in the Ruhr coalfield between 1841 and 1849, while new sources of zinc (Dortmund and Bonn), lead (Aachen) and blackband iron (Dortmund) were discovered and exploited in the late 1840s and early 1850s. Prussia's output of iron rose sharply, from 0.5 million to 1.29 million tons between 1852 and 1857, due to rapid conversion from charcoal smelting to coke smelting.

Although private capital was of prime importance, government legislation again played a helpful role in Prussia. The Mining Laws of 1851 and 1860, for instance, freed mine owners from strict state supervision and halved taxes upon their output. The laws, subsequently, did much to free mine labour from the old guild restrictions upon mobility.

> **Alfred Krupp (1812–1887)**
> A German industrialist whose success was founded upon a process of steel production suitable for the manufacture of improved artillery barrels (1847). He introduced the Bessemer process to Germany (1862) and founded one of the greatest industrial conglomerates in Europe.

The growth of the Prussian steel industry may be measured by the rise of its greatest enterprise, the Krupp factories in Essen. Based upon a successful method of producing cast steel, Alfred Krupp's enterprise grew, between 1826 and 1861, from a single foundry employing seven men to a vast complex employing 2,000. In the next three years alone, thriving on military orders from the Prussian government, especially for modern artillery, the workforce trebled again. In all, Prussian steel production was seven times greater in 1864 than in 1848. The rate of economic growth within the *Zollverein* boundaries may be gauged from the table below.

Indicators of economic activity in the states that formed the Zollverein, *1820–1870*

	1820	1840	1850	1870
Railways (km)	–	549	5,821	8,560
Coal (million tons)	1.0	–	6.9	29.4
Pig iron (million tons)	0.046	0.17	0.53	1.4

Railway construction

Both Bavaria (1835) and Saxony (1837) made an earlier contribution than Prussia to the construction of German railways. The Prussian government was, initially, just as suspicious about the new mode of transport as many other states had been. The 1840s and 1850s, however, saw a rapid change in this attitude. Having appreciated the advantages of east–west communications for economic and strategic purposes, Prussia constructed Germany's second state-owned line (1847), and then sought consistently to extend state influence over the system as a whole. By 1860, 55% of Prussian railways were worked by the state. Quite apart from its economic significance, the growth of the German railway system, as a whole, played a considerable role in the process of 'shrinking' the country and in stressing the insignificance of the lesser states. At every turn, therefore, in an examination of Prussian and German economic growth in the 1850s

**John Maynard Keynes
(1883–1946)**
British economist. As a
delegate to the Versailles
peace conference in 1919, he
became convinced that the
economic terms imposed upon
Germany were unjust and
would lead to further political
difficulties in Europe. After the
Wall Street Crash in 1929, he
defined the principles of
'Keynesian' economics. These
included the contention that a
degree of government
intervention would always be
necessary to combat such
undesirable factors as
unemployment.

**1. In what respects did the
Prussian economy become
stronger in the first half of the
19th century?**

**2. Explain the statement that
'Prussia's dominance of
Germany in the late 19th
century was based upon coal
and iron.'**

and 1860s, one is reminded of the famous judgement of John Maynard
Keynes that 'the German Empire was not founded on blood and iron, but
on coal and iron'.

What was the overall role of economic factors in German unification?

The claim made by Keynes raises the question of the relationship between
the economic growth of Germany, and of Prussia in particular, and the
political achievement of Bismarck. The traditional view has been to see
Bismarck as exploiting the economic advantages of his time to gain the
political ends that he sought. More recently, a school of historians led by
Helmut Böhme has concluded that the dynamics of the German economy
were of greater importance than the political priorities of the Prussian
government. In this light, Bismarck might be seen, less realistically, as the
exploiter of these economic forces, than as a politician whose course was
largely determined by them and by the social forces that arose from them.
Historian Geoff Eley (1992) reflects this line of thought when he
summarises Böhme's views on the reduction of Austrian influence in
Germany.

'The struggle for the control of the *Zollverein* was decisive between 1853
and 1868 in destroying Austrian efforts at reducing Prussia to secondary
status. Therefore, 1858 and the opening of a 'New Era' in Prussian government becomes less crucial than 1857 and the economic depression, which
widened the gap between the Austrian and Prussian-led economies; 1862
is important less for Bismarck's appointment as Minister-President of
Prussia, than for the treaty of free trade with France; Austria's defeat in
1866 is less decisive than its exclusion from the Zollverein two years
before.'

3.4 Why was there a constitutional crisis in Prussia in 1860–1862, and why did it bring Otto von Bismarck to power?

The accession of King Wilhelm I

The period 1858–62 saw a transformation of Prussian domestic politics
that turned a decade of sterility into a period of crisis that threatened to
bring down the monarchy. The first element in this transformation was a
change of monarch. In October 1858, the mental illness of Friedrich
Wilhelm required the appointment of his brother, Prince Wilhelm, as
regent. He succeeded to the throne upon his brother's death in 1860.
Already 63 years old, Wilhelm's first political memories dated from the
Napoleonic Wars and, by 1848, he had the reputation of a strict conservative. This, however, was an oversimplification. He was, indeed, deeply
attached to the principle of legitimate monarchy and to the traditions of
Prussian military glory, but he had been convinced of the need to adapt in
the face of modern forces. As a man of honour, he stood by the constitution that his brother had granted, 'not,' as Golo Mann has written (*The
History of Germany since 1789*, 1974), 'because he liked it, but because a
king must stand by his sacred word.'

The resurgence of nationalism and liberalism

The second major development during this period was the revival of the
German national movement in the last years of the 1850s. The national
question, in Agatha Ramm's words (*Germany 1789–1919: a Political*

History, 1968), had 'barely retained public interest' in the early 1850s. In a negative sense, the lack of any German influence over events in the Crimea played a role in its revival. More positively, the partial success of Italian nationalism in 1859 also had an impact north of the Alps. Also important were the consistent efforts of the lesser German princes to reform the Confederation with a view to increasing its influence over foreign affairs. The revival led to the formation (1859) of the National Association (*Nationalverein*), directly inspired by the Italian National Society. The Association was banned in all major German states, but continued to look to Prussia for leadership, as Italians had looked to Piedmont. The journalist J. Froebel wrote, in 1859, that 'the German nation is sick of principles and doctrines, literary greatness and theoretical existence. What it demands is power, power, power. And to the man who offers it power it will offer honour, more honour than he can imagine.'

Thirdly, whether as a cause or result of the nationalist revival, came a marked resurgence in liberal political activity. In Prussia, it had manifested itself especially in the emergence of the Progress Party (*Fortschrittpartei*). Raised upon the anti-Austrian, anti-Russian and theoretically anti-militaristic foundations of traditional Prussian liberalism, it enjoyed great success in the first elections of the new decade. In the elections to the *Landtag*, in January 1862, it won 83 seats in an assembly that contained only 16 conservatives. Three months later, its strength rose to 136 seats, while the conservatives fell to 11 and the 'old' liberals fell from 95 to 47.

Von Roon and military reform

The War Minister Von Roon's plans to reform the Prussian Army were the immediate cause of a crisis between *Landtag* and the Prussian king. These proposals were also, in part, the result of the crisis of 1859. The government's prime concern was with the size of the army for, while the Prussian population had doubled since 1814, the annual intake of recruits had remained static at 40,000. Von Roon now proposed to increase this to 63,000 and to create 53 new regiments. He also proposed to change the nature of the army by limiting the role played by the reserve militia (*Landwehr*). This was composed of part-time soldiers who had finished their three years' training and who, in his view and on the evidence of the mobilisation in 1859, 'lacked the genuine soldierly spirit and had no firm discipline'. To the liberal majority, however, the *Landwehr* had the advantage of being freer from the detested spirit of Junker militarism and of costing them far less in taxes. It also recalled fond memories of the 'people's war' against Napoleon in 1813. Thus, Roon was not only fighting a technical battle, but also facing a class struggle.

The appointment of Otto von Bismarck

By 1862 the dispute was already two years old, and the government had twice deceived the assembly into making temporary grants of money for the army. Angry and alienated, the assembly now refused to sanction the national budget, leaving Wilhelm to contemplate the possibility of **abdication**. Only as a desperate measure, and at the prompting of von Roon, did Wilhelm take the most important political decision of his life. He summoned to office a man closely identified with the far right of Prussian politics, the ambassador to Paris, Otto von Bismarck-Schönhausen.

Bismarck was not a man to be impressed by abstract principles, whether of legitimism or of **constitutionalism**. Nevertheless, his first moves aimed at finding ground for compromise with the *Landtag*. Only when that failed did he take the determined course of adjourning their sitting (October

Landtag: The representative assembly of an individual German state or province.

Albrecht von Roon (1803–1879)
Served in Prussian army from 1821, and wrote a number of texts on army reform. Active against radicals in 1848. As Minister of War (1859) and Minister of the Marine (1861), he collaborated with Moltke and Edwin von Manteuffel in the reform and modernisation of the Prussian Army. He became Minister President of Prussia (1871) when Bismarck vacated the post to take the office as Chancellor of the Reich.

Abdication: The constitutional process whereby a monarch gives up his or her throne.

Constitutionalism: Belief in a constitutional system of government.

1862) and collecting and spending the national budget whether they liked it or not. As theoretical justification, Bismarck exploited the 'gap theory' (*Luckentheorie*). He claimed that the constitution made the budget the joint responsibility of the two houses of the assembly and the monarch, but failed to cater for the eventuality of a dispute between them. In that event, he claimed, without much justification, the executive power reverted to the king.

More important than any theory, however, was the knowledge that real power lay in the hands of the government, the more so now that it had 53 new regiments at its disposal. 'The great questions of the day', Bismarck told the *Landtag*, in the first and most famous speech of his ministerial career, 'will not be decided by speeches and the resolutions of majorities – that was the great mistake of 1848 and 1849 – but by iron and blood.' For four years, and through two wars, Bismarck was to direct Prussian affairs without a constitutionally approved budget, and in the face of continued parliamentary opposition.

1. What was the Prussian constitutional crisis in the early 1860s about?

2. What do we learn about Bismarck's political priorities from his conduct during the constitutional crisis in 1862?

3.5 What were the bases of Bismarck's political beliefs and foreign policy?

What were the bases of Bismarck's political beliefs?

The new Minister President of Prussia, in 1862, was a man of 47 without any ministerial experience, and with extremely limited experience of government administration. Greatly though he stressed his origins among the Prussian feudal aristocracy, Bismarck was no ordinary Junker. His middle-class mother had insisted upon an education in Berlin and at the University of Göttingen, where he acquired a veneer of student liberalism and literary radicalism, to go with his Junker swordsmanship and love of riotous living. By nature, Bismarck was intensely ambitious, rightly convinced of his superiority over the narrow-minded conservatives that made up the Junker ranks, and intolerant of criticism to an extent that often brought on physical illness. From the time of his marriage (1847), he professed a simple, personal Protestant faith, but was able to divorce personal from political morality.

This strange semi-Junker gained his first political experience almost by accident, sitting in the Prussian *Landtag* in 1847 only as a substitute for a sick member. From this experience, and from the events of 1848–49, he derived an intense hostility towards radicalism. This was matched by his disdain for parliamentary 'talking shops' and contempt for policies that were based upon abstract romanticism. Having gained a powerful reputation on the extreme right of Prussian politics, he bitterly opposed the Erfurt Union as 'a shameful union with democracy' and rejoiced at the restoration of the *status quo* after Olmütz. The 1850s formed a crucial period in Bismarck's personal and political development. From 1850 to 1858, he sat as Prussian representative in the federal assembly (*Bundestag*), apparently ideally suited to aid reconciliation between the two great conservative forces in Germany. Indeed, contrary to his later autobiographical claims, his stance remained pro-Austrian until 1854. Many commentators have interpreted the transformation as the result of Austria's attempts to change the German *status quo* in its favour. For A.J.P. Taylor it was rather that the events surrounding the Crimean War convinced Bismarck that Austria was now unable effectively to protect conservative interests in Germany. Indeed, Bismarck wrote at the time, 'I should be very uneasy if we sought refuge from a possible storm by hitching our trim and sea-worthy frigate to that worm-eaten old Austrian man-of-war.'

Bundestag ('Federal Assembly'): The representative assembly of the German Confederation (Bund).

Germany and Central Europe,
1815–1866

The Kingdom of Prussia

The Austrian Empire

— Boundaries of the German Confederation

By 1859, Bismarck was so out of sympathy with Austria that he could advise General von Alvensleben, during the Italian crisis, to 'march southwards with our whole army with boundary posts in our soldiers' knapsacks and drive them into the ground either at Lake Constance or where Protestantism ceases to prevail'. His view was so out of keeping with Prince Wilhelm's concern for legitimacy that his reward was to be packed off as ambassador, first to St Petersburg (1859) and then to Paris (1862). Despite this, and despite the outbreak of three wars in his first eight years in power, we should not regard Bismarck as a warmonger. He followed Clausewitz in believing that 'war is the continuation of politics by other means', but generally he regarded those 'other means' as dangerous and to be avoided whenever possible.

In conclusion, Bismarck's beliefs and motives may be sorted into three categories.

● Firstly, his political instincts were conservative, although his intellect taught him that conservative ends could now only be attained by

A cartoon published in 1862 in the Prussian liberal magazine *Kladderadatsch*. Bismarck holds the Prussian constitution at arm's length and declares 'I cannot govern with this'.

1. What lessons had Otto von Bismarck learned from his political experiences in the years 1848–1862?

2. Who were Bismarck's main allies and main opponents within German politics when he came to power in 1862?

harnessing more modern notions, such as industrialism and nationalism.

- Secondly, his allegiance was to Prussia. It was not an allegiance to 'the people' or to 'the nation' as that of the German nationalists was, but to the monarchical, Junker-dominated state which he valued as 'an organ of power, a principle of order and authority'. Only when that state became, nominally, a German state did Bismarck's allegiance become German.

- Thirdly, Bismarck believed unswervingly in his own superior claim to exercise political power. 'He claimed', wrote A.J.P. Taylor, 'to serve sometimes the King of Prussia, sometimes Germany, sometimes God. All three were cloaks for his own will.'

What were the bases of Bismarck's foreign policy?

Principle or pragmatism?

The British statesman, Benjamin Disraeli, recounted in later years a conversation that he claimed to have had with Bismarck in 1862. According to Disraeli, Bismarck laid down a clear programme. 'As soon as the army shall be brought into such a condition as to inspire respect, I shall seize the first best pretext to declare war against Austria, dissolve the

German Diet and give national unity to Germany under Prussian leadership.' Recent historians have usually reacted to this either by dismissing the conversation, or by minimising it as the barest outline of long-term aims by a man as yet unaware of the complexities of politics at the highest level. The subjection of Austria, at least in northern Germany, as well as the destruction of the Confederation, probably represent Bismarck's ultimate hopes well enough. In power, however, he found repeatedly that a master plan was impossible, and that the only means of progress was the piecemeal exploitation of external events. In the 1860s, he became the supreme realist and **pragmatist**, learning to declare in later life that 'man cannot create the current of events. He can only float with it and steer.'

It is also possible to view Bismarck's spectacular foreign policy, in the 1860s, in a completely different light. Many recent writers on German history have tended to lay stress upon the importance of domestic politics, and to interpret foreign policy mainly as a means by which politicians sought to achieve domestic ends. Accordingly, Bismarck's policies in the 1860s are now sometimes interpreted mainly as a continuation of his domestic struggle to contain liberal, constitutional trends within Prussia. No sooner had he come to power in 1862 than the conservative *Kreuzzeitung* predicted that he would 'overcome domestic difficulties by a bold foreign policy'. Bismarck himself observed, at the same time, that 'as long as we gain respect abroad, we can get away with a great deal at home'. His ambiguous attitude towards liberal principles and his bid for a *rapprochement* with the liberals from a position of great strength after the victory of Sadowa both suggest that there are grounds for viewing the events of the 1860s from this domestic angle.

Prussia and the Polish revolt

Prussia's relations with its major European neighbour, Russia, were improved by factors arising from the Polish revolt of January 1863. The reaction of the Prussian government was to send General von Alvensleben to St Petersburg (February 1863) to offer a convention whereby Russian troops would be allowed to pass through Prussian territory in pursuit of Polish rebels. It was not a startling concession, considering what Prussian Junkers stood to lose from a peasant revolt, but it contrasted favourably with France's pro-Polish stance and with Austria's Crimean 'betrayal'. Historians have found it hard to agree upon the merits of the so-called 'Alvensleben Convention'. Erich Eyck followed a traditional line in viewing it as a significant diplomatic success, guaranteeing the future goodwill of Russia. D.G. Williamson and others have disagreed, seeing the Convention in the short term as a serious error, which alienated Prussian liberals and made it harder to achieve the *rapprochement* that Bismarck was seeking with France. In the longer term, however, it remains true that Russia was to acquiesce in Prussia's destruction of the central European balance of power. There was to be no Olmütz in the 1860s.

Austria and the Zollverein, *1862–1865*

Two further issues cemented Prussia's position within Germany. By signing a trade agreement with France in 1862, Prussia theoretically violated existing *Zollverein* treaties. This gave Austria the chance, its last as it happened, to make alternative economic proposals to the princes. Their rejection of these approaches, their acceptance of the Franco–Prussian agreement, and their conclusion of a renewed *Zollverein* treaty excluding Austria (1865), confirmed Prussia's economic leadership of Germany.

Austria seemed to be on firmer ground in terms of political leadership. The Emperor's decision (August 1863) to summon an Assembly of Princes (*Fürstentag*) to discuss reform of the Confederation, seemed likely to

Pragmatist: Someone who approaches problems in a practical and realistic manner, rather than with an ideal solution in mind.

Kreuzzeitung: A contemporary Prussian newspaper (*Zeitung*) that reflected the conservative views of the governing classes. It took its name from the principal military decoration of the Prussian army, the Iron Cross (*Kreuz* – cross).

Rapprochement: A French term indicating a coming together, or a resolution of different opinions. It is usually used to indicate the reestablishment of friendly relations between states or between political groups.

Fürstentag: An assembly of the German princes, occasionally convened by the Austrian Emperor as a forum for the discussion of German affairs.

1. What did Bismarck do between 1862 and 1865 (a) to strengthen Prussia's position within Germany, and (b) to improve its diplomatic position within Europe?

2. 'Bismarck's conduct of Prussian politics between 1862 and 1865 was entirely conservative.' Do you agree with this statement?

confirm its position and the duality of power within Germany. At Bismarck's insistence, Wilhelm refused to acknowledge Austrian leadership by attending, and refused to accept the reform proposals drafted there. As events were to prove, this was Austria's last attempt to unite Germany by princely consent. Thus, Austria's traditional claim to speak and act for the princes as a whole was already open to doubt at the moment when the next crisis of German nationalism erupted.

3.6 By what means, and by what stages, was Austria excluded from German politics between 1863–1866?

The Schleswig-Holstein crisis of 1863–1864

The issue of the two duchies on the borders of Germany and Denmark was an old one, and had last come to a head in 1848. The problem arose from a mixed population and from a confusion of dynastic and semi-feudal claims. Schleswig, to the north, was predominantly Danish, while Holstein had a substantial German majority and was actually a member of the German Confederation. The territories were technically subject to the King of Denmark, but enjoyed a large degree of legal and administrative independence. The crisis of 1848 had arisen from the support of the middle-class nationalist Holsteiners for the Duke of Augustenburg, whose son continued the family's bid for local power in the 1860s. The pre-1848 status of both Schleswig and Holstein was confirmed by the major powers, in 1852, by the so-called London Protocol. This confirmed both Danish overlordship and the liberties of the duchies and thus left both parties dissatisfied.

A renewed crisis resulted, in 1863, from the decision of the new Danish monarch, Christian IX, to regulate the situation in his country's favour. The reaction of German nationalists to this initiative is well illustrated by the declaration of the Prussian liberal, Karl Twesten, that he 'would rather suffer the Bismarck ministry for some years longer than allow a German land to be lost to us'. Bismarck, too, stood to benefit from intervention. In the first place, he could not tolerate the increase in the prestige of the German Confederation that would result from an easy victory over Denmark. It seems clear, too, that he always had in mind the ultimate annexation of the duchies, predominantly as a means by which to confirm his position in the eyes of King Wilhelm.

At no stage did Bismarck pretend to be acting in the interests of nationalism, writing that 'it is no concern of ours whether the Germans of Holstein are happy'. Nor is it seriously maintained any longer that this was a trap to lure Austria into military commitment and to create the basis for future tensions. The alliance by which the two German powers agreed to joint action (January 1864) was necessary to avoid Austrian jealousy, to prevent it leading a force on behalf of the Confederation, and to minimise the fears and resentments of the other signatories of the London Protocol. The war itself was a one-sided affair, concluded by the treaty signed in Vienna, in October 1864, whereby King Christian renounced both Schleswig and Holstein. After years of wrangles in which the Confederation had put forward the German viewpoint, that body was now totally excluded from the settlement. The claims of the Duke of Augustenburg were also conveniently ignored, and the newly acquired territories were placed under the joint administration of Austria and Prussia. Squabbles, accusations and threats of war marked their ten months of joint rule. Yet, rather than start a confrontation, Bismarck accepted the conciliatory Convention of Gastein (August 1865), which formally divided the administration. Prussia took responsibility for Schleswig and Austria for Holstein.

The impact of the crisis on German politics

At the close of 1865, Bismarck had some cause for satisfaction. Quite apart from influence over Schleswig, his actions had demonstrated once more the impotence of the Confederation. Also, far from opposing him, Austria had been party to that demonstration. For the first time in German political affairs in the 19th century, Prussia had led while Austria followed.

Bismarck was also entitled to suppose that he had reduced the hostility of the Prussian liberals towards him. Otto Pflanze, in *Bismarck and the Development of Germany* (1963), has claimed that, as a result of the blow apparently struck for the German cause, 'almost overnight the Bismarck cult was born. Its devotees began to reinterpret their hero's actions during the preceding four years. They excused his infringements of the constitution in view of what they presumed to have been his hidden purpose.' Others, such as Golo Mann, do not accept that Prussia's liberals were won over so easily. There is little doubt, however, that within the next year Bismarck was to score remarkable triumphs over all his opponents within Germany.

The Austro-Prussian War: diplomatic preparations

The idea that the Gastein Convention was a trap deliberately laid by Bismarck to lure Austria into war is no longer widely accepted. It might be seen as a semi-satisfactory compromise over a delicate set of problems, which allowed Bismarck to gain time. In 1864 and in early 1865, war with Austria still posed too much of a risk. By late 1865 and early 1866, however, several of the outstanding uncertainties had been resolved in a manner satisfactory to Prussia. The first such uncertainty was the attitude of France. Bismarck's meetings with Napoleon III at Biarritz and at St Cloud (October–November 1865) left him confident of French neutrality in the event of an Austro-Prussian conflict. It is far from certain that any promises of territorial compensation were made and it may be that the most important outcome was Bismarck's realisation that Napoleon's main desire was to remain at peace.

Secondly, the attitude of Italy was clarified. A new trade treaty with the *Zollverein* (December 1865) had not fully won Italy over to the Prussian camp, but the failure of its friendly approaches to Austria had decided its course by April 1864. By the military alliance then signed, Italy agreed to fight with Prussia against Austria, with Venetia as its reward. The condition was also laid down that the war should begin within three months. Bismarck had ensured, by this diplomacy, that he would fight only on one front, while Austria fought on two. He had also ensured that the issue would be decided by war. In May, as a last bid for peace, Austria actually agreed to acknowledge Prussian supremacy in northern Germany, but demanded the retention of Venetia as a condition, forcing Bismarck to reject the offer because of his commitment to Italy.

The war and its outcome

Superficially, the war that began with the Prussian invasion of Holstein, in June, was about the administration of the duchies. Prussia accused the

Refugees: People who are forced to leave their country because there is a war or because of their political or religious beliefs.

Austrian authorities of violating their mutual agreements by sheltering **refugees** from the harsh Prussian rule in Schleswig. Austria was also in breach of the Gastein Convention, it was claimed, when it referred this dispute to the German Confederation. These were obviously convenient excuses. The war was really a trial of Prussian strength, postponed from 1850, against Austria and against the Confederation, which was Austria's main power base within Germany. It was significant that Prussia also went to war with Saxony, Hanover, Bavaria, Würtemberg, Baden, Hesse-Darmstadt, Hesse-Cassel and Nassau. In a very real sense, this was a war for the conquest of northern Germany at least.

In the war itself, the German states proved to be ineffectual allies. Their forces failed to link effectively with those of Austria, and they were eliminated from the conflict in a series of engagements, conveniently ignored by subsequent nationalist historians, at Langensalza, Dormbach, Kissingen and Rossbrunn. On the all-important Bohemian front, the decisive action was fought at Sadowa (otherwise known as the battle of Königgrätz), on 3 July. Superior Prussian infantry tactics and **armaments** ensured heavy Austrian losses (roughly 20,000 to Prussia's 9,000), and left open the road to Vienna. The rapid conclusion of an armistice at Nikolsburg three weeks later was the result of compelling pressures on both sides. The Austrians were motivated by nationalist 'rumblings' in Bohemia and Hungary, while Bismarck had reason to fear the reactions of France and Russia to Prussia's extraordinary triumph. In combating the strong desire of King Wilhelm and his generals for territorial gains, Bismarck was thinking not only of foreign jealousy and the future balance of power, but also of the danger of the conservative Prussian state and administration overreaching itself. 'Our power finds its limits,' he wrote at the time, 'when the supply of Junkers to fill official posts gives out.'

Armaments: Weapons and military equipment belonging to an army or a country.

1. What steps did Bismarck take, between 1863 and 1866, to ensure that Prussia would be successful in a war against Austria?

2. How important was Bismarck's diplomacy in bringing about Prussia's victory over Austria in 1866?

3.7 What had Bismarck achieved by 1866?

The Treaty of Prague

Prussia's defeat of Austria, which was enshrined in the Treaty of Prague (23 August 1866), caused a greater disruption to the European state system, and to the balance of power, than any other event since the defeat of Napoleon. The contemporary German historian Ferdinand Gregorovius captured the importance of the event with only a little exaggeration:

> 'The entire Prussian campaign has no parallel in the history of the world. The consequences of the Battle of Sadowa are at least as follows: the unification of Germany through Prussia, the consummation of Italian independence, the fall of the temporal power of the Papacy, the deposition of France from the dominion she has usurped over Europe.'

In more sober detail, the treaty allowed Prussia to annex Hanover, Hesse-Cassel, Nassau, Frankfurt and Schleswig-Holstein. By recognition of its right to form all German territories north of the river Main into a new North German Confederation, Prussia achieved the death of the old German Confederation. A seven-week military campaign had thus untied a knot that had defied decades of diplomatic wrangling. Austria suffered no territorial loss, apart from Venetia. Instead, it surrendered to Prussia the only prize that Bismarck had really desired, its prestige and status within Germany. Nevertheless, the defeat had profound long-term effects upon the Austrian Empire. At a stroke, it was banished from the political affairs of both Germany and Italy. The only direction in which it could now seek prestige and expansion was towards the south-east, towards the Balkans. This was a factor that was to have grave consequences in 1914. For the time being, it turned in on itself, reassessing its internal strength and revising its internal organisation. The most important product of these processes was the Compromise (*Ausgleich*) of 1867, by which Hungary was recognised as a constitutional monarchy, free from Austrian interference in its internal affairs and united to it only through the person of its king.

The 'surrender' of the Prussian liberals

The events of 1866 also provided Bismarck with a notable domestic triumph. The Prussian liberal movement had now to decide upon its reactions to this partial unification of Germany. It had sought unification for decades, but had consistently condemned the means by which it had now been achieved. Many were intoxicated by Bismarck's success. 'I bow before the genius of Bismarck,' wrote a previously consistent critic, von Schering. 'I have forgiven the man everything he has done up to now. More, I have convinced myself that it was necessary.' Johannes Miquel insisted that his fellow liberals should now be practical. 'Today more than ever before politicians must ask, not what is desirable, but what is attainable.'

In this atmosphere, Bismarck chose the moment perfectly to approach the **Reichstag** with an admission that he had acted illegally over the past four years. He requested their pardon in the form of an **Act of Indemnity**. He was duly pardoned by 230 votes to 75. The Progress Party split on the issue and a new political party emerged, the National Liberals. The new party remained devoted to the principles of free trade and the rule of law, but, for the time, shared common ground with Bismarck in its enthusiasm for a strong German state.

Did Prussian liberalism 'sell out' to Bismarck?

The answers of historians have tended to reflect their views on liberalism, or on the German state founded by Bismarck. To Heinrich von Sybel, a patriotic contemporary, the Act of Indemnity was an enlightened and moderate compromise. More recently, Otto Pflanze has accused the liberals of surrendering to success. They were the victims, he claims, 'of their own limited ends, their lack of genuine popular support, and their lust for national power'. It is also important to understand that the relationship between Bismarck and the liberals was more complex than simple confrontation. Although the division between them over constitutional issues was deep, there was scope for genuine co-operation on other, more practical matters. Bismarck retained genuine sympathy for some of the economic priorities of the liberals, and promoted them in the aftermath of the constitutional crisis. His succession of trade treaties, for instance, with Belgium, Britain, France and Italy served both parties, catering for the economic principles of the liberals and confirming, at the same time, Prussia's dominance within the *Zollverein*.

Equally, as the 1860s progressed, both sides could find much to attract them in a policy of *kleindeutsch* national unity. It is not satisfactory to see Bismarck's confrontation with the Prussian liberals, in 1862–63, simply as a prelude to the 'real' business of foreign policy. Until the late 1870s, it remained an important priority for Bismarck in domestic politics to maintain some form of working relationship with the liberals. This factor must be borne in mind in assessing what passed between them in 1866.

Reichstag: The parliament of the united German Empire (Reich). This name was used for the assembly of the North German Confederation even though, technically, Germany did not become an 'empire' until 1871.

Act of Indemnity: A legal act which pardons an individual, or a group, for illegal acts that he/she/they have committed in the past.

Prussian dominance of the North German Confederation

The most important characteristic of the new North German Confederation, created by the Treaty of Prague, was that it rested upon the military power of Prussia. The true nature of Prussian domination was clearly illustrated by the case of Hanover, where a long-established dynasty was deposed and the fortune of its king confiscated. Similarly, in Schleswig-Holstein, Prussia continued to ride roughshod over the Augustenburg claims. Of the 23 states that associated themselves by treaty in the North German Confederation, Prussia supplied five-sixths of the population. The constitution of the Confederation, however, was a compromise. It was a synthesis of Bismarck's original, rigidly conservative ideas, and liberal attempts to preserve some measure of parliamentary liberty. Why, given the power of his position, did Bismarck compromise? The historian Gordon Craig believes that Bismarck deliberately attempted to create a viable parliament so as to play it off against the separatist tendencies of the governments of the member states. Perhaps, as the historian Erich Eyck has suggested, Bismarck also made liberal concessions in the hope that future membership would thus be more inviting to the southern states.

As a result of these concessions, the North German Parliament (*Norddeutscher Reichstag*) was elected, by universal manhood suffrage and by secret ballot. It enjoyed both freedom of speech and the freedom to publish its debates. The liberals also succeeded in forcing the administration to submit the budget, which was nearly all for military expenditure, for the Reichstag's approval every four (later extended to every seven) years.

On the other hand, Bismarck retained substantial freedom of action. Most taxes were indirect, from *Zollverein* customs and duties, and were therefore beyond the control of the Reichstag. The Federal Chancellor (Bismarck himself) was the only 'responsible' minister, and it was far from clear to whom he was 'responsible'. Indeed, there were no other federal ministers to impede Bismarck. Finally, the initiation of legislation was in the hands of the Federal Council (*Bundesrat*), made up of appointed representatives of the states' governments. This was, effectively, the old Federal Diet, but was now firmly under the presidency and control of Prussia.

1. What did Bismarck and Prussia gain from the victory over Austria in 1866?

2. How justifiable is the claim that the North German Confederation was nothing more than an expanded version of the Prussian state?

3.8 What factors forced Bismarck to go beyond the settlement achieved in 1866?

The position of the southern states

It is probable that Bismarck had no clear plans for further action at the end of 1866. 'There is nothing more to do in our lifetime,' he had written to his wife. Yet the southern German states continued to pose complex problems for Prussia. Strong separatist forces survived south of the River Main. Of four southern states, only Baden, whose Grand Duke was son-in-law to the King of Prussia, showed any real enthusiasm for union with the north. In Hesse, popular enthusiasm for union was offset by the hostility of the government while, in Bavaria and Würtemberg, opposition to the north was more general. A strong Democratic Party in Würtemberg remained hostile to Prussian absolutism, while in Bavaria dynastic jealousy and staunch anti-Protestantism combined with a widespread dislike of Prussian **militarism**. As late as 1869, the election of a large Catholic majority in the Bavarian assembly seemed to confirm the strength of **separatism**.

Militarism: A philosophy or policy that emphasises the importance and the value of military strength and military success.

Separatism: A political belief, or movement, that advocates the separation of one territory or political grouping from a larger political unit.

Friedrich Ferdinand von Beust (1809–1896)
Served in the government of his native Saxony as Foreign Minister (1849–53) and Minister of the Interior (1853–66). Upon the defeat of Saxony by Prussia in 1866, he transferred to the service of Austria. He held office as Imperial Austrian Chancellor (1867–71), in which capacity he was responsible for the early implementation of the *Ausgleich* (Compromise) with Hungary, and for important measures against the Catholic Church. Ambassador to London (1871–78) and to Paris (1878–82).

Why, then, could the south not be left alone? In part, there was the danger of what allies the southern states might find if they were not the friends of Prussia. The Austrian Emperor, for instance, had given clear notice that he did not necessarily regard the Treaty of Prague as a final and irreversible settlement by appointing the former Saxon premier, Friedrich Ferdinand von Beust, as his Foreign Minister. France, too, tentatively sought friends south of the Main. In addition, pressure for further progress towards unity came from the liberal nationalists of the north who, like Johannes Miquel, refused to see the river Main as more than 'a preliminary stop where the engine has to refuel and take on water in order to continue the journey'. More important still was the fact that the separate existence of the southern states was a sham. Mainly because of the mutual jealousy of Würtemberg and Bavaria, the southern states were unable to translate the vague phrases of the Treaty of Prague concerning a southern union into any form of reality. As a result, they were effectively dependent upon Prussia in both military and economic terms. As members of the *Zollverein* already, the southern states had little choice, after 1866, but to accept Prussian proposals for a 'Customs Parliament' that would add political links to existing economic ones. Even so, by electing a majority favourable to separatism, the southern states continued to keep their distance.

The most effective link between the new Confederation and the south was, therefore, the string of military treaties that Bismarck concluded with the southern states, in August 1866. These placed Prussia in the position recently vacated by Austria, as their protector. Already, by the end of 1866, war appeared the most likely cause of further German unification.

Germany and France: the Luxembourg question

The key diplomatic questions raised by the events of 1866 concerned future German relations with France. In the memoirs that he published after his fall from office, Bismarck claimed to have believed that a conflict with France was an inevitable step along the path to further national unity. In fact, his view at the time was certainly less clear than that. It was based upon the assumption that Napoleon III could not simply accept the changes of 1866, but was not based upon any clear notion of how the Emperor would respond. 'Napoleon III,' he wrote at the time, 'has lost more prestige than he can afford. To recover it he will start a dispute with us on some pretext or other. I do not believe that he personally wishes war, but his insecurity will drive him on.'

After initial probes in the direction of Belgium and the Rhineland, Napoleon's 'policy of compensation' came to focus upon the Grand Duchy of Luxembourg. It does not seem possible, any longer, to maintain that Bismarck trapped or tricked the French Emperor over the Luxembourg question. On the contrary, most recent commentators have agreed that he was quite content to give up the territory and its fortifications to France as the price for placating it and preserving the stability of his new North German creation. What he would not do was to commit himself publicly to that policy when he badly needed the support of the liberal nationalists in the Reichstag.

The insistence of the King of Holland that he would not sell Luxembourg without the specific agreement of Prussia was thus the factor that killed the deal. Bismarck did not initiate the nationalist outcry that now condemned the loss of any 'ancient German land', but he was power-less to act against it. Prussia effectively gained nothing from the international conference (May 1867) that agreed to the neutralisation of Luxembourg and to the removal of the Prussian garrison. France was not pacified, and the strategic position of Germany was not strengthened.

1. What problems did Bismarck encounter in German politics in the years immediately after his victory over Austria?

2. Do the political events of 1867 suggest that Bismarck was losing control of German politics?

Bismarck's only consolation came from the increased unease that now arose in the southern states about French ambitions. When Erich Eyck wrote, in *Bismarck and the German Empire* (1968), that 'the Luxembourg affair was the turning point in Bismarck's development from a Prussian to a German statesman', he meant it, not in the sense that the Chancellor had undergone a conscious conversion, but in the sense that, for the first time, he had lost the initiative. He had been carried along further than he wished by a force that he had previously exploited with confidence.

3.9 Why, and with what consequences, did Prussia go to war with France in 1870?

The Hohenzollern candidature

The peace of western Europe was not seriously threatened by the Luxembourg crisis, but it was shattered, three years later, by a less predictable confrontation. In September 1868, revolution in Spain overthrew the ruling house of Bourbon. By the beginning of 1869, the Spanish throne had already been rejected by a number of candidates who placed too high a value upon a quiet life. Prince Leopold von Hohenzollern-Sigmaringen, a member of the Catholic branch of the Prussian ruling house, then took up the candidature. By the following February, Spanish representatives were busy overcoming the misgivings of the prince, of his father, Prince Karl Anton, and of the Prussians. The Prussian government insisted throughout that the candidature must, at no time, appear to be official state policy. With King Wilhelm's permission grudgingly given (June 1870), the project seemed able to go ahead as long as speed and secrecy presented France with a *fait accompli*. Under such circumstances their obvious objections to a monarch with Prussian sympathies on their southern border, would be outflanked. That hope, however, was thwarted by misunderstanding and delay in Madrid. In early July, before the Spanish parliament could formally decide upon their king, the French ambassador received official confirmation of the rumours that he had already heard.

The reaction of the French foreign ministry was strong enough, and had sufficient backing elsewhere in Europe, to kill off the Hohenzollern candidature. Clumsy French attempts, however, to extract a promise from King Wilhelm that the project would never be renewed, seemed to call into question the royal and the national honour. This gave Bismarck the chance to snatch from the Spanish affair greater advantage than had ever seemed possible. By releasing to the press an edited version of the telegram in which the king reported his conversation with the French ambassador at Bad Ems (the 'Ems Telegram'), Bismarck gave the impression that a blunt exchange of diplomatic insults had taken place. He once more took control of the nationalist forces that had served him so well in the past. Faced with the choice of retreat or further confrontation, France declared war (19 July), initiating a conflict in which a united German state was to be forged.

What was Bismarck's role in the candidature?

In his memoirs, Bismarck was eager to convey the impression of total detachment from the Hohenzollern affair, and to charge the disruption of European peace to the insolence and instability of the French government. Later research, especially by G. Bonnin and Erich Eyck, however, clearly demonstrated Bismarck's close links with the candidature. These range from the initial distribution of bribes, through the difficult process of

Fait accompli: A French term signifying an 'accomplished fact', something that is over and done with, and is not subject to further negotiation.

convincing King Wilhelm of the strategic advantages of the project, to the final affair of the 'Ems Telegram'. It is difficult to doubt that Bismarck engineered the candidature, but that does not necessarily mean that he did so with a view to starting war. Indeed, it was only by accident that the French government found out about the candidature in time to react at all. It is better, therefore, to see Bismarck's aim as being to outmanoeuvre and surround France in such a way as to force it to accept further Prussian aggrandisement without a fight. The thwarting of the plan, rather than the plan itself, left him with no other means than war by which to create stronger links between the northern and southern German states. He could have had unity without war, but only through war could he guarantee that such unity would rest upon a basis of Prussian military domination. This was the only basis acceptable to Bismarck and to those he served.

1870: the completion of German unity

> **Eduard Lasker (1829–1884)**
> Liberal politician of Jewish origins. Active amongst student revolutionaries in Vienna in 1848. Elected to Prussian Landtag (1865) and to the assembly of the North German Confederation (1867). One of the founders of the National Liberal Party which he represented in the Reichstag from 1871. Played a major role in the drafting and codification of German law after unification.

Of greater importance than the military victory in the Franco-Prussian War were the political developments by which the German Empire was formed. At the outbreak of the war, a powerful combination of factors ensured that the southern states would honour their treaty obligations to Prussia. Not least among these was the popular enthusiasm that Karl Marx dismissed contemptuously as 'south German beer patriotism'. Much pressure also came from the leaders of the National Liberals, especially from Eduard Lasker, who organised persuasive propaganda campaigns south of the river Main. The Crown Prince of Prussia, Friedrich, was also a consistent advocate of unity and of the claim of the Hohenzollerns to the Imperial German crown. Although, once more, events were moving beyond Bismarck's control, he too played his role by the well-timed publication of France's earlier compensation proposals, a frightening revelation for the southerners.

While the generals, to the chagrin of the Chancellor, kept the conduct of the war closely under their own control, Bismarck's prime concern was to negotiate a settlement with the southern states that would turn a wartime alliance into a permanent union. In this task three main obstacles needed to be overcome: the respective desires of Würtemberg and of Bavaria to maintain their own independence, and the determination of King Wilhelm not to accept a 'popular' crown, nor to see the Prussian monarchy diminished by becoming a wider, German one. In the long run, the position of the major southern states was hopeless. They could not rely on each other, could not risk an isolated existence outside an otherwise united Germany, and could scarcely resist the growing nationalist enthusiasm inside their own boundaries. Continued separatism, as King Ludwig of Bavaria conceded, 'would be completely impossible politically because of opposition from the army and the people, as a result of which the Crown would lose the support of the country'.

German unity without Austria was assured in November 1870, when a mixture of threats and bribes from Prussian state funds persuaded Ludwig to sign a treaty accepting unification. Bavaria and Würtemberg preserved a number of symbols of independence. They retained control over their postal and railway systems, and over their armies in peacetime. This was a small price for Bismarck to pay for an assurance that Wilhelm would now be offered the German crown by the princes, and not by the Reichstag. In the event, that body was merely asked to approve the offer, and did so with enthusiasm. Wilhelm, himself, had many reservations and regrets about the transformation of his beloved Prussian kingdom. He could at least console himself with the fact that the assembly that proclaimed him

A painting by the German court artist, Anton von Werner, showing the acclamation of Wilhelm I as German Emperor by the German princes in the Hall of Mirrors in Versailles, 18 January 1871.

Werner's painting draws attention to specific elements which he suggests were responsible for German unification. Identify them.

'German Emperor' (not 'Emperor of Germany', for that would have offended Bavarian feelings, and would have raised awkward questions about the extent of 'Germany') at Versailles, on 18 January 1871, was an assembly of his fellow monarchs. He had thus remained true to his legitimist philosophy, and had not 'picked up a crown from the gutter'.

1. What were the immediate causes of the Franco-Prussian War?

2. How convincing is the claim that Bismarck planned the Franco-Prussian War and its outcome?

3. Why did the war between Prussia and France in 1870–71 end in the declaration of a united Germany?

Conclusion

Bismarck's great achievement, by 1871, was not that he had created a united German state. Many other forces – nationalism and industrialisation, for example – had given him invaluable aid in that process. His great achievement had been to bring about German unity without damaging important conservative elements within the Prussian state. His triumph was a great one. It was a triumph over the radicals, who wanted a different kind of Germany, and over the conservatives, who had been reluctant to take Prussia into any kind of united Germany. His was a united Germany without true democracy, without parliamentarianism and without Austria.

3.10 Was German unification primarily the result of successful Bismarckian diplomacy?
A CASE STUDY IN HISTORICAL INTERPRETATION

When C. Grant Robertson wrote, in *Bismarck* (1919), of German unification as a 'marvellous march of events, in which each stage seems to slip into its pre-appointed place,' he was perpetuating a tradition established some years earlier in Germany itself. A generation of German historians had interpreted German unification as the premeditated design of a master politician, and had portrayed Bismarck as the supreme statesman, leading Germany to its rightful destiny. Prominent in this school of thought was the Prussian academic Heinrich von Treitschke, whose *German History in the Nineteenth Century* (1879–94) traced the 'inevitable' rise of Prussian mastery, with Bismarck portrayed as the chosen instrument of Germany's fate. Bismarck himself was happy to convey a similar impression in his memoirs, eager as he was to maintain his status as a national hero after being forced from office. In such an interpretation, the diplomacy of the great Prussian minister is seen as the primary factor in the sequence of events that created the united German state. He successfully outmanoeuvred Austria over the Schleswig-Holstein affair, isolated it from Russia and from France in preparation for the conflict of 1866, and subsequently goaded France into the war by which the German states were finally welded together.

A very different view of Bismarck's work and of German unification was provided after the Second World War by A.J.P. Taylor, in *Bismarck: the Man and the Statesman* (1968). Taylor ascribed to Bismarck a great deal of political skill, but much more limited aims and vision. Bismarck's primary concern was merely to establish Prussian hegemony in northern Germany, as a means to guarantee that its freedom of political action would not be limited by the influence of Austria. In effect, he had achieved these goals by 1866, through the defeat of Austria, the establishment of a North German Confederation dominated by Prussia, and the acquisition of new territories in northern Germany. The subsequent confrontation with a hostile France was certainly not part of a Bismarckian master plan. On the contrary, he was surprised and frightened by it, and attempted to deflect it by concessions over Luxembourg, and by diplomatic intrigues with Spain. When these proved unsuccessful, the creation of a 'wartime coalition' involving other German states, was primarily a pragmatic measure to avert a Prussian defeat. At much the same time, the German-American historian Otto Pflanze was arguing, in *Bismarck and the Development of Germany* (1963), that the whole notion of a movement within Germany towards unification was a 'fiction of nationalistic historians'. It was not something broadly desired by public opinion, and was engineered by Bismarck mainly to serve his own political ends.

Other historians have taken a different route towards diminishing the role played by the genius of Bismarck. These have concentrated less upon the Prussian statesman himself, than upon the environment in which he operated. W.E. Mosse, in *The European Powers and the German Question* (1958), examined the wider diplomatic environment of the 1850s and 1860s, and stressed the favourable circumstances which made Bismarck's task easier. The major obstacles at the start of the 1850s to Prussian aggrandisement or to German unification were the hostility of Austria, Russia and France. In the course of the 1850s, Austria was weakened and discredited by defeats in Italy and by the breakdown of its relations with Russia, while France under Napoleon III became isolated and the object of suspicion. None of this owed anything to the work of Bismarck, or of any other German politician, but these developments created favourable circumstances, which a clever opportunist could exploit. 'If he played his hand with great skill,' Mosse concluded, 'it was a good one in the first place.'

Much as these interpretations differ over the vision and premeditation employed by Bismarck, they all view diplomacy as the primary force driving Germany towards unification. The British economist J.M. Keynes laid the foundations for a very different interpretation many years ago with his famous judgement that 'the German Empire was created more by coal and iron than by blood and iron' (*The Economic Consequences of the Peace*, 1919). Subsequently, an influential school of German historians has substituted the 'primacy of economics' for the 'primacy of diplomacy'. The most notable work, in this area, has been that of Helmut Böhme who, in *Germany's Path towards Great Power Status* (1966), concentrated upon the social and economic development of contemporary Germany. For Böhme and the writers who have followed his lead, the most important factor in German history in the 19th century was the development of its economic life, and especially the development of an industrial economy in Prussia. This emphasis leads historians to consider how far the Prussian state was in control of such forces. There is ample evidence that, in the years before 1860, Prussian ministers took important steps to exploit the growing industrial economy in the interests of the state. The creation of the *Zollverein* is a prime example of this, emphasising the growing attractions of a German national market. Indeed, Böhme believed that Prussian diplomacy, itself, was founded upon this economic dynamic. The political struggles of the early 1860s arose largely from Prussia's awareness of the importance of such economic leadership, and the desire to protect it against economic challenges from Austria. 'The *kleindeutsch* national state,' he claimed, 'arose chiefly from the Prussian defence against the economic order conceived by Austria for the great Central European region.'

An examination of Germany's development after 1871, however, makes it equally clear that the interests of German industrialists did not fully coincide with the interests of the Prussian-dominated state. It is tempting to conclude, therefore, that although Bismarck rode such economic forces with great skill in the 1860s and the 1870s, he found himself in an unfamiliar Germany during the latter part of his political career. He governed a state with a highly traditional political structure, contrasting starkly with a modern, dynamic economy. This was not something that he had desired, and certainly not something that he had planned.

1. What different views have been taken by historians of the role played by Bismarck in the unification of Germany?

2. Why have some historians in recent years attached less importance to the work of Bismarck as a cause of German unification?

Source-based questions: The Hohenzollern candidature

SOURCE A

Your Majesty,
Will I trust, graciously permit me with my humble duty to summarise the motives which in my modest opinion speak in favour of the acceptance of the Spanish Crown by His Serene Highness, the Hereditary Prince of Hohenzollern, now that I have already respectfully intimated them by word of mouth.

For Germany it is desirable to have on the other side of France an ally on whose sympathies (1) we can rely and with whose feelings France is obliged to reckon. During a war between Germany and France it would be necessary to keep at least one French Corps stationed on the Spanish frontier. We have in the long run to look for the preservation of peace not to the good will of France but to the impression created by our position of strength (2).

No danger to the person of the Hereditary Prince need be anticipated. In all the revolutions which have convulsed Spain the idea of an outrage against the person of the Monarch has never arisen, no threat has ever been uttered (3).

I feel a personal need to make it plain by the present humble memorandum that if the outcome is a refusal the responsibility will not lie at my door, especially if in a near or remote future historians and public opinion were to investigate into the grounds which have led to rejection (4).
Von Bismarck (5).

Bismarck to the King of Prussia, 9 March 1870.
(The numbered notes are referred to in Source B.)

SOURCE B

(1) How long would these sympathies last?
(2) Agreed.
(3) But the expulsion of the dynasty did take place.
(4) The above marginal notes make it clear that I have strong scruples against the acceptance of the Spanish Crown by the Hereditary Prince of Hohenzollern and would only consent to his acceptance of it if his own conviction told him that it was his duty to mount the Spanish throne, in other words, that he regarded his act as a definite vocation. In these circumstances I am unable to advise the Hereditary Prince to such an act. Wilhelm.
(5) At the discussion which took place in my presence the majority gave adherence to the view put forward by the Minister-President, namely the acceptance of the Spanish throne by the Hereditary Prince. Since, however, the latter upheld his verbal and written declaration that he could only decide on acceptance on my command, the discussion was thereby brought to an end. Wilhelm.

Notes made by the King of Prussia in the margins of Bismarck's letter (Source A).

SOURCE C

When the King heard that the candidature was being further discussed he said that it was 'very extraordinary that this sort of thing was going on without his authorisation'. He wanted to be informed 'of everything that Prim's agent brings either by word of mouth or in writing before any action is taken'.

Report from Thile, Bismarck's principal aide in the Foreign Office, to Bismarck, 19 June 1870

SOURCE D

That beats everything! So his Majesty wants the affair treated with official royal interference? The whole affair is only possible if it remains the limited concern of the Hohenzollern princes.
It must not turn into a Prussian concern, the King must be able to say without lying: I know nothing about it.

Bismarck's comments on Thile's report (Source C).

SOURCE E

Preparations for war on a large scale are in progress in France. The situation is, therefore, more than serious. Just as I could not bid your son accept the crown, so I cannot bid him withdraw his acceptance. Should he, however, so decide, my 'adherence' will again not be wanting.

King Wilhelm I to Prince Karl Anton, 10 July 1870

Source-based questions: The Hohenzollern candidature

SOURCE F

During dinner at which Moltke and Roon were present, the pronouncement came from the embassy in Paris that the Prince of Hohenzollern had renounced his candidature in order to prevent the war with which France threatened us. My first idea was to retire from the service because I perceived in this extorted submission a humiliation of Germany for which I did not desire to be responsible. I was very distressed for I saw no means of repairing the corroding injury I dreaded to our national position from a timorous policy, unless by picking quarrels clumsily and seeking them artificially. I saw by that time that war was a necessity, which we could no longer avoid with honour.

Bismarck discussing the events of 12 July 1870 in his memoirs, *Reflections and Reminiscences*, published in 1898.

1. Explain briefly the following references:

(a) 'it must not turn into a Prussian concern' (Source D)

(b) 'your son' (Source E)

(c) 'the corroding injury I dreaded to our national position' (Source F)

2. Study Sources B, C and E.

(a) From a comparison of these sources, assess the consistency of the King's attitude to the Hohenzollern candidature.

(b) On the evidence of these sources, consider the view that Bismarck treated the opinions of the King with barely concealed contempt.

3. Study all of the sources.

From these documents, and any other evidence known to you, how far would you agree that by 12 July 1870 Bismarck had sustained a major diplomatic defeat entirely of his own making?

Further Reading

The Unification of Germany, 1815–70 by Andrina Stiles (Hodder & Stoughton, Access to History series, 1989)

Imperial Germany 1850–1918 by Edgar Feuchtwanger (Routledge, 2001)

4 Germany under Bismarck, 1871–1890

Key Issues

- What problems confronted Bismarck in the government of united Germany, and how effectively did he deal with them?

- In what ways did Germany's economy and society develop in the years after unification?

- How well did the diplomacy of the united Reich serve the interests of Germany and of European peace?

4.1 What were the main political features of the Bismarckian state?

4.2 Why, and with what results, did Bismarck enter into an electoral alliance with the National Liberals between 1871 and 1878?

4.3 What was the purpose of the *Kulturkampf*, and to what extent was it achieved?

4.4 Why did Bismarck abandon the National Liberals for a more conservative stance in 1878?

4.5 How successful was Bismarck in his attempt to combat socialism?

4.6 Historical interpretation: To what extent was Bismarck responsible for the authoritarianism and intolerance of the German state in the early 20th century?

4.7 To what extent did Bismarck's foreign policy succeed in defending German interests in the 1870s?

4.8 Did Bismarck's alliance with Austria after 1878 represent the failure of his diplomatic system?

4.9 Why did Bismarck launch a German colonial policy in his last years in power?

4.10 What was the impact of unification upon German economic development?

Framework of Events

1871	January: Proclamation of German Empire
	May: Franco-Prussian War concluded by Treaty of Frankfurt
1872	June: Expulsion of Jesuits from Germany as part of *Kulturkampf*
	September: Formation of 'League of the Three Emperors'
1874	Introduction of May Laws, limiting the independence of Catholic clergy
1875	March: Publication of papal bull *Quod Nunquam* attacking May Laws
	April: 'War in Sight' crisis
1878	June–July: Congress of Berlin resolves the international crisis arising out of the Russo-Turkish War
	July: Major conservative gains in Reichstag elections at expense of National Liberals
	October: Introduction of anti-socialist laws
1879	July: Passage of new tariff laws, introducing economic protectionism
	October: Conclusion of Dual Alliance between Germany and Austria
1880	Conclusion of revised Three Emperors' Alliance between Germany, Russia and Austria
	Introduction of accident insurance – part of Bismarck's 'state socialism'
1882	Formation of Triple Alliance, involving Germany, Austria and Italy
1883	Introduction of sickness insurance as part of Bismarck's policy of 'state socialism'
1884	Renewal of Three Emperors' Alliance
1885	German East Africa Company created. Annexation by Germany of Tanganyika and Zanzibar
1886	Anglo–German agreement on spheres of influence in East Africa
1887	Conclusion of Reinsurance Treaty between Germany and Russia

1888	March: Death of Emperor Wilhelm I; succession of Friedrich III
	June: Death of Friedrich III; succession of Wilhelm II
	March: Dismissal of Bismarck as Chancellor of Germany.

Overview

In order to understand the methods by which Otto von Bismarck governed the German Empire between 1871 and 1890, it is necessary to understand the complex origins of that Empire. Important as the personal role of Bismarck was in bringing about German unification, other forces impersonal and perhaps more powerful were also at work. Since the 18th century nationalist theorists had preached that it was Germany's destiny to rise above the selfish interests of individual German princes and to create a united state that might allow Germans at last to play a positive and dominant role in European affairs. Such beliefs had been stimulated by the disturbances of 1848, which seemed to promise the collapse of the old political order in Europe, and by events in Italy in the 1850s, which began to undermine the conservative influence of the Austrian Empire. Alongside such theories, the advance of industrialisation in Germany created economic interests that orthodox politicians found difficult to ignore and impossible to resist. The advantages of easier trade and communications between the states were such that, as early as 1834, a range of north German states had associated themselves in a customs union, the *Zollverein*, that involved a high degree of economic co-operation decades before any political union was envisaged.

These forces were confronted by other, more conservative, interests. Austria and Russia had enormous traditional interests to defend in central and eastern Europe. Not only were the rulers of both states dedicated to the defence of **legitimist** interests, including those of the individual German princes, but both governed such a mixture of racial groups that the very existence of their empires was threatened by the principles of nationalism. In Prussia, too, conservative instincts were likely to oppose any attempt to establish a unitary, popular German state. Under Friedrich Wilhelm IV (1840–61), and under his brother and successor Wilhelm I (1861–88), the Prussian monarchy was equally devoted to legitimist principles, and equally hostile to the notion that political power should lie in the hands of the nation. In Prussia's feudal landowning class, the **Junkers**, the kings of Prussia found ample support for such conservative ideas.

From 1862, Bismarck himself acted as the leading servant of this conservative Prussian monarchy, and as the willing representative of Junker interests. As such, he had little sympathy for the causes of national unity or of liberal reform, yet he was equally hostile to the authority of Austria within the **German Confederation**, and to the claims of the Austrian Emperor to be able to dictate to Prussia over the affairs of Germany. Bismarck's primary aim in the 1860s was to readjust the political balance within Germany, guaranteeing the security of Prussian interests, while controlling those political forces within Prussia that threatened the interests of the governing class. If his aims were essentially conservative, Bismarck's methods were subtle and imaginative. Contemporary diplomatic circumstances in Europe enabled him to isolate and confront Austria, and the promise of significant changes in German politics won the consent of liberals within Prussia and other German states.

Legitimist: A theory of monarchy which considers that each state has a ruler, or ruling family, designated by God as the only 'legitimate' or true ruler. Thus the Hohenzollern family were the 'legitimate' rulers of Prussia.

Junkers: The aristocratic landowners, with extensive estates predominantly in East Prussia, who formed the governing class of the Prussian state.

German Confederation: The alliance of German states, under the presidency of the Austrian Emperor, established in 1815 to guarantee the security of its members in the aftermath of the Napoleonic Wars.

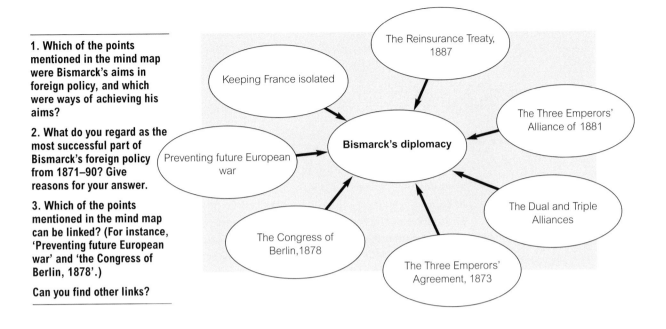

1. Which of the points mentioned in the mind map were Bismarck's aims in foreign policy, and which were ways of achieving his aims?

2. What do you regard as the most successful part of Bismarck's foreign policy from 1871–90? Give reasons for your answer.

3. Which of the points mentioned in the mind map can be linked? (For instance, 'Preventing future European war' and 'the Congress of Berlin, 1878'.)

Can you find other links?

North German Confederation: A revised version of the German Confederation, established as a result of Prussia's victory over Austria in 1866. It comprised those German states north of the river Main, and Prussia was the dominant political influence within the confederation.

Reich: The German state or Empire.

How successful was Bismarck in the 1860s? It is quite possible that he had achieved all that he aimed for by 1866. At that stage, he had isolated and defeated Austria, effectively ending its influence over the affairs of northern Germany. It may well be the case that Bismarck visualised the **North German Confederation**, under Prussian leadership, as the ideal outcome of this struggle. Other factors, however, forced him to go further. Unsuccessful in his attempts to appease or to deflect French suspicions over the growth of Prussian influence, Bismarck accepted an unlikely alliance with nationalist enthusiasm in the course of the Franco-Prussian War (1870–71). The most important outcome of the war was the transformation of the wartime coalition of German states into a formal and permanent political union. By 1871, his achievement was not so much that a united German **Reich** emerged from that war, but that it emerged in a form acceptable to the conservative forces that Bismarck represented:

● Austria was excluded.

● The existence and independence of the German princes were maintained to a degree. Indeed, the Imperial authority of the Kaiser was based upon the support and acclamation of the German princes.

● The Imperial constitution guaranteed the political interests of Prussia's governing classes in all important respects.

Inevitably, one of the dominant themes of German domestic politics during the 1870s and the 1880s was the government's attempt to keep political power predominantly in the hands of these traditional, conservative classes. However strong nationalist sympathies may have been in some areas of German politics, Bismarck's domestic policies were directed more by considerations of class struggle. Aware of the potential challenge from middle-class interests and from the

Coalition: A government or a parliamentary majority consisting of people from two or more political parties who have decided to work together.

Reichstag: The parliament of the united German Empire (Reich).

increasing political organisation of the working classes, Bismarck worked to ensure that no direct political power fell into the hands of these groups. In this undertaking he was only partly successful. Appearing to work with the National Liberals in the 1870s, Bismarck successfully placed his emphasis upon policies that consolidated the Bismarckian state, rather than any that strengthened the direct political interests of the Liberals. Bismarck's great political re-alignment in 1879, however, represented a shift to a **coalition** in which he was no longer the undisputed senior partner. In a climate of economic recession he could not afford to ignore the demand of Junker agriculturalists, and of industrialists, for economic protection. Although it was not wholly distasteful to Bismarck to abandon the Liberals for more conservative allies, the move demonstrated the limits of his success in the long term. While he could control the parliamentary aspirations of the industrial middle classes, he could not ignore their economic power, for that formed a fundamental basis of the power and prosperity of the German state. Able to manipulate the **Reichstag**, but not the economic might of the Ruhr, Bismarck was forced now to seek a path equally acceptable to Junkers and industrialists. In the course of the next three decades, this 'alliance of rye and steel' would lead German policy into paths that Bismarck would never willingly have contemplated. He had indeed ensured that the united Reich would be based upon conservative interests, but not exclusively upon those of the Prussian Junkers.

Bismarck's attitude towards the other major component of German industrialisation – the urban working class – was much clearer. He regarded them as a consistent threat to the aristocratic society, from which he came, and remained unconditionally hostile to their political ambitions. Bismarck was a sufficiently subtle politician, however, to know that such ambitions had to be deflected, rather than suppressed. He therefore pursued a dual policy that sought to obstruct the growth of the leading socialist parties, while introducing a programme of social reforms promoted and funded by the state.

1. What do you regard as Bismarck's greatest achievement in domestic policy after 1871? Explain your answer.

2. What do you regard as Bismarck's greatest failure?

3. From the factors mentioned in the mind map, place what you regard as Bismarck's achievements in one column and his failures in another.

4. On balance, do you regard Bismarck as being successful in domestic policy after 1871?

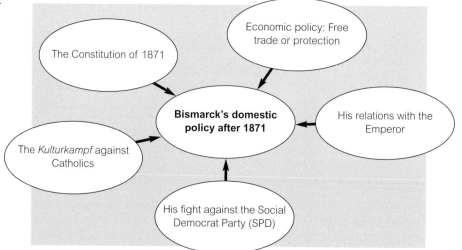

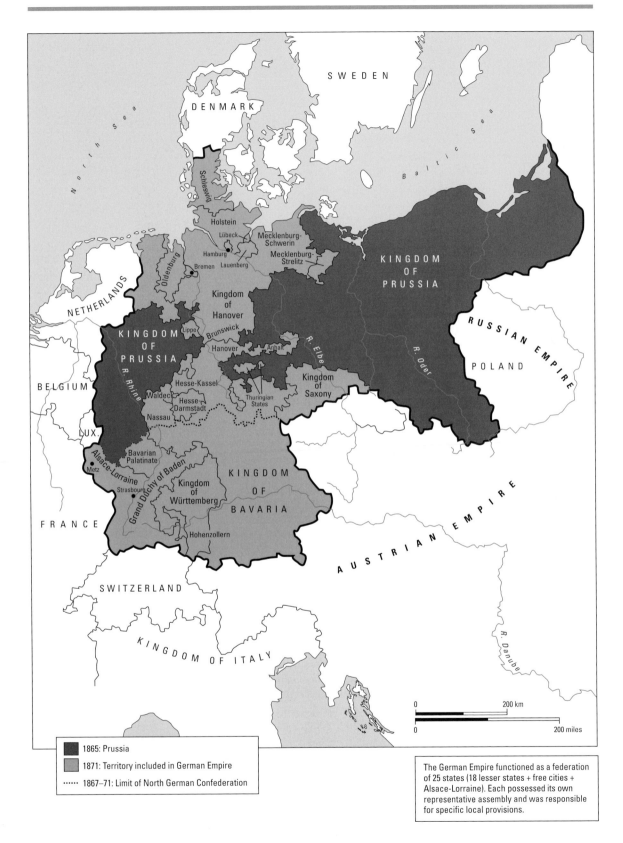

The German Empire functioned as a federation of 25 states (18 lesser states + free cities + Alsace-Lorraine). Each possessed its own representative assembly and was responsible for specific local provisions.

The German Empire in 1871

How successful was Bismarck in these domestic policies? To a remarkable extent, he succeeded in preserving the political structures that he valued. At the end of his career, the Prussian monarchy and the army were stronger than they had ever been, and the Junker class continued to dominate the high offices of state. The economic and social structure of Germany, however, had not stood still. German industry had continued to develop, its growth directly stimulated by political unification. Bismarck contributed to this growth by his strategy of coalition, compromise and concession to these economic forces. At his fall from power, he left one of the most modern and dynamic economies in Europe in the hands of rulers and politicians whose attitudes and political priorities were those of the mid-19th century.

The newly unified German state also faced another major challenge. Unification brought about a transformation in the European balance of power. Germany had to confront the mistrust, if not the downright hostility, of states whose interests had been damaged or threatened by this transformation. Although three wars were fought in the process of unification in the 1860s, Bismarck had little to gain from further warfare. Utterly opposed to a *grossdeutsch* union that would bring Austria back into German politics, he had no further territorial ambitions. German diplomacy in the 1870s and 1880s was dominated by the desire to isolate France, the state most likely to challenge the new Germany, and to maintain a system of alliances that would prevent conflict between Austria and Russia. For all his shifts and compromises in the course of two decades, that system remained essentially intact at the end of Bismarck's career. It is tempting to view the fall of Bismarck in 1890 as a key factor in the transformation of European diplomacy from stability and balance to ambition and confrontation.

Grossdeutsch ('Great German'): Term used to describe the concept of a united Germany in which all ethnic Germans are included.

4.1 What were the main political features of the Bismarckian state?

Kaiser Wilhelm I (1797–1888)
Saw action in the Napoleonic Wars, and developed a reputation in Prussia as a conservative and militarist. He became regent of Prussia upon the breakdown of his brother, King Friedrich Wilhelm (1858), and succeeded as king upon his brother's death (1861). He appointed Otto von Bismarck as Minister President (1862) to stave off constitutional challenges, and supported his minister through successful wars with Denmark, Austria and France. Upon the formation of the German Reich in 1871, Wilhelm became the first Kaiser (Emperor) of united Germany. He remained a symbol of conservative values, and of the dominance of the Prussian elite within united Germany until his death at the age of 91.

In theory, the German Empire created in 1871 was a voluntary association of German states, governed by as free a constitution as existed anywhere in Europe. The Empire was a federal state, consisting of four kingdoms (Prussia, Bavaria, Württemberg and Saxony), 18 lesser states, three free cities, and the imperial territory (Reichsland) of Alsace-Lorraine. Each of these, with the exception of Alsace-Lorraine, retained a great deal of its former autonomy in regard to its own domestic administration. Yet Prussia was by far the largest and most powerful of Germany's constituent parts. It comprised over 60% of the area of the Reich (134,000 out of 208,000 square miles) and a similar proportion of its population (24.7 million out of 41 million). It was hardly surprising, therefore, that the power and influence of Prussia lurked behind each article of the German constitution.

The Reichstag

The basis of the Reich's parliamentary constitution was adapted directly from that of the North German Confederation. The Imperial Assembly (Reichstag) was elected by universal manhood suffrage, but was subject to a number of limitations which prevented its growth into a true parliamentary body. It had the power to question the Chancellor (which office fell of course to Bismarck) and to initiate debate upon any point of his policy, but neither he nor any other minister was responsible to the assembly for their actions. The Reichstag had theoretical control over any alteration to the military budget, but largely sacrificed this weapon by agreeing in 1874, mainly through fear of starting a new constitutional conflict, to approve that budget for a period of seven years. It repeated this process in 1881 and 1887. This 'loss of the full right of budget approval', argues historian Hajo Holborn, 'blocked the growth of a parliamentary system in Germany.' Furthermore, the bulk of the remainder of the Reich income, from indirect taxation, posts and from the contributions of member states, lay wholly beyond the control of the Reichstag.

The Bundesrat and the Emperor

Bundesrat: Upper house of the Reichstag which represented the independent interests of the states.

In reality, political power lay outside the Reichstag. In part, it lay with the upper house, the *Bundesrat*, but for the most part it rested with the Prussian hierarchy. The *Bundesrat* had the power to initiate legislation. Also, with the assent of the Emperor, it had the authority to declare war and to settle disputes between states. With the interests of the Reich and of the individual states thus balancing each other out, real power lay with Wilhelm I and his ministers. Wilhelm was by hereditary right German Emperor, with full powers over the appointment and dismissal of ministers, who were responsible only to him. He also had full control over foreign affairs, and had the right to the final say in any dispute over the interpretation of the constitution. By virtue of its size, Prussia possessed 17 of the 58 seats in the *Bundesrat* at a time when 14 votes constituted a **veto**. The body therefore served the important dual purpose of maintaining the separate political identity of Prussia within the Reich, and of blocking any steps towards a radical, unitary state. Indeed, the balance of forces in the German constitution as a whole indicated clearly that it was designed to block and to prevent any major constitutional change or development in the future.

Veto (**Latin – 'I forbid'**): A negative vote exercised constitutionally by an individual, an institution or a state. It has the effect of automatically defeating the motion against which it is cast.

The Treaty of Frankfurt and the annexation of Alsace-Lorraine

The outcome of the Franco-Prussian War and the ultimate shape of the German Reich were decided simultaneously by the terms of the treaty signed at Frankfurt on 10 May 1871. France was compelled to pay a **war indemnity** of 5 billion francs over a period of three years. It also had to accept substantial territorial losses. German nationalists had claimed Alsace unsuccessfully in 1815, in the 1820s and again in 1848–49, and now that desire was supplemented by power, annexation was perhaps inevitable. 'This territory,' wrote the nationalist historian von Treitschke, 'is ours by right of the sword, and annexation follows from the right of the German nation to prevent the loss of any of its sons.'

War indemnity: A payment made by the defeated side in order to pay the costs incurred by the victors in the war.

Northern and eastern Lorraine, with the great fortress of Metz, also became German territory. There was far less justification for regarding these as German lands, and for many years the standard view on this issue was that Bismarck bowed reluctantly to the pressure of the army, the king and the nationalists. More recent research has suggested that Bismarck may have had some role in the formation of this public mood. His motives, however, are unlikely to have been ideological. On a practical level, historian Gordon Craig points out in *Germany 1866–1945* (published in 1981) that French bitterness was likely to be just as great, whatever the terms of the surrender, and Bismarck himself wrote in similar vein to his ambassadors abroad. 'We cannot look to the French temper for our guarantees. What the French nation will never forgive is their defeat as such. In German hands Strasbourg and Metz will take on a purely defensive character.'

Political parties

The parties that competed for seats in the Reichstag were very different

Pressure groups: Political organisations who wish to influence political decision making but do not wish to gain political power.

organisations from their English counterparts. They were predominantly **pressure groups** representing the sectional interests of one part or another of the diverse German nation, and they remained social phenomena rather than instruments for winning the struggle for power.

The Conservatives

On the right wing of the Reichstag stood two major groups, the Conservatives (from 1876 the 'German Conservatives') and the Imperial Party (*Reichspartei*). The former had its strength in Prussia itself, among Protestant, aristocratic landowners. Concerned at, and sometimes openly hostile towards, Bismarck's flirtations with liberalism and nationalism, it remained a moderate force in the Reichstag, but a major one in the Prussian Landtag, which it dominated through local influence. The *Reichspartei* enjoyed a broader geographical basis of support, among landowners and industrialists alike. Also, its support for the Imperial Chancellor was much more consistent, in admiration of his great achievement in the foundation of the Reich.

Composition of the Reichstag, 1871–1890

	1871	1874	1877	1878	1881	1884	1887	1890
German Conservatives	57	22	40	59	50	78	80	73
Reichspartei	37	33	38	57	28	28	41	20
National Liberals	125	155	141	109	47	51	99	42
Progress Party	46	49	35	26	60	–	–	–
Centre Party	61	91	93	94	100	99	98	106
Social Democrats	2	9	12	9	12	24	11	35
Guelphs	9	4	10	4	10	11	4	11
National groups (Alsatians, Poles, Danes)	14	30	30	30	35	32	29	27

Total seats = 397 (1871: 382)

Ludwig Windthorst (1812–1891)
Deputy (1849) and Minister of the Interior in Hanover, and hostile to the Prussian annexation of that state. Leader of the Centre Party (*Zentrum*) in the Reichstag after unification, fiercely opposing Bismarck in the course of the **Kulturkampf**.

Kulturkampf: German term meaning 'struggle for civilisation': the clash with the Catholic Church in Germany in the 1870s. For German liberals, the Catholic Church was the 'old enemy'. For Bismarck, it was not so much a struggle between belief and unbelief, more a 'matter of a conflict between monarchy and priesthood. What is at stake is the defence of the state.'

The Centre Party

The Centre Party (*Zentrum*), founded in 1870, still tends to be described as the party of Germany's large Roman Catholic minority. In fact it was more than that. Primarily dedicated to the defence of the interests of the Catholic Church, it also attracted others with a partisan objection to the recent work of Bismarck, such as the Protestant 'Guelphs', who were embittered supporters of the deposed King George of Hanover. Particularly strong in Bavaria and in the Rhineland, the Centre Party was led in the Reichstag by a Catholic Hanoverian, Ludwig Windthorst. One of the few great parliamentarians of the 'Bismarck era', greatly respected even by those who loathed his views, Windthorst has been characterised by historian Golo Mann as 'a sly idealist, a devout fox, a man of principles and a very clever politician, dignified and cunning'.

The Liberals

In the 1870s the National Liberals were Bismarck's most enthusiastic supporters in the Reichstag. They were at one with him in their enthusiasm for a centralised state, if increasingly at odds with him in their support for progressive social and constitutional legislation. To their left stood the Progress Party (*Fortschrittpartei*), diminished but unbowed by the liberal split of 1866. They shared the National Liberals' enthusiasm for free trade and the rule of law, but were opposed to the centralism and militarism of the Bismarckian state. In Eugen Richter and Eduard Lasker they had effective parliamentary leaders, the latter so consistent a critic of the

Chancellor as to be described by Bismarck as 'even more of a vile louse than Windthorst'.

The Left
German socialism in 1871 was as yet a modest force, based upon Ferdinand Lassalle's General Workers' Association (*Allgemeiner Arbeiterverein*) founded in 1863, and the Social Democratic Workers' Party formed by Wilhelm Liebknecht and August Bebel at Eisenach in Saxony in 1869. Its day was, however, soon to come.

---

1. By what means did Prussia exert influence over the politics of united Germany after 1871?

2. What different interests were represented by the political groups within the Reichstag between 1871 and 1890?

3. How convincing is the claim that 'the constitution of the German Reich in 1871 was one of the most democratic in Europe'?

Wilhelm Liebknecht (1826–1901)
A socialist, active in 1848, and subsequently in contact (1850) with Karl Marx. One of the founders of the First International (1865) and of the German Social Democractic Party (1869). Deputy in the Reichstag from 1874 to 1900.

August Bebel (1840–1913)
Worked with Liebknecht on the foundation of the First International (1865) and of the German Social Democratic Party. Subsequently, leader of the SPD and a prominent member of the Second International.

Ferdinand Lassalle (1825–1864)
Radical socialist, a friend of Karl Marx. Active in the Ruhr in 1848–49 and subsequently founder of the first German trade union.

4.2 Why, and with what results, did Bismarck enter into an electoral alliance with the National Liberals between 1871 and 1878?

How much common ground existed between Bismarck and the National Liberals?

The first seven years of Bismarck's government of a united Germany, 1871–78, are frequently described as his 'liberal era'. While Bismarck was by no stretch of the imagination a true liberal, he found it convenient during this period to co-operate in the Reichstag with the National Liberal party. In the first place, they were the dominant party in an assembly where the Chancellor had no party of his own. Secondly, the spirit of conciliation that had motivated the **indemnity of 1866** remained alive. The National Liberals remained broadly sympathetic towards Bismarck as the architect of their major policy aim, national unity. Most important, their immediate aims coincided with Bismarck's in such areas as the consolidation of that national unity and the centralisation of the administration of the Reich.

To conservative critics it often seemed that the alliance with the National Liberals was carrying Bismarck too far to the left. Lothar Gall, in *Bismarck, the White Revolutionary* (1986), describes Bismarck as being 'the stirrup-holder of liberalism'. In fact it is clear that the Chancellor gave his 'supporters' nothing that involved any immediate political power. The Press Law (May 1874) provided little protection for editors against government prosecution. Attempts in the Reichstag to limit the influence of the Junkers in Prussian local government achieved little of practical value. Also, as we have seen, the Reichstag failed to maintain control over the vital area of government military expenditure.

It is equally important to establish, however, that the measures undertaken in 1871–78 should not merely be written off as 'sops' offered by Bismarck to 'fool' the National Liberals and to maintain a convenient political understanding in the short term. The economic and administrative

Indemnity of 1866: One of Bismarck's first actions upon coming to office in 1862 was to ignore liberal objections to taxation needed by the state to increase the size of the army. The taxes were levied without parliamentary permission, in defiance of all liberal and constitutional principles. Following his success against Austria in 1866, and the creation of a North German Confederation, Prussian liberals voted to 'pardon' Bismarck for this action. This is widely interpreted as a sacrifice of constitutional principles in the interests of nationalism.

Enabling Laws: Laws which confer the legal freedom to take certain actions, although they do not make these actions obligatory.

Kleindeutsch ('Little German'): Term used to describe the concept of a united Germany (favoured by Prussia) from which Austria is excluded.

legislation of his 'liberal era' was of the greatest importance in the formation of the German state. It illustrates very clearly the complex relationship between Bismarck and the German liberals. The period produced, in the words of historian Geoff Eley, 'an impressive concentration of forward-looking economic legislation [and] an elaborate framework of capitalist **enabling laws**'. Although Bismarck refused to grant the liberals the kind of political framework that they desired for Germany, the *kleindeutsch* state of 1875 was, in economic terms, very much what liberal thinkers had always envisaged. Only time would tell whether this delicate balance of socio-economic progressiveness and political conservatism could be maintained.

Administrative and financial consolidation

The state created by Bismarck was a curiously disunited entity. It lacked religious unity and unity of economic interests. It contained national minorities with little or no desire to be part of the German Empire. There is thus much truth in the historian A.J.P. Taylor's description of the Reich in 1871 as merely a 'wartime coalition'. Such were the separatist feelings of the states, for instance, that Germany had no national flag until 1892 and no national anthem until after the First World War. For Bismarck, with his desire for closer political control, and for the National Liberals, with their enthusiasm for national unity, it was vital that this situation be improved. The first session of the Reichstag, therefore, saw the passage of over 100 acts to this end. The currencies of the states were unified into a national currency, all tariffs (taxes) on internal trade were abolished, and a uniform body of commercial law was introduced. The Prussian State Bank became the Reichsbank, and Germany adopted the gold standard. Uniformity of legal procedures was achieved in 1877. A national Appeals Court was established by 1879, although the codification of German civil law did not come into effect (January 1900) until long after Bismarck's fall from power.

The problem of the national minorities

Edwin von Manteuffel (1809–1885)
One of the main influences behind Prussian army reform in the early 1860s and active in the wars against Denmark, Austria and France. Commanded army of occupation in France (1871–73). Governor of Alsace-Lorraine (1880–85).

Chlodwig von Hohenlohe (1819–1901)
Prime Minister of Bavaria (1866–70) in which office he supported the idea of German unity under Prussia. German ambassador to Paris (1874–85); Governor-General of Alsace-Lorraine (1885–94); Chancellor of Germany (1894–1900).

After administrative separatism, the second major area of disunity concerned the national minorities within Germany's borders. For nearly 20 years, by a mixture of coercion and conciliation, Bismarck attempted to tie these minorities more closely to the German state, but had no significant degree of success. In Alsace-Lorraine the decision to allow French or pro-French elements to leave the territories resulted in the migration of 400,000 people between 1871 and 1914. The remainder found themselves governed by Prussian civil servants, with the German language imposed in schools and in local administration. From 1874 they were represented in the Reichstag, and the choice of governors for the territories showed some tact and commonsense. Edwin von Manteuffel (1809–1885) was a humane and conscientious administrator. His successor, Prince Chlodwig von Hohenlohe, was a south German Catholic and had more in common with the people of Alsace than with many Protestant Prussians. The consistency with which the people of Alsace voted for deputies in favour of separation from the Reich showed, however, that such attempts at conciliation were largely unsuccessful.

In the case of the Poles, conciliation was much less in evidence. When the state sought to reduce the influence and independence of the Catholic Church within Germany, Polish clergy in the eastern provinces were particularly hard hit. Their leader, Cardinal Ledochowski, was imprisoned and his office left vacant for 12 years. The use of the Polish language was outlawed in education and in the law courts. State funds were used to finance the purchase of lands in Polish hands for the purpose of settlement

Plebiscite: A direct vote of all of the electors of a state to decide a question of public importance. Otherwise known as a referendum.

1. What measures were taken in the 1870s to consolidate the unity of the German state?

2. How accurate is the description of the years 1871–78 as a 'liberal era' in the government of Germany?

by Germans, although the Poles were rather more successful in raising funds for the reverse purpose. It is scarcely surprising that, given these tactics, the Polish problem remained unsolved.

Finally, the problem of the Schleswig Danes was largely ignored. In 1879, on the eve of the Dual Alliance, Austria agreed to allow Germany to abandon the **plebiscite** in North Schleswig promised by the Treaty of Prague in 1866. It took a world war to revise the status of North Schleswig and of Alsace-Lorraine, and to resolve the problems of Germany's Polish subjects.

4.3 What was the purpose of the *Kulturkampf*, and to what extent was it achieved?

German liberalism and the Catholic Church

The first decade of domestic politics in the German Reich was dominated by the clash with the Catholic Church. It was branded at the time as the 'struggle for civilisation' (*Kulturkampf*). It is difficult for us to grasp today, in a generally more secular age, the feelings aroused by this legal assault upon Germany's substantial Catholic minority. We shall miss its significance altogether unless we accept that, as historian Erich Eyck tells us in *Bismarck and the German Empire* (1968), 'in those years many of the most enlightened and highly educated men believed that the future of mankind was at stake'.

The view that Bismarck artificially engineered this confrontation as a means of uniting various strands of German opinion against a common enemy is no longer tenable. The roots of the *Kulturkampf* stretch deep into German history, certainly back to Prussia's acquisition of the largely Catholic Rhineland in 1815, and possibly to the Reformation. This was not even exclusively a German issue, for reforming politicians in Italy, and in France during the Third Republic, had also felt obliged to confront the conservative principles of the Catholic Church. In those states, too, it seemed to many that the authority and the teachings of the Church were incompatible with the principles of a modern society based upon national identity. In the case of Germany in the early 1870s the struggle was really made up of two separate clashes. For the German liberals, the Catholic Church was an old enemy. Precursors of the *Kulturkampf* can be seen even in the southern states, as in the Church Law (1860) and the Elementary School Law (1868) passed in Baden. The offence of the Catholic Church had been compounded in 1864 with the publication of Pius IX's *Syllabus of Errors*, in which the Pope condemned every major political and social principle for which German and Italian liberals stood. Pius had declared moral warfare, and for the liberals the battle appeared to be one for the future of human thought.

Bismarck and the Catholic Church

For Bismarck the issue was less abstract. Despite the fact that he and most of the Prussian Junkers were Protestant, his battle had little to do with doctrine. 'It is not a matter of a struggle between belief and unbelief,' he declared. 'It is a matter of the conflict between monarchy and priesthood. What is at stake is the defence of the state.' For him the origins of the *Kulturkampf* lay in the events of 1866–70, during which Prussia had replaced Austria as the dominant force in German politics. In the process, tens of thousands of German Catholics had been transformed from sympa-

Papal Infallibility: The principle defined by Pope Pius IX in 1870, whereby the Pope, as God's representative on Earth, was inevitably correct in any doctrinal statement that he made. As a denial of freedom of opinion, and as a potential challenge to the authority of national governments, this doctrine isolated the Catholic Church from most of the other major political and philosophical forces in western Europe.

Jesuit order: A religious order founded by St Ignatius Loyola in the 16th century. The founder's principle that members owed direct obedience to the Pope alone caused the order to be viewed with great suspicion in most European states. The order's close association with education also caused it to be viewed as a major channel by which the influence of the Catholic Church might be spread.

Excommunication: Expelled from the Church; destined for eternal damnation.

thetic *grossdeutsch* supporters of the Habsburg monarchy into reserved followers and subjects of Prussia. Its origins also lay in the recently declared doctrine of **Papal Infallibility** (July 1870). By aiming to tie Catholic loyalties directly to the Papacy, instead of to the national state, the doctrine was a clear challenge to state power. The launching of this struggle offered Bismarck other political advantages, such as closer ties with the anti-clerical Italian government, with Russia, themselves greatly troubled by Catholic Poles, and with the National Liberals. His major motive, however, was probably the desire to combat those whom he felt genuinely to be 'enemies of the Empire' (*Reichsfeinde*). The Catholics were thus the first of many minority groups to play this role in 'united' Germany.

The May Laws

The spearhead of the attack upon the Catholic Church was formed by legislation framed, under Bismarck's instructions, by Adalbert Falk, the Prussian Minister of Religious Affairs. First, in 1872, came the cutting of diplomatic relations with the Vatican (May) and the expulsion of the **Jesuit order** from German soil (July). In the following year came the main onslaught in the form of Falk's notorious 'May Laws'. The education of clergy, clerical appointments and the inspection of Church schools were all brought under state control. Appointments to German ecclesiastical positions were limited to those educated in Germany, and priests were forbidden to use the threat of **excommunication** as a means to compel opponents. In a further series of measures, civil marriage – strenuously opposed by Bismarck – in 1849 became compulsory in the Reich, and most religious orders in Germany were dissolved (1875).

The results of the Kulturkampf

In 1874–75, Church and state remained locked in conflict. Eight of the 12 Catholic bishops in Prussia were deprived of their offices and more than 1,000 priests were suspended from their posts. However, the desired political effect was not achieved. Spiritually the Church thrived upon its 'martyrdom', and politically the increase in the representation of the Centre Party in the Reichstag frustrated Bismarck's hopes of a quick surrender. There were also other unhappy side-effects. The anti-Catholic stance endangered good foreign relations with Austria and the threat of an Austro–French understanding grew. Prussian conservatives, although staunchly Protestant, disliked the liberals' hostility to all religious instruction in schools and distrusted Bismarck's liberal 'alliance' in general. Indeed, the price demanded by the liberals for their further support – the extension of free trade and ministerial office for members of their party seemed to Bismarck himself to be unreasonably high. The death of Pius IX (1878) and the election of the more conciliatory Leo XIII provided an opportunity that Bismarck seized with enthusiasm. With the repeal of the bulk of the May Laws (1878) and the symbolic dismissal of Falk (July 1879), the *Kulturkampf* came to an abrupt end. Of the great 'struggle for civilisation', only the laws on civil marriage, state supervision of schools and those against the Jesuits remained.

1. What measures were taken against the Catholic Church in Germany in the course of the *Kulturkampf*?

2. Why did Bismarck launch the *Kulturkampf* in the 1870s?

3. What, if anything, did Bismarck gain by his measures in the 1870s against the Catholic Church in Germany?

Did Bismarck, therefore, lose the *Kulturkampf*? Certainly the struggle did much to damage his earlier work of unification, and made the majority of German Catholics more sympathetic to Papal authority than they had been before. On the other hand, reconciliation did largely transform the Centre into a purely religious party. If we see Bismarck's aim as the preservation of his state in the longer term, then perhaps we should accept the verdict of historian C. Grant Robertson that 'Bismarck deliberately sacrificed victory in the *Kulturkampf* to victory in other issues, more important in his judgement.'

4.4 Why did Bismarck abandon the National Liberals for a more conservative stance in 1878?

The 'Great Depression' and its impact upon German politics

War reparations: Payments made by a defeated state to compensate the victorious state(s) for damage or expenses caused by war.

Cartels: Economic arrangement whereby major manufacturers agree to share markets, rather than to compete for them. The aim is usually to fix prices for the benefit of the manufacturers and to guarantee levels of sales and profits.

For all the issues of principle at large in the 1870s, German politics did not operate by ideology alone. For much of the so-called 'Bismarck era' the political life of Germany was played out against a background of economic anxiety and depression. Germany's 'Great Depression' was a classic case of economic recession. The economic history of the Reich opened with a short period of 'boom', fuelled by over-generous credit policies on the part of German bankers, and by the large amounts of capital pumped into the economy by French **war reparations**. These stimuli set off a wave of unsound investment projects whose eventual collapse, in the same fashion as the Wall Street Crash, struck a blow to business confidence whose effects could still be felt nearly 20 years later. It is important to appreciate the exact nature of the impact made by this 'Great Depression'. In terms of production and of economic growth, Germany recovered relatively quickly. The production levels of 1872–73 had been restored by 1880; urban growth continued unabated, especially in Berlin and in the Ruhr; the development of **cartels** allowed major industrial enterprises to maintain their stability. After 20 years of uninterrupted economic growth, however, the psychological impact of the slump was considerable, and the effect of the depression on political mentalities was to last well beyond 1880. Its main political impact was to mobilise and to polarise conservative economic thinking, and to create a powerful lobby in favour of economic protection. The rejection of liberal, free-trading policies by the leaders of German industry soon became evident in the formation of such pressure groups as the League of German Iron and Steel Manufacturers (1873) and the Central Association of German Industrialists (1876). When Junker agriculturalists also became convinced that their interests were threatened by free trade, Bismarck was faced by an enormously powerful coalition in favour of protective tariffs.

The real impact of the depression, therefore, was that it undermined the political basis upon which Bismarck had founded his power in the early 1870s. It forced him to adapt once more to the prevailing circumstances within Germany. As historian D.G. Williamson puts it, in *Bismarck and Germany, 1862–90* (1986), the economic developments of the later 1870s 'discredited both economic and political liberalism and enabled the conservatives and the survivors of the pre-capitalist era successfully to attack the liberal ethos'.

The significance of the reforms of 1878–1879

The ending of the *Kulturkampf* cannot be seen merely as a tactical withdrawal, cleverly calculated by a master politician. In 1878–79, Bismarck was faced once again with a crisis of the utmost gravity, which forced him to adapt and revise his policies. The change of direction that he undertook at the end of the 1870s has often been interpreted as political opportunism. More recently, historians have come to view this period as a key stage in the development of the German Reich, as significant in its way as the events of 1870–71. Helmut Böhme, for instance, argues in *An Introduction to the Social and Economic History of Germany* (1978) that the Franco-Prussian War established a viable form of unity between the German states, but did not establish a satisfactory socio-economic balance within the new Reich. It became increasingly clear in the course of the 1870s that Bismarck's alliance with German liberalism failed to meet the interests of many influential groups within the Reich. The dramatic switch to economic and political conservatism at the end of the decade represented an acceptance on Bismarck's part of conservative social and economic values more closely in keeping with the conservative structure of the state. Historian Agatha Ramm confirms this interpretation in describing these reforms as a 'coherent and systematic revision of policy in relation to the economic, social and financial needs of the Reich'.

The introduction of protectionism

Protectionism: The economic practice whereby a country's domestic industries are protected from foreign competition by the imposition of high import duties placed upon foreign goods.

Bismarck now felt compelled to meet the growing demand for measures of economic **protectionism**. While free trade remained an essential principle of the National Liberals, demands for higher protective tariffs increased from other quarters. These demands had been heard from the iron and steel industries from the mid-1870s, but now Prussia's Junker landowners added their voices to the argument. Instead of aiming at free access to the markets of Britain and France, they now found themselves threatened by the cheap grain arriving from the United States of America. The adoption of protective tariffs by France, Russia and Austria–Hungary over this same period seemed to make it all the more desirable for Germany to follow suit. Apart from this impressive array of industrialist and Junker opinion, the government itself had pressing motives. Protection would aid the growth of national self-sufficiency in the event of a future crisis, and tariffs provided the government with a valuable source of income independent both of the Reichstag and of the member states.

From 1876, the path chosen by Bismarck became clearer. In April of that year he accepted the resignation of Rudolf von Delbrück, head of the Chancellor's Office and architect of the earlier free-trade policies. In early 1878, the refusal of the Liberal leaders to join Bismarck's government unless they were given guarantees over ministerial appointments and policy decisions, sealed their fate in the eyes of the Chancellor. When the new tariff laws were enacted in the Reichstag (July 1879) they imposed duties of between 5% and 7% on imported foodstuffs, and of 10%–15% on imported industrial goods. An amendment proposed by Freiherr zu Frankenstein limited Bismarck's triumph: it fixed an upper limit of 180 million marks in tariff income to be retained by the Reich, and ensured that any surplus would be distributed among the states. If this provided those states with some little satisfaction, there was none for German liberalism. A substantial step had been taken back to the path of conservatism, and the 'liberal era' in the history of united Germany was effectively at an end. In the view of one of the most influential of recent German historians, Helmut Böhme, these measures constituted the establishment of an interest-based coalition that would dominate the politics of Imperial Germany up to 1918. So important was this step, Böhme believed, that it amounted to nothing less than a 're-founding of the German Empire.'

Rudolf von Delbrück (1817–1903)
Prussian statesman. Active (1864–66) in the reorganisation of the *Zollverein*. As President of the Imperial Chancellery (1871) he was prominent in the drafting of Reich laws. A supporter of free trade, he resigned in 1876 over Bismarck's promotion of protective tariffs.

1. In what ways were the economic policies of the German Reich changed in the late 1870s?

2. Who gained and who lost from the introduction of economic protectionism in Germany in the late 1870s?

4.5 How successful was Bismarck in his attempt to combat socialism?

Reichsfeind (German – 'enemy of the Empire'): In Bismarck's Germany this came to indicate the deliberate policy whereby one particular group (e.g. Catholics or Socialists) was held up as an enemy in order to unite other groups against them and in support of the state.

Bismarck's fear of socialism

The second compelling motive for Bismarck's change of course in the late 1870s was his desire to combat what he saw as the menace of socialism within Germany. Although the weakness of the socialists in the Reichstag might seem to make them unlikely candidates for the role of *Reichsfeind*, Bismarck, like most European statesmen, was genuinely shaken by recent

Paris Commune: A radical political regime set up in Paris (March 1871) in the aftermath of France's defeat in the Franco-Prussian War. It lasted only until May 1871, when it was brutally crushed by French troops, but it created such an impression that it remained a powerful symbol of radical, socialist excesses for more than a generation.

events such as the **Paris Commune**. The 'Eisenach' socialists had, after all, refused their support for the war in 1870. Many remembered August Bebel's claim in the Reichstag in May 1871 that 'before many decades pass the battlecry of the proletariat of Paris will become that of the whole proletariat of Europe'. It seems probable that if Bismarck's opposition to Catholicism was not primarily ideological, his opposition to socialism was. In A.J.P. Taylor's words, he 'genuinely believed in the turnip-ghost which he conjured up'.

The anti-socialist law

Bismarck's opportunity came in mid-1878 when two attempts upon the life of the Kaiser gave him the chance to raise the cry of 'the Fatherland in danger', to dissolve the Reichstag and to hold fresh elections. Although neither would-be assassin had any clear association with the Social Democratic Party, the mood of the electorate was patriotic and conservative. 'The Emperor has the wounds, the nation the fever,' commented a liberal observer. The Social Democrats themselves had few seats to lose and the real losers of the election were the National Liberals. A majority was returned in favour of economic protection, the repeal of the 'May Laws', and the passage of Bismarck's anti-socialist measures (*Sozialistengesetz*). This law (19 October 1878) did not ban the Social Democratic Party directly, but crippled its organisation by banning any group or meeting aimed at the spread of socialist principles, outlawing trade unions, and closing 45 newspapers. It was originally in operation, thanks to a liberal amendment, for only two and a half years, but was renewed regularly until 1890.

'State socialism'

It was clear to Bismarck that socialism could not be conquered by oppression alone. The second string of his anti-socialist policy was thus a programme of 'state socialism'. This involved a series of measures to improve the conditions of the German workers. In 1883, medical insurance and sick pay were introduced. Although these were largely financed by the workers themselves, the employers were responsible for the funding of the scheme of insurance against industrial injuries introduced in the following year. Finally, in 1889, old age pensions were introduced, some two decades before their appearance in Britain.

Did such measures bring Bismarck more success against socialism than he had enjoyed against Catholicism? Historians have differed in their assessments of 'state socialism'. Some, like Erich Eyck, have seen the policy as a fraud, pursued for short-term political advantage. They point out how much more advantageous it would have been to relax the restrictions upon trade unions to allow workers to fight their own battles. They note that old age pensions were paid only to those who reached the age of 70, a ripe old age indeed for an industrial worker. Certainly, Bismarck failed to check the growth of the Social Democratic Party. Its membership increased from 550,000 in 1884 to 1,427,000 in 1890, suggesting that the workers saw 'state socialism' as a fraud and gave their support to the left. Gordon Craig, however, believes that it is possible to trace such paternalism in Bismarck's policies right back to 1862. 'State socialism', therefore, was based upon genuine conviction. Certainly Bismarck gained enthusiastic support from 'academic socialists' (*Kathedersozialisten*), such as Franz Brentano and Max Weber. He also horrified some liberals who accused him of attempting to found communism in Germany.

The historian A.J.P. Taylor regarded Bismarck's policies as successful in some important respects. He noted how subservient the German working class was to government policy in the years leading up to 1914 and

1. By what means did Bismarck check the political influence of socialism within Germany in the 1880s?

2. Did Bismarck succeed in containing the threat of socialism to the German state?

concluded that Bismarck's policy had at least defused the threat of working-class opposition to the state. More recently David Blackbourn has reinforced this observation in slightly different terms. In *The Fontana History of Germany 1780–1918: the Long Nineteenth Century* (1997), Blackbourn notes that 'more generally, organised German workers wrestled with their desires to be good socialists and good Germans – what historians refer to as the problem of "double loyalty".'

4.6 To what extent was Bismarck responsible for the authoritarianism and intolerance of the German state in the early 20th century?
A CASE STUDY IN HISTORICAL INTERPRETATION

Historiography: Different historical views by historians. Another term for historical interpretation.

Few 19th-century figures have attracted the attention and controversy that surround the achievement of Otto von Bismarck. This is easy to understand when one considers the tremendous impact of German unification upon European history in the 75 years after 1871. Even in his own lifetime, the perception that Bismarck's work was central to that unification created a strand of German **historiography** that portrayed him as the master statesman, successfully manipulating events in order to lead Germany to its rightful destiny. Prominent in this school of thought was the Prussian academic Heinrich von Treitschke, whose monumental *German History in the Nineteenth Century* (1879–94) traced the 'inevitable' rise of Prussian mastery, with Bismarck portrayed as the chosen instrument

---

The constitution of the German Empire 1871–1918

'The fig leaf of democracy covering naked Prussian absolutism [dictatorship]'

Karl Liebknecht (one of the founders of the SDP)

Federal state

The German Empire was a federal state. This meant political power was divided between the central government, based in the capital Berlin, and the state governments. State governments had responsibility for internal law and order, education and social welfare. However, some states had even greater responsibilities. Baden, Wurtemburg and Bavaria (The South German States) had their own postal services. Bavaria ran its own railway system and retained control over its army in peacetime.

However, the largest state by far was Prussia, which comprised over 60 per cent of the national territory. It also had the two most important industrial areas within its frontiers – the Ruhr and Upper Silesia.

Head of state: the Emperor

The Emperor was the King of Prussia. He was also the Supreme War Lord with control over the army. The Emperor appointed each minister, who was personally responsible to him. He could also sack any minister.

Head of government: the Chancellor

The Chancellor was chosen, and could be sacked, by the Emperor.

The National Parliament

The National Parliament contained two houses:

The **Reichstag** was the Lower House, which was elected democratically. Every male German over 25 had the right to vote.

The **Bundesrat** was the Upper House. It contained representatives of the states. Prussia had by far the largest representation of any state (17 out of a total of 58).

Local states

In Prussia the state parliament (*Landtag*) was chosen on a three-class suffrage. This meant that one third of all seats went to rich landowners (*Junkers*) even though they comprised a small percentage of the population. Some states, like Hamburg and Frankfurt, had democratic methods of electing their state parliaments. Mecklenburg Strelitz had no state parliament!

Do you think Karl Liebknecht was right?

of Germany's fate. Two ruinous world wars naturally had a considerable effect upon Bismarck's reputation among historians, within Germany and abroad. If he was indeed so great and successful a statesman, and if the Germany that he governed was his conscious and deliberate creation, then he should naturally assume much responsibility for the actions, and the subsequent development, of that state.

This view was widespread in the years after the Second World War. As historians in Germany and abroad searched for the origins of the disasters caused by Nazism, they looked to the growth of the German state before the Hitler era. They examined the role of Bismarck in the political development of that state. German liberals such as Erich Eyck, in *Bismarck: Life and Work* (1941–44), and the academic Friedrich Meinecke, in *The German Catastrophe: Reflections and Recollections* (1960), led the attack by stressing Bismarck's repression of political freedom after 1870. By crippling the development of democratic institutions in Germany, Bismarck had laid the country open to future dictatorships. Such views were understandably popular with Germany's wartime opponents. In one of the most popular English summaries of modern German history (*The Course of German History*, 1945) A.J.P. Taylor wrote that 'during the preceding 80 years the Germans sacrificed to the Reich all their liberties; they demanded as reward the enslavement of others'. Led by Gerhard Ritter, in *Europe and the German Question* (1948), German conservatives continued to argue that Bismarck could not be held responsible for later developments. His semi-feudal brand of conservatism, they argued, along with his religion and his *kleindeutsch* views, all distanced him greatly from the principles of Nazism. As Hans Rothfels put it, in *Bismarck and the State* (1954), 'we may criticise Bismarck for paving the way to some fatal trends of our day, but we cannot very well overlook the fundamental fact that Hitler did precisely what the founder of the Reich had refused to do'.

Did Bismarck create an authoritarian state?

If we try to answer this question by examining the constitution of the united Germany, we find that the evidence is ambiguous. On the one hand, the Reichstag displayed some democratic features.

- It was elected by universal manhood suffrage, and its assent was required for all legislation, including the periodic renewal of the military budget.

- It contained a wide variety of independent political parties, representing the full range of German political interests.

Yet the assembly lacked many of the powers of a full parliamentary democracy.

- Its members had no direct control over the actions of the Chancellor, nor over foreign policy, nor – beyond the voting of the army grant – over the conduct of the army.

- With the Chancellor and other leading ministers standing aloof from the party system, the political parties could not play any direct role in the formulation of government policy.

In short, the constitution embraced two different political mentalities: one with its roots in German liberalism, and the other with its roots in the authoritarian government that had been the norm within the individual German states. Its future depended upon which would emerge supreme.

Clearly, in the course of the 40 years after 1871, conservatism came out on top. In part, this was due to the preferences of Bismarck himself. It is clear that he saw the Reichstag as a body to be manipulated, rather than as a mirror in which to discover the will of the German people. His primary aims were not to advance German democracy, but as the historian Wolfgang Mommsen puts it, in *Imperial Germany 1867–1918* (1995), to 'preserve the pre-eminence of the traditional elites despite the changes that were taking place in German society'.

One influential view of German history, however, credits Bismarck with much less direct influence over the political development of the infant Reich. Helmut Böhme, in *Germany's Path to Great Power Status* (1966), not only placed economic trends at the heart of the process of German unification, but also saw in economics the main factors behind the shaping of politics within the new state. For Böhme, the crucial factor was the great economic depression that affected Germany between 1873 and 1879. From this crisis emerged a coalition of conservative interests, linking industrial and Junker agrarian interests, that would dominate the Reich until 1918. Liberalism was thrust into the margins of German politics, and such 'anti-modern' notions as anti-socialism and anti-semitism thrived in so conservative an environment. Socialism, in particular, was a direct product of the economic depression, and an obvious threat to the interests of these economic elites. Political oppression of the German socialist movement, therefore, was a logical product of these forces and not merely a whim or a political expedient employed by Bismarck. Geoff Eley concludes in 'Bismarckian Germany' in *Modern Germany Reconsidered 1870–1945* (1992), that 'the politics laid down in the Bismarckian period cast a long shadow. They established powerful continuities that extended through the imperial period to that of Weimar and played the key part in rendering German society vulnerable to Nazism.'

This impersonal emphasis, however, does not get Bismarck off the hook altogether. It must be pointed out that fear of revolution and of social radicalism was a fundamental element in Bismarck's political make-up and that he thus served as a major component in this conservative alliance, and a driving force behind its political measures. Several of the political elements within this alliance – leading industrialists for example – might have been identified in other states with more advanced causes. In Germany, however, under Bismarck's influence, they assented to authoritarian government, they contributed to the hostility that existed in educational and other professional circles towards democracy, and they helped to emphasise the authority and the mystique of the state. It seems necessary, therefore, to accept a consensus which, as Geoff Eley puts it, 'casts German state making in the light of social and economic history, but without turning Bismarck into the cipher of impersonal forces'.

Viewed in this way, the indictment against Bismarck is not that he created political conditions that were later used by German dictators, but that he used political forces and conditions that already existed, and which continued to exist in subsequent generations. It is hard to resist the conclusion that he did so willingly and eagerly, and that in the 1880s he presided deliberately over a political system based upon narrow conservative interests, and upon the restriction of the political activities of certain groups identified as 'enemies of the state'. The notion that German prosperity and security were threatened by hostile groups within Germany or abroad was central to Bismarck's political style. It is scarcely surprising that the next generation accepted so readily the claim that neighbours sought to restrict and restrain Germany's legitimate growth. Although Bismarck may not have approved of some of the ends to which Wilhelm II turned his political authority from 1890 onwards, he was directly responsible for the fact that the new Kaiser possessed the political authority, and the necessary political support, in the first place. It is far less credible to blame Bismarck for the power that fell into Hitler's hands in the 1930s. Where Wilhelm II acted largely within the structure of the Bismarckian constitution, and of the conservative coalition that Bismarck bequeathed to him, Hitler began his period in power by deliberately demolishing large portions of the Bismarckian structure. Not only was the Reichstag undermined by his assumption of emergency powers in 1933, and rival political parties banned, but the more traditional elements of the conservative coalition were steadily excluded from political influence. Above all, the federal structure of the Reich, so important for the preservation of Prussia's distinct political identity, was demolished and replaced by a centralised state system. *Anschluss* – the integration of Austria into a greater German state – was, of course, the opposite of everything that Bismarck had worked for in the 1860s.

1. On what grounds have historians reached different conclusions about Bismarck's government of the united German Reich?

2. How convincing is the argument that Bismarck set up a repressive, authoritarian state in Germany?

4.7 To what extent did Bismarck's foreign policy succeed in defending German interests in the 1870s?

Before 1870, Bismarckian foreign policy had aims, more or less specific, that were pursued and eventually achieved by the skilful exploitation of external circumstances. Chief among these were the desire to substitute Prussian influence for that of Austria in the affairs of the German states, and subsequently to deflect the hostility of France, aroused by Prussia's success. After 1871 the essential principles of German foreign policy underwent a substantial change. In the eyes of Bismarck the *kleindeutsch* settlement of that year was final, and Germany was a state without further territorial ambitions. As he himself remarked, 'when we have arrived in a good harbour, we should be content to cultivate and hold what we have won'. It was now Bismarck's primary aim to prevent external events from disrupting the settlement that he had created. In this undertaking he was to achieve far less success than he had enjoyed in the first decade of his diplomatic career.

The *Dreikaiserbund*

For some years after 1872 the mainstay of Bismarck's delicate diplomatic balance was the understanding between the rulers of Germany, Russia and Austria–Hungary, known as the 'League of the Three Emperors' (*Dreikaiserbund*). First projected at a meeting of the monarchs in 1872, it was confirmed the following year (22 October 1873). It was given a more solid form by a series of military agreements promising aid to any party attacked by a fourth power.

In concluding this general and formless agreement, Bismarck probably had three main motives, although authorities disagree as to where the main emphasis should be placed. Firstly, the *Dreikaiserbund* represented a natural union of conservative ideals against disruptive forces such as nationalism and socialism. Secondly, the League ensured that neither Austria–Hungary nor Russia was available as an ally for France. A.J.P. Taylor preferred to emphasise the third potential benefit to Germany from the League. 'Its object insofar as it had one, was to prevent a conflict between Austria–Hungary and Russia in the **Eastern Question**.' Preoccupied by domestic issues for much of the decade, Bismarck sought to ensure that Europe remained peaceful by leading a combination of three of Europe's five main powers.

Eastern Question: A term used to describe the political and diplomatic problems posed by the decline of the Turkish Empire. This decline raised the prospect of Russian expansion in the eastern Mediterranean, the Middle East and the Balkans. Such prospects threatened the interests of Great Britain, France and Austria–Hungary.

The 'war in sight' crisis

Behind the superficial unity of the *Dreikaiserbund* lay self-interest and mutual suspicions that were always likely to undermine it. Two crises in the 1870s demonstrated the instability of the League. The first, the so-called 'war in sight' crisis of 1875, was the result of a major diplomatic miscalculation on the part of Bismarck. He had estimated, since 1871, that his purposes were best served by the survival of a republican government in France, as this would strengthen Russian and Austrian suspicions of France and keep that country in isolation. Bismarck even went so far as to dismiss and humiliate his ambassador in Paris, H. von Arnim, when the latter disagreed and promoted royalist interests. In 1875, however, political developments in France indicated a rise in royalist support and there were disturbing signs of military preparations. Bismarck's reaction was to allow threats of a preventative war, which he certainly never intended to fight, to circulate from unofficial sources. These came to a head with an article in the *Berliner Post* (9 April 1875) entitled 'Is war in sight?' Far from leading to the desired French embarrassment and retreat, the article caused France to appeal to the other powers to prevent a further German assault upon it. Britain and Russia led the protests to Berlin, and the crisis ended as suddenly as it had begun, with a German retreat. The limits of Russia's confidence in Germany had been clearly illustrated.

The Eastern Crisis

The second crisis, the Eastern Crisis of 1875–78, was not of Bismarck's making. It arose from the general revolt of the South Slav peoples, with Bulgarian support, against their Turkish overlords in 1875–76. Panslavism and practical political interests encouraged successful Russian intervention and resulted in the Treaty of San Stefano (3 March 1878). By the terms of this treaty European Turkey was substantially reduced in size by the creation of large Russian **client states** in Bulgaria, Romania, Serbia and Montenegro. Bismarck had disclaimed any interest in the Eastern Question, using the famous phrase that no Balkan issue was 'worth the healthy bones of a single Pomeranian musketeer'. Even so, he could not fail to be concerned at the prospect of a clash between Russia and Austria–Hungary, which now saw its only remaining sphere of influence in the Balkans threatened. The only alternative to war was a conference of the great powers, and this met in Berlin (June–July 1878) under the presidency of Bismarck. There he played the role of the 'honest broker', not aiming for personal profit, but for a peaceful settlement between his 'clients' Russia and Austria–Hungary. The interests of the other major powers, including Britain, ensured that Russia would not be able to maintain the San Stefano settlement.

Superficially, the Congress of Berlin marked a highpoint in Bismarck's diplomatic career. In the short term, he had preserved peace and confirmed Berlin as the centre of European diplomacy. Erich Eyck, on the other hand, was one of those historians who preferred to see the congress as marking the beginning of the end of the Bismarckian system. Russian opinion was bitter at the loss of Slav territory, won at the cost of Russian blood, even though they kept their substantial Asian gains from Turkey. Tsar Alexander II was not alone in seeing the Congress of Berlin as 'a European coalition against Russia under the leadership of Prince Bismarck'. The introduction of protective tariffs against Russian agriculture in 1879 only confirmed this impression. Quite apart from the chill that entered into Russo-German relations, the *Dreikaiserbund* was further undermined by the occupation of Bosnia and Herzegovina by Austria–Hungary against the will of the local population.

Client states: Nations receiving support in the form of money, services and weapons from a more powerful nation.

1. What diplomatic steps did Bismarck take to defend German interests between 1871 and 1878?

2. How successful was the Congress of Berlin from Bismarck's viewpoint?

4.8 Did Bismarck's alliance with Austria in 1879 represent the failure of his diplomatic system?

German and Austrian motives behind the Dual Alliance

Anti-German feeling in Russia arose after the Congress of Berlin as a result of thwarted pan-Slav ambitions and of the wounded pride of Alexander Gorchakov, the Russian premier, rather than as the result of any deliberate re-orientation of German policy. It had great, long-term importance in that it confirmed the impressions that Bismarck had derived from the events of 1875–78. He felt that the time had come to put Germany's relations with Austria–Hungary on a surer footing. His motives were undoubtedly complex, but were dominated by the desire to avoid diplomatic isolation, and perhaps by the hope of frightening Russia back on to better terms with Germany by the prospect of its own isolation. It was also certain that a clear commitment to Austria would be the most popular of the diplomatic options within Germany, especially at a time when his own domestic policy relied so heavily upon conservative support. As Bismarck wrote to the reluctant Kaiser Wilhelm: 'German kinship, historical memories, the German language, all that makes an alliance with Austria more popular in Germany than an alliance with Russia.' Nevertheless, it was only with great difficulty that the Emperor's scruples about the 'betrayal' of Russia and of his fellow monarch were overcome.

In Austria, on the other hand, the prospect of an alliance was greeted with great enthusiasm. The chief minister, Count Andrassy, was reported to have 'jumped for joy' at news of the German proposals. By the terms of this Dual Alliance (October 1879), both powers committed themselves to aid the other in the event of a Russian attack, but only to neutrality if the attack came from another power. Austria–Hungary, therefore, was not committed to aid Germany in hostilities against France – an inequality that drew further criticism from the Kaiser.

In the following years the Dual Alliance became the centre of a system of German diplomacy. The agreement has been variously interpreted by different historians, some seeing it as the salvation of European peace in the 1880s, and others seeing it as confused and contradictory. In May 1882, the alliance became the Triple Alliance through the association of Italy with Germany and Austria–Hungary. This extension of the Bismarckian system had real advantages for Germany in that its mutual undertakings with Italy were specifically anti-French. This provided Germany for the first time with a committed ally against that country. On the other hand, Austria's alliances with Serbia (June 1881) and Romania (October 1882) drew Germany even deeper into areas where it had no direct stake or interest.

The Reinsurance Treaty and its significance

Meanwhile, what of Russia? In the short term, Germany was able to maintain friendly relations with its neighbour. Fear of diplomatic isolation encouraged Russia to agree to the renewal of the *Dreikaiserbund* on a more formal basis (June 1881). The three powers agreed to remain neutral in the event of one of their number going to war with a fourth power. Russia and Austria–Hungary also defused tension in the Balkans for the time being, by acknowledging each other's spheres of influence in the region.

In the late summer of 1886, however, a new crisis arose over Russia's virtual deposition of Bulgaria's independent-minded King Alexander (August–September 1886). It raised the likelihood of an Austro–Russian clash more starkly than at any time since 1878, and the resultant collapse

A famous *Punch* cartoon of 1890, entitled 'Dropping the Pilot'. Commenting on Bismarck's resignation, it shows Wilhelm II watching the Iron Chancellor leave the 'ship' of the German state, which he had guided for so long.

1. What changes took place in Germany's relations with Austria and with Russia in the years between 1878 and 1890?

2. Does Bismarck's foreign policy after 1871 suggest that he was more concerned to consolidate German power in Europe than to expand it?

3. How secure was Germany's position in European diplomacy by the time Bismarck left office in 1890?

of the *Dreikaiserbund* threatened the whole basis of Bismarckian diplomacy. In an attempt to plug the gap and to retain some influence over Russia's actions, the Chancellor was able to conclude (June 1887) a secret agreement with Russia, known as the Reinsurance Treaty. By its terms, both powers agreed to remain neutral in the event of a dispute with a third power. Germany also recognised Russia's greater interest in Bulgaria. As these neutrality clauses did not apply in the event of a German attack on France, or of a Russian attack upon Austria–Hungary, Bismarck did in fact gain some means of preventing the latter eventuality. Much controversy has centred upon the question of whether the Reinsurance Treaty was compatible with the Dual Alliance. In fact, there was no contradiction in the letter of the two agreements. They placed Germany in the position of having to decide, in the event of a clash between Russia and Austria–Hungary, who was truly the aggressor and thus which treaty Germany would honour. Bismarck's achievement in the Reinsurance Treaty was that he preserved Germany's power to arbitrate between the two powers.

The 'balance sheet' of Bismarckian diplomacy

What, then, was Bismarck's diplomatic legacy? The historian John McManners, in *Essays in Modern European History*, concludes that, by his commitment to Austria–Hungary, Bismarck bequeathed potential political disaster. 'Two years before Bismarck's fall from office, his system was shaking and the shadow of a Franco-Russian alliance was creeping into the horizon.' This judgement is harsh in that it attaches too little importance to the forces driving Bismarck in his decision in 1879, and underestimates the subtlety of the Reinsurance Treaty. It was, after all, Wilhelm II who allowed the treaty to lapse in 1890 when Russian enthusiasm for its renewal remained high. Nor did Bismarck create the eastern European tensions that erupted in 1914. If Bismarck's work as a diplomat can be criticised it is perhaps on the grounds that he monopolised power to such an extent that, after his fall, the diplomatic future of Germany would inevitably lie in the hands of less able men.

4.9 Why did Bismarck launch a German colonial policy in his last years in power?

The acquisition of colonies

In the mid-1880s, the otherwise consistent course of German foreign policy took an unprecedented twist. Bismarck gave his government's support to the formation of a far-flung, but important, body of German colonial possessions. This contrasted starkly with the fact that in 1871 he had refused to annex French colonial possessions in place of Alsace-Lorraine, and that as late as 1881 he had declared that 'so long as I am Chancellor we shall pursue no colonial policy'. Germany's part in the 'scramble for Africa' was concentrated in the years 1884–85, establishing sovereignty in areas where German trading interests had been developed by private firms over the previous decade or so. In April 1884, the state agreed to 'protect' a strip of territory at Angra Pequena, in what is now Namibia, which had been secured from the Nama tribesmen by the Bremen merchant, Franz Lüderitz. Within the year, to the deep concern of British interests in southern Africa, this had grown into the colony of South-West Africa. In July of the same year the government appointed Gustav Nachtigal as German Consul-General in Togoland and the Cameroons, where he had previously been representing a group of Hamburg businessmen. Karl Peters, a businessman and adventurer of dubious reputation, acquired most of German East Africa (now Tanzania) for the Reich, in February 1885, through a series of shady deals with local chiefs. Further afield, the establishment of Imperial control over northern New Guinea (May 1885) and over the Samoan Islands in the Pacific (1899) completed the shape of the German colonial empire.

What were Bismarck's motives?

The reasons for this abrupt departure from tradition have exercised historians ever since, and there is still no general agreement as to Bismarck's motives. The traditional view of nationalist historians was that Bismarck had always hoped for imperial greatness, and was merely awaiting his opportunity. More recently, the most widely accepted explanation has been that the German Chancellor had to conform to dominating trends in German society. German industry was now powerful enough to seek new outlets and new sources of raw materials abroad. It was perhaps natural that, after the introduction of protective tariffs in 1879, many businessmen should seek similar protection for their interests abroad from the state. This enthusiasm found expression in the formation of such successful pressure groups as the German Colonial Union (*Deutscher Kolonialverein*, 1882) and the Society for German Colonisation (*Gesellschaft für Deutsche Kolonisation*, 1884). Nationalist feeling also proclaimed that the German state, having established its European position, now had to make its power felt in the wider world. Lastly, Bismarck may have been influenced by the arguments of the political conservatives, who saw foreign adventures as a welcome distraction from domestic tensions at a time when the struggle against socialism was in full swing.

Whatever the rationale behind it, German colonial policy was generally sterile. Bismarck had hoped that colonisation would not become a financial burden upon the Reich, but would be financed by private enterprise. 'I do not wish to found provinces,' he told the Reichstag in 1884, 'but to protect commercial establishments in their development.' These hopes were ill founded. By 1913 colonisation had cost the German taxpayer over

Imperialism: The practice whereby a state acquires economic and/or political power over other territories, usually with a view to commercial/industrial expansion.

1. What colonial territories did Germany acquire in the 1880s?

2. What benefits and what disadvantages did Germany derive from the acquisition of colonies in the 1880s?

1,000 million marks in direct government aid. Only Togoland and Samoa had proved to be self-supporting. In almost every respect the results of 30 years of **imperialism** had been a disappointment. The total German population of the colonies amounted to only 24,000, most of them officials. Only South-West Africa, where diamonds were discovered in 1907, fulfilled hopes of valuable natural resources. The native populations, poor and under-developed, were unable to play the role of consumers of German industrial produce. Worst of all, the limited colonial experiment of 1884–85 provided the basis for German pretensions to a 'world policy' in the next decade, and thereby played no small role in the events that led to war in 1914.

4.10 What was the impact of unification upon German economic development?

The stimulus of unification

The establishment of the Reich in 1871 provided a number of direct stimuli to an economy that already possessed a substantial base for prosperity. Alsace-Lorraine, for example, contained Europe's largest deposits of iron ore. Production increased rapidly under German control, from 684,000 tons in 1872 to 1,859,000 tons in 1882. The injection of part of the French indemnity payments into the national economy caused a spectacular, if short-lived, boom in 1871–73. This was felt especially in the building and railway industries. Lastly, unity provided the opportunity for a burst of legislation designed further to unify the economic life of the Reich.

Simply in terms of output, the 'Bismarck era' provided further dramatic advances for the German economy. Coal production soared, steel production increased by some 700%, and the German merchant marine advanced from virtual non-existence to the position of second largest in the world. The table below, by contrasting German development with that of Great

Economic comparisons between Great Britain, France and Germany, 1870–90

	1870	1890
Population (millions)		
Germany	41	49
Britain	32	38
France	36	38
Coal production (million tons)		
Germany	38	89
Britain	118	184
France	13	26
Steel production (million tons)		
Germany	0.3	2.2
Britain	0.6	3.6
France	0.08	0.6
Iron ore production (million tons)		
Germany	2.9	8
Britain	14	14
France	2.6	3.5

Britain and France, gives an impression of its advance as a world industrial power. Apart from the doubling of the railway network, it is also important to note the extent of nationalisation that took place during these decades. Out of Prussia's 28,000 kilometres of track, 24,000 kilometres passed into state ownership between 1879 and 1884.

Banking, finance and industrial cartels

In these respects the 1870s and 1880s formed part of a steady and consistent development. What was unique to this period was the development of two important features in the economy. Firstly, the post-war boom provided a considerable stimulus to the German banking industry. By the mid-1870s, Germany had a remarkably well-endowed system. Apart from the Reichsbank, there were six other banks which dominated commerce and industry with a combined capital of 2,500 million marks. They participated widely in the arrangement of private loans to industry and of public loans to the state, in the encouragement of new industries such as electricity and chemicals, and in the development of foreign and colonial ventures. With their representatives sitting on the boards of many leading companies, the co-operation between bankers and industrialists – known as 'finance capitalism' – reached a high stage of development during this period. Such bankers could also provide important services for the state. Bismarck's own banking adviser, Gerson Bleichröder, helped to finance the expensive military campaigns of 1863–66 at a time when state reserves were low, and later stage-managed the policy of railway nationalisation in the 1870s and 1880s.

The second distinctive feature of contemporary economic development was the growth of cartels. There were four such cartels in 1865, and only eight a decade later. Harder times made such arrangements more attractive and Germany boasted 90 in 1885 and 210 five years later. The largest cartels, such as the Rhenish Steel Syndicate and the Ruhr Coal Syndicate, headed by such men as Alfred Krupp, Hugo Stinnes and Fritz Thyssen, exercised enormous influence over the economic and political development of the Reich. Their demands for protective tariffs in the 1870s, and their later campaigns for naval and colonial development, clearly demonstrate this influence. A further result of these cartels was that safe home markets enabled German industrialists increasingly to break into foreign markets by 'dumping' goods cheaply.

Therein lay the seeds of the ultimate failure of Bismarck's conservative system. For all his fear of Catholics or Socialists, the greatest danger to Junker, Prussian Germany arose from the increasing demands and ambitions of German financiers and industrialists.

1. What were the major features of Germany economic and commercial development in the 1870s and the 1880s?

2. In what ways did German economic developments in the 1870s and the 1880s change the state and the society that Bismarck had created in 1871?

Source-based questions: Bismarck as pragmatic politician

Study Source 1 below and then answer questions (a) to (c):

SOURCE 1

(Bismarck explains the motives behind his policies in a speech to the Reichstag, 1881)

I have often acted hastily and without reflection, but when I have had time to think I have always asked: what is useful, effective, right for my fatherland, for my dynasty – so long as I was merely in Prussia – and now for the German nation? I have never been a doctrinaire. Liberal, reactionary, conservative – these I confess seem to me to be luxuries. Give me a strong German state, and then ask me whether it should have more or less liberal furnishings, and you'll find that I answer: Yes, I've no fixed opinions. Make proposals, and you won't meet any objections of principle from me. Sometimes one must rule liberally, and sometimes dictatorially, there are no external rules.

(a) Study Source 1.

What, according to Source 1, were Bismarck's main priorities in his government of Germany between 1870–90? [5 marks]

(b) On what issues did Bismarck most strongly disagree with the German liberals? [7 marks]

(c) What are the main arguments for and against the claim that 'Bismarck was primarily a conservative influence upon German politics between 1870–90'? [18 marks]

Further Reading

Texts designed for AS and A2 Level students

Bismarck and Germany, 1862–90 by D.G. Williamson (Longman, Seminar Studies series, 1986)
Bismarck and the German Empire, 1871–1918 by Lynn Abrams (Routledge, Lancaster Pamphlets, 1995)

More advanced reading

The most influential biographies of Bismarck are probably:
Bismarck and the German Empire by Erich Eyck (Allen & Unwin, 1968) which provides a classic, German liberal view of the subject.
Bismarck: the Man and the Statesman by A.J.P. Taylor (New English Library, 1968) which remains a classic interpretation of Bismarck's career.
Bismarck, the White Revolutionary by Lothar Gall (Allen & Unwin, 1986)
> A more concise summary is provided in 'Bismarckian Germany' by Geoff Eley, in *Modern Germany Reconsidered, 1870–1945*, G. Martel (ed.) (Routledge, 1992).

5 Wilhelm II's Germany, 1888–1918

Key Issues

- How important were the personality and priorities of Wilhelm II in shaping German politics in this period?

- What pressures and priorities guided German government in this period?

5.1 What was the impact upon German politics of the accession of Wilhelm II in 1888?

5.2 What was the extent and what were the consequences of German economic growth between the accession of Wilhelm II and the outbreak of the First World War?

5.3 To what extent did Chancellor von Caprivi pursue a 'new course' in German domestic politics?

5.4 How effective were the major institutions of government within Wilhelmine Germany?

5.5 What were the main aims of German domestic policies between 1890 and 1914?

5.6 Was social democracy a serious threat to the stability of Wilhelmine Germany?

5.7 What were the results of Germany's decision to pursue a 'world policy'?

5.8 Was Germany's position in European diplomacy strengthened or weakened by its policies between 1894 and 1905?

5.9 What was the impact of the First World War upon German domestic politics?

5.10 Historical interpretation: What forces shaped the political policies of Wilhelmine Germany?

Framework of Events

1888	February: Publication of German commitments to Austria-Hungary in the Dual Alliance
	March: Death of Kaiser Wilhelm I
	June: Death of Kaiser Friedrich III; accession of Wilhelm II
1890	January: Reichstag refuses to renew Anti-Socialist Laws
	March: Resignation of Bismarck as Chancellor of Germany
	June: Reinsurance Treaty between Germany and Russia allowed to lapse
	October: Expiry of Anti-Socialist Law
1891	Renewal of Triple Alliance between Germany, Austria and Italy for 12 years
1894	Dismissal of Caprivi. Hohenlohe appointed Chancellor of Germany
1897	von Tirpitz is appointed as German naval secretary
1898	First German Naval Bill
1900	von Bülow replaces Hohenlohe as Chancellor of Germany
1904	German attempts to initiate an alliance with Russia fail
1905	First Moroccan crisis, started by Kaiser's visit to Tangier
1906	Third German Naval Bill
1908	Fourth German Naval Bill. Publication of interview in *Daily Telegraph* causes embarrassment for Kaiser
1909	Germany recognises French interests in Morocco
	von Bülow is replaced as German Chancellor by Bethmann-Hollweg
1911	Second Moroccan Crisis
1912	Elections leave Social Democrats as strongest party in Reichstag
1913	'Zabern Incident' in Alsace-Lorraine embitters Franco-German relations
1914	June: Assassination of Archduke Franz Ferdinand in Sarajevo

1914	July: Austria-Hungary declares war on Serbia
	August: Germany declares war on Russia and on France
1916	Hindenburg becomes Chief of the General Staff
1918	Armistice ends the First World War.

Overview

A KEY issue in any political appraisal of Wilhelmine Germany is to establish whether or not the events of 1890 really constituted a new departure in German history. In that year Wilhelm II, only 18 months into his reign, dismissed Otto von Bismarck from his post as Chancellor. The traditional view of historians is that the removal of Bismarck's caution and realism, and of his fundamental concern for a peaceful diplomatic balance in Europe, set Germany and Europe on the road to the disaster of 1914.

Yet it may also be argued that little changed in 1888 in terms of the fundamental forces that drove German politics. These emerged in the late 1870s when, against a background of severe economic depression, Bismarck formed a formidable conservative alliance to resist the economic and political demands both of liberals and of the working classes. Industrialists and Junker landowners alike demanded policies that resisted the growth of genuine political freedom, which favoured the protection and development of their own economic interests, and which deflected the demands of the lower orders in German society. The emergence of a colonial programme, largely at odds with most of the principles that Bismarck had followed earlier in his political career, may be taken as a prime example of such policies. The departure of Bismarck, the argument continues, had little impact upon this situation. The essential conservative power-base of the German government, and the essential threats to that power-base, remained unchanged, and future Chancellors came under equal pressure to respond to these factors.

On the other hand, in social and economic terms, a great deal changed in Germany after 1888, and it changed very quickly. In the first decade of the 20th century the German Reich was barely recognisable as the state that Bismarck had founded in 1871. Its industrial economy had grown spectacularly, becoming the strongest in Europe, employing some 60% of the working population. In combination with this development, trade unionism expanded rapidly and the Social Democrats (SPD) attracted votes at such a rate that, by 1912, they constituted the largest single party in the Reichstag. Despite the enormous political and economic successes that Germany had achieved in the past few decades, or perhaps because of them, the Reich that entered the 20th century was full of contradictions. Economically and socially it was a modern and dynamic state; in political terms, however, it remained dominated by traditional elites who clung to their power and privileges, with little sympathy for political reform. Unsurprisingly, these elites supported policies that might have the widest appeal to the population, which might attract or at least isolate those who would otherwise favour more radical politics. The most striking political features of the Wilhelmine period, therefore, were not constructive measures of social development and reform, but measures and gestures designed to promote Germany's international status and prestige.

Superficially, Wilhelm II was well suited to act as the focus for this *Sammlungspolitik*. He relished military affairs, and delighted in grand gestures

Sammlungspolitik (German – 'policy of gathering together'): Term used to describe the attempt by the German government in the 1890s and 1900s to pursue policies that would have an equal appeal to the many different political and economic interest groups that existed within the Reich.

which made him the centre of public attention. Unfortunately, he was not a good judge of such gestures, and failed to appreciate the impact that they might have upon Germany's neighbours. It was one of the great ironies of the Wilhelmine period that Germany – perhaps the most secure and prosperous state in Europe – appeared to believe itself threatened and restricted on all sides by jealous enemies. The most dangerous and damaging elements of this *Sammlungspolitik* were the building of a German battle fleet, and the decision to pursue *Weltpolitik*. Even if the aim in both cases, as many historians now argue, was to win popularity at home, rather than really to challenge foreign powers abroad, the very nature of that policy made it impossible to reassure those foreign powers. In attempting to avoid the consequences of domestic instability, therefore, Germany made a substantial contribution to international instability.

In both international and domestic terms, the First World War provided an enormous test for the German state and society. In retrospect, the decision to enter the war, in the hope of a quick and rewarding victory, was disastrous, for the impact of the war upon domestic politics was exactly the opposite of that which Germany's leaders had envisaged in 1914. The economic prosperity of the country was wrecked by the enormous costs of the war and by the economic blockade which was imposed by Germany's enemies. The political differences that the war was intended to heal, or at least to mask, opened wider than ever. In the final stages of the war Germany was a country in crisis: the rift between the most conservative and the most left-wing elements in German politics were such that the state stood on the verge of civil war. In addition, the economic confidence and security that had been the most striking features of pre-war Germany lay in ruins. Although the Kaiser abdicated and fled into exile, the military and industrial conservatives who had supported him remained, eager to preserve their pre-eminence, and to shift the blame for the disaster onto other shoulders. The scene was set for the darkest decades in German history.

Weltpolitik (German – 'world policy'): Term used to describe the policy of the German government in the 1890s and 1900s whereby it sought to establish and advance German interests in all parts of the world, rather than concentrating upon European affairs.

1. Of the factors mentioned in the mind map, which do you think was Wilhem II's greatest success? Explain your answer.

2. Can you link any of the factors mentioned in the mind map? (For instance, the 'Introduction of Weltpolitik'can be linked to 'acquiring overseas colonies' and the 'naval race with Britain'.)

Can you find any other links?

3. Was Wilhelm II the person most responsible for the outbreak of the First World War? From the points mentioned in the mind map, which link William II's policies and the outbreak of war?

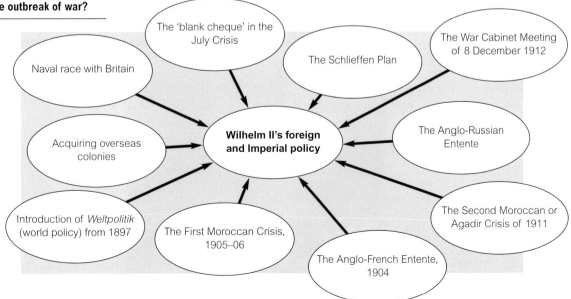

5.1 What was the impact upon German politics of the accession of Wilhelm II in 1888?

The long reign of Wilhelm I ended in March 1888, in the Kaiser's 92nd year. His son, briefly Kaiser as Friedrich III, had only months to live. He had suffered for a year from cancer of the throat, which had already deprived him of speech, and which ended his life in June. The imperial throne of Germany thus passed to his own son, and the 30-year reign of Wilhelm II began.

The personality and aims of Wilhelm II

The personality and psychology of the new Kaiser, now 29 years of age, have been a source of fascination for historians. His relationship with his parents, especially with his English mother, was tense and uneasy, and his personal sensitivity was undoubtedly increased by an accident at birth which left him with a withered arm and partially deaf. At Bonn University he showed far less interest in systematic study and learning than in the company of student **aristocrats**, and discovered the true passion of his youth in his years as an officer in the Potsdam Guards. Dismissed by his own father as 'inexperienced, immature and presumptuous', Wilhelm has not been kindly treated by historians. A typical judgement is that of Gordon Craig, in *Germany 1866–1945* (1978). 'Wilhelm had as much intelligence as any European sovereign and more than most, but his lack of discipline, his self-indulgence, his overdeveloped sense of theatre, and his fundamental misreading of history prevented him from putting it to effective use.'

The age of the young Kaiser was also significant. He belonged to a new, confident generation unaware of the dangers that German conservatism had narrowly survived in 1848 and in 1862. As historian Golo Mann put it, 'his memories began in 1870. He regarded the position which he owed to brilliant manoeuvres and clever acts of violence as the gift of God, as the natural order of things.'

Aristocrats: People whose families have a high social rank, especially those who hold a title. Their wealth is passed down the generations by inheritance.

Delusions of grandeur: a photograph of Wilhelm II, dated 1908.

Divine Right of Kings: The political view that claims that royal authority derives directly from God. As a consequence, a particular family or individual is designated by the will of God as ruler in a particular state.

Alfred von Kiderlen-Wächter (1852–1912)
Prominent German diplomat. Ambassador to Denmark (1894), to Romania (1900) and to Turkey on several occasions. Foreign Minister (1910) under Bethmann-Hollweg's administration. An enthusiastic supporter of *Weltpolitik* in general, and of the Triple Alliance in particular.

What did the personality of the new Kaiser mean for the conduct of the German government? Firstly, it meant that Wilhelm II would not be content with the passive role played by his grandfather. He believed passionately in the **Divine Right of Kings**, and from this derived a notion of the mystical link between the ruler and his people. Not for him a reign based upon the narrow interest of Junker landowners, or dictated by the advantage of Prussia alone. Wilhelm, in the words of the historian A.J.P. Taylor, 'desired an absurdity – to be Emperor of all of the Germans'. In a state built by Bismarck upon division and confrontation, the prospects of harmonious relations between monarch and Chancellor were dim.

Strong though he was on principle, the new Kaiser's style of government was hectic, spectacular and shallow. He travelled obsessively, rarely spending as much as half the year in his capital and earning the nickname of *Der Reise-Kaiser* ('the travelling Emperor'). He had views on everything, but rarely bothered to back his 'inspiration' with hard information. 'He just talks himself into an opinion,' remarked the German diplomat Alfred von Kiderlen-Wächter in 1891, while Wilhelm's biographer M. Balfour has remarked that 'his fluency in speaking meant that he approached all questions with an open mouth'. It was a fair summary of the man and the monarch that he openly boasted that he read neither the newspapers nor the German constitution. The outcome was a 30-year reign of great spectacle, constant motion, but little positive content. It amounted, in the words of the future Weimar minister, Walter Rathenau, to a 'dilettante foreign policy, romantic conservative internal policy and bombastic and empty cultural policy'.

The collapse of Bismarck's political system

For all the monumental achievements of the previous three decades, Bismarck's position as Chancellor of the Reich had remained dependent, in practice, upon the goodwill of the monarch. That position had appeared for some years to be threatened by the prospect of the succession of Crown Prince Friedrich, with his allegedly liberal sympathies, and his English wife, the Crown Princess Victoria. The death of Friedrich saved Bismarck from one challenge to his authority only to confront him with another. The political sympathies of Wilhelm were less liberal, but he differed fundamentally with his Chancellor as to methods of government.

The issues that divided the two men in 1888–90 were, in reality, merely symptoms of their different interpretations of the Reich and of the role of the Kaiser. A strike by miners in the Ruhr (May 1889) gave Wilhelm the chance to display his brand of paternalism towards the German working class. While he prepared a programme of social reforms, including a ban on Sunday working, Bismarck rejected the principle of conciliation and concession. Instead he aimed to continue a policy of hostility and confrontation. Bismarck's plans to make the renewable Anti-Socialist Laws permanent not only provoked a clash in the royal council (January 1890), but had severe repercussions in the Reichstag elections in the following month. Bismarck's coalition of Conservatives and National Liberals lost 85 of their 220 seats, and the Social Democrats nearly doubled their share of the vote. Deprived of the support of both monarch and Reichstag, Bismarck had only intrigue to fall back on. His attempts to force through a package of measures to revise the constitution, to help his political control, forced the Kaiser's hand. Wilhelm chose the path of conciliation, demanded Bismarck's resignation, and received it on 18 March 1890.

Bismarck's legacy

For all his earlier achievement, Bismarck bequeathed to Germany a legacy of tension and troubles. The concentration of power in his own hands meant he had consistently obstructed the growth of truly representative institutions in Germany. As Max Weber commented, 'Bismarck left behind him as a political heritage a nation without any political education ... a nation without any political will, accustomed to allow the great statesman at its head to look after its policy for it.' Undoubtedly, Bismarck had governed with great shrewdness, but the sad result of his political egoism was that his great power now passed into the hands of an irresponsible and unstable monarch. Furthermore, Wilhelm inherited a variety of thorny problems, especially in colonial and foreign policy, which Bismarck had allowed to develop for reasons of short-term political advantage. Despite his famous announcement upon Bismarck's resignation that 'the ship's course remains the same; "Full steam ahead" is the order', Wilhelm's fundamental misunderstanding of recent German and European history was to guarantee the destruction of most of the essential principles of Bismarckian Germany within the next 30 years.

1. What were the main political beliefs of Kaiser Wilhelm II?

2. Why did Otto von Bismarck fall from power in 1890?

5.2 What was the extent and what were the consequences of German economic growth between the accession of Wilhelm II and the outbreak of the First World War?

The years of Wilhelm II's reign to 1914 saw German industry build upon its Bismarckian foundations to take its place among the foremost industrial economies of the world. In this respect, the character of the country matched that of the Kaiser. It was young, dynamic, and outwardly confident.

Population growth, heavy industries and communications

Underlying Germany's economic acceleration was a continued rapid growth in population, providing native industries with a greater labour force and with more consumers. Between 1870 and 1890, Germany had experienced a population rise of 21%, from 40.9 to 49.5 million. In the next two decades, the rate of increase was half as great again, leading to a population of 65 million.

The traditional heavy industries of the Reich maintained the direction that they had followed in 1870–90, but they experienced a spectacular acceleration in the pace of output. Coal production was challenging that of Britain by the outbreak of the First World War, while steel output had surpassed that of Great Britain in 1900, and was nearly double that of its rival by 1910. The necessary corollary of these increases in German production was the expansion of its communication system. The Wilhelmine period saw a steady continuation of the growth in the railway system that had been a central feature of economic expansion since the foundation of the Reich. A system that extended 19,480 kilometres in 1870, and 41,820 kilometres in 1890, had grown to 59,016 kilometres by 1910.

The development of a German merchant navy was even more spectacular. The total tonnage of steamships registered at Hamburg rose from 99,000 in 1880 to 746,000 in 1900, while the figures for Bremen in the same period were 59,000 and 375,000. Germany's total merchant marine in 1914 amounted to 3 million tons, only a quarter of the British total, but nearly three times that of the USA.

Key economic indicators, 1890–1913

	Coal and lignite (million tons)	Pig iron (million tons)	Steel (million tons)	Exports (£ million)	Imports (£ million)
1890	89.1	4.66	3.16	170.5	213.6
1900	149.8	8.52	7.37	237.6	302.1
1910	192.3	14.79	13.15	373.7	446.7
1913	279.0	–	–	504.8	538.5

The 'new' industries

Nor was German expansion limited to traditional industries. By the outbreak of the First World War, Germany had established a substantial lead over all other European powers in the new chemical and electrical industries. Germany came to produce 75% of the world's output of chemical dyes by 1914, and played a prominent role in the development of agricultural fertilisers, pharmaceutical products and the industrial uses of sulphuric acid, sodium and chlorine. In electronics, Werner von Siemens had already contributed the electric dynamo (1867), and important work on electronic traction (1879 onwards). There was also the development of the two biggest electricity combines in Europe, Siemens/Halske, and AEG (*Allgemeine Elektrizitäts Gesellschaft* – General Electricity Company). By 1913 half of the world's electro-technical trade was in German hands. Such household names as Daimler and Diesel also attest to German achievement in engineering. In short, Germany's economic position within Europe was being transformed, not merely by industrialisation, but by the creation of 'young' industries, emerging at a time when older industrial economies were beginning to feel the need for reinvestment and modernisation.

National wealth and living standards

The total wealth of the German Reich increased in the peaceful years of the Wilhelmine era, according to the contemporary economist, Karl Helfferich, from 200,000 million marks to 300,000 million. The table below relates to Prussia alone. It indicates the increase in the number of great personal fortunes in this period. Other evidence suggests that the increase in German prosperity was more generally felt. For example, per capita income doubled in the course of 40 years. It rose from 352 marks per year (1871–75), through 603 marks per year (1896–1900) to 728 marks per year in 1911–13. The dramatic decrease in the rate of emigration, from 134,200 in 1880–89, to 28,000 in 1900–10, also indicates the relative rise in German living standards by the latter decade.

It should be noted, however, that this overall prosperity was not shared by German agriculture. It was not that agriculture stagnated: scientific methods of cultivation had spread rapidly since 1870, with an estimated

The rise in incomes – in the German Imperial currency of Reichmarks (RM)

Total fortune of:	1895	1911
Between 100,000 & 500,000 RM	86,552	135,843
Between 500,000 & 1 million RM	8,375	13,800
Between 1 and 2 million RM	3,429	5,916
Over 2 million RM	1,827	3,425

fourfold increase in mechanical harvesting between 1882 and 1907 alone. Yet German grain producers could not compete adequately with American imports, especially when large ocean-going steamers and low freight charges cheapened imports further. By 1900, it was cheaper to import grain from America than to transport it 400 kilometres within Germany. Grain prices dropped and heavy internal tariffs were needed to enable the Junker farmers of East Prussia to pay their debts. Economically, therefore, the Germany of Wilhelm II presented a subtly contrasted picture of modern dynamism and embattled conservative interests.

Inevitably the dramatic expansion of German industry involved substantial changes in the distribution and the living standards of the working population. Already evident in Bismarckian Germany, these changes accelerated dramatically in the decades that immediately preceded the First World War. In particular, they took the form of a large-scale movement of the population to urban centres, and from agricultural to industrial employment. In the four decades up to 1907, it has been estimated, something like 40% of the population of united Germany moved from one region of the Reich to another, and the proportion of the population employed in industrial production increased from 31% to 40%. Some spectacular examples of urban growth had occurred in the years since unification. Between 1870 and 1910, for example, the population of Leipzig grew from 107,000 to 679,000. Equivalent figures for Cologne (129,000 to 517,000), Essen (52,000 to 295,000) and Duisburg (32,000 to 229,000) tell the same story, and must be placed in the context of an overall rise in the German population of only 44%. Apart from the growth of individual towns, the nature and function of whole regions were sometimes transformed. In the Ruhr, in the Saarland, in Upper Silesia and elsewhere, new industrial conglomerations had been created as villages developed into towns, and merged with each other in the process of industrial growth. Such regions naturally experienced the same social problems that had arisen in other parts of Europe where rapid industrialisation had taken place. 'Overcrowding,' writes David Blackbourn (*Germany 1780–1918: The Long Nineteenth Century*, 1997), 'was exacerbated by the conditions to which the occupants of attics, cellars and tenements were exposed – damp, lack of natural light, primitive sanitary conditions that made the perfect breeding ground for infectious diseases. Periodic outbreaks of cholera and typhus were the most vivid symbol of dangerous, degraded living conditions.' A major outbreak of cholera in Hamburg in 1892 was the worst of many such epidemics.

What were the political implications of such developments?

It would be easy to see these developments as a classic case of industrial expansion alienating the industrial workforce, and preparing the ground for class conflict. In the case of Germany, however, the effects may have been more complex. The nature of Germany's economic growth in the Wilhelmine years, for instance, also produced a rapidly expanding lower middle class, with less radical political aspirations, alongside the industrial workers. It has been estimated that, in the 25 years leading up to 1907, the number of 'white collar workers' (clerical, rather than manual workers) roughly tripled in Germany to a total of 3.3 million. At the time of unification there were more than ten manual workers to each clerical worker. On the eve of the First World War the ratio had been reduced to 3.5 to 1. A number of social historians have also stressed that regional and religious identities remained strong in Germany, often cutting across traditional conceptions of class-consciousness. A further factor to be taken into account is the fact that the vast bulk of this urban population

1. In what respects did the German economy make the most spectacular progress between 1890 and 1914?

2. Who benefited most and who benefited least from the trends in the German economy during these years?

found work during the Wilhelmine period. In only one year between 1900–14 did unemployment rates in Germany rise above 3%. Wilhelmine Germany never had to cope with the impact of economic depression upon this industrial population. There can be little doubt that the governing elites of the period regarded the industrial masses with suspicion, and often with fear. Whether they were right to do so is a question on which historians have yet to reach agreement.

5.3 To what extent did Chancellor von Caprivi pursue a 'new course' in German domestic politics?

The search for a German consensus

Leo von Caprivi (1831–1899)
Entered the Prussian army in 1849 and fought in the conflicts with Denmark (1864), Austria (1866) and France (1870–71). Head of Admiralty (1883–88). Imperial German Chancellor (1890–94).

Bismarck's successor as Chancellor of the Reich and as Prime Minister of Prussia was General Leo von Caprivi. He brought to these offices the prestige of high military rank, personal honesty and modesty, but none of the political experience or deviousness necessary to master the complexities and contradictions of the Bismarckian state. 'The primary problem of the Caprivi Era,' in the opinion of historian J. Alden Nichols (*Germany after Bismarck*, 1958), 'was how to handle a complex political creation that had finally escaped from the control of its creator.' The new Chancellor, like the Kaiser, desired greater conciliation and less confrontation in domestic politics. He refused to regard any political grouping as a *Reichsfeinde* (see page 72) and was willing to accept the assistance of any group in furthering his projects. Both Caprivi and the Kaiser claimed not to be initiating a 'new era', an indication of how little they understood of Bismarck's rule.

Reform of the Bismarckian system

The years 1890–94 saw systematic inroads made into the domestic system established by Bismarck.

● The Anti-Socialist Laws were allowed to lapse.

● Attempts were made to win the working classes over to the Reich with a series of reforms that included: – a ban on Sunday working– the limitation of working hours for women and children and the establishment of courts for industrial arbitration.

● Confrontation with national minorities in Posen and in Alsace-Lorraine was eased by the relaxation of rules governing the use of German in administration and education.

● A moderate reduction was sought in the privileges of Prussia within the Reich. Prussia's independent foreign ministry was abolished, its tax system reformed and a graduated income tax introduced.

Of much more direct offence to the Prussian Junkers was Caprivi's new economic course. In the interests of increased trade and of cheaper food, he abandoned Bismarckian protectionism, that great guarantee of the Junkers' agricultural prosperity. A series of trade treaties – with Austria-Hungary and Italy in 1892, with Belgium, Switzerland and Romania in 1893, and with Russia a year later – greatly stimulated Germany's industrial progress but involved, as their price, the reduction of German agricultural tariffs. The unfortunate coincidence of these measures with the increase in cheap American corn exports drove not only the Junkers, but also most farmers into opposition to the government. The Federation of Agriculturalists (*Bund der Landwirte*), founded to organise this opposition (February 1893), boasted 250,000 members within the year and constituted one of several new conservative forces in German politics.

The fall of Caprivi and the return to conservatism

The fate of two pieces of projected legislation illustrated the deterioration of Caprivi's political position. A bill by the Prussian Ministry of Education, proposing religious segregation of schools, and closer control of religious education by the Churches (1892), was defeated by the opposition of all liberal groups in the Reichstag. The defeat brought about Caprivi's resignation as Prime Minister of Prussia, which further weakened his political base. More surprisingly, a new Army Bill also ran into opposition. Presented to the Reichstag in 1892, it was only passed after a dissolution and new elections in which the conservative parties and the Social Democrats prospered at the expense of the Liberals.

Four years in office served to convince Caprivi that he had underestimated the selfishness of the various political interests in the Reichstag. In the same period, the initial, superficial 'liberalism' of the Kaiser had faded. Wilhelm accepted his Chancellor's resignation in October 1894. He was disillusioned at the failure of the workers to desert the Social Democrats and rally to him, perturbed at the resurgence of political violence especially evident in the assassination of the French president by anarchists, and perplexed at the rift between the government and Junker conservatism.

Did Caprivi abandon Bismarck's foreign policy?

Friedrich von Holstein (1837–1909) Entered the Prussian diplomatic service in 1860. Became a *protégé* of Bismarck, but lost favour through his disagreement with the Chancellor's policy of alliance with Russia. Returned to prominence after Bismarck's fall. Head of Foreign Ministry (1900–06), losing office in the aftermath of the Moroccan crisis.

It is a more complex matter to decide whether Caprivi departed from the traditional Bismarckian course in handling Germany's foreign affairs. Certainly he presided over the destruction of a central element in the Bismarckian diplomatic system when in March 1890 he refused to renew the Reinsurance Treaty with Russia. In this, he was not acting with any anti-Russian motive; instead he hoped to maintain friendly relations with the great eastern power. Caprivi was influenced, however, by personalities in the foreign office, such as Friedrich von Holstein whose general leanings were anti-Russian. Their convincing arguments concerned the incompatibility of sections of the treaty with German undertakings to Austria and to Romania, and the undoubted fact that its terms gave far greater advantages to Russia than to Germany. In short, Caprivi acted honestly where deviousness might have served better. The result of his action was the almost immediate confirmation of Bismarck's nightmare, a diplomatic understanding between Russia and France. Furthermore, by agreeing to the renewal of the Triple Alliance with Austria and Italy in 1891 he made a contribution to the formation of hostile camps in Europe that eventually undermined the peace.

Caprivi remained Bismarckian in the sense that he continued to resist the considerable pressures within Germany for a 'world policy' (*Weltpolitik*). He saw little realistic future in the acquisition of colonies. The essence of his policy remained European, to consolidate and improve Germany's position in Central Europe. This aim was served by his system of economic agreements with Germany's neighbours and by the confirmation of the Triple Alliance.

It had its most controversial display in the Anglo-German treaty of July 1890. By this treaty Germany transferred to Great Britain all rights to the island of Zanzibar, and to large areas of the adjacent African mainland, in

Pan-German: The policy which dictates that all those of German racial origin should be united in a single German state. This naturally involved the union of Germany with those parts of the Austro-Hungarian Empire whose population was ethnically German.

1. Which of Bismarck's policies were abandoned when Caprivi held office?

2. In what ways did the priorities of Caprivi's government differ from those of Bismarck's government?

return for the strategic North Sea island of Heligoland. If, however, the Zanzibar agreement was an opening move in a plan to tempt Britain into closer relations with Germany in place of the Russian alliance, it was a failure. Caprivi underestimated the reluctance of the British to get involved in binding continental commitments. He also found that his concept of Germany's continental future was not widely popular at home. The **Pan-German** League (*Alldeutscher Verband*), which took form between 1891 and 1894, was a deliberate attempt to encourage the Reich to pursue a more energetic, prestigious and cosmopolitan foreign policy. Thus, although Caprivi rejected some of the methods most dear to Bismarck, the brief span of his government did represent the last attempt to limit Germany to European commitments before his opponents launched it on the ultimately disastrous course of 'world policy'.

5.4 How effective were the major institutions of government within Wilhelmine Germany?

The office of Chancellor

The German Reich was to have three more chancellors between the fall of Caprivi and the outbreak of war in 1914. The first of these was a Catholic, Bavarian aristocrat, Prince Chlodwig von Hohenlohe-Schillingsfürst (1894–1900). After a lifetime in state service, he reached the highest office at the age of 75. He was, frankly, a stop-gap. His conservative views on domestic matters and his pro-Russian sympathies recommended him to the German right, and his lack of any coherent programme of his own fitted in well with Wilhelm's ambitions of personal government. Primarily, in the words of the contemporary German politician Friedrich Naumann, Hohenlohe was 'an artist in the avoidance of catastrophe'. His years in office constituted, in retrospect, a lull before the diplomatic storm of the new century.

Hohenlohe's resignation in 1900 was precipitated by the Kaiser's persistent failure to consult him on important policy matters. His successor was to be a prime accessory in Wilhelm's irresponsible political meddling. Bernhard von Bülow (1900–09) was a more cosmopolitan and, it was felt, more modern man than Hohenlohe. There was too much of the flattering courtier about Bülow for him to have been a safe, moderating influence on the Kaiser, as Hohenlohe had been.

Many historians have laid upon Bülow much of the blame for Germany's diplomatic irresponsibility during the period. The circumstances of Bülow's fall are thus ironic. Although his resignation in June 1909 was ostensibly due to the defeat in the Reichstag of his project for a tax on inherited wealth, the real cause of his downfall was, like Bismarck's,

Bernhard Prince von Bülow (1849–1929)
Chancellor of the German Empire (1900–09) under Kaiser Wilhelm II. Having risen through the Foreign Office, where he had been Minister since 1897, von

Bülow was closely identified with German colonial expansion and seemed to share the Kaiser's enthusiasm for a 'world role'. He had a reputation for brilliance, but superficial polish was not

backed by firm principles or broad vision, and he deserved the nickname of 'the eel' bestowed upon him. Bülow adopted attitudes to France and Russia that unintentionally reinforced the trend

towards opposing European power groups. He resigned after losing the confidence of Wilhelm II and the Reichstag.

the loss of the monarch's confidence. This arose from Bülow's carelessness the previous year in allowing the publication of an interview given by Wilhelm to the British newspaper *The Daily Telegraph*. Characteristic irresponsibility on the Kaiser's part led to utterances offensive to Britain and to Russia, and highly embarrassing to Germany. Most Germans, he suggested, were hostile to Britain, and he was the only force that restrained their hostility. An outcry in the Reichstag brought Wilhelm to the verge of a nervous breakdown and ended the 'golden age' of his personal government. In the long run, as many foreign observers have pointed out, the Reichstag missed the opportunity for long-term constitutional change afforded by the *Daily Telegraph* incident, and Bülow alone paid a high price for the affair.

The last peacetime Chancellor of Imperial Germany was Theobald von Bethmann-Hollweg (1909–17). A man of personal courage and honour, he seemed an ideal choice from the point of view of domestic affairs. However, his crippling disability was his total inexperience in foreign or military affairs. While this certainly recommended him to a Kaiser who desired supremacy in those areas, it was part of Germany's tragedy that such a man led the government at the time when the fate of Europe depended upon such matters.

In a sense such changes in personnel were of secondary importance. Of greater significance in the years 1894–1914 was the erosion of the overall power of the Chancellor, perhaps the most important of all the departures from Bismarck's system of government. In part, this was due to an 'invasion from above', to the Kaiser's consistent desire for personal rule. At the same time the power of the Chancellor was eroded from below, by the loss of control over various, previously subordinate, ministries. Caprivi had allowed far greater freedom to other departments than Bismarck had ever tolerated, and Admiral Tirpitz at the Naval Ministry provided a good example of an independence of action inconceivable before 1890.

The Reichstag

Although it is clear that Wilhelmine Germany was not a true constitutional monarchy, it would be inaccurate to dismiss the Reichstag as an ineffective sham. There is much evidence of improved party organisation in the assembly after 1890, and evidence too of occasions when the Reichstag showed concerted opposition to the government. The most notable example occurred in 1913, when deputies were united in outrage over the behaviour of the military in the Zabern Affair. Yet the fact remains that the government was able largely to ignore such pressure and the Reichstag was never able to bring down a government or to restrict its actions, as its British or French equivalents might have done.

In part this was because the Chancellor was not a parliamentary party leader and could not be undermined by the reduction of his majority. There were also other serious weaknesses in the German parliamentary system, which prevented it from playing a more positive role in government. As a representative assembly, it was unsatisfactory in several respects. Its constituencies, for instance, were notoriously uneven, their boundaries remaining unchanged between 1871 and 1914. By the time of the 1912 elections, the largest were ten times the size of the smallest. They did not reflect population changes, and it took far more votes to elect a Social Democratic representative in an industrial region than to elect a conservative or a member of the Centre Party in a rural constituency.

Yet the Social Democratic Party steadily increased its parliamentary representation. Why then could parties not put effective pressure upon the government in the Reichstag? To a large extent, this was due to their

---

Theobald von Bethmann-Hollweg (1856–1921)
Started his career as a civil servant in Brandenburg, served in the Prussian Ministry of the Interior, and became Secretary of State in the Imperial Office of Internal Affairs (1907). Bethmann-Hollweg was appointed Chancellor in 1909. He was a competent administrator, but lacked knowledge and experience of foreign and military affairs. He became increasingly dependent on non-Parliamentary centres of influence such as the court, army and bureaucracy.

Alfred von Tirpitz (1849–1930)
Founder of the German navy. Served in the Prussian navy from 1865. Chief of Staff of Navy High Command; Rear Admiral (1895); Secretary of State of Imperial Navy Department (1897–1916), in which capacity he was an advocate of submarine warfare. Drafted Germany's first Navy Law (1898) and the many subsequent laws. He became an admiral in 1903; Grand Admiral in 1911. Tirpitz was a nationalist deputy in the Reichstag (1925–28).

inability to form effective coalitions. This, in turn, was due to divisions and resentments arising from the party politics of previous decades. The National Liberals had supported Bismarck's anti-socialist laws and had been enthusiastic promoters of the *Kulturkampf* (see Chapter 3). The Social Democratics Party and the Centre Party could not easily forget or forgive this. Such differences were eventually overcome under the pressures of war, and a coalition emerged between these groups that formed the basis of the Weimar Republic (see Chapter 11), but there was no such urgency in the 1890s or the 1900s. Historian David Blackbourn, in *The Fontana History of Germany 1780–1918: the Long Nineteenth Century* (1997), emphasises how these parties never had to concern themselves with practical issues or effective compromises. This was because they were never in power in this period, or seriously in pursuit of power. Instead, they could afford the luxury of ideological rhetoric, which distanced them from each other. This was especially true of the Social Democrats. Theoretically a Marxist party, it turned its face against alliances with 'bourgeois' parties, and preached radical social and political change to an extent that created fear and hostility among political groups with whom the Social Democrats might profitably have formed an electoral alliance. It must also be remembered that the German state was **federal**, and that significant differences existed between political conditions in one state and in another. Party co-operation on a national level became even more difficult when party attitudes and relations differed greatly in the provinces.

Federal: A system of government which consists of a group of states controlled by a central government. The central government deals with things concerning the whole country, such as foreign policy, but each state has its own local powers and laws.

The army in the German mentality

The decline of the Chancellor's office, the personal unreliability of the monarch and the failure of the Reichstag to seek fundamental political change, were different elements in the severe weakening of civil government in Germany. The most important result of this was that the German army occupied a status unparalleled in Europe. In part, it owed this status to the role that it had played in Germany's growth. The nation suffered from what the historian A.J.P. Taylor called a 'Sadowa–Sedan complex', based on the memories of the great victories of the past. Glorification of war and conquest was commonplace in contemporary German thought and writing. 'The whole nation,' remarked the socialist August Bebel, 'is still drunk with military glory and there is nothing to be done until some great disaster has sobered us.'

Two illustrations may help to indicate the independence of the army from German government. In November 1913, a series of disturbances broke out in the garrison town of Zabern (Saverne) in Alsace. They were evidently triggered by the arrogant behaviour of garrison troops, and resulted in arbitrary arrests, the use of force to disperse crowds, and the declaration by the military authorities of a state of siege. Fearful for public order, the civil authorities sought to discipline the soldiers involved, but were directly overruled by the Kaiser himself. The 'Zabern Affair' escalated and caused an outcry in the Reichstag comparable with that over the *Daily Telegraph* interview. The vote of censure against the government and its support of the military authorities was carried by 293 votes to 54. Yet the matter ended there. As in 1908, the Reichstag hesitated to take further action, and the Kaiser and his ministers firmly maintained their support of the army. The failure to take any effective action against excesses illustrates the virtual immunity of the army from political control.

A similar point is made by a study of the contemporary development of military strategy. Under Count von Schlieffen (Chief of the General Staff 1891–1906), the army command had come to terms with the problems of war on two fronts. Their strategy – the 'Schlieffen Plan', formulated in

1. What evidence is there of the political influence and independence of the German army during the reign of Wilhelm II?

2. What were the strengths and weaknesses of the Chancellors who served Wilhelm II between 1894 and 1914?

3. In what respects can it be argued that the government of Germany during the Wilhelmine period was undemocratic?

1897 – called for a rapid outflanking movement through Belgium and Luxembourg to eliminate France from the war before Russian mobilisation was completed. Sections of that force could then be transferred to the Eastern Front to meet the Russians. Militarily, it was a daring plan, yet it was politically indefensible, as Germany was among those nations who guaranteed Belgium's neutrality. Nevertheless, the strategy became the basis of German military planning for the next 15 years. Gerhard Ritter, who saw the growth of unrestrained military independence in Germany as one of the main causes of the disaster of 1914, has outlined the reason for this. 'To raise political objections to a strategic plan worked out by the General Staff would have appeared in the Germany of Wilhelm II unwarranted interference in a foreign sphere.' In the years preceding 1914, and in that fateful year itself, the German military establishment differed from those of other European powers, not in the degree of its preparedness for war, but in the degree of its freedom from civil governmental restraint.

5.5 What were the main aims of German domestic policies between 1890 and 1914?

For many years after the collapse of the German Reich in 1918, it was usual for historians to conclude that the policies of Wilhelmine Germany had been shaped primarily by foreign aims and ambitions. In recent years, however, a new 'school' of German historians has insisted upon the 'primacy of domestic affairs'. They argue that domestic struggles were the prime preoccupation of German politicians, and that even the great adventure of *Weltpolitik* was in truth only a foreign means to a domestic end. Hans-Ulrich Wehler, in *The German Empire 1871–1918* (1985), states that the true theme of Wilhelmine, and indeed of Bismarckian, politics was 'the defence of inherited ruling position by pre-industrial elites against the onslaught of new forces – a defensive struggle which became even sharper with the erosion of the economic foundations of these privileged leading strata'.

Government through repression or through national consensus?

Certainly, the years of Caprivi's chancellorship had seen the vested interests of the Junker class threatened by the benevolent attitude of the Kaiser towards social problems, and by the sympathy of the Chancellor for industrial economic interests. The fall of Caprivi, largely the work of the Junkers themselves, forced future chancellors to seek new tactics against the dual threats of socialism and industrialism. The first tactic was repression. After 1894, the expressed desire of Wilhelm II to be 'King of the Beggars' was rarely in evidence. Instead, the Kaiser pointedly withdrew his original instructions to Protestant pastors to concern themselves with social questions. The five years between 1894 and 1899 witnessed a stream of anti-socialist and anti-union legislation proposed in the Reichstag, mostly without success.

The refusal of the Reichstag – in which conservative representation dropped 21% between 1893 and 1898 – to support a policy of repression, forced a change of tack. Under Bülow's administration, the government embraced a principle defined in 1897 as *Sammlungspolitik*. In other words, it sought to 'gather together' behind a common policy all the major propertied and conservative interests in the Reich. If the hostility between Junker and the industrialists could be bridged, a formidable front could be presented to social democracy. Bülow's policy had two 'prongs':

1. The reorientation of economic policy, evident in 1902 when Bülow abandoned Caprivi's system of trade treaties, to replace them with a set of high tariffs protecting agriculture and certain key German manufacturers from foreign competition. Russian corn, incidentally, was largely excluded thereby from the German market, to the relief of the Junkers. The discontent of German heavy industry, meanwhile, was relieved by the start of Germany's massive naval construction programme. Aptly this conciliation of conservative economic interests became known as the 'Alliance of Rye and Steel'.

2. Meanwhile, the wider policy of *Weltpolitik* played the same role. Bülow's explanation of his policy in 1897, while superficially declaring the 'primacy of foreign affairs', in fact betrayed the true nature of *Weltpolitik*. 'I am putting the main emphasis on foreign policy. Only a successful foreign policy can help to reconcile, pacify, rally, unite.'

Parties in the Reichstag, 1890–1912

	1890	1893	1898	1903	1907	1912
Conservatives	93	100	79	75	84	57
National Liberals	42	53	46	51	54	45
Left Liberals	76	48	49	39	49	42
Centre	106	96	102	100	105	91
Social Democrats	35	44	56	81	43	110
National minorities (e.g. Poles, Danes, Alsatians)	38	35	34	32	29	33
Anti-Semites	5	16	13	11	21	13

Germany and its minorities

A lesser, but nevertheless significant, feature of the domestic politics of 1894–1914 was the reversal of Caprivi's policies towards national minorities within the Reich. In Prussia, for example, Bülow rigorously enforced the laws banning the use of Polish in education, and passed a law in the Landtag (1908) allowing the confiscation of Polish estates for the settlement of German farmers. It is true that in 1911 Alsace and Lorraine received a new constitution integrating them more closely into the normal political system of the Reich. However, the 'Zabern Affair' of 1913 showed clearly that the brutal mentality of military occupation still predominated.

The position of Germany's Jewish population during the Wilhelmine years is not easy to define. **Assimilation** had produced some impressive success stories. Families such as the Warburgs, the Rothschilds and the Ballins had established themselves with enormous success in banking and in shipping. Middle-class Jews had little difficulty carving out successful careers in medicine, science or journalism. On the other hand, more traditional career areas, such as government, the army and the judiciary, remained closed. Wilhelmine Germany also boasted a variety of anti-semitic political parties, who admittedly won relatively few votes, but provided fertile soil for a growing tradition of pseudo-intellectual anti-semitism. Ernst Haeckel's *Riddle of the Universe* and Houston Stewart Chamberlain's *Foundations of the Nineteenth Century* were both published in 1899. Both adopted a pseudo-scientific approach to the question of race, 'proving' the superiority of Germanic races, and that this superiority would

Assimilation: The process by which one group adapts itself to the culture and traditions of the society in which it lives. In particular, this has come to be associated with European Jewish communities who have faced the choice of adapting to become part of national communities, or of maintaining a distinct cultural identity.

be undermined if Jews were allowed to 'dilute' German racial characteristics by intermarriage.

Even so, recent historical research has suggested that such 'scholastic' reasoning played little part in the growth of German anti-semitism. Jack Wertheimer and Egmont Zechlin have both suggested that a more significant role was played by the influx of some 79,000 Jews from eastern Europe who flooded into Germany from Russian territory in the years shortly before the First World War. The element of class threat posed by these poor and unassimilated Jews, together with the element of patriotic mistrust generated by the war, formed the true basis of the anti-semitic explosion of the 1930s.

---

1. What was *Sammlungspolitik*, and why did the German government pursue such a course during this period?

2. What evidence is there of intolerance towards minority groups within Germany at this time?

5.6 Was the rise of social democracy a serious threat to the stability of Wilhelmine Germany?

The growth and development of social democracy

We have already seen that this was a period of dramatic social and economic change in Germany, and that these changes caused alarm among the governing classes. Alongside those changes, and perhaps because of them, electoral support for the Social Democratic Party also increased considerably. As the table on page 99 shows, a temporary lapse in Social Democrat support in 1907 was reversed so effectively that by 1912 the party was the most powerful in the Reichstag. If one were to judge from these figures alone, one would conclude that *Sammlungspolitik* failed to secure the state against the threat of socialism. Their triumph certainly had an effect upon the Kaiser and his government. 'The German parliamentarian,' Wilhelm declared in 1913, 'becomes daily more of a swine.' Yet how much of a threat did **social democracy** pose to the Imperial system of government? For all its Marxist origins, the German socialist movement by 1912 was broadly committed to the 'revisionism' proposed by Eduard Bernstein in 1898 in his work, *The Presuppositions of Socialism and the Tasks of Social Democracy*. Bernstein's conclusion was that Marx had been mistaken about the approaching crisis of capitalism, as the rising living standards of German workers proved, and that change should not be sought through the active promotion of revolution. Historian David Blackbourn summarises the position of the Social Democratic Party neatly: 'It believed that history would deliver the future into its lap. Waiting for revolution, it was caught between accommodation and action.' From 1906 onwards, leading social democrats were willing to make electoral pacts with the Liberals to forward desirable social policies. They were willing, in general, to subscribe to an Imperial foreign policy which they interpreted as primarily opposed to reactionary Tsardom. They even supported the financial provisions of the Army Bill in 1913, because of the government's proposal that these should be paid for by a property tax.

Social democracy: A kind of socialism in which people are allowed a relatively large amount of freedom.

The 'threat' of social democracy

Nevertheless, it is possible to understand the apprehension of the ruling classes at the electoral success of social democracy which destroyed the conservative 'Bülow bloc' of parties, and replaced it with a bloc effectively able to resist any unpopular government legislation. The 1912 elections, wrote Wolfgang Mommsen (1995), thus created the 'stalemate of the party system'. The Zabern incident, although it demonstrated the practical weaknesses of the Reichstag, also provided a disturbing

<table>
<tr><td>

Karl Liebknecht (1871–1919)

Son of Wilhelm Liebknecht, founder of the Social Democratic Party. After an early career as a radical lawyer, Karl Liebknecht was active in the Social Democrats resisting moves to direct the party away from its Marxist roots. Entered the Reichstag

</td><td>

(1912), voted against war credits (1914), and served during the war as a non-combatant. Expelled from the Social Democrats (1916), he helped to found the Spartacus League. A leading figure in German communism at the end of the war, Liebknecht was killed in the course of the Spartacist rising.

</td><td>

Rosa Luxemburg (1871–1919)

Born in Poland and active in Polish radical politics before emigrating to Switzerland in 1889. Joined German Social Democratic Party, and actively resisted Bernstein's revision of its Marxist doctrine. An advocate of the general strike as a revolutionary

</td><td>

weapon. Formed the Spartacus League with Karl Liebknecht (1916), and like him was killed in the course of the Spartacist rising.

</td></tr>
</table>

1. In what ways had leading theorists of German social democracy revised the revolutionary doctrines of Karl Marx by the beginning of the 20th century?

2. How realistic were the fears felt by the German governing classes at the increase in support for the Social Democrats?

illustration of the fact that massive anti-government feeling could now be mobilised within that assembly. The Social Democratic Party, furthermore, did possess an active left wing, led by Karl Liebknecht and Rosa Luxemburg. It maintained an orthodox Marxist line, and was to show its revolutionary potential in 1918. Lastly, we should not ignore the fact that the prospect of power in the hands of industrial workers appeared outrageous and highly dangerous to many conservatives, regardless of the uses to which those workers might turn their power. With or without justification, therefore, the election results of 1912 ensured that domestic political tensions were as high as ever as the conservatives of the German government and General Staff approached the international crisis of the last years of peace.

5.7 What were the results of Germany's decision to pursue a 'world policy'?

The nature of *Weltpolitik*

In the years that followed the fall of Caprivi, a revolutionary new factor came to dominate the foreign policy of the Reich. That policy departed from the essentially European concerns of Bismarck and came, more and more, to demand a world role for Germany. By enlarging its interests in non-European affairs Germany was to become a 'world power' (*Weltmacht*). The reasons for this fundamental change were complex and varied, yet on the whole this 'world policy' (*Weltpolitik*) must be seen as an external reflection of internal German developments.

Firstly, it undoubtedly reflected the mentality and personality of the Kaiser. *Weltpolitik* consisted of a headstrong and incoherent insistence that Germany should have a say in all major issues, just as Wilhelm intruded his half-formed opinion into all aspects of domestic government. As the historian Imanuel Geiss puts it, in *German Foreign Policy, 1871–1914* (1976), 'German foreign policy during this time bore the personal stamp of the Kaiser. He found it more or less congenial and in keeping with his personal ambitions and his style of behaviour.' Certainly, Wilhelm made a direct practical contribution to this policy by his appointment to high office of its enthusiastic supporters. In 1897 alone, the promotions of Johannes von Miquel to the vice-presidency of the Prussian ministry, of Alfred von Tirpitz to the naval ministry and of Bernhard von Bülow to the head of the foreign ministry provided the core of the *Weltpolitik* 'crew'.

Weltpolitik was not merely a result of the Kaiser's whim. The expansion of German industry had renewed and increased the national sense of power, and many leading figures expressed the fear that existing resources and markets would soon prove insufficient and that emigration to the USA might rob Germany of its most dynamic sons. 'Our vigorous national development,' claimed Bülow himself, 'mainly in the industrial sphere, forced us to cross the ocean.' The historian Treitschke and the statesman Delbrück publicised a variation upon this theme. Since German unification, the colonial expansion of other powers had cancelled out Germany's advance in status. Germany was faced with the choice of colonial expansion or stagnation as a major power. This theme of world expansion as a logical sequel to unification was most eloquently expressed by the sociologist Max Weber in his inaugural lecture at Freiburg University in 1895. 'We have to grasp,' he stated, 'that the unification of Germany would have been better dispensed with because of its cost, if it were the end and not the beginning of a German policy of World Power.'

Lastly, many recent historians concentrating upon the domestic affairs of the Reich have interpreted *Weltpolitik* as essentially an element in the solution of Germany's internal political problems. At a time when the apparent factional divisions in German politics were widening, it provided a means of uniting national opinion and neutralising the disruptive opposition of the Social Democrats. The patriotic stance of the Social Democrats in 1914 certainly suggests that *Weltpolitik* succeeded where the reform programmes of Bismarck and of Caprivi had failed. Most historians would now agree with the conclusion stated by Imanuel Geiss, that '*Weltpolitik* came into existence as a red herring of the ruling classes to distract the middle and working classes from social and political problems at home'. Where Bismarck (in 1890) and Wilhelm II (in 1894) had toyed with the idea of a *coup d'état* as the answer to domestic pressures, Germany now turned to the glamour and excitement of *Weltpolitik*.

Coup d'état: The process whereby a small political group seizes control of the state by force.

The acquisition of colonies

In the last four years of the 19th century the mentality of *Weltpolitik* manifested itself in all those quarters of the globe subject to European penetration. In Africa it took the form of a masquerade as protector of the Boers in their confrontation with British imperialism in the Transvaal, under President Kruger. After the Boers had thwarted an ill-organised, British-backed coup, Wilhelm dispatched his famous 'Kruger Telegram' congratulating them on maintaining their independence 'without having to appeal to friendly powers for assistance'. With German naval power in its infancy, it was an empty gesture, whose only lasting effect could be to cause offence to a potentially friendly European power.

The first tangible reward of *Weltpolitik* was reaped in China in 1897. There, alarmed at the extent of Japan's success in its war against China (1894–95), Germany acted, together with Russia and France, to modify the original Japanese gains, and to ensure that China remained open to European penetration. Its own private gain was a 99-year lease of the port of Kiaochow as a trading and naval base. The following year the small groups of Pacific Islands, the Carolines and the Marianas, were purchased from Spain. In 1899, Germany declared that its joint control with Britain and the USA over the islands of Samoa was dissolved, and assumed possession of the eastern portion of the islands.

Patently trivial as such gains were, the extension of German interests in the Middle East had more serious international implications. As early as 1888, the Deutsche Bank had agreed with the Turkish government to finance the projected railway from Baghdad to the Persian Gulf. It was clearly a region sensitive to both British and Russian interests. While Bismarck had specified at that time that German money implied no direct German political interest, Wilhelm II showed none of his restraint. In a typically pretentious speech (1898) he referred to himself as 'the protector of 300 million Muslims', and openly referred to 'my railway'. The compensation for strained relations with Britain and Russia was the attraction of the Turkish Empire into the German orbit – yet the First World War proved Turkey to be an ally of doubtful worth.

The birth of the German navy

The most spectacular and damaging manifestation of Germany's new ambitions was the growth of its naval power. The development of a mighty battle fleet, like *Weltpolitik* itself, served several purposes. For many, like its founder Admiral von Tirpitz, it was an assertion of the nation's new status. 'The fleet, he declared, 'is necessary to show that Germany is as well born as Britain.' In so saying, he betrayed the essential feature of naval development. It was aimed at, and bound to offend, Great Britain. It was the one major European power with whom Germany had no potential continental argument, and whose friendship might have offset the Franco-Russian alliance. Equally, the decision to develop the fleet provided a huge new outlet for German heavy industry. It was no coincidence that so great an industrialist as Alfred Krupp was a leading member and backer of the Naval League (*Flottenverein*), founded in 1898. To the politically-minded middle classes, the fleet represented a national weapon relatively free from the influence of the Prussian Junkers.

The first Naval Bill, of March 1898, envisaged an eventual force of 19 battleships, 12 heavy cruisers and 30 light cruisers. The launching of the revolutionary British battleship, 'HMS Dreadnought' (February 1906), had a double impact upon the naval question. By rendering obsolete all existing battleships, it opened up the real possibility that a German fleet could compete with its British counterpart. At the same time, it necessitated an urgent rebuilding of the German fleet. In retrospect, further German bills in 1906, 1907 and 1908 constituted a double misfortune for the German state. They resulted in a tremendous financial undertaking, and signalled the beginning of a naval arms race between Britain and Germany. It is in these respects that we may accept the verdict of historians Ian Porter and Ian Armour, in *Imperial Germany 1890–1918* (1991), that 'the whole naval programme was an expensive failure'.

Weltpolitik: *the balance sheet*

With the exception of the new battle fleet, the physical results of *Weltpolitik* were meagre, even absurd. By 1914, Germany possessed a colonial 'empire' of only about a million square miles. Total German investment in those colonies was only 505 million marks. The colonies were dotted about the globe, almost indefensible and totally vulnerable to the attack of an enemy – as their fates in 1914 were to prove. In terms of Germany's overall diplomatic position, the decision to move towards 'world power' was of enormous negative importance. It completed the destruction of the Bismarckian European balance and prepared the way for Germany's isolation and encirclement. The historian Bernadotte Schmitt summarised the error of *Weltpolitik* as follows:

1. Into what areas did German influence spread as a result of *Weltpolitik*?

2. Summarise the impact of *Weltpolitik* upon Germany's diplomatic relations with other European powers.

3. Why did Germany decide to build a major battle fleet at the end of the 19th century?

> 'A policy of naval expansion, the development of an African empire, commercial and financial penetration of the Near East could each be justified. But to pursue all three courses at the same time was the worst possible policy, for it kept alive the distrust and suspicion of the *Entente* powers, convinced them of the dangerous reality of German militarism, and made them more anxious than ever to act together.'

Source-based questions: The construction of the German navy

Study the following source material and then answer the questions which follow.

SOURCE A

Record of a conversation between the Chancellor, Hohenlohe-Schillingfürst, and the Kaiser, March 1897

His Majesty received me with great affability, listened approvingly to my explanation, and then indulged himself in a highly detailed lecture on the navy. He enumerated the ships that we have and the ones we would need in order to survive a war. He emphasised that we had to have an armoured navy to protect our trade and to keep ourselves supplied with provisions; and was of the opinion that our fleet would have to be strong enough to prevent the French fleet cutting off food supplies that we needed. If the Reichstag didn't approve this, he would nevertheless carry on building, and would present the Reichstag with the bill later. Public opinion didn't concern him.

SOURCE B

Part of an article in Nauticus, a journal published to promote the German navy (published in 1900)

The concept of the navy has indeed been the hearth around which the German attempts at unity have clustered and warmed themselves. Thus it has already helped to fulfil a great national mission. It has also, however, been allotted the further task of overcoming the discord between the parties in the united German Empire, and directing the minds of the disputants towards the greatness and the glory of the Fatherland. Today millions of our compatriots are spiritually alienated from the state and the prevailing economic order: the concept of the navy possesses the power to revive the national spirit of the classes and fill them once again with patriotic loyalty and love for Kaiser and Reich.

SOURCE C

Part of a secret communication from the German ambassador in London to the Chancellor, von Bülow. He reports conversations with senior British ministers. (The comments in brackets are those written by the Kaiser in the margins of the original document.) July 1908.

Both ministers considered that the situation between England and Germany turned on the question of the fleet. Expenditure on the British navy had risen as a result of the German programme ('False! As a result of British greed for power, and their fear of bogeymen.'), and in proportion to the increased speed of construction ('There has been no increase'). Every Englishman would spend his last penny to maintain naval superiority ('According to *Nauticus* they have it threefold'), on which depended England's existence as an independent state.

I replied that a 'German invasion' existed only in the British imagination. No reasonable being in Germany thought of it ('Very good'). The invention of the Dreadnought had unfortunately made ship-building dearer and had caused Britain to forfeit her immense advantage, but whose fault was that?

(a) Use Source C and your own knowledge.

Explain briefly the reference made in Source C to 'the invention of the Dreadnought'. [3 marks]

(b) Use Sources A and B and your own knowledge.

Explain how Source A differs from Source B in its explanation of the motives behind the development of a German navy. [7 marks]

(c) Use Sources A, B and C and your own knowledge.

Explain the impact of the German decision to build a navy upon German domestic and foreign politics in the years between 1897 and 1914. [15 marks]

5.8 Was Germany's position in European diplomacy strengthened or weakened by its policies between 1894 and 1905?

Germany and Russia

The weakening of the Bismarckian system of alliances left Germany's European diplomacy with two central themes in the decade after the fall of Caprivi. The first was the desire to maintain friendly relations with Russia in the hope of detaching it from its new-found friendship with France. The year 1894 provided two sources of hope in this respect, with the replacement of Caprivi by the more conservative and 'Bismarckian' Hohenlohe, and with the accession of Nicholas II. The new Tsar, a cousin of the Kaiser, enjoyed friendly personal relations with his fellow Emperor, and was susceptible to Wilhelm's entreaties to pursue a civilising mission against the 'yellow peril' in eastern Asia. The 1890s saw common action against excessive Japanese gains from China, but the logical outcome of Russian commitment was its involvement in the Russo-Japanese war of 1904. Although such distractions suited Germany's purposes, the conviction in St Petersburg that such a war had always been the German goal merely compounded the damage done by the cancellation of the Reinsurance Treaty. Nevertheless, Wilhelm came close to success in a final effort to separate Russia and France. In a meeting at Björkö (July 1905) he persuaded the Tsar to conclude an agreement whereby both states undertook to aid the other in the event of an attack by another European power in Europe. The success was, however, merely superficial. The Tsar had undertaken more than his ministers would allow him to fulfil. The implications for the loss of French economic aid alone were so serious that they refused to endorse the agreement, and the Treaty of Björkö remained a 'dead letter' from the moment of its signature.

Germany and Britain

A logical response to the growing intimacy of Russia and France would have been to cultivate relations with Great Britain more closely. German attitudes to Britain, though, remained highly ambiguous. The ambassador to London, von Hatzfeldt, hoped and believed Britain might be drawn into the Triple Alliance and consistently condemned *Weltpolitik* as a tactless means of alienating a valuable ally. The Kaiser himself was certainly attracted to some elements of British society, but had an intense dislike for others, such as its constitutional monarchy. Such ambiguity was mirrored in the diplomatic history of the 1890s. The promise of the agreement over Heligoland and Zanzibar contrasted with the lively hostility created by the 'Kruger Telegram'. Germany's official, and vaguely benevolent, neutrality during the Boer War (1899–1900) was offset by the violently anti-British propaganda of the Pan-German League and the Naval League. Thus, when a Conservative government in Britain abandoned the **isolationism** of the Liberals and put out feelers for a formal alliance, the opportunity was missed.

Isolationism: The policy by which a state withdraws from international commitments to pursue the development of its own domestic interests.

The first British approach (March 1898) collapsed because of German fears that a treaty might fail to achieve parliamentary ratification, and that relations with Russia might be strained to no avail. The second approach (January 1901) was killed by a series of miscalculations by the German Foreign Office. In the first place, senior officials remained convinced that a German alliance was Britain's only option. Speaking of British hints of an approach to France, Bülow declared that 'in my opinion we need not worry about such remote possibilities'. Secondly, Germany set excessively strict conditions upon an understanding with Britain. It was to tie itself, not

1. What changes occurred in Germany's diplomatic relations during this period

(a) with Russia and

(b) with Great Britain?

2. Compare the strengths and weaknesses of Germany's diplomatic position in 1890 and in 1910.

simply to Germany, but to the Triple Alliance as a whole. Finding the prospect of commitment to the maintenance of Austria-Hungary quite unacceptable, Britain had within three years informally associated itself with the Franco-Russian Entente.

The so-called 'free hand' policy of the German Foreign Office, by rejecting British overtures, and by overestimating the significance of the Björkö agreement, had by 1905 left Germany isolated but for its partners in the Triple Alliance. Given the vacillation of Italy and its improving relations with France, this effectively meant dependence upon Austria–Hungary as Germany's sole reliable ally.

5.9 What was the impact of the First World War upon German society and politics?

In Germany, as in other combatant states, the war provided an unprecedented test of national unity and of national identity. Indeed, like conservatives all over Europe, many German politicians led their country into the conflict in the hope that the crisis would submerge differences and tensions, and would unite the population behind the governmental system. In the early stages of the war the gamble appeared to be justified. Governmental claims that this was a defensive war, necessary to prevent Germany being stifled by jealous neighbours, seemed generally to be accepted, and Germans of all political persuasions rallied to the cause. The SPD, so critical recently of most aspects of the Kaiser's policy, voted in favour of war credits, and intellectuals who should have known better issued manifestoes in which they justified the war as a necessary defence and safeguard of superior German 'Kultur'. Programmes demanding large-scale territorial annexations after Germany's inevitable victory were extremely popular, as the historian David Blackbourn has indicated:

> 'Annexationist ambitions were not confined to soldiers like Hindenburg and Ludendorff, or to Pan-Germans or other super-patriots. They were shared by civilian ministers, civil servants, Catholic and liberal politicians, liberal intellectuals, even by some Social Democrats. The point is not that there were no differences between extreme annexationists and moderates – there were – but that the moderates were not really so moderate.'

Burgfriede (literally, 'Castle peace'): The term refers to the way in which the garrison of a besieged castle puts aside its differences in the face of a common threat. The term comes to mean, therefore, a political truce at a time of crisis.

Germans of all descriptions appealed to the concept of *Burgfriede*, the abandonment of differences that occurs within a castle that is under siege.

Why did the political unity of 1914 degenerate as the war progressed?

The maintenance of this *Burgfriede* depended upon a speedy victory and, as the war entered its second year, the first cracks in the political solidarity of 1914 began to appear. In particular, these were provoked by the economic effects of the war, which were complex and far-reaching. Problems quickly arose in terms of manpower and of its organisation. By the end of 1914, one-third of Germany's pre-war industrial labour force was in uniform, and with little prospect of their immediate return, new sources of labour had to be found. The number of women employed in factories rose by 50%, foreign labour was conscripted from occupied areas, especially from Belgium and Poland, and new industrial workers were recruited from the countryside. These new urban workers were subjected to an increasing level of governmental regulation. The War Raw Materials Office (KRA – *Kriegsrohstoffabteilung*) was quickly established (August 1914), co-ordinating the private companies that were to produce and distribute the raw materials required for the war effort, and this set the pattern for increasing government intervention in the economic life of the state. In 1916, the introduction of the Auxiliary Labour Law made it obligatory for all German males between the ages of 17 and 60 to work for the war effort if so required, and left them with little independent choice as to where and how they would be employed. Although arbitration boards were established to resolve disputes, and trade unions were allowed an unprecedented role, there can be no doubt that these developments represented a substantial extension of military control over the working population. Political tensions arose from a variety of associated factors. Little seemed to be done to limit the profits made by key war industries, and no minister dared to reduce the fiscal privileges of the Junker agriculturalists. Inflation eroded wage levels in all industries, and government attempts to requisition food from the countryside caused considerable resentment among farmers. There is evidence of growing opposition to the war in the countryside some time before it manifested itself in the cities.

In addition, the attempts by the allies to blockade Germany, and to cut off imports of food and raw materials, were hugely effective. The impact upon a country that imported a third of its foodstuffs was bound to be serious, and problems of malnutrition were widespread even before the notorious 'turnip winter' of 1916–17. Over the whole course of the war, it is believed, as many as 750,000 German deaths could be attributed to starvation. In addition to the material hardships, the government's attempts to regulate food supplies caused considerable bitterness and political division. Rationing was not implemented efficiently, with different official levels applying in different areas, and a flourishing black market existed throughout the war.

The waning of popular enthusiasm coincided directly with the tightening of conservative, military control over the direction of the war. The disastrous losses at Verdun led to the dismissal of Field Marshall von Falkenhayn, and control of the Supreme Command (OHL – *Oberste Heeresleitung*) passed into the hands of Paul von Hindenburg and his second-in-command Erich von Ludendorff. This was of the greatest importance in terms both of German military strategy and of the direction of domestic politics. Both men set their faces against any suggestion of a compromise peace, and sought to prosecute the war by all available means to a successful conclusion. Some of the available means, such as unrestricted submarine warfare in the west, or a draconian peace settlement with Russia in the east, had serious military and political implications. On the domestic front, meanwhile, it became increasingly clear that political power had fallen into military hands to an extent that was unprecedented even in recent German experience. In July 1917, Bethmann-Hollweg, increasingly aware that it was in Germany's interests to seek a negotiated peace, lost the confidence of the military leaders and was forced out of office. His fate was later shared by the Secretary for Foreign Affairs, von Kühlmann, who was forced to resign as late as July 1918 for suggesting in the Reichstag that the allies might be approached for a negotiated peace.

It was clear that the tripartite governmental structure of Wilhelmine Germany no longer existed. The new Chancellor, Georg Michaelis, was effectively controlled by the army, and the Kaiser no longer exercised any realistic authority. The army was now in control, to the extent that historian Martin Kitchen refers to this period as the 'Hindenburg dictatorship'. The army acquired domestic powers, restrictions upon public assemblies, supervision of political meetings, the use of troops as strike-breakers, which were not at all what left-wing politicians had originally envisaged as the results of their cooperation with the war effort. The German experience of war now aggravated the very divisions that it had been intended to heal. The SPD, for example, was increasingly at odds with the military leadership. As early as December 1915, some members had proposed a motion in the Reichstag opposing annexations in Belgium at the end of the war, and threatening to oppose the voting of further war credits. That threat surfaced once more in July 1917 when the fall of the Tsarist government in Russia raised the possibility of moderate peace proposals which might encourage Russia to leave the war. April 1917 saw major strikes in several German cities and, while the SPD in general remained loyal to the patriotic cause, some of its more radical members took a different route. At a conference in Gotha in April 1917, Hugo Haase, former chairman of the party, led a group of dissidents to form a new party, the Independent Social Democrats (USPD – *Unabhängige Sozialdemokratische Partei Deutschlands*). Three months later the SPD renewed its threat to vote against further war credits. Then, in January 1918, at least a million workers participated in the biggest strike that Germany had witnessed during the war.

At the same time, this movement to the left was offset by a rallying and consolidation of right-wing patriotic elements. 1917 also witnessed the formation of the Fatherland Party, a coalition of traditional conservative groups, which quickly boasted 1.25 million members and included some prominent conservative names among its membership. Admiral Tirpitz was its chairman, and Wolfgang Kapp, soon to give his name to one of the most dangerous assaults upon the Weimar Republic, was one of its primary administrators. A much less prominent member, Anton Drexler, was shortly to found another extreme nationalist organisation, the National Socialist Party. By early 1918, the battle-lines within domestic German politics had become more rigidly defined than they had ever been before the war.

What was the significance of the wartime experience for Germany's political future?

The political polarisation that took place in the course of 1917–18 serves to illustrate how important Germany's wartime experience is in understanding the events of the next two and a half decades. It is commonplace to emphasise the role played by the 1919 peace settlement in creating the divisions that crippled the Republic and eventually brought Adolf Hitler to power. More recently, however, historians have been eager to stress that most of these factors had their origins in the war itself. Edgar Feuchtwanger (*Imperial Germany 1850–1918*, 2001) has explained how most of the major difficulties facing Weimar politicians had their genesis in the war. By an early stage in the war the small business man, later the target of much Nazi propaganda, already felt himself severely damaged by the privileges and incentives offered by the military and the government to large-scale industrial producers. The crippling inflation that constituted one of the most spectacular problems of the 1920s was the direct result of inadequate financing of the war. The fact of an extended conflict left the German government with severe financial problems. Able to cover only 16% of the costs from taxation, and unwilling to extend the tax liability of the privileged classes, the German government gambled on other means. On the assumption of eventual victory, and subsequently of imposing heavy reparations upon their opponents, they printed extra cash to finance the war, so that 'Germany floated through the war on a sea of paper money' (Ian Porter and Ian Armour, *Imperial Germany 1890–1918*, 1991). Another method of financing the war was through the large-scale issue of war bonds. Prosperous members of the middle classes invested patriotically in such bonds, only to find that the prospects of repayment receded with the prospects of victory. For many such Germans the war destroyed the social status and the financial security to which they had been accustomed, and left them adrift in an uncertain and threatening world. In effect, the

Weimar Republic in 1919 inherited an economic situation that was more or less hopeless, not because of the terms of the peace, but because of the nature of the war itself.

5.10 What forces shaped the political policies of Wilhelmine Germany?
A CASE STUDY IN HISTORICAL INTERPRETATION

One of the most important and persistent themes in historical revisionism in recent decades has been the tendency to question the roles and the importance of 'great men' in shaping historical events. This tendency has been particularly evident in recent work on German history, where traditional interpretations have laid great emphasis upon the roles of such individuals as Otto von Bismarck and Adolf Hitler. Although historians have rarely accorded him the same status as these men, Kaiser Wilhelm II was also believed to have made an important impact upon the course of German politics in the two decades before the outbreak of the First World War. His accession to the throne in 1888 was held to signal a significant change in the exercise of state power within the Reich. Where his grandfather, Wilhelm I, had largely entrusted Bismarck with his executive authority, and had allowed his Chancellor a wide freedom of action, the young Kaiser insisted upon direct, personal control. Distinct differences were therefore discernible between the priorities of 'Bismarckian' and of 'Wilhelmine' Germany. Tentative and insincere colonialism, for instance, gave way to full-blown *Weltpolitik*. The alliance with Austria, once a tool for maintaining the balance of Europe, became the basis for a wartime alliance. J.G. Röhl, in *Germany without Bismarck: the Crisis of Government in the Second Reich, 1890–1900* (1967), made a characteristic case for this point of view when he wrote that between 1897 and the crisis of the *Daily Telegraph* interview, Wilhelm 'dictated policy to an amazing extent. All appointments, all bills, all diplomatic moves were made on his orders.' This emphasis upon the personal authority of the Kaiser was widely accepted, both by contemporaries and by historians. In 1918, the army's Junker commanders believed that they could convince enemy politicians that fundamental change had taken place in the political structure of Germany simply by forcing the abdication of the Kaiser.

This comfortable consensus was one of the casualties caused by the important work of the German historian Fritz Fischer. In such books as *War of Illusions: German Politics, 1911–1914* (1969) and *World Power or Decline: The Controversy over Germany's War Aims in the First World War* (1975), he claimed that elements in German society pressed the state into policies which made Germany directly responsible in large part for the outbreak of war in 1914. It was not satisfactory either to pin blame solely upon the Kaiser's erratic personality, or to deny Germany's overall responsibility. Although Fischer's main concern was with the origins of the war, his conclusions had important implications for the writing of Wilhelmine history. In the place of a stable society, dominated by a powerful Kaiser, Fischer portrayed a society in crisis, whose governors sought desperately for policies that might provide a degree of national unity.

The body of work that followed in support of the 'Fischer thesis' was largely synthesised by Hans-Ulrich Wehler in his influential book, *The German Empire* (1973). Wehler, too, portrays Wilhelmine Germany as a cynically anti-democratic state, in which elite groups, industrialists, Junkers, and certain agencies in which their influence was entrenched, such as the army and the diplomatic corps, placed enormous pressures upon the Kaiser and his government to protect their vested interests. The

Zabern Incident in Alsace-Lorraine in 1913, or the wide acceptance of the dangerous and irresponsible Schlieffen Plan, might be taken to represent one strand of these influences. The authority of Friedrich von Holstein in the Foreign Ministry (1900–06) might be taken to represent another.

In its turn this 'new orthodoxy' has been challenged in recent years, especially by the work of a school of British historians that includes Richard Evans (editor, *Society and Politics in Wilhelmine Germany*, 1978), David Blackbourn and Geoff Eley (co-authors of *The Peculiarities of German History: Bourgeois Society and Politics in Nineteenth-century Germany*, 1984). Their main criticism of Wehler and his school is that they have underestimated the complexity of Wilhelmine society, and have thus overestimated the ease with which that society could be manipulated by the government. They have concentrated less upon the upper strata of German society, and are less convinced of the coherence and control of its governing elites. Instead their emphasis falls upon non-elite groups in the lower-middle or working classes, which they see as exerting enormous and disruptive pressures, to which the governors of Germany were forced to respond. The growth of the Social Democratic Party in the Reichstag in the last years of peace provides specific evidence of the pressure emanating from the industrial working classes. David Blackbourn's work on the Centre Party at this time also indicates that it was no longer a strictly clerical party, but increasingly a party that reflected middle-class and lower-middle-class interests. The government was forced to adopt policies that would court the parliamentary representatives of these classes, or which would deflect them from social and economic demands more threatening to the interests of the political elites. In particular, this might be seen in the more active and expansionist foreign policy of the Wilhelmine period. Volker Berghahn also placed the history and development of the German navy in this context, seeing it as a focus for popular, patriotic emotion, rather than as a strategic military weapon in its own right.

Where once the German Reich between 1890 and 1914 was seen as a stable and orthodox, semi-autocratic state, the question of political control now seems to be more difficult and confused. No new consensus has emerged to replace the traditional interpretation, and the picture created by recent research is rather of lack of control, of a state attempting to reconcile many conflicting forces and interests. This is the view and the social diversity that James Retallack refers to, in *Modern Germany Reconsidered* (1992), when he writes that 'the Empire was not entirely bad. It was neither completely urban nor completely rural. Aristocrats did not exclusively set the tone of everyday life – but neither did the Social Democrats. Manipulative strategies to deflect change did not always work as planned [and] often they went disastrously wrong.'

Source-based questions: The government role of Wilhelm II

Study the following four passages and answer both of the sub-questions that follow.

SOURCE A

From: Edgar Feuchtwanger, Imperial Germany 1850–1918, published in 2001. This historian ascribes an important role to the Kaiser, at least in the early stages of his reign.

The first three years of Hohenlohe's chancellorship saw the 'personal regime' at its height. Most of the Kaiser's assertions of self-will had to do with personalities, the 'fight against revolution', and most importantly with the complex of foreign and defence policy, including the building of an ocean-going fleet. In fact the Kaiser interfered often decisively in most major decisions and the only limit to the personal regime was his own ignorance, inconsistency and lack of a coherent plan. This still left the chancellor and the bureaucracy room for manoeuvre.

Source-based questions: The government role of Wilhelm II

SOURCE B

From: Katherine Anne Lerman, Kaiser Wilhelm II. Last Emperor of Imperial Germany, published in Heinemann History Briefings, 1994. This historian largely rejects the idea that historical events are determined by the influence of one man.

Many historians have been understandably reluctant to accept the thesis that the Kaiser personally ruled Germany before 1914. Not only does this thesis seem perilously close to the 'great man' theory of history, but it also appears to underestimate the complexity of the imperial German political system, the influence of the other states and political institutions within the Empire, and the inevitable constraints on the exercise of monarchical authority. Moreover, on close examination of policy issues, it is quite clear that the Kaiser did not rule Germany on a day to day basis or have command of the details of government work. His knowledge and understanding of political matters was always very superficial; he disliked routine work and read newspaper cuttings in preference to political reports. The one major issue on which Wilhelm II's will is generally seen to have been decisive is in the building of a German navy. A preoccupation with the Kaiser's political initiatives and actions tends to encourage the conclusion that his 'personal rule' was a myth, and that the monarchy merely interfered with or meddled in political decision-making, thereby contributing to, but in no sense determining the erratic course of German policy before 1914.

SOURCE C

From: Hans-Ulrich Wehler, The German Empire 1871–1918, published in 1985. This historian suggests that no individual or interest was able to dominate German politics during this period.

A power vacuum was created [by the fall of Bismarck] and subsequently a climate arose in which various personalities and social forces appeared in an attempt to fill it. Since neither they nor Parliament succeeded, there existed in Germany a permanent crisis of the state behind its façade of high-handed leadership. This in turn resulted in a variety of rival centres of power. It was this system that caused the zigzag course so often followed by German politics from that time on. First the young Kaiser tried to be both Emperor and Chancellor in one, in Bismarck's mocking phrase a brand of 'popular absolutism'. But this never received constitutional sanction: nor did Wilhelm II succeed in changing constitutional reality for any length of time, however much his clique of advisers tried to surround the decision-making process with the illusion of monarchical power.

SOURCE D

From: D. Blackbourn, Germany 1780–1918; the Long Nineteenth Century, published in 1997. This historian emphasises the role that Wilhelm was able to play in German government by his indirect influence, rather than by direct constitutional authority.

Recent writers have devoted much attention to the Kaiser's state of mind. Whether he suffered from arrested development, megalomania or manic-depression, the point is that his personal flaws mattered because he mattered. The Kaiser exercised an influence on German politics in many different ways. He was a powerful symbolic figure who helped to set the tone of public life and seduced many younger middle-class Germans by acting out the role of 'strong man'. The Kaiser also exercised his prerogatives. He took his power of appointment seriously, and used it, often against the advice of responsible ministers. He absorbed the influence of courtiers and favourites, and he interfered in decision-making by personal vetoes, marginal notes on official documents, and endless policy pronouncements. While ministers dealt with elected politicians, they also had to cope with demands and initiatives that came directly or indirectly through the Kaiser from various sources – powerful economic interests, court favourites, aides-de-camp and generals.

(a) Compare the views put forward in Sources B and D on the role played by Wilhelm II in the direction of German government.   [15 marks]

(b) Using these four passages and your own knowledge, evaluate the claim that 'the major problem in German politics between 1890 and 1914 was not the power of Wilhelm II, but the absence of any dominant political power'.   [30 marks]

Further Reading

Texts designed for AS and A2 Level students

From Bismarck to Hitler: Germany 1890–1933 by Geoff Layton (Hodder & Stoughton, Access to History series, 1996)

Imperial Germany 1890–1918 by Ian Porter and Ian Armour (Longman, Seminar Studies series, 1991)

More advanced reading

Germany 1866–1945 by Gordon Craig (Oxford University Press, 1978)

The German Empire, 1871–1918 by Hans-Ulrich Wehler (Berg, 1985)

From Kaiserreich to Third Reich: Elements of Continuity in German History, 1871–1945 by Fritz Fischer (Unwin Hyman, 1986)

Society and Politics in Wilhelmine Germany by R.J. Evans (ed.) (Croom Helm, 1978)

Imperial Germany 1850–1918 by Edgar Feuchtwanger (Routledge, 2001)

The Fontana History of Germany 1780–1918: the Long Nineteenth Century by David Blackbourn (Fontana, HarperCollins, 1997) provides an excellent introduction to recent work on German history in this period.

6 From democracy to dictatorship 1918–1945

Key Issues

- How stable was the Weimar Republic in the 1920s?

- Why was Hitler able to establish such a powerful dictatorship in Germany in the course of the 1930s?

- What were the effects of the Nazi dictatorship upon German politics and society?

Framework of Events

1918	November: Abdication of Kaiser Wilhelm II. Armistice signed to end First World War
1919	February: Friedrich Ebert elected President of the German Republic
	July: Adoption of Weimar constitution. Spartacist rising
1920	March: Failure of Kapp *Putsch*
1921	May: Germany agrees to pay reparations demanded by allies
1922	April: Treaty of Rapallo between Germany and Russia
1923	January: Occupation of the Ruhr by French and Belgian troops
	August: Appointment of Gustav Stresemann as Chancellor
	November: Failure of Hitler's Beerhall *Putsch*. Introduction of *Rentenmark* as German currency
1924	September: Introduction of Dawes Plan
1924	April: Election of Paul von Hindenburg as President of German Republic
	December: Signature of Locarno Treaties
1926	September: Germany admitted to League of Nations
1929	February: Germany accepts Kellogg–Briand Pact
	October: Collapse of American Stock Market

1930	March: Brüning becomes German Chancellor
	September: Nazis win 107 seats in Reichstag elections
1931	June: Hoover moratorium on reparation payments
1932	April: Hitler wins 13 million votes in presidential election, but is defeated by Hindenburg
	June: Von Papen becomes Chancellor
	July: Nazis win 230 seats in Reichstag elections
	December: Von Schleicher becomes Chancellor
1933	January: Hitler appointed German Chancellor
	February: Reichstag fire
	March: Enabling Law grants Hitler emergency powers
	April: National boycott of Jewish businesses
	October: German withdrawal from League of Nations
1934	January: German–Polish non-aggression pact
	June: Purge of SA leaders in 'Night of the Long Knives'
	August: Death of President Hindenburg; Hitler assumes title of *Führer*
1935	January: Plebiscite authorises return of Saarland to Germany
	September: Nuremberg Race Laws against Jews
1936	March: German remilitarisation of Rhineland
	August: Introduction of compulsory military service
	October: Introduction of economic Four-Year Plan
1938	March: German *Anschluss* with Austria
	October: German occupation of Sudetenland
	November: 'Crystal Night' (*Kristalnacht*) anti-Jewish pogrom
1939	March: Germany renounces non-aggression pact with Poland
	May: Conclusion of 'Pact of Steel' with Italy
	August: Conclusion of pact with Soviet Union
	September: German invasion of Poland. Britain and France declare war on Germany
1941	September: Removal of teachers considered disloyal to Nazis
	December: 'Rationalisation Decree'
1942	May: Start of bomber raids on German cities
1944	July: Attempt to assassinate Hitler.

Overview

THE Weimar Republic was not simply an artificial regime brought into existence by the peculiar circumstances that prevailed in 1918. In part, it had its roots in a tradition of German social democracy that can be traced back, through the Bismarckian period, to the 1848 revolutions and beyond. This tradition, committed to constitutional government and to the rule of law, had attracted sufficient support in the pre-war years to make the Social Democrats the largest party in the Reichstag (German parliament). The Social Democrats were hurried into power in 1918, not by the due process of parliamentary election, and certainly not by significant long-term shifts in social and economic structures. Instead the change was precipitated by the catastrophe that overtook the German war effort in that year. At that point, finding themselves at a military disadvantage from which there seemed to be no escape, the German generals sued for peace in the full expectation that the terms would reflect the even nature of the long conflict. As a means to that end, they entered into an unlikely alliance with Social Democrat politicians, and abandoned the Kaiser who had seemed hitherto to provide the best guarantee of their interests. When much harsher peace terms were put to them, they had no choice but to accept them, given the military situation on the Western Front and the political instability at home.

After such promising parliamentary progress in peacetime, therefore, German social democracy was catapulted into power with three substantial handicaps. One, of course, was its share of responsibility for the harsh peace terms imposed upon Germany by the Treaty of Versailles. Another was that social democracy had to compete in the years after 1918 with other powerful political traditions and with new political forces. Even if the German army had been defeated, and that certainly was not the case on the Eastern Front, German conservatism and German nationalism remained strong and influential. From the east, too, came the influence of the Russian Revolution to make German Communism a far stronger force than it had ever been in the pre-war years. The third handicap was of a more practical nature, for this new government was obliged to meet the enormous economic demands imposed upon it by the victorious allies.

However, the Weimar Republic survived in spite of, and perhaps because of, these circumstances. It survived the challenge of political extremism in the years immediately after the war because conservative elements, such as the army, were willing to support it against the 'greater evil' of Communism. It survived the economic chaos of 1923 for two main reasons. In part its image was enhanced by the patriotic stance that it was able to strike when French forces occupied the Ruhr. It was also of the greatest importance that the subsequent collapse of the German currency convinced the United States of America that they should participate actively in a more moderate enforcement of the peace terms. It was possible to believe, in the later 1920s, that the German Republic was edging towards normality.

A second catastrophe – the collapse of the American stock market in 1929 – undermined the Republic's position altogether. The very nature of the crisis ensured that Germany would receive no further assistance from the powerful capitalist economies that had come to its aid in 1923. In the early 1930s, moreover, social democracy faced a new threat from the right wing of German politics. After their failure to seize power by naked violence in the early 1920s, the National Socialists (Nazis) had reinvented themselves as a parliamentary party with a manifesto that embraced the whole range of German political discontent. In these catastrophic economic circumstances, their appeal as a new and radical force proved irresistible to many German voters and, ultimately, to Germany's political hierarchy.

Adolf Hitler came to office with an insane vision of Germany's political future, but with a remarkable talent as a pragmatic politician. The circumstances under which the Nazis came to power imposed two priorities upon them. One was the elimination of rival political forces in what was still, in 1933, a constitutional state; the other was the solution of the enormous social and economic problems that had played such a major role in the Nazis' success. Both of these goals had been achieved to a large degree by 1937 by ruthless and single-minded means. Many historians doubt the long-term viability of the Nazi economy by this date, and some have recently begun to question whether Nazism had indeed overcome all differences of political opinion within Germany. Nevertheless, it is clear that the Nazi regime was turning in the late 1930s towards the fulfilment of its wider ideological aims. Whether Nazi anti-semitism, the revision of the Versailles Treaty, and the pursuit of territorial expansion in eastern Europe followed a master plan, or whether Hitler improvised such policies as circumstances allowed, these were clearly among the priorities of German politics in the late 1930s. They led German policy into a wider arena. If they were not the sole causes of the world conflict that developed between 1939 and 1941, they contributed enormously to the destruction of the German state and to a dramatic redirection of German history in the second half of the 20th century.

1. What do you regard as the most important reason why the Weimar Republic failed? Explain your answer.

2. Place the reasons in the mind map in order of importance. Which do you regard as more important – economic reasons or political reasons? Give reasons for your answer.

3. Can you find links between reasons? (For instance, the 'Wall Street Crash' led to a 'rise in unemployment' and increased 'the appeal of Hitler' and the Nazis.) Can you find any other links which contain economic and political factors?

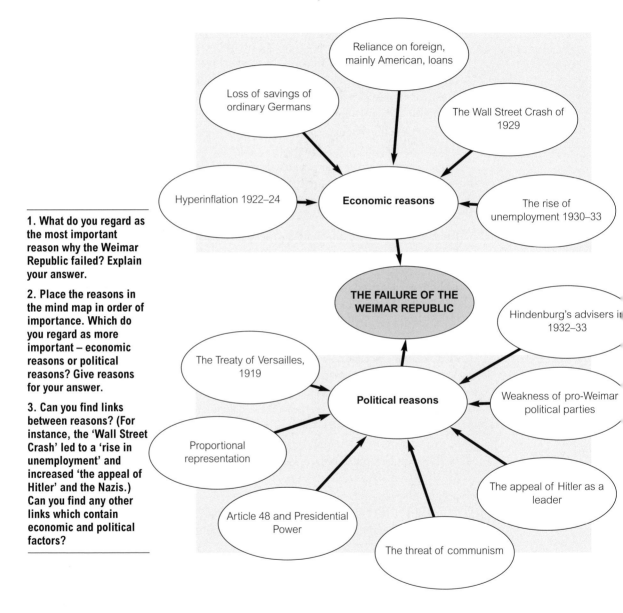

6.1 How true is it that the Weimar Republic was brought into being by, and represented, democratic interests in Germany?

The political forces within the Republic

Republican government in Germany was born (9 November 1918) under the most unfavourable circumstances. Quite apart from the imminent collapse of the war effort, and the abdication of the Kaiser, the fleet was in mutiny at Kiel and at Wilhelmshaven. Soldiers' and workers' councils had appeared in Berlin, Cologne and Munich, where a Bavarian Republic had been declared. The name by which the German republic is commonly known derived from the fact that the dangerous condition of the capital in 1919 obliged the newly elected National Assembly to meet in the small provincial town of Weimar. The early failure of successive emergency governments, the desire of many conservatives to present a liberal front to the allies, and the radical nature of much anti-government agitation, all placed the Social Democratic Party (SPD) at the forefront of events. The shape of the Weimar Republic was to be determined by the state and by the aims of that party.

The German socialist movement was deeply divided. An Independent Social Democratic Party (USPD) had broken away from the SPD (April 1917), and a more extreme Communist Party (KPD) had been formed in November 1918. While the Communists supported the seizure of power and the implementation of radical programmes, the SPD followed the lead of its chief, Friedrich Ebert, in preferring peaceful, democratic change through an elected assembly. The non-revolutionary nature of Ebert's government was confirmed on the first day of the Republic's life, when he accepted the offer from General Groener of army assistance against the forces of the left. His decision undoubtedly strengthened his government by alliance with such a traditional and respected force. Groener possibly saved Germany from the intervention of allied troops. Naturally, however, the decision drew fierce criticism from the left. This was increased in the next few weeks when army units, aided by a newly formed Volunteer Corps (*Freikorps*), bloodily suppressed a Communist ('Spartacist') rising in Berlin (January 1919) and dispersed the 'Soviet' that had briefly held power in Munich (April 1919). Thus, while the Republic came to power across the corpses of some of its enemies, it owed that passage to a force that was merely a temporary ally. In the light of subsequent events, it was ominous that Groener had made no promise to protect the Republic from the forces of the right.

The Weimar constitution

The elections to the National Assembly (January 1919) placed the SPD at the head of the poll, but without an overall majority. It was thus obliged to enter a coalition with the Centre Party and the Democratic Party (DDP), which was to characterise the fragmented nature of political life in the Weimar Republic. The constitution drafted by the Assembly (July 1919) nevertheless represented a considerable democratic advance since 1914. It named the Reichstag as the sovereign authority of the state, and decreed that it should be elected every four years by **proportional representation**, by all men and women over the age of 21. The President, elected every seven years, was subject to the authority of the Reichstag, although he also possessed special powers for use in an emergency. A further outstanding break from the principles of the Bismarckian constitution concerned the powers of the upper house (*Reichsrat*). This continued to represent the interests of the component parts of the federal state, but was now

---

Friedrich Ebert (1871–1925)
Of relatively humble background, Ebert joined the SPD in 1889; as a trade union activist, he was on the police 'black list'; he held assorted jobs, until elected to the Reichstag in 1912; and became joint leader of the SPD in 1913. Nominated first Chancellor of the newly declared Weimar Republic on the Kaiser's abdication on 9 November 1918, Ebert oversaw the armistice and the difficult transition to parliamentary democracy. He became Weimar's first President in August 1919, and used Article 48 to stabilise Weimar democracy. Ebert was criticised by the left for using the Army and Free Corps units to suppress workers' uprisings, and for failing to engage in a radical revolution; he was criticised by the right for his support of trade unions and workers' rights. Died prematurely from appendicitis in 1925.

General Wilhelm Groener (1867–1939)
Military commander and politician. Succeeded Erich von Ludendorff as head of General Staff (1918). Subsequently Minister of Transport (1920–23) and Minster of Defence (1928–32) under the German Republic.

Proportional representation: System of voting in which each political party is represented in the parliament in proportion to the number of people who vote for it in the election.

A satire by artist George Grosz on the conservative triumph in the early years of the Weimar Republic. The caption reads: 'Cheers. Noske! The Young Revolution is Dead.'

Prost. Noske! Die junge Revolution ist tot!

subservient in all respects to the Reichstag. These component parts, instead of existing as sovereign kingdoms or duchies, were now designated merely as provinces (*Länder*).

A vigorous historical debate has surrounded the events of 1918–19 and their significance. For historian A.J. Nicholls they represented a true democratic advance for Germany (*Weimar and the Rise of Hitler*, 1968), bringing peace and a more genuinely representative system in place of the parliamentary 'charades' of Bismarck's time. Yet to Gordon Craig (*Germany 1866–1945*, 1978) these events constituted an 'aborted revolution' which failed to change basic political attitudes and prejudices, and which thus condemned the republic to failure in the long run. John Hiden has compromised between the two positions, seeing the 1919 constitution, like the events that gave birth to it, as 'a synthesis between progressive political and social ideas and the desire to protect traditional institutions'.

1. What reasons led to the formation of a republican government, under Social Democrat leadership, in Germany in 1918?

2. To what extent was a democratic form of government established in Germany 1918–1919?

6.2 What forces in Germany opposed the Weimar Republic and for what reasons?

As imminent defeat in war brought the Republic into being, so its most pressing task was the conclusion of peace. In this task its freedom of action was almost nil. Advised by the military chiefs that continuation of hostilities was impossible, and forced to accept the allies' terms as the only alternative to invasion, the Weimar Republic nevertheless inherited a

Fourteen Points: The 'Fourteen Points' were listed in a speech by President Woodrow Wilson in January 1918, intended to set out a blueprint for lasting peace in Europe after the First World War.

Social democracy: A kind of socialism in which people are allowed a relatively large amount of freedom.

Reparations: Payments made by a defeated state to compensate the victorious state(s) for damage or expenses caused by the war.

legacy of bitterness and resentment at its actions. German hopes that peace would be based upon Woodrow Wilson's '**Fourteen Points**', and that the replacement of the Kaiser by **social democracy** would incline the allies to leniency, proved misplaced. The terms that the republican ministers Müller and Bell finally accepted caused resentment. Among the causes of resentment were the following:

- Germany would not be accepted into the League of Nations.

- Germany lost eastern territories to states that could not pretend to have defeated it.

- Future German industry would pass the fruits of its labour to foreign capitalists in the form of **reparations**.

Worse, it was claimed that the German armies had not been beaten by the allies at all, but betrayed by the secret enemy at home – the socialist and the Jew. The myth of the 'Stab in the Back' (*Dolchstoss*) was born.

Despite the widespread feeling that 'the true basis of the Republic is not the Weimar Constitution but the Treaty of Versailles', it is not fair to imagine that the regime was doomed by the circumstances of its birth. For all its losses, republican Germany still had potentially the strongest economy in Europe, and its recovery was rapid. The political demoralisation caused by Versailles was a more serious problem, for it not only guaranteed a constant right-wing opposition to the Republic, but also undermined the initial enthusiasm of more moderate patriots for the regime. The future of the Weimar Republic, therefore, depended upon surviving long enough for such passions to cool.

Opponents on the left

The acceptance of the Weimar constitution in the Reichstag, by 262 votes to 75, and the success of the more moderate political parties in the elections of 1919, should not obscure the hostility that existed in Germany to the new regime. The election result, as the left-wing commentator E. Troeltsch explained it, was not really a vote of confidence, for 'this democracy was in essence an anti-revolutionary system, dedicated to the maintenance of order and opposed to the dictatorship of the proletariat'. On the left extreme of the Republic's enemies stood the KPD, separated from the regime by a gulf of bitterness formed during the risings of 1919, and by the brutal murders of Communist leaders Karl Liebknecht and Rosa Luxemburg by *Freikorps* men. By December 1920, when its decision to join the International (the International Organisation of Communist and Socialist Parties) attracted many converts from the USPD, the KPD could boast a membership of 400,000 with 33 daily newspapers at its disposal. Although closely tied to a pro-Moscow policy by the leadership of Ernst Thälmann (1925–33), the party pursued a cautious policy, preferring to consolidate its strength, membership and influence steadily, rather than undertaking further adventures of the sort that had failed in 1919. Its achievement was, however, unimpressive. It failed to win any great influence among the trade unions, and alienated many potential supporters by its pro-Soviet stance. Nevertheless, the hostility between communists and social democrats continued into the next decade and helps to explain the failure of the left in Germany to resist the rise of Nazism.

Ernst Thälmann (1886–1944)
Originally active in the trade union movement and in the Social Democratic Party, Thälmann joined the German Communist Party in 1924. Party Secretary, and twice party candidate in presidential elections. Arrested by the Nazis (1933), and died in Buchenwald concentration camp.

Opponents on the right

A more daunting array of political opponents lay to the right of the Republic. The nationalists, grouped especially around the German National People's Party (DNVP) represented the brand of conservatism

Völkisch: German adjective used to describe a policy or idea based upon the principle of race. The *völkisch* groups laid their stress upon the concept of race (*Volk*), preaching the superiority of German racial characteristics and culture, and the need to protect them against alien influences, especially the harmful influence of the Jews.

Putschism: Violent insurrection. *Putsch* is a German word indicating the violent seizure of power by a group or party. It is the equivalent of the French *coup d'état*.

Stormtroopers: Small groups of well-armed foot soldiers. The *Sturmabteilung* (SA or Brownshirts) was a paramilitary force in Germany in the early 1930s. It was an organisation of about 4.5 million men who fought street battles against their opponents.

Gregor Strasser (1892–1934)
Joined the Nazi Party in 1920 and took part in the Beerhall *Putsch* (1923). Favoured the left-wing elements of National Socialist doctrine and opposed Hitler's alliances with 'big business'. Strasser resigned his party office in protest in 1932, and was murdered during the 'Night of the Long Knives'. His brother Otto (1897–1974), also prominent on the left wing of the movement, left the Nazi Party in 1930, and fled into exile in Canada.

---

1. What reasons did German nationalists and German communists have to feel that they had been betrayed by the Weimar Republic?

2. To what extent do you agree with the claim that 'the greatest handicap of the Weimar Republic lay in the fact that it had accepted the terms of the Versailles Treaty'?

---

that desired a return to the principles and institutions of Wilhelmine Germany. The DNVP had influential support in the civil service, within the legal system, among industrialists, and in the churches. Indeed, the hostility of the legal system towards the Republic was clearly shown in the lenient sentences passed against right-wing terrorists and rebels. The nationalist threat to the regime was, nevertheless, limited by several factors. The leadership of the DNVP was divided over the issue of co-operation with the republican regime, and the whole emphasis of the party's policies was upon principles partly compromised by the defeat of the old Germany in the First World War.

In the course of the later 1920s, the nationalists began to surrender the leadership of the right-wing opposition to the National Socialist German Workers' Party (NSDAP or 'Nazis'), the most successful of the *völkisch* groups that appeared on the right of German politics. Founded in 1919 by Anton Drexler, but soon dominated by the brilliant orator Adolf Hitler, the Nazis came close to ruin in their early life by placing their trust in a policy of *putschism*. This resulted in public discredit and in the imprisonment of their leaders. Although the subsequent change of tactics – whereby the NSDAP now sought power by parliamentary means – led to poor results, the party had hidden strengths. Its local organisation, although uneven, was especially strong in Bavaria. Elsewhere it employed some notable local leaders, such as Gregor Strasser and Julius Streicher, who ensured tight local discipline.

It also deployed a powerful paramilitary force, the **stormtroopers** (*Sturmabteilung* or SA), which proved more than a match for its Communist rivals in the street violence that scarred the political life of the Weimar Republic. Lastly, its broad policy appealed to the resentments of defeated Germans, both 'national' and 'socialist'. Although this policy had little success in the years of republican prosperity, it promised to serve the party well should Germany once more fall upon hard times.

It is open to dispute whether the German Army (*Reichswehr*), in its reduced, post-Versailles form, should be numbered among the Republic's enemies. Although it had done a great deal to enable the Weimar government to survive its first weeks, there was much in the principles of the traditional officer class, which still drew 21% of its membership from the nobility, that was at odds with the philosophy of the social-democratic Republic. The view of Hans von Seeckt (Chief of Army Command 1920–26) was that the *Reichswehr* should be an apolitical body, preserving its traditional values above the hurly-burly of party rivalry. Comparison between *Reichswehr* action in 1919, and its refusal to act against army veterans in *Freikorps* units during the Kapp *Putsch*, clearly showed that its attitude towards the government was merely lukewarm. In the words of John Hiden, in *The Weimar Republic* (1974), it 'would tolerate the Republic for the time being in its own interests'.

6.3 Why were the years 1920–1923 a period of crisis for the Weimar Republic?

The Kapp *Putsch* (1920) and the Beerhall *Putsch* (1923)

Matthias Erzberger (1875–1921)
Reichstag deputy (1903) and leader of the Centre Party. Favourable to a peace settlement from 1916, he was a member of the delegation that signed the armistice in 1918. Foreign Minister in the German Republic, he was assassinated by nationalists.

In its first months the Weimar Republic fought for its life against the hostility of the left, surviving by virtue of its temporary allies. In the next four years, however, there was much to maintain the sense of crisis and bitterness. The publication in April 1921 of the magnitude of Germany's reparation payments to the allies, combined with Matthias Erzberger's plans to strengthen the national economy by taxes upon war profits and inherited wealth to create enormous resentment on the right. This merged with existing nationalist hostility to subject the Republic to increasing right-wing violence. During these stages of the Republic's life, wrote historian Gordon Craig, 'its normal state was crisis'.

The first of these violent assaults was the Kapp *Putsch* (March 1920). Although this attempted coup was a symptom of wider right-wing discontent, the immediate trigger was the government's attempts to disband a *Freikorps* unit under Captain Ehrhardt at the request of the allies. Ominously, the *Reichswehr* took up a neutral stance, claiming that 'obviously there can be no talk of letting *Reichswehr* fight against *Reichswehr*'. Wolfgang Kapp's plans were frustrated instead by Berlin workers and civil servants who refused the orders of the rebels and denied them transport facilities and publicity. Unfortunately, this action was not repeated in later moments of republican peril.

Walter Rathenau (1867–1922)
President of the AEG electrical company, and director (1915) of Germany's war economy. Foreign Minister of the German Republic (1922) and signatory of the Treaty of Rapallo, he was assassinated by nationalists.

Meanwhile, Germany experienced political violence and assassination unparalleled in its history. The most spectacular examples were the murders of Matthias Erzberger (August 1921) and of Walter Rathenau (June 1922). The final drama of this period of right-wing pressure was played out in Munich in November 1923, when Hitler and some Nazi followers attempted to exploit a clash between the reactionary government of Bavaria and the federal authorities. Their aim was a 'March on Berlin' after the style of Mussolini's recent 'March on Rome'. Police action reduced the so-called 'Beerhall *Putsch*' to a fiasco. Taken out of context the activities of Kapp and Hitler appear to pose little threat to the Weimar Republic. Nevertheless, the lenient sentences passed on the offenders – five years' imprisonment for Hitler and no punishment for any of Ehrhardt's *Freikorps* men – made clear the sympathy for their cause in high places. The Reichstag elections held in June 1920 added further indications of the ascendancy of the right.

The French invasion of the Ruhr

By 1920 the bases of French security proposed at Versailles lay in ruins. Domestic developments in Germany offered little prospect of its willing acceptance of the settlement and an increasing reluctance to maintain its reparation payments. By the Wiesbaden Accords (October 1921), France agreed to help German payments by accepting a proportion in raw materials and industrial produce, rather than in cash, but in the next year these payments in kind had slipped into arrears.

Faced with the choice of using conciliation or confrontation to exact its due from Germany, public and political opinion in France inclined more and more toward the latter solution.

In November 1922 Germany requested a suspension of its payments for up to four years in the face of domestic economic difficulties. It was Germany's third such request in three years and strongly suggested that the whole question of enforcing the Versailles settlement was at stake. It was this vital issue that prompted France, with support from Italy and Belgium, to send troops across the Rhine and into the industrial heartland of the Ruhr in January 1923. Protesting, with justification, that the invasion of its sovereign territory was against the terms of the peace treaty, the German government appealed with great success for a policy of passive resistance in the Ruhr. In February 1923, coal production there fell to 2.5 million tons, where 90 million had been mined in 1922. Three iron smelting furnaces operated in March where 70 had worked in the previous year. Occasional terrorist attacks on troops and military action against German demonstrators raised the overall tension.

Value of the Reichsmark *against the dollar*

July 1914	4.2
July 1919	14.0
July 1920	39.5
July 1921	76.7
July 1922	493.2
Jan. 1923	1 7,972.0
July 1923	353,412.0
Aug. 1923	4,620,455.0
Sept. 1923	98,860,000.0
Oct. 1923	25,260,208,000.0
15 Nov. 1923	4,200,000,000,000.0

Source: Gordon Craig, *Germany 1866–1945*

1. What evidence was there of political and economic instability in Germany in the years 1919–23?

2. What were the main causes of the inflation that struck Germany in 1923, and upon whom did it have the greatest impact?

Inflation

Here we have to consider the domestic effects of the occupation of the Ruhr upon Germany. The most sensational of these was the acceleration of the decline of the *Reichsmark* (German currency) that had been in progress since the war. The initial blame lay, not with the French invasion, but with the crippling cost of the war, the pressure of reparation demands, and the Republic's misguided policy of printing money to meet budget deficits. As the table shows, the decline now raced out of control. Apart from its role in the origins of inflation, the government bore some responsibility for not checking it at an early stage. 'Cheap money' had its attractions for industrialists who now found plant and wages cheap, and for landowners whose mortgages were easier to pay off. Some enormous fortunes, such as that of the industrialist Hugo Stinnes, were forged out of this financial chaos. Inflation, on the other hand, had no consolations for the small saver or investor whose carefully accumulated sums and guaranteed interest became worthless in a matter of days.

The collapse of the value of pensions and savings ruined many, and the number of recipients of public relief in 1923 was three times that in 1913. 'Millions of Germans,' wrote Gordon Craig in *Germany 1866–1945* (1981), 'who had passively accepted the transition from Empire to Republic suffered deprivations that shattered their faith in the democratic process and left them cynical and alienated.' As a further ominous by-product many trade unions, unable in the crisis to protect their members' interests, suffered a sharp drop in their rolls and in their political influence.

6.4 In what respects did the years 1924–1929 constitute 'the golden age of the Weimar Republic'?

Stable political leadership: Gustav Stresemann and Paul von Hindenburg

The Weimar Republic not only survived, but launched upon the most successful period of its life, a period when long-term survival at last seemed possible. Two factors contributed greatly to this recovery. For the first time, the Republic had leaders who commanded respect, for the fall of Chancellor Cuno (August 1923) brought into office the major political figure of the Republic, Gustav Stresemann. Stresemann became republican because he was horrified by the more radical alternatives. His political

<table>
<tr><td>**Gustav Stresemann (1878–1929)** Elected to the Reichstag in 1907; became leader of the National Liberal Party in 1917. Formed the German People's Party (DVP) in 1918. As Chancellor of a coalition government from 13 August to 23 November</td><td>1923, Stresemann successfully resolved the major crises of that year (French occupation of the Ruhr, massive inflation). From 1924 until his untimely death from a stroke in 1929, Stresemann served as Foreign Minister. Although initially an</td><td>authoritarian and supporter of the use of military force, Stresemann became convinced of the need to support the Republic and to find peaceful solutions to Germany's problems; the renegotiation of reparations in the Dawes Plan (1924) and Young</td><td>Plan (1929), and the diplomatic achievements of the Locarno Pact (1925), the Treaty of Berlin (1926) and Germany's admission to the League of Nations (1926), were key elements in the potential stabilisation of Weimar democracy.</td></tr>
</table>

background, nevertheless, was that of an orthodox conservative, and made him acceptable to many people who could barely tolerate his predecessors. Although Chancellor for only three months, he continued to exert a profound influence upon German politics from the Foreign Ministry until his death in 1929.

Shortly after the emergence of Stresemann, the death of Friedrich Ebert (February 1925) brought to the presidency of the Republic the wartime hero Field Marshal Paul von Hindenburg, a man of impeccable patriotic credentials. His election was largely an expression of nostalgia for the stability and strength of the 'old' Germany. 'The truth is,' Stresemann testified, 'that Germans want no president in a top hat. He must wear a uniform and plenty of decorations.' Hindenburg, however, wore both his uniform and his office with tact, and effectively defended the Republic from the worst barbs of its right-wing opponents.

The second vital factor in the recovery of the Republic was the desire of the wartime allies to prevent the collapse or political disintegration of Germany. Foreign co-operation was central to the regime's new lease of life.

The establishment of financial stability

The first achievements of the revived Republic were the rescue of the German currency and the regulation of reparations. At the end of 1923, thanks to the work of Hans Luther at the Ministry of Finance, the discredited *Reichsmark* was replaced by the so-called '*Rentenmark*'. In the absence of sufficient gold reserves, the new currency was backed in theory by Germany's agricultural and industrial resources. It was a new, largely fictitious, form of security, which relied heavily upon foreign goodwill for its general acceptance. There was enough of this goodwill, however, not only to support the stabilisation of the currency, but also to regulate the question of Germany's reparation payments through the formulation of the Dawes Plan in 1924. Outwardly, the German economy presented a picture in the later 1920s of stability and prosperity. The emergence of giant industrial combines such as I.G. Farben and United Steelworks (*Vereinigte Stahlwerke*) in 1926 seemed to testify to the renewed dynamism of German heavy industry. In 1927, overall production figures at last matched those of 1913.

Chancellors of Weimar Germany 1919–1933

Paul Scheidemann	1919 (Feb.–June)	W. Marx	1923–1924
G. Bauer	1919–1920	Hans Luther	1925–1926
H. Müller	1920 (March–June)	H. Müller	1929–1930
C. Fehrenbach	1920–1921	Heinrich Brüning	1930–1932
Joseph Wirth	1921–1922	Franz von Papen	1932 (May–Nov.)
Wilhelm Cuno	1922–1923	Kurt von Schleicher	1932–1933
Gustav Stresemann	1923 (August–Nov.)	Adolf Hitler	1933–

The achievement of domestic political stability

Financial stability was accompanied by a greater degree of political stability. Apart from the acceptability of Stresemann and Hindenburg, the economic recovery blunted nationalist opposition to the Republic by appeasing the industrialists who played a substantial role in the DNVP. The armed forces, too, seemed to be on better terms with the Republic after the resignation of von Seeckt (October 1926) as commander of the *Wehrmacht*. After the appointment of General Groener (December 1927) as Defence Minister, 1928–29 provided two pieces of electoral comfort for the government. The Reichstag elections in May 1928 provided the worst results for a decade for the parties of the political extremes. Between them the DNVP (14.2%), the NSDAP (2.6%) and the KPD (10.6%) secured less than 30% of the popular vote. In December 1929 a **referendum** took place, forced by a coalition of nationalists and Nazis, trying to condemn the Young Plan and proposing treason charges against the government for doing deals with foreign interests. Only 13.8% of the votes cast agreed with this interpretation of government policy.

Referendum (or plebiscite): A form of political consultation in which the electorate is asked for its response to a specific measure proposed by the government.

Why, and with what success, did Weimar Germany adopt a 'policy of fulfilment' in foreign affairs?

'For most Germans,' writes John Hiden in *The Weimar Republic* (1974), 'foreign policy meant an unremitting effort to revise the terms of the Treaty of Versailles.' Successive German governments sought to remedy the dangerous diplomatic isolation that resulted from defeat, and to restore the degree of national independence lost to the allies and to their occupation agencies. The first method they used was the simple tactic of sullen obstruction.

● The clauses of the treaty directed against the Kaiser and other alleged war criminals were never effectively enforced.

● The disbanding of paramilitary organisations was slow and unreliable.

● The clauses relating to disarmament were implemented only under constant allied supervision.

Such a policy could not be successful for long against opponents with both the determination and the means to enforce the treaty terms. German policy thus changed under the chancellorship of Joseph Wirth (May 1921–November 1922) to one of 'fulfilment' (*Erfüllingspolitik*). This apparent co-operation with the allies was one of the greatest causes of bitterness among the right-wing opponents of the regime. It played a direct role in stirring the political violence of the period.

It was, nevertheless, a sensible and realistic policy. It was designed to encourage future allied leniency towards Germany, and its introduction coincided with a successful solution to the problem of diplomatic isolation. The conclusion of the Treaty of Rapallo with the Soviet Union in April 1922 created investment opportunities for Germany. It also greatly improved the prospects of evading the military restrictions imposed at Versailles. However, it may also be argued that it did a great deal, in combination with the chaos caused by French occupation of the Ruhr, to frighten the western allies into taking a more reasonable attitude towards Germany.

The greatest successes of *Erfüllungspolitik* were achieved whilst Gustav Stresemann controlled the Foreign Ministry. He combined the broad principles of 'fulfilment' with an attempt to lay foundations for the revision of the peace treaties. Stresemann was portrayed by liberal historians as a 'good European', eager to put co-operation in the place of confrontation, while historians of the Marxist left saw him as a capitalist reaching an accommodation with the other western powers for essentially anti-Soviet reasons. The publication of his official papers indicated that Stresemann was neither of these things. His primary aim was to rid Germany of foreign restraints, and to regain full sovereignty and freedom of political action. Thus the Locarno Pact of 1925 guaranteed Germany's western borders against further incursions, without committing Germany to acceptance of the hated territorial settlement in the east. It also paved the way for Germany's acceptance into the international community of the League of Nations. The agreement of the Dawes Plan in 1924 and the Young Plan in 1929 were classic examples of this policy of 'fulfilment'. They reduced Germany's total reparations debt, and gained foreign recognition of its difficulties in paying it off at all.

Steadily, from January 1926, Germany began to reap the fruits of this policy. In that month, British withdrawal from Cologne marked the first major reduction of the occupying forces. This was followed in January 1927 by the withdrawal from Germany of the Inter-Allied Control Commission, the major 'watchdog' of the Versailles terms. Before the fall of the Republic, the evacuation of foreign troops was completed by the French withdrawal (August 1929). Within two years, the continuation of reparation payments had been dealt a near fatal blow by Chancellor Brüning's successful application to the USA for a '**moratorium**' (June 1931). No area of policy under the Weimar Republic could claim to rival the success of its foreign policy. Its tragedy was that the government failed consistently to convince the political extremists of the constructive good sense of that policy. When the international economic crisis undermined the Republic, its foreign policy of restrained national reassertion was to be one of the first casualties of its collapse.

Moratorium: A legally authorised delay in the performance of a legal duty or obligation. From the Latin *mora* – delay.

Was the Republic secure at the end of the 1920s?

For all these shifts in policy, and for all the improvements that had taken place in its status and stability, the Weimar Republic still had its weaknesses. It seemed to be winning the public relations battle as the end of the 1920s approached, but it had established few durable institutions to sustain it in time of crisis. The lukewarm toleration of the regime shown

---

Political parties in Weimar Germany

DNVP (the German National People's Party): a conservative, nationalist party that was opposed to the creation of German democracy. Wanted a return to the authoritarian type of government under Wilhelm II. Supported the large-scale landowners of eastern Germany. Wanted protective tariffs against imported foodstuffs. Developed from the Fatherland Front and the Conservative Party of the last years of the Kaiser's reign.

DVP (the German People's Party): Weimar equivalent of the National Liberal Party of Bismarck's and Wilhelm II's Germany. Represented the interests of 'big business'. Most prominent politician was Gustav Stresemann.

Zentrum (the Centre Party): represented the interests of the Catholic Church in Germany. Linked with the BVP (Bavarian People's Party) which represented Catholic interests in Bavaria.

DDP (the German Democratic Party): supported German democracy. Weimar equivalent of the Progressive Liberal Party of Bismarck's and Wilhelm II's Germany. Supported by the middle class. Electoral support declined rapidly from 1920.

SPD (the Social Democratic Party): the largest party in Germany for most of the Weimar period. Represented the interests of the German working class. It had existed since 1875 and supported the creation of a socialist state through democratic means.

KPD (the Communist Party): formed in 1920 from the Spartacists and elements of the Independent Social Democratic Party. Wanted to create a communist state. Opposed to democracy. Main rival for working-class support of the SPD.

NSDAP (the National Socialist German Workers' Party, or Nazi Party): Hitler's party. Wanted to over-throw Weimar democracy and the Treaty of Versailles. Initially planned to achieve this through revolution. After 1925 Hitler attempted to achieve power through the ballot box and intimidation by the SA stormtroopers. Largest party in the Reichstag by 1932 but never gained more than one-third of the votes before January 1933.

by the *Reichswehr* was not widely imitated by the civil service, the universities or the schools. The historian K.S. Pinson describes in detail the atmosphere of German education in the 1920s.

'The essential control of both lower and higher education remained in the hands of those who had nothing but contempt for the Republic and who therefore made no effort to prepare the German youth for republican citizenship. Not a single school text in Weimar Germany presented the true story of German defeat in 1918. Germany geography texts still inculcated in the minds of the young the definition that Germany was a country surrounded on all sides by enemies.'

Nor had the Republic developed a system of parliamentary parties strong enough to give stability to its democracy. The classic Weimar coalition parties – the Social Democrats, the Democratic Party and the Centre Party – remained divided on many points of economic, political and religious doctrine. Their lack of cohesion in the face of the rise of a popular anti-democratic movement would play a major role in the disasters of the early 1930s.

Lastly, for all the appearance of superficial prosperity, the basis of the German economy was unsound. Industrial investment and government expenses were not adequately financed from German capital or German profits. More than a third of all capital invested in Germany in the late 1920s came from foreign loans. Imports between 1924 and 1930 were always greater than exports. The total deficit of the German budget over these years amounted to nearly 1.3 billion *Reichsmarks*. It is impossible to deny that in the years 1924–29 the Weimar Republic was progressing and was achieving some signs of permanency. In that limited period, however, normality was never quite achieved, and when it appeared close it proved only a brief interlude between two disasters.

---

1. In what respects were domestic politics in Germany more stable between 1924 and 1929 than they had been in the previous five years?

2. How convincing is the claim that 'the Weimar Republic was on the verge of success until undermined by the international economic crisis of 1929'?

3. Did the foreign policy of the Weimar Republic serve Germany's best interests?

6.5 Why was the Weimar Republic unable to survive the crisis generated by the Wall Street Crash?

The economic impact of the crash upon Germany

Stresemann had warned in 1928, 'Germany is dancing on a volcano. If the short-term credits are called in a large section of our economy would collapse.' Indeed, within days of Stresemann's premature death (3 October 1929), the slump in the Wall Street stock market (24 October 1929) triggered off just such a phenomenon. Germany's foreign capital, which had stood at 5 billion marks in 1928, dropped by half in 1929, and shrank to a mere 700 million marks in 1930. Loans began to be called in and bankruptcies multiplied. With the government consistently reluctant to set off renewed inflation, the crisis manifested itself primarily as massive unemployment. The problem had haunted Germany since the recovery of 1925, with 2 million out of work in the winter of 1925–26 and 1.5 million jobless a year later. The rise towards the disastrous figures of the Depression began in the summer of 1928. In mid-1929, 1.5 million were unemployed and in the following year the figures soared out of control. Three million were affected in the winter of 1929–30, 5 million by the end of the following summer and 6 million in January 1932.

Extremism: The behaviour or beliefs of people who wish to bring about political or social change by doing things that other people consider too severe or disruptive, often using violence.

The political impact of the crash upon Germany

The main political result of the economic slump was a substantial revival of **extremism**. As the table on page 127 indicates, the elections of 1930–32 were marked by a dramatic growth of influence for those parties that offered extreme solutions to the contemporary distress. The KPD achieved greater support than it had ever had before, but above all it was the Nazis that benefited from the economic tragedy.

Elections to the Reichstag, 1919–1932

	Jan. 1919	June 1920	May 1924	Dec. 1924	May 1928	Sept. 1930	July 1932	Nov. 1932
NSDAP	–	–	32	14	12	107	230	196
DNVP	44	71	95	103	73	41	37	52
DVP	19	65	45	51	45	30	7	11
Centre	91	85	81	88	78	87	98	90
DDP	75	39	28	32	25	20	4	2
SPD	165	102	100	131	153	143	133	121
USPD	22	84	–	–	–	–	–	–
KPD	–	4	62	45	54	77	89	100

There can be no doubt that the economic crisis played a major role in the increasing popularity of the NSDAP. For example, the research of historian Martin Broszat, in *The Hitler State* (1981), has established that, of all the working class recruits joining the Nazi Party in 1930–33, some 55% were unemployed. Nevertheless, there was nothing inevitable about the Nazi advent to power. They never represented a majority in the Reichstag and their electoral fortunes were in decline by late 1932. Their triumph resulted from the degeneration and miscalculations of republican politics in the years of economic crisis.

Brüning's administration

Heinrich Brüning (1885–1970)
A leading figure in German Catholic politics, prominent in the Centre Party (becoming its leader in 1929). Brüning was a social, political and economic conservative, a war veteran, and hostile to the principles of social democracy. Appointed Chancellor (1930), and Foreign Minister (1931). Resigned both offices in 1932, and lived in exile in the USA.

The resignation of Chancellor Müller's cabinet (March 1930) – the Republic's last Social Democrat administration – marked the end of majority government in Germany. As the political parties of the centre continued to place sectional interests before national needs, the effective government of the state fell into the hands of President Hindenburg and advisors such as General Groener and General von Schleicher. Their primary aim was less the protection of democracy and parliamentary government than the formation of a more authoritative and authoritarian government to face the economic crisis. Their first choice as Chancellor, Heinrich Brüning, had admirable qualifications for the office. He sought to cement his administration with some foreign success, such as the suspension of reparation payments, and he tackled Germany's domestic crisis by orthodox, deflationary economic tactics. Reductions in social services and in unemployment benefits, at the time when they were needed most, were unlikely to rally wide support, and they led to Brüning's damaging reputation as the 'Hunger Chancellor'. They also drove many of the unemployed into the ranks of the paramilitary organisations. Meanwhile, military expenditure and subsidies to the *Junker* farmers were maintained.

Franz von Papen (1879–1969)
Member of the Centre Party and deputy in the Prussian *Landtag* (1923–32). Chancellor of the German Republic (1932). Narrowly escaped assassination during the 'Night of the Long Knives'. Tried at Nuremberg for his role in assisting the Nazis to power, but acquitted.

Brüning's greatest political error, however, was the dissolution of the Reichstag (July 1930) in search of a secure majority. Instead, at a time of mounting crisis, he found the political extremism and the violence of the streets translated into Reichstag seats. Continued failure to curb economic depression, and to achieve ministerial stability, finally encouraged the President to replace Brüning with Franz von Papen in May 1932. This was the move which, according to the liberal historian Erich Eyck, 'killed not only the German Republic, but the peace of Europe'.

General Kurt von Schleicher (1882–1934)
After active service in the Imperial German Army, he became a senior officer in the *Reichswehr* (1919–29). Appointed Defence Minister in von Papen's government (1932), he then served briefly as Chancellor. Unable to reach agreement with Hitler, Schleicher resigned (1933), and was murdered during the 'Night of the Long Knives' (1934).

1. What was the economic and political impact of the Wall Street Crash upon Germany?

2. How did the economic crisis of 1929 help to bring Hitler and the Nazis to power in Germany?

3. Why did the Weimar Republic survive the crisis of 1923, but not that which began in 1929?

Papen, Schleicher and the advent of the Nazis

Franz von Papen's responsibility for the advent of the Nazis was great. In June, he lifted the ban that Brüning had placed upon the *Sturmabteilung*. In July, he used the resultant street violence, and the spate of deaths in clashes between Nazis and Communists, as the pretext to dismiss the Social Democrat provincial government in Prussia, one of the last strongholds of democratic government in Germany. Like Brüning before him, his decision to hold new elections (July 1932) played into the hands of the Nazis with their increasing support. Papen's efforts to establish an electoral alliance with Hitler as the junior partner were frustrated, both by Hitler's refusal to accept any office less than that of Chancellor, and by the aged President's personal and social dislike of Hitler. With Papen's resignation, the President had only one alternative to Hitler himself. When Kurt von Schleicher failed in his brief chancellorship (December 1932 – January 1933) to split the Nazi leadership by negotiating with Gregor Strasser, Hindenburg at last accepted Adolf Hitler as the only alternative to political chaos and possible civil war.

Hitler thus became Chancellor on 30 January 1933, with a cabinet of three Nazis and ten conservatives, the latter representing the vain hope of the traditional German right that they might still use the dynamic force of Nazism for their own purposes. A seven-hour torchlight parade by the SA in the streets of Berlin formed the funeral celebrations of the Weimar Republic.

6.6 What was the contribution of Adolf Hitler to the rise of Nazism?

Adolf Hitler (1889–1945)

Judaism: Religion of the Jewish people, which is based on the Old Testament of the Bible and the Talmud (book of laws and traditions).

Born in the small Austrian town of Braunau am Inn (20 April 1889), Hitler was the son of a customs official already well into middle age. Academically and socially, the young Hitler was a failure. His inability to gain admission to the Academy of Fine Arts in Vienna (1907) formed the prelude to 'five years of misery and woe', living by odd jobs and occasional artistic work. Hitler's 'Greater German' nationalism was already formed, and he later claimed that it was in Vienna that he first formulated the intense hatred of Jews and **Judaism** that was thereafter a central feature of his political beliefs. Convinced of the decadence of the Austro-Hungarian Empire, and of the invincibility of the racially purer German Reich, Hitler evaded Austrian conscription in 1914 to serve in a Bavarian regiment. After a creditable military career at the Western Front, he was stunned by the sudden collapse of the German war effort in November 1918. For him, there could be no other explanation than that all patriotic Germans had been vilely betrayed by the socialists, Marxists and Jews prominent in the November 'revolution' and in the subsequent Weimar Republic. In subsequent years, Hitler propagated the myth of the 'stab in the back', not only because of its propaganda value, but also because he was personally convinced of its truth. His natural place thereafter was in the ranks of the extreme nationalist opposition to the Republic. In September 1917 he joined the German Workers' Party which shortly afterwards changed its name to the National Socialist German Workers' Party (NSDAP). By July 1921 Hitler was its chairman.

Hitler as orator and publicist

Hitler's tenure of power in Germany lasted only 12 years. His tenure of real international power was shorter by half. Yet the fact that his is undoubtedly the best known face, and his the best documented political career of the century, bears witness to the extraordinary impact of the man. Hitler's primary qualification for a political career was his extraordinary talent as an orator. In part, this was based upon careful study of all the elements of public speaking, and brilliant mastery of the tactics of dogmatic assertion, sarcasm and emotional appeal. As W. Carr wrote in *History of Germany, 1815–1985* (1987), 'a Hitler speech was superb theatre. Hitler was his own script writer, choreographer and actor-manager all rolled into one.'

His success was not wholly explained, however, by contrived effects, but was largely due to the intense sincerity of his nationalistic feelings, and by his ability to communicate with the outrage and frustration of millions of Germans. A contemporary, Otto Strasser, described the effect of a speech as follows.

> 'He enters a hall. He sniffs the air. For a moment he gropes, feels his way, senses the atmosphere. Suddenly he bursts forth. His words go like an arrow to their target; he touches every private wound on the raw, liberating the mass unconscious, expressing its innermost aspirations, telling it what it most wants to hear.'

Such skills were more than adequate for one who saw himself at first only as a 'drummer' preparing the way for a greater leader, a John the Baptist, smoothing the way for Germany's true saviour. The stage at which he came to believe in himself as that saviour is unclear; perhaps as he reformulated his political views after the failure of the Munich *Putsch* of 1923. The years after 1923 saw the emergence of Hitler as unchallenged party leader.

Hitler achieved and fulfilled this role in an unorthodox fashion, for his were not the usual talents of political organiser and administrator. He was lazy, and often bored by practical detail. Administrative inefficiency, however, was outweighed by a remarkable political instinct, an unconquerable will power and self-confidence, total ruthlessness, and a talent for winning the dogged devotion of individuals. It is quite possible that Hitler cultivated his disinterest in detail and practicalities to maintain party unity, and to present the image that he maintained so well as the man of destiny, far above the petty wrangling that corrupted mundane politics. These were the talents that transformed Adolf Hitler from the 'nobody of Vienna' into the most dynamic and fateful figure in German history.

1. What was the impact of Germany's defeat in the First World War upon Adolf Hitler's political thinking?

2. To what extent do Hitler's personal talents explain the rise and the appeal of Nazism in the late 1920s and the early 1930s?

6.7 What were the main political and social doctrines of National Socialism?

The ancestry of Nazism

The intellectual roots of Nazism must be sought in a variety of locations. Many commentators, especially in the years immediately after the Second World War, interpreted Nazism as a movement that grew naturally from the authoritarianism and nationalism of earlier German history. It is hardly surprising that many German historians, such as Gerhard Ritter in *The Historical Foundations of the Rise of National Socialism* (1955), favoured a different view of Nazism. They saw it, not as the product of German history, but as the product of the unprecedented social and economic pressures upon Europe in the 1920s and 1930s. Another prominent German authority, Karl Bracher, in *The German Dictatorship* (1978), may be closest to the truth when he combines the two schools of thought. 'Past research has made clear that an examination of the roots of National Socialism must be conducted simultaneously on two levels; the German and the overall European.'

Essentially a distillation of resentments and fears, Nazism was a rag-bag of elements borrowed from most of the major political tendencies of the last century. From Germany alone it borrowed the conservative **Realpolitik** of Bismarck, the nationalism of Johann Fichte and the godless humanism of Friedrich Nietzsche. Its racial theories leaned heavily upon those of the Comte de Gobineau (*Essay on the Inequality of the Human Races*, 1855) and of Houston Stewart Chamberlain (*Foundations of the Nineteenth Century*, 1899). Both men had argued from the lunatic fringes of **Darwinism** that the key to human development lay in the inevitable triumph of the **Aryan races** over 'lesser varieties of mankind'. From further afield, and more recently, came the practical examples provided by Italian Fascism, with its attractive trappings and its bold seizure of national power. Also there was the ruthless example of Stalin in his consolidation of power in the Soviet Union. Although he was distanced from Stalin's political aims, Hitler could only feel the greatest respect for Stalin's coldly logical methods. 'Stalin and I,' he was to declare, 'are the only ones who see the future.'

The philosophy of *Mein Kampf*

Some semblance of cohesion and consistency was given to this variety of influences by the initial programme of the National Socialist Party (February 1920) which predated Hitler's dominance over the party and, more importantly, by Hitler's own political testament *My Struggle* (*Mein Kampf*). This was written during his imprisonment after the failure of the 1923 coup, and published in 1925. A rambling and highly personal work, *Mein Kampf* provided no precise manifesto for future government, but made clear the essential principles upon which the Nazis and their leader intended to proceed.

Central to Hitler's argument was the conviction that the only true basis of the state was not that of class interest (an invention of Marxism and Judaism) or of community or economic interest, but that of race. It was thus the primary duty of the German state to unite within its borders all those of common racial origin, and to eliminate alien elements that might weaken or corrupt the ethnic community (*Volksgemeinschaft*). In the case of Germany, this meant the elimination of the influence of the Jews. In Hitler's view their international conspiracy bore the responsibility for all Germany's recent ills. Subsequently, the major duty of the state would be the provision of adequate resources and 'living space' (**Lebensraum**) for the population that dwelt by right within its boundaries. As the preservation of its people was the reason for the state's existence, it was not only permissible, but positively desirable, for the state to acquire this *Lebensraum* by struggle against neighbouring races. Nor did Hitler attempt to dodge the implications of this doctrine in the specific case of Germany. 'History proves', he declared in *Mein Kampf*, 'that the German people owes its existence solely to its determination to fight in the east and to obtain land by military conquest. Land in Europe is only to be gained at the expense of Russia.'

Political authority: the *Führerprinzip*

To provide the dynamism and the unity of purpose necessary for the achievement of such a visionary programme, Nazism defined the 'leader principle' (*Führerprinzip*). Thereby, each level of Nazi organisation was committed to unquestioning obedience to its chief, with ultimate allegiance owed to the man at the apex of the pyramid of command, the *Führer*. This gave the appearance of consistency to a divided movement

Realpolitik: Policy that is based upon real, practical considerations, rather than upon abstract principles or ideals.

Darwinism: The views of Charles Darwin (1809–1882), the great British biologist, who defined the principles of evolution among animal species. Some political and social commentators believed that similar laws of development applied to the human race as well, and that some races were thus more highly developed than others. Such views are usually referred to as 'Social Darwinism'.

Aryan races: Term used by racists to indicate those Nordic and Anglo-Saxon races which the Nazis supposed to be superior to others.

Lebensraum (German – 'living space'): That foreign territory which, in the view of extreme German nationalists, had to be seized for the proper future maintenance of the German race.

Führer (German – leader): Name for the person in charge of the Nazi organisation, namely Adolf Hitler. An essential feature of Nazism. 'The *Führer*,' wrote Nazi theorist Ernst Huber in 1933, 'is the bearer of the people's will; he is independent of all groups, associations, and interests. In his will the will of the people is realised.'

1. What were the main racial theories and beliefs of the Nazi Party when it came to power in 1933?

2. What was the relative importance of nationalism and socialism in the doctrines of the Nazi Party?

and ensured Hitler's personal authority. It also appealed to millions of Germans for whom representative democracy seemed a short road to economic ruin and to national humiliation. This principle allowed the Nazis to pose not merely as the latest candidates for party political power, but as the appointed guardians of the destiny of the whole German nation.

6.8 How did Hitler ever become Chancellor of Germany?

Totalitarianism: This term has been defined in a variety of ways: it generally refers to a streamlined state with one leader, one party and one ideology, based on repression and indoctrination, and it emphasises the similarities between dictatorships of the Right (Hitler's Nazism, Mussolini's Fascism) and the Left (Stalin's Communism).

Fascism: Originally referring to Mussolini's Italy, this concept has been generalised by some historians to encompass modern right-wing dictatorships, including Nazism.

Given the appalling consequences, the arguments about who or what was responsible for Hitler's rise to power range over an immensely wide terrain. Historical controversies range from detailed empirical questions – such as which social groups voted for the NSDAP, or what was the role of big business in financing Hitler – to much wider interpretations of the period as a whole.

Some historians emphasise long-term peculiarities of German history, appealing to notions of a *Sonderweg* ('special path') to modernity; others point to features common to many European states after the First World War. For some, the problem has to do with 'modern mass society' and hence Nazism is an instance of **totalitarianism**; for others, adopting a Marxist approach, Nazism has to do with 'crises of capitalism' and is hence a variant of **fascism**. And some concentrate primarily on one individual: Hitler. Hitler's personal power has been emphasised – indeed over-emphasised – in many popular biographies and films, as well as historical works, as though Hitler's 'spell' had been something people could not resist. Even among those historians focusing on the same period, there are often huge differences of emphasis in choosing where precisely to lay the blame.

It is possible to simplify this complex story somewhat by analysing two separate but closely interrelated developments. One was the instability and eventual destruction of democracy in Weimar Germany. The other was the rise of a mass party under Hitler's leadership. It was when the political and economic crises came to a head that the combination proved fatal. Those individuals who played a key role in destroying democracy were unable to find a stable solution on their own; they thought that in 'taming' Hitler, they could harness the power of the masses to the purposes of the elites. This final gamble proved tragically flawed.

Thus Hitler benefited from much wider historical currents. Only in very specific circumstances was this Austrian drifter able eventually to gain a position of power in the German state, from which he could go on to shape European and world history.

Was Weimar democracy 'doomed from the start'?

The legacies of the First World War
As Ian Kershaw has aptly written, the First World War 'made Hitler possible'. The experience and aftermath of war shaped Hitler's outlook and gave him the opportunity to enter post-war German politics; at the same time it created an audience receptive to his prejudices. Kershaw continues: 'Without the war, a Hitler on the Chancellor's seat that had been occupied by Bismarck would have been unthinkable' (Kershaw, *Hitler 1889–1936: Hubris*, p.73). But – as Kershaw also reminds us – making 'Hitler possible' does not mean making Hitler inevitable. How important, then, was the war in explaining the collapse of Weimar democracy?

Versailles Treaty, 1919

Territorial changes:

- Loss of colonies abroad
- Alsace-Lorraine to be returned to France
- France to benefit from the coal production of the Saar
- West Prussia, Upper Silesia and Posen to go to a reconstituted state of Poland
- Danzig to become a free city under the supervision of the new League of Nations
- Demilitarisation of Germany's border areas
- Left bank of the Rhine to be under Allied supervision for 15 years

Restrictions on power:

- No union of Germany and Austria permitted
- German Army to be reduced to 100 000 men, for domestic and border-guard duties only
- Restrictions on German Navy, and submarines forbidden
- No German Air Force permitted

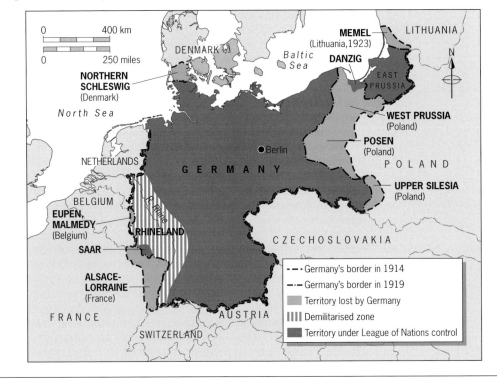

The psychological and social consequences of the 'Great War' of 1914–18 were undoubtedly of massive significance. The experience of 'total war' involved not merely soldiers but also civilians on the home front: women and young people participated in economic production, and in food riots and strikes. For some soldiers at the front, the experience of the mud-filled trenches, the daily witnessing of the maiming and deaths of comrades in stalemate battles over a few yards of territory, aroused a hatred of war itself. For others – like Hitler – it fed into rabid hatred of the culprits allegedly responsible for German defeat, the 'Jews' and 'Bolsheviks', and a determination to take revenge. This 'stab in the back' myth proved to be of major importance in the turmoil and upheavals of the post-war years. So too, in very different ways, did the shell-shock, the sense of disorientation, and the difficulties of reintegration into civil society following demobilisation. The immediate post-war years were characterised by widespread hunger and high death rates from diseases such as influenza, as well as rioting, strikes, political instability and violence. Many people in this devastated post-war society – with its high numbers of war widows, orphans, teenagers without fathers or elder brothers – had a totally unrealistic set of expectations about what the new Republic could offer, as Richard Bessel has shown (*Germany after the First World War*, 1993).

In this wider context, the harsh terms of the Versailles Treaty of 1919 caused massive resentment. Loss of colonies abroad and territory at home, the ban on an air force, restrictions on the size of the army and navy, and demilitarisation of border areas, were heavy blows, as was the infamous 'War Guilt clause' laying primary blame for unleashing the war on Germany and her allies. Weimar was born of a humiliating defeat, and the nationalist resentment caused by the Versailles Treaty could readily be exploited as a binding force across different social groups who would otherwise have had little in common.

Reparations, when the extent was revealed in 1920, also proved to be a long-running source of discontent. However, there is controversy over precisely why reparations were such a liability. For a long time it was held that the absolute level of reparations was indeed a major economic millstone, rendering Weimar capitalism intrinsically weak. More recently, as Theo Balderston outlines (*Economics and Politics in the Weimar Republic*, 2002), historians have argued that the major problems were the ways in which reparations were perceived and presented, in terms of Germany's 'capacity to pay' (or not), and the ways in which politicians chose to deal with reparations. Inflation, already rooted in the financing of the war through bonds rather than taxes, was made very much worse by the government's decision simply to print more and more paper money, leading to the massive inflation of 1923. Whatever the balance of these debates, the reparations issue dogged Weimar's brief life.

More generally, the balance between structural economic and political weaknesses on the one hand, and the 'freedom of manoeuvre' or choices available to politicians on the other, are common general themes underlying a number of debates over the collapse of Weimar democracy.

Intrinsic political weaknesses?

It has often been argued that further weaknesses were rooted in the constitution and political system. On further inspection, this view proves somewhat problematic, since aspects of political culture affected the way in which the constitution worked in practice.

The Weimar Republic appeared to be immensely democratic: women as well as men over the age of 20 had the right to vote; and the system of proportional representation meant that all votes cast were given appropriately weighted representation in the Reichstag (national parliament). Yet, in a country where there were numerous political parties representing very narrow sectional – religious, regional or social class – interests, this in effect led to a multiplicity of small parties gaining parliamentary representation. With no single party able to acquire a majority of seats on its own, parties were in a constant process of negotiating unstable coalitions on the basis of one or another shaky compromise, and there were frequent changes of government. It was not necessarily the system of proportional representation as such that was the problem therefore, but rather the character of Weimar parties under particular social and economic circumstances.

The role of the President, who was voted in for seven years by direct popular vote, was often said to be that of an *Ersatz Kaiser*: a 'substitute Emperor', with considerable personal powers. In particular, the President's powers to appoint and dismiss Chancellors, and to rule by emergency decree under the notorious Article 48, have been the subject of much

The role of the President of the Weimar Republic:
● Elected directly by the people, to serve for a seven-year term
● Has power to appoint and dismiss Chancellors
● Article 48: power to rule by emergency decree

critique. But such powers could be used to stabilise, as well as to undermine, democracy: it was not Article 48 itself, which was used by Weimar's first President and committed democrat, Friedrich Ebert, to stabilise the Republic, but rather its later misuse by President Hindenburg to undermine democracy, which proved problematic.

Flawed revolution and fatal compromises?

Weimar Republic: The Republic was created following the abdication of the Kaiser in November 1918 and named after the town of Weimar in which its first parliament met, because of the continuing political unrest in Berlin at the time.

The birth of the **Weimar Republic** – a result of sailors' and soldiers' mutinies and massive revolutionary unrest, causing the flight of the Emperor and the ad hoc declaration of a Republic – was accompanied by a series of compromises which dogged its brief life.

One such compromise was the agreement made between the civilian government under Friedrich Ebert, and the Army under General Groener, in November 1918. Ebert's pact with the Army has been criticised as unnecessary, allowing the old regime to retain its power and regroup; it has been defended as essential to orderly demobilisation and maintaining order in a time of crisis. The result was that the Army continued to play a powerful role in politics, which was eventually to prove fatal in undermining democracy. It also played a role in unleashing bitter splits among the left. Along with the so-called 'Free Corps' units, the Army was involved in suppression of popular unrest, particularly that of a left-wing persuasion. The murder of the Spartacist (left-wing communist) leaders Karl Liebknecht and Rosa Luxemburg in January 1919 led to lasting hosility between Social Democrats and Communists, making co-operation against Nazism much more problematic a decade later.

Another key compromise was that between the employers' organisations and the trade unions, in the Stinnes-Legien agreement of November 1918. This gave trade unions formal recognition and rights which, in employers' eyes, were fundamentally linked to the democratic system as such. Although the institutional framework was partially dismantled within a matter of years, and the resources and strength of trade unions declined massively with widespread unemployment after 1929, this too would prove to be a highly problematic legacy in discrediting democracy in the eyes of many leading industrialists.

Ebert has been further criticised for failing to engage in full-scale social revolution, resting content with a mere political revolution, leaving the power of the old elites intact. A committed democrat, Ebert felt people should be able to make their preferences known through the ballot box. In the event, the ballot box proved indecisive, the early 'Weimar coalition' of moderate parties led by the SPD lasting little over a year.

On both the left and the right, massive discontent continued. There were repeated attempts to take political control by violence, from the left-wing uprisings in Munich in 1919 and in Thuringia and Saxony in 1923, to the rightwing Kapp Putsch of 1920 and the Nazi 'Beer Hall Putsch' of 1923. Amidst continued violence on the streets, there were frequent political assassinations, including that of the Foreign Minister Walter Rathenau in 1922.

Was there the potential for stabilisation?

For all these undoubted weaknesses, the 'doomed from the start' school of historians have not clinched their case. Hitler's first unsuccessful attempt at seizure of power, in November 1923, was in the very year in which Weimar democracy suffered its worst early crises, with the French and Belgian occupation of the Ruhr, and massive inflation spiralling out of control. Hitler's miserable attempt to emulate Mussolini's successful march on Rome ended as a damp squib, the hoped-for 'march on Berlin' stopped dead in its tracks, still in the centre of Munich within hours of its muddled

Munich Putsch, 8–9 November 1923. A special unit of Putschists.

launch. Despite a successful propaganda stand by Hitler at his trial, which received national publicity, by 1924 the early troubles of the Weimar Republic seemed effectively over, the chances of a Hitler ever becoming German Chancellor effectively nil.

In the middle years of the 1920s, with inflation under control, reparations repayments renegotiated under the Dawes Plan of 1924, and considerable foreign policy successes under the long-serving Foreign Minister, Gustav Stresemann – known as a *Vernunftrepublikaner* ('Republican of conviction') – the Weimar Republic looked set for long-term stabilisation (for a recent evaluation, see Jonathan Wright, *Gustav Stresemann*, 2002). Historians dispute the extent of 'stabilisation' in Weimar's middle years, which were not entirely the 'golden twenties' they are sometimes portrayed as being; but war-time legacies, new political structures and the general turbulence of the early years do not, on their own, amount to a sufficient explanation of Weimar's eventual collapse a decade later.

How important were attacks on the system by elites?

The various weaknesses and ambiguous legacies of Weimar's difficult birth need not inevitably have caused serious problems. It was rather the ways in which they were represented (in the case of German defeat) or dealt with (in the case of reparations) that led to the real problems. Such perceptions and choices were, moreover, rooted in a wider problem: that of a lack of widespread support for democracy in principle.

The real problem of Weimar was, it is sometimes suggested, that it was a 'Republic without Republicans'. The right criticised Weimar for being an ineffective parliamentary democracy tainted by dishonourable defeat and by forms of cultural modernism; and on the left, socialists were critical of the ills of capitalism, while Communists were not committed to the democratic political system either. Thus a highly divided political culture was a key ingredient in Weimar's fragility. But we have to be very clear about where precisely to lay the blame for bringing democracy down.

The roles of key elites
Weimar democracy was ironically itself arguably a victim of a 'stab in the back' – and this precisely by those most important individuals and groups who should have shouldered the responsibility of upholding the political system.

Coalition government: A government made up of more than one party, in coalitions which, during the Weimar period, were generally very unstable.

President Paul von Hindenburg (1847–1934)
A military man – who had fought already in the Austro-Prussian War of 1866 and the Franco-Prussian War of 1870 – Hindenburg was brought out of retirement to serve in the First World War. Having scored a notable victory at the battle of Tannenberg in 1914, Hindenburg went on to play a prominent role in the war, as Field Marshal and then Army Chief of Staff. Widely popular as a military hero, despite his advanced age Hindenburg was elected President on Ebert's death in 1925, and narrowly re-elected on a second ballot in 1932. By the time he appointed Hitler Chancellor in 1933 – a mere 18 months before his own death – he was already suffering from senility.

'The real meaning of the Hitler salute': famous poster by political photomontage artist John Heartfield (1891–1968) of Hitler receiving a backhander.

The 'revolution' of 1918 was only a partial one. Many of the traditional elites – the civil service, the judiciary, the Army, teachers in universities and schools, business elites – were far from enthusiastic about the new political system, and harked back to the 'good old days' of Imperial Germany. Thus, for example, the lenient sentences meted out by judges to those found guilty of political crimes on the right contrasted strongly with the very harsh sentences given to those found guilty of similar offences on the left. The frequent changes of **coalition government** gave rise to widespread criticisms of the 'system' with its party squabbling; many thought that the real problem was the 'emergence of the masses' in a democracy, and that the old authoritarian political system had been a great deal more effective.

President Paul von Hindenburg, a military hero from the Great War, replaced Weimar's first president, Friedrich Ebert, when the latter died prematurely from appendicitis in 1925. Although constitutionally empowered to uphold the Republic, Hindenburg from the very start yearned for a more autocratic form of government. Hindenburg's use of presidential rule under Article 48 from 1930 onwards effectively brought democracy to an end well before he made the final mistake of appointing Hitler to the Chancellorship. The Army leadership, too, under General von Von Schleicher from 1926, held anti-democratic views, and was deeply committed to revision of the Treaty of Versailles. Von Schleicher was to become particularly important in the political machinations of 1932–3.

Economic elites were not on the whole convinced democrats either, associating democracy with increased power and voice for workers and trade unions. Many agrarian elites – particularly the landowners who in Prussia, known as *Junkers*, had long held a dominant political position – were severely hit by an agrarian crisis in the 1920s, which set in well before the Wall Street Crash; they also generally favoured a return to authoritarian government along the lines of Imperial Germany.

The role of big business in the rise of Hitler has been a particular focus of historical controversy. According to the orthodox Marxist interpretation, Nazism was a variant of the wider phenomenon of 'fascism', the last ditch of modern capitalism in a period of crisis. The famous John Heartfield poster, showing Hitler with his hand outstretched backwards to receive a wad of money, fed the myth that business tycoons 'paid Hitler'. However, research by Henry Ashby Turner (*German Big Business and the Rise of Hitler*, 1985) and others has revealed a far less simplistic picture.

Many businessmen were against the Weimar system of parliamentary democracy and political parties. They were against Marxism, which, like Hitler, they understood to include Social Democrats and other non-Marxist socialists as well as Bolsheviks; and they were opposed to what they saw as the power of trade unions which appeared to be guaranteed by the system. Most wanted some form of authoritarian government. In all of this, their general aims were compatible with those of Hitler.

However, this did not by any stretch of the imagination make most of them pro-Nazi. Many despised Hitler, who did not fit in well with their social circles; very few were actually supporters of the NSDAP. The handful of exceptions included the long-time financial supporter and Ruhr steelworks magnate, Fritz Thyssen; the relatively small businessman and organiser of the 'Keppler circle' of economic advisers to Hitler, Wilhelm Keppler; the right-wing President of the Reichsbank Hjalmar Schacht, who finally broke with Hitler's government in 1937; and the Cologne banker Baron Kurt von Schroeder, whose capacity to speak on behalf of the wider business community appears to have been greatly over-estimated.

After the election of 1930, however – when the NSDAP gained a surprising 18.3 per cent of the vote – and in face of the growing political and economic crisis, many businessmen began to hedge their bets. At the same time, Hitler seized the opportunity to woo the business vote, or at least to neutralise potential hostility. He had greatly benefited from association with the conservative press baron Hugenberg (leader of the **DNVP**) in campaigning against the **Young Plan** (to replace the **Dawes Plan** on reparations) in 1929. He remained associated with – though keeping some distance from – the forces of 'national opposition' in the **Harzburg Front** of 11 October 1931, and followed this up with a speech at the Düsseldorf Industry Club on 27 January 1932.

Many businessmen remained unconvinced by Hitler's (often deliberate) vagueness on economic policies, and continued to greet Nazism with a degree of scepticism. Nevertheless, in 1932, in the context of growing political crisis, attitudes were shifting. A small number of businessmen and bankers handed in a petition to Hindenburg on 19 November 1932, which falsely gave Hindenburg the impression of a far wider basis of support among this community for Hitler. Some key individuals were also involved in the final discussions of late January 1933.

Thus, while business antipathy to 'the system' was an element in the destruction of Weimar democracy, on the whole big business played much less of an active role in levering Hitler into power. Even Hitler's attempted neutralisation of the business community had a price to be paid, since it aroused disquiet among some of his own more radical supporters in the NSDAP. The difficulties of juggling the demands and interests of both radical followers and powerful traditional elites were to become increasingly evident once Hitler was in power.

The two separate strands – the disillusionment of the elites with the system of Weimar democracy, and Hitler's own pursuit of power – were increasingly flowing together. But it took conditions of major crisis for the NSDAP to become a genuinely mass party, and for the old elites to run out of alternative strategies, and to turn in desperation to Hitler.

How did the Nazis achieve political breakthrough?

In 1925, when Hitler returned to political life, the NSDAP was disintegrating into squabbling factions. He soon found a capacity to unite different wings under loyalty to his own person as undisputed Leader. Yet in the relatively stable period of the mid-1920s, the party itself was little more than a tiny drop in the complex ocean of Weimar politics: in the elections of 1928, the NSDAP scored a mere 2.6 per cent of vote, with twelve deputies in the Reichstag. Its staggering rise in the following years can only be explained in terms of the way in which it was able to exploit and benefit from the mounting economic and political crises following the Wall Street Crash of 1929.

Nazi ideology, propaganda, organisation and tactics
Most Weimar political parties appealed to the particularistic interests of different sections of the community, with material interests directly opposed to each other (conservative nationalists versus Communists, for example) or specific religious interests to defend (the Catholic Centre Party). The NSDAP, by contrast, claimed to be a *Volkspartei* ('People's Party'), capable of healing the divisions of modern society and uniting all Germans together in a harmonious 'national community'. Most Weimar parties projected a somewhat dry, dull and bureaucratic image, an image of

DNVP: The national conservative, and under Hugenberg increasingly right-wing, 'German National People's Party' (*Deutschnationale Volkspartei*).

Young Plan/Dawes Plan: The Dawes Plan of 1924 regularised Germany's reparations payments in the short term and promoted an influx of foreign loans to boost the German economy.
The **Young Plan** of 1929 was designed to be a final settlement of a much-reduced reparations bill, to be paid over a long period (59 years).

Harzburg Front: A loose right-wing grouping resulting from a meeting of nationalist opposition forces in Bad Harzburg, including the DNVP and the veterans' organisation, the *Stahlhelm*.

middle-aged men embroiled in self-serving coalition squabbles. The NSDAP by contrast appeared youthful, dynamic, and vigorous, as well as totally untainted by power and responsibility.

The NSDAP was not even saddled with any very specific policies. Nazi ideology was both grandiose and vague. Vehemently nationalist, Nazis railed against the Treaty of Versailles, the '**November criminals**', Jews and Bolshevists. On capitalism, the arguments were equally negative: against large department stores which were increasingly threatening the livelihood of small shopkeepers; against 'international finance capital', behind which allegedly lay the hand of 'international Jewry'; against all the cultural evils of 'modern capitalism', including 'decadent' jazz music, the emancipation of women, and 'degenerate' morals. At the same time the Nazis were virulently anti-Communist, and again saw the hands of Jews lurking behind Bolshevism. There was a scapegoat for everything.

> '**November criminals**': Those accused of being responsible for Germany's military defeat in November 1918.

The Nazi message was put across through well-targeted propaganda and clever organisational tactics. An extensive regional system allowed the infiltration and on occasion take-over of social and professional organisations, targeting groups such as small farmers, lawyers, doctors and teachers, women and students. In an age before television, and with slowly increasing but still limited radio ownership, personal appearances and well-orchestrated campaign meetings were of vital importance. Perhaps the first modern politician to make major use of the aeroplane to speak in as many places as possible, Hitler was able to exploit campaign meetings with enormous success, developing his oratorical powers and other tricks for heightening audience expectations.

Who voted for the NSDAP?

Yet without the economic and political crises unleashed by the withdrawal of short-term American loans from the already fragile German economy following the Wall Street Crash of 1929, the NSDAP might still have remained a fringe party. Its growing electoral support in the elections of 1930 and July 1932 was directly related to the growth of mass unemployment, and the growth of political instability, in this period.

The SPD-led Müller coalition cabinet of 1928–30 eventually fell apart over the question of whether to deal with rising unemployment by lowering unemployment benefits, or raising taxes. Müller's successor as Chancellor, Brüning, was unable to command a parliamentary majority. When, in the elections of September 1930, the NSDAP suddenly scored 18.3 per cent of the vote, and a threatening phalanx of 107 Nazi deputies

> Campaigning in front of a polling station for the presidential elections in March 1932, Berlin.

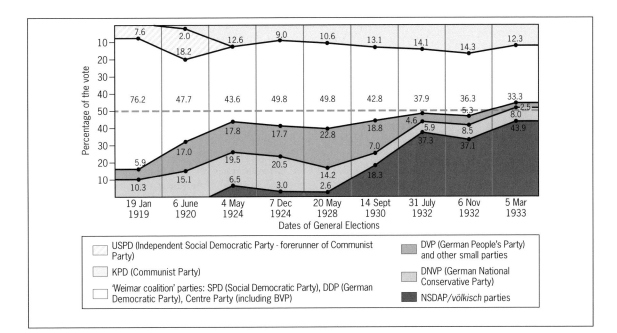

Dates of General Elections

USPD (Independent Social Democratic Party - forerunner of Communist Party)

KPD (Communist Party)

'Weimar coalition' parties: SPD (Social Democratic Party), DDP (German Democratic Party), Centre Party (including BVP)

DVP (German People's Party) and other small parties

DNVP (German National Conservative Party)

NSDAP/*völkisch* parties

The vote for the Catholic Centre Party (and its Catholic 'sister party', the BVP) remained remarkably constant. It was primarily the parties of the 'bourgeois centre' which catastrophically lost votes to the NSDAP. Had the Social Democrats (SPD) and Communists (KPD) combined forces, they would have presented stronger opposition to the Nazis.

marched into the Reichstag, many parties including the SPD decided it would be better to tolerate the Brüning government rather than risk further elections. Thus from 1930, Weimar democracy was essentially at an end, as Presidential use of Article 48 allowed Brüning to put through unpopular legislation against the wishes of the majority of members of parliament.

Brüning's economic policies have been the subject of massive controversy among historians. Brüning chose to adopt deflationary measures, preferring rising unemployment to other possible strategies for tackling the growing crisis. By 1932, six million people – around one in three of the workforce – were unemployed. Historians (notably Carl-Ludwig Holtfrerich and Knut Borchardt) disagree about the extent to which alternative policies were or were not available to Brüning, or the extent of his 'freedom of manoeuvre' (see Balderston, and Holtfrerich's essay in Ian Kershaw (ed.), *Weimar: Why did German Democracy Fail?*, 1990). But there is no doubt about the consequences: as unemployment rose, so too did support for the Nazis.

This is not because the unemployed voted for the NSDAP. As the research of Thomas Childers (*The Nazi Voter*, 1983) has shown, it was the fear of unemployment, rather than unemployment itself, which tended to make people look to the Nazi party for ways out of the crisis. The NSDAP vote was concentrated particularly among the agrarian and small-town lower middle classes, in the predominantly Protestant areas of northern and eastern Germany; in other words, among those who still had something to lose, and who feared loss of social status. Catholics tended to remain loyal to the Catholic Centre party; and the workers who were laid off first, and hence were unemployed, tended to remain loyal to the traditional parties of the working class, the SPD and KPD. The NSDAP appears to have benefited from what Larry Eugene Jones (*German Liberalism and the Dissolution of the Weimar Party System*, 1988) has called the 'collapse of the bourgeois middle'. While never genuinely representing the whole 'national community', the NSDAP nevertheless was able to mobilise a relatively wide cross-section of society in times of crisis. At its peak, it drew not only on the core voters mentioned above, but also garnered significant support among some sections of the working class – particularly those in small enterprises who had not been organised in unions or other workers' movements – and among the middle and professional classes.

The Brüning government fell, not because of increased support for Nazism – there was no further general election during Brüning's Chancellorship – but because Brüning lost the support of President Hindenburg (in part because of Brüning's mismanagement of Hindenburg's campaign to stand again as President when his seven-year term came to an end in 1932). Brüning's successor, Franz von Papen, was totally unable to cobble together any kind of parliamentary support. In the elections of July 1932, following his appointment as Chancellor, his position worsened dramatically: the NSDAP won a staggering 37.8 per cent of the vote – their highest under more or less genuinely democratic conditions, – and, with their 230 deputies in the Reichstag alongside the equally anti-democratic communist bloc, there was an anti-democratic 'wrecking majority' that could block normal parliamentary processes. The government seemed to be caught in deadlock, with Hitler as leader of the largest party.

How did Hitler finally get appointed Chancellor?

Yet Hitler was not offered the Chancellorship in the summer of 1932. The most that Hindenburg could bring himself to offer was the Vice-Chancellorship, a suggestion which Hitler greeted with derision, much to the dismay and anger of many members of his party who felt he had thrown away the best chance they would ever get. Von Papen limped on for a few more months, losing a vote of no confidence in the Reichstag on 12 September by 512 votes to 42.

Nazi fortunes apparently on the wane
During the autumn of 1932, the first signs of economic recovery began to be felt. Meanwhile, the fortunes of the Nazi party appeared to take a turn for the worse, with funds and energy exhausted by the almost constant electioneering of the year. In the elections of 6 November 1932, the Nazi vote declined to 33.1 per cent of the vote, with 196 deputies in the Reichstag. The party itself was split further by the willingness of its more radical wing, in the person of Gregor Strasser, to enter into discussions with the new and short-lived Chancellor, General von Schleicher, who had finally taken over government after playing a key role in many of the political machinations of preceding months.

Ironically, it was precisely because Hitler had been losing popular support – while yet remaining leader of the largest party in the Reichstag – and because his party appeared split and weakened, that Hitler no longer appeared quite so much of a threat. Thus, it looked more likely that he could be co-opted and 'tamed' by those who wished to harness his mass following for their own purposes.

Political deadlock: the apparent lack of any stable alternative
Von Schleicher's Chancellorship of a matter of weeks from December 1932 to January 1933 was even more short-lived than that of his predecessor. During this period, he failed to gain the support of trade unionists and the 'left wing' of the NSDAP, and at the same time managed to antagonise industrialists and agrarian elites. By January 1932, there was almost total political deadlock in Germany. Von Schleicher himself had commissioned a report (the 'Ott Report') the previous autumn which claimed to show that the Army could not control the rising levels of political violence on the streets, particularly in the event of civil war.

The final 'backstairs intrigue'
In late January 1933, the fatal combination came together. Elites were not prepared to uphold democracy at any cost; most wanted some form of

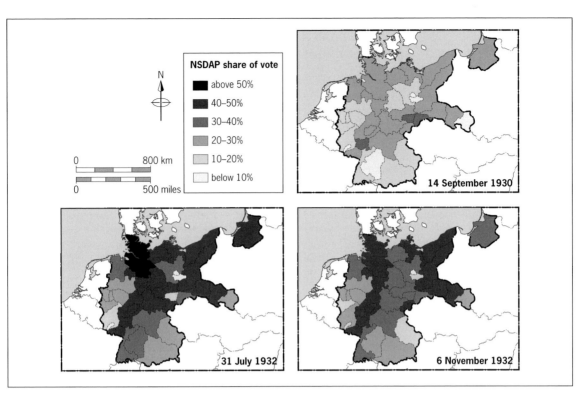

The electoral performance of the NSDAP 1930–33.

SA: The brown-shirted *Sturmabteilung* ('storm troopers'), a paramilitary organisation of the NSDAP.

Reichstag fire: The German parliament building (Reichstag) was set on fire by an arson attack which the Nazis blamed on Communists and used as a pretext for declaring a state of emergency in the run-up to the election.

authoritarian government. Hitler, as leader of the largest party, was insistent on the Chancellorship or nothing. With loss of votes, morale and membership, organisationally split, and suffering heavy debts, the NSDAP no longer seemed so dangerous. In these circumstances, an ageing Hindenburg was persuaded, by a small group including his own son and von Papen, to appoint Hitler leader of mixed cabinet in which there were only two other Nazis.

On the evening of 30 January 1933, the SA celebrated Hitler's appointment as Chancellor with a torch-lit parade through the centre of Berlin; within days, political opponents were being rounded up, brutally beaten and tortured, while Hitler unveiled his megalomaniac plans for the future. Following the **Reichstag fire** of 27 February, under conditions of intimidation and violence, the Nazi party still failed to gain an absolute majority of the vote; in the elections of 5 March 1933, the NSDAP polled just under 44 per cent of the vote. Hitler had been handed power by the old guard, while a majority of the population remained unwilling to support him. It did not take Hitler long to ensure he would no longer need to pay heed to such electoral matters.

The death of Weimar democracy: accident, suicide or murder?

The answer to this question is complex: there was an element of each. 'Accident', because had the Wall Street crash not occurred there would have been some chance for continued stabilisation over time; 'suicide', because key elites had no will to uphold democracy and took the wrong decisions, most tragically at the very end; and 'murder', because Hitler made no secret of his intention to destroy democracy, having abused the democratic system to attain power by constitutional means. On balance, Hitler had a great deal of luck as well as political ability; he was the beneficiary of developments which had taken place for reasons not of his own making.

1. Identify the main groups that supported Hitler in Germany in 1933.

2. Explain the popularity of the Nazis in Germany in 1933.

6.9 How was Nazi power consolidated after 1933?

1. Which of the reasons given in the mind map was the most important in explaining Hitler's creation of a dictatorship?

2. Can you identify any other possible reasons which explain Hitler's creation of a dictatorship?

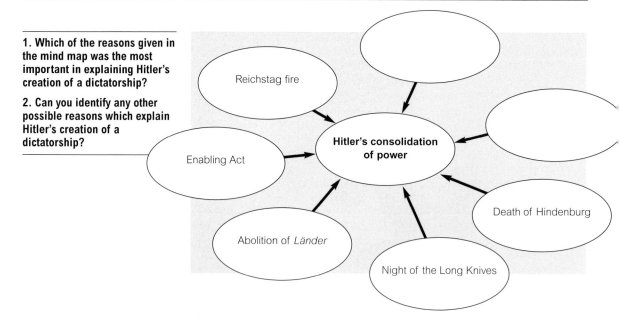

The Reichstag fire and the Enabling Act

Hermann Goering (1893–1946)
Joined the Nazi Party (1922) after distinguished war service as a pilot. President of the Reichstag (1932–45). Minister President of Prussia and Minister for Aviation (1933–45). Commander-in-Chief of the *Luftwaffe* (1934–45). Responsible for the Four-Year Plan (1936–45). Convicted and condemned at Nuremberg, he committed suicide before execution.

Despite their popular pose as a revolutionary party, the Nazis had come to power by constitutional means. Nevertheless, the years after 1933 witnessed a Nazi takeover of the machinery of the German state that was little short of revolutionary. Like Mussolini in 1923, Hitler was never likely to be satisfied with power limited by a constitution and by the presence in the state of parties and interests potentially hostile to his own. At first, his tactics for strengthening his position centred upon the Reichstag election to be held in March. He prepared for this with a massive propaganda campaign that stressed the continuity between Nazism and other forms of German conservatism, and by practical measures such as Hermann Goering's rapid extension of Nazi control over the police and civil service in Prussia. The result still left the Nazis with the direct support of only 43.9% of the population, but by then a whole new range of possibilities had opened up for Hitler.

The fire that destroyed the Reichstag building (27 February 1933) provided such a convenient crisis for the Nazis that it was supposed for many years that their agents had started it. It now seems that van der Lubbe, the Dutch Communist who was accused of the crime, really did commit it. The government may merely have exploited the happy coincidence. This powerful illustration of the 'Communist threat', upon which Nazi propaganda had long insisted, went a long way to ensuring public acceptance in the arrest of Communist deputies and in the passage of two measures central to the collapse of German democracy. The arrests themselves strengthened Hitler's position in the Reichstag. The Decree for the Protection of People and State (28 February) suspended the essential freedoms of the individual, giving the state unprecedented rights of search, arrest and censorship. The Enabling Law (23 March), which only the SPD opposed, transferred full legislative and executive power to the Chancellor (Hitler) for a period of four years. Undoubtedly, German democracy was destroyed by Hitler, but he was abetted in the crime by so-called democrats who lacked the determination to keep liberty alive.

Title page of a pamphlet placing blame for the Reichstag fire on communists, 1933.

Gleichschaltung

Long before the expiry of that four-year period, Hitler had destroyed or neutralised all those groups and institutions in a position to impose limits upon his power. This policy was referred to by the term *Gleichschaltung* (co-ordination). In some cases, the weapon used was the naked exercise of state or party power. By the Law against the New Formation of Parties, the KPD and the SPD were formally outlawed and their property seized, and all other political parties, except the Nazis, were declared illegal. By accepting this law such well-established organisations as the Catholic Centre Party effectively dissolved themselves and accepted Nazi dictatorship. In January 1934, Hitler abolished the provincial assemblies of the *Länder*. In their places he put Nazi governors (*Reichstatthalter*), and made Germany a centralised, unitary state for the first time.

Other institutions weakened their positions by attempts to compromise with the new government. The socialist trade unions had already guaranteed their non-intervention in political questions. They had also accepted the supervision of a Nazi *Reichskommissar* when, on 2 May 1933, stormtroopers occupied their offices throughout Germany, dissolved them, and began the enrolment of all labour into a German Labour Front. Other institutions lost their independence by a process of subtle infiltration. The Prussian civil service was brought under firmer control by the dismissal of nearly 30% of its officers on racial grounds or on grounds of 'incompetence'. The legal and academic professions became subject to Nazi 'fronts' or 'academies' outside which there was little hope of practice or of professional advancement.

Winning over other conservative elements in German politics

Three major elements in German society were too powerful to be directly coerced, and perhaps bear more guilt for the accommodations that they reached with Hitler. The support of German industry for Hitler had got seriously underway in 1928–29. His disciplining of the Strasser 'wing' of the party, and his subsequent alliance with the conservative Nationalist Party had convinced its leaders that the Nazis were not, as the contemporary joke had it, 'like a beefsteak, brown on the outside but red in the middle'. At this early stage, substantial financial contributions to the party were made by a variety of banking and mining interests, headed by the steel magnate Fritz Thyssen. Hitler's consistent policies of anti-socialist legislation and subsequent rearmament earned much wider support in these areas in the years immediately after his seizure of power.

The Catholic Church, too, was quick to seek an arrangement with the new regime, which now found it convenient to play down its essentially anti-Christian nature. A Concordat (July 1933) was concluded with the Nazi state in an attempt to preserve the Church's educational influence and similar privileges. In this agreement the Church authorities undertook to dissuade Catholic priests from political activity, and did much to hasten the collapse of the Centre Party. Unlike the Lateran Accords concluded with Mussolini, the Concordat represented almost complete surrender to the new political leadership. Certain elements in the Lutheran Church, by agreeing to the formation of a Reich Church (*Reichskirche*), surrendered in similarly abject fashion. In this case, however, a breakaway Confessional Church managed to survive as a symbol of Christian opposition to Nazism.

Like the major industrialists, the German army (*Reichswehr*) shared a community of interest with the Nazi *Führer*. Its commanders had little objection to his declared nationalist aims, while the realisation of those aims seemed unlikely without heavy industry to produce weapons and without soldiers to use them. Although elements of suspicion remained, the army accepted the promises that had been made to it in February and March 1933 as to its future role. While this gave Hitler the support of the army, he had to wait longer for any substantial element of direct control. The death of President Hindenburg (August 1934) not only made possible the combination of the offices of President and Chancellor in the new office of 'Führer and Chancellor', but also gave Hitler the chance to revise his relationship with the army. By imposing a new oath of allegiance upon all ranks (August 1934), he ensured their commitment directly to 'the Führer of the German Reich and People, Adolf Hitler'. The later dismissal of the War Minister, General von Blomberg (January 1938), over the scandal of his marriage to a former prostitute, and of the Army Commander-in-Chief, General von Fritsch (February 1938), over trumped-up charges of homosexuality, reinforced Hitler's control over the army at a time of increasing foreign commitment.

The Night of the Long Knives

For all these successes in 'co-ordinating' influential elements in the state into the Nazi system, Hitler could not feel wholly secure by the beginning of 1934. Ironically, the greatest surviving threat to him and to his policies came from within the Nazis' own ranks. The paramilitary SA had been formed in the early days of the movement to provide physical protection for Nazi meetings and to disrupt those of their opponents. Its attraction for

---

Ernst Röhm (1887–1934)
Röhm was an early member of the NSDAP, a close friend of Hitler, and a participant in the unsuccessful 1923 Beer Hall Putsch (which ended his career in the Army). Röhm built up the NSDAP's paramilitary wing, the SA (*Sturmabteilung* or Stormtroopers). The SA under his leadership became an ever larger and more radical force in German politics, greatly contributing to the political violence of the late Weimar years. By 1933–4, an increasingly powerful and independent SA posed a threat to the Army and to Hitler's strategies of 'legality' once in power. Röhm was thus the prime target of the 'Night of the Long Knives' in 1934. Röhm himself was arrested and shot in a prison cell after he refused to commit suicide.

former soldiers, as well as for hooligans, was enormous, and by late 1933 its numbers had swollen to some 2.5 million men. To its leader, Ernst Röhm, it represented the central weapon of the Nazi Revolution, the German equivalent of Trotsky's Red Army. It would guarantee the radical transformation of German society and, by taking over the functions of the *Reichswehr*, would guarantee the Nazification of the state. To Hitler, the SA was an embarrassing legacy of the years of struggle. It had fulfilled its street-fighting purpose and served now only to scare industrialists and conservative army officers by its radical posturing. Besides, with the SA under his command, Röhm stood as the only man in the Nazi Party realistically able to challenge the power of Hitler.

There has been much dispute among historians over the process by which Hitler reached the decision to eliminate the threat of the SA. Joachim Fest (*Hitler*, 1973), and Martin Broszat (*The Hitler State*, 1981) picture Hitler upon a deliberate collision course with Röhm since the beginning of 1934. Alan Bullock argued that Hitler would have been willing to delay, had it not been for mounting pressure from the *Reichswehr*. Another important factor was the ill-health of President Hindenburg, which made it imperative for Hitler to enjoy full *Reichswehr* support when the opportunity arose for him to take over the dead President's functions. In any case, the decision had been taken by late June when Hitler unleashed the purge known since as the 'Night of the Long Knives' (29–30 June 1934). A pretext was provided by a series of bogus SA 'revolts' in Berlin and Munich, staged by Himmler, Goering and their agents.

The estimates of the numbers murdered by SS (*Schutzstaffel*) squads, with material support from the *Reichswehr*, range from a low of 77 to a high of 401. The bulk of these were SA men, including Röhm himself, shot in prison without trial. The opportunity to settle diverse scores with old rivals was too good to miss. The dead also included General von Kahr, who had deserted Hitler in the 1923 *Putsch*, Gregor Strasser, who had long opposed him within the party, and a number of other non-Nazi political figures.

The 'Night of the Long Knives' was Hitler's most spectacular, and probably his most successful, piece of *Realpolitik*. For all the initial shock that it caused, it had eliminated the threat from the left of the party and removed important conservative interests outside the party. Less than three weeks after the event, 38,000,000 Germans gave their tacit support by accepting in a plebiscite vote Hitler's assumption of the office of '*Führer and Chancellor*'.

Schutzstaffel (SS – 'protection squad'): Paramilitary force, originally recruited as Hilter's protection squad. Subsequently entrusted with many of the main policy tasks of the Nazi regime including responsibility for the operation of the concentration camps. Headed by Heinrich Himmler.

1. What obstacles were there to Hitler's overall political control of Germany when he came to power in 1933?

2. How true is the claim that Hitler had complete control over German domestic politics by the end of 1934?

Source-based questions: The political role of the SA

SOURCE 1

Ernst Röhm, writing in June 1933, outlines his views of the role of the SA.

A tremendous victory has been won. But not absolute victory! The new state did not have to disown the bearers of the will to revolution as the November men had to do. In the new Germany the disciplined brown storm battalions stand side by side with the armed forces. But not as part of them. The *Reichswehr* has its own undisputed task: it is committed to defend the borders of the Reich. The police have to keep down the lawbreakers. Beside these stand the SA and the SS as the third power factor of the new state with special tasks, for they are the foundation pillars of the coming National Socialist State. They will not tolerate the German revolution going to sleep or being betrayed at the halfway stage by non-combatants.

If the bourgeois simpletons think that the 'national' revolution has already lasted too long, whether they like it or not, we will continue our struggle with them; if they are unwilling, without them; and if necessary, against them.

(a) Study Source 1.

What do we learn from Source I about the role that Röhm believed the SA should play within the Nazi state?
[5 marks]

(b) How did Hitler deal with the threat that Röhm and the SA posed to his own vision of Nazi policy?
[7 marks]

(c) What reasons did some elements in German politics and society have for rejecting the message put forward by Röhm, and yet still supporting the Nazi Party?
[18 marks]

6.10 How did the Nazi state impose its authority?

Centralised authority, or a confusion of administrations?

In theory, the power structure of the Nazi state was extremely simple. The far-reaching process of *Gleichschaltung* had transformed Germany into a state dominated by its single political party. 'The party,' declared Hitler in mid-1933, 'has now become the state', and that principle was legally enshrined in the Law to Ensure the Unity of Party and State (December 1933). Behind the authority of the party lay, in principle, the authority of one man. Thus, in 1939, the Nazi theorist Ernst Huber could define the basis of the Nazi constitution as follows: 'we must speak, not of state power, but of *Führer* power, if we want to describe political power in the national Reich correctly. The *Führer* power is not hemmed in by conditions and controls, and jealously guarded individual rights, but is free and independent, exclusive and without restriction.'

In reality, the smoothly functioning Nazi state was never much more than a myth, for government consisted largely of a jostling for influence between the old ministerial hierarchies and a variety of party bodies that sought to supervise or to control them. In several cases, ministers who were Nazis only in the sense of collaboration, such as Schwerin von Krosigk at the Ministry of Finance and Hjalmar Schacht at the Ministry of Economics, were highly successful in preserving the traditions of their departments. On the other hand, the Minister of the Interior, Wilhelm Frick, a Nazi himself, ultimately failed to prevent the infiltration of his

Martin Bormann (1900–1945?)
Joined the Nazi Party in 1925. Deputy to Rudolf Hess (1933–41). Personal secretary to Hitler (1941–45). Assumed to have died during the last days of the war although his body was never identified.

Alfred Rosenberg (1893–1946)
Joined the Nazis in 1919, and became one of their leading theoreticians. Editor of the Nazi newspaper *Völkische*

Beobachter (1921). Head of the party's office for foreign affairs. Minister for the occupied territories (1941–45). Condemned at the Nuremberg Trials and executed.

Joachim von Ribbentrop (1893–1946)
A late convert to membership of the Nazi Party (1932). Adviser to Hitler on foreign affairs. Ambassador to London (1936–38); Foreign Minister (1938–45). Condemned to death at Nuremberg and executed.

Heinrich Himmler (1900–45)
Himmler participated in the 1923 Beer Hall Putsch and was appointed head of the SS (*Schutzstaffel*) in January 1929. Himmler organised the purge of the SA and built up the SS, which became the key instrument of terror in the Nazi state. In 1936 Himmler became 'Reichsführer SS and Chief of the German Police in the Ministry of the Interior', thus controlling both the regular police force and the security police. During the war, he

controlled a veritable empire of power through the 'Reich Security Main Office' (RSHA), the criminal police and the Gestapo, as well as the various sections of the SS and Waffen-SS. He also oversaw and masterminded the 'Final Solution of the Jewish Question'. On being arrested by the British at the end of the war, Himmler committed suicide with a poison pill.

Gauleiters: Nazi Party officials at regional and district level, who could build up considerable local power bases.

department by the Party Chancellery under Martin Bormann. The Foreign Office found itself in competition with the Nazi Bureau for Foreign Affairs, headed by Alfred Rosenberg, and with the specialist agencies headed by Joachim von Ribbentrop, before he himself became Foreign Minister in 1938. The pattern of 'dualism, struggles over competence, and duplication of function' was repeated at local government level between local administrators and Nazi provincial chiefs (*Gauleiters*). In all cases, a high price was paid in terms of administrative efficiency.

Some have claimed that this confusion arose from Hitler's great failings, his boredom with administrative detail, and his preference for wider questions, especially in foreign affairs. It is also quite possible that Hitler saw the departmental in-fighting as a deliberate means of maintaining his personal power, being the great arbiter in any such dispute. He was satisfied with a system that enabled him to block any initiative or individual unacceptable to him.

The roles of propaganda and terror

The Nazi state had two great cohesive agents, both directly responsible to the *Führer*. One of these was the Ministry of Propaganda under the guidance of Joseph Goebbels. This reached new heights of sophistication through more complex and powerful media than had been available a generation earlier. The second body was the SS, with its secret police offshoot, the 'Gestapo' (*Geheime Staatspolizei*: Secret State Police).

Founded in 1925, but transformed four years later with the appointment of Himmler as its commander, the SS differed from the SA in several important respects. Whereas the SA was a mass organisation, relying upon force of numbers for its effect, the SS was an elite force, under Hitler's direct control. As such, its role extended rapidly once the Nazis were in power. From 1932 it dominated the party's intelligence work, from 1934 it had effective control of the nation's police system, and under the emergency laws of 1933, the SS controlled the concentration camps which sprang up to receive political opponents of the Nazi regime.

If there ever was such a thing as a Nazi state, it was primarily an organism for ensuring the maintenance of power, and the SS was at its centre. Surveying the general incoherence of Nazi administration, historian Gordon Craig concludes that 'the force that prevented the regime from

1. By what means did Hitler and the Nazi Party maintain their authority over Germany between 1933 and 1939?

2. How important was the element of terror and intimidation in the maintenance of Nazi authority in Germany in the 1930s?

3. What evidence is there to support the claim that the administration of the Nazi state was confused and incoherent?

dissolving into chaos was terror, and its instrument was the SS'. The activities of the SS therefore expanded further as war increased the need for cohesion in Nazi policy after 1939. Its members dominated the administration of the occupied territories. Its military wing, the 'Waffen SS', sought to exert more and more influence over military affairs, resurrecting the threat that the army appeared to have conquered in the 'Night of the Long Knives'.

There is no doubt that this power was hugely effective in the negative sense of destroying opposition. What it succeeded in creating now remains to be seen.

6.11 How radical were the economic changes that the Nazis brought about in Germany?

1. Which of the policies in the mind map best explains why Hitler was able to keep power from 1933?

2. Place the policies in the mind map in order of importance to explain why Hitler was so popular in Germany from 1933 to 1939.

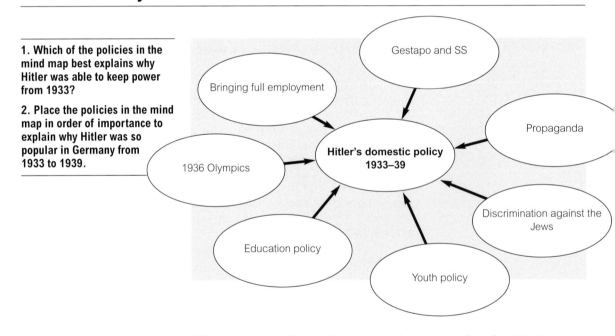

Whatever the effects of terror and propaganda, the Nazi regime depended for its survival upon the solution of the economic problems that had caused so many voters to turn to the party in 1929–32. Yet at no time, as Karl Bracher writes in *The German Dictatorship* (1978), 'did National Socialism develop a consistent economic or social theory'. In place of such a theory, Nazism had a set of fixed and sometimes contradictory commitments. Within the context of those commitments its economic achievements were considerable.

● **The drive for full employment** Firstly, to maintain popular sympathy and industrial support, an expansion of industrial activity and a dramatic reduction of unemployment were necessary. Without departing from the essential principles followed by Papen and Schleicher, the government poured money into public works. The most spectacular example of this was the construction of 7,000 kilometres of motorway (*Autobahn*). Aided by the recruitment of many of the unemployed into the Reich Labour Service, the unemployment figures fell from nearly 6 million to 2.5 million within 18 months of the Nazis' advent to power. With the subsequent expansion of heavy industry to meet the needs of rearmament, and the reintroduction of military conscription (1935), the Nazis could claim almost complete success by 1939, when unemployment figures stood at less than 200,000.

● **Nazism and the 'little man'** The second range of commitments was met with less consistency and with less obvious success. A complex programme of legislation was introduced to preserve the German peasantry from the twin curses of rising industrial prices and falling prices for their agricultural produce. All peasant debts, totalling 12 billion *Reichsmarks*, were suspended between March and October 1933, and many imported foodstuffs were subjected to higher tariffs. The Hereditary Farm Law (October 1933) gave the small-scale farmer security of tenure by forbidding the sale, confiscation, division or mortgaging of any farm of between 7.5 and 10 hectares, owned by farmers of Aryan blood. While this ensured the permanence of the peasant food producer – the very foundation of the German race in the view of many Nazi theorists – the law militated against the development of larger farming units and new farming methods. Ultimately, it worked against the self-sufficiency that was a major economic aim of the Nazi state. By 1936 the price of many basic foodstuffs had increased by up to 50% since the Nazis came to power.

The urban equivalent of the peasant, the small-scale trader or business man, gained still less from the regime that he had helped to bring to power. A number of laws – such as the Law for the Protection of the Retail Trade (May 1933) which was designed to protect the trader against the influence of the larger concerns – were far outweighed by the continued advance of 'big business'. This can be shown by the 1,500 new **cartel** arrangements between mid-1933 and the end of 1936. Whereas only 40% of German production was in the hands of monopolists in 1933, the proportion had grown to 70% by 1937.

Cartel: Economic arrangement whereby major manufacturers agree to share markets, rather than to compete for them. The aim is usually to fix prices for the benefit of the manufacturers and to guarantee levels of sales and profits.

Nazism and 'big business'

Ultimately the regime would support the larger enterprises, given that its long-term priorities were rearmament and self-sufficiency in all strategic products. This was perhaps the only economic goal towards which Nazi Germany moved with any consistency in the 1930s. The first phase of the policy was supervised by Hjalmar Schacht as President of the Reichsbank (from May 1933) and Minister of Economics (from June 1934). His major achievement was to limit the drain of Germany's foreign exchange by paying foreign debts in *Reichsmarks*. He also concluded a series of trade agreements, notably with Balkan and South American states, whereby Germany paid for its purchases in *Reichsmarks*, which thus encouraged its trade partners to purchase German goods in return. Schacht's great weakness, from the Nazi point of view, was his financial orthodoxy. His reluctance to spend more than Germany was earning threatened to put the brake on the process of rearmament. It became necessary to devise machinery for this task, which was directly under the control of the *Führer*. Thus, in August 1936, the Four-Year Plan was announced, and its direction was entrusted to Hermann Goering, a man of no economic talent, but with impeccable Nazi credentials. The primary aim of the Four-Year Plan was to achieve self-sufficiency in strategic industrial and agricultural products, either by increasing production or by developing synthetic substitutes. The plan had its important 'showpiece' successes, such as the Hermann Goering Steelworks erected at Watenstedt-

Salzgitter. It established a complicated system of controls over prices, and the distribution of raw materials, but in some important respects – in fuel, rubber and light metals – Germany remained well short of self-sufficiency in 1939.

Conclusions

By most orthodox economic criteria, the economy of Nazi Germany was chaotic. Its reserves of foreign currency remained low, and its balance of payments remained dramatically in deficit. Karl Bracher and other historians have painted a picture of the ruination of the economy by Nazi exploitation. On the other hand, B.H. Klein (*Germany's Economic Preparations for War*, 1959) denies that preparation for war totally dominated German economic activity, stressing that production of consumer goods rose steadily right up to the eve of war in 1939. Certainly, by a mixture of Schacht's clever financing and 'windfalls' such as the confiscation of Jewish property and the seizure of Austrian assets after the *Anschluss*, the economy produced impressive results.

The German economy under the Nazis

	Unemployed (million)	Coal (million tons)	Iron ore (million tons)	Pig iron (million tons)	Steel (million tons)	Arms budget (billion RM)
1932	6.042 (January) 5.392 (July)	118.6	2.6	6.1	8.2	1.9
1935	2.974 (January) 1.754 (July)	143.0	6.0	12.8	16.2	6.0
1938	1.052 (January) 0.218 (July)	186.4	12.4	18.1	21.9	17.2

1. Which sections of the German population benefited from Nazi economic policies in the 1930s?

2. Is there any justification for the claim that the Nazis brought about an economic revolution in Germany in the 1930s?

From the 1930s, Marxist historians were eager to portray the Nazi regime as a political 'front' working in effect for Germany's capitalists, and essentially serving their economic interests. According to this interpretation, the suppression of trade unions and the expansion of heavy industrial output were among the 'tasks allotted by finance capital to its Fascism' (D. Eichholtz, 1969). More recent writers on the political left, however, have been forced to accept that it was Nazi ideology, rather than capitalist interests, that held the upper hand in this relationship. T.W. Mason, for instance (*Nazism and the Third Reich*, 1972), has shown convincingly that, although there was a degree of co-operation between industry and Nazism up to 1936, thereafter all major decisions were taken with the regime's political objectives in view. Often these decisions involved consequences of which the business community heartily disapproved, as in the case of attacks upon Jewish financial and industrial institutions. The decline of Hjalmar Schacht's influence, culminating in his resignation from the Reichsbank (January 1939), typifies the dominance of Nazism in its grim alliance with capitalism. Historian Karl Bracher has supported these views in his conclusion that 'the basic principle of National Socialist economic policy was to use the traditional capitalist structure with its competent economic bureaucracy to move towards its prime objective: acceleration of rearmament'.

6.12 Did the Nazis bring about social and cultural revolutions in Germany?

Promise of radical social change probably ranked only a little lower than the prospect of economic recovery and national resurgence as a vote winner for the Nazis in 1929–32. In the event, hopes of a 'social revolution' were frustrated. The dominant classes continued in most cases to exercise their social and economic functions, and the Nazi advocates of radical change were eliminated. What change there was served not as a revolutionary end in itself, but as a means towards the broader Nazi aims of the consolidation of power and the preparation of the nation for war.

The living standards of the German worker

The emptiness of Nazi promises of a 'social revolution' should not lead one to suppose that German workers gained nothing from their industrial co-operation with Nazi strategy. Many contemporary commentators, such as R.A. Brady (1937) and F. Neumann (1942), stressed the class nature of the Third Reich and saw it primarily as a middle-class mechanism for the exploitation of the working class. More recent authorities, such as D. Schönbaum, in *Hitler's Social Revolution* (1967), have indicated instead the solid benefits that many German workers received during this period. Although they lost important rights, such as that of union representation, it may be that they were awarded prosperity as a consolation prize for the loss of political freedom. Their greatest gain was, of course, employment. Arguments about the wage levels of the Third Reich are theoretical in view of the fact that 6 million workers were not receiving a salary of any sort in 1932. In any case, there is evidence that although average wages remained around the 1932 levels, skilled workers and workers in strategic industries such as metallurgy, engineering and building benefited markedly from Nazi industrial expansion with wage increases of up to 30%. Production and sales figures for consumer goods in the immediate pre-war years suggest a distinct rise in the standard of living.

Nor should the activities of the 'Strength through Joy' (*Kraft durch Freude*) programme, for all their propaganda content, be dismissed solely as 'window dressing'. In 1938 alone, 180,000 Germans enjoyed holiday cruises under its auspices, while 10 million took holidays of one kind or another. Its activities also extended to evening classes, and a large variety of cultural and sporting activities.

Yet material rewards were often offset by declining conditions of employment. Above all, the German worker frequently put in far longer hours than any of his or her counterparts in western Europe or the USA. The industrial demands of the regime made 10% increases in hours commonplace, with rises of 25% in some specialised areas of employment. The national average working week lasted 49 hours in 1939, rising to 52 by 1943, with an increase of 150% in the number of industrial accidents in 1933–39, and a 200% increase in occupational diseases. Remarkably, such increases appear to have been broadly accepted by the majority of German workers, whether motivated by material gain or by patriotism. Whatever the motive, we have to accept the verdict of the historian Richard Grunberger: 'the working class that Karl Marx had seen as being in the van of the proletarian revolution significantly extended the lifespan of the Third Reich by exertions that came very close to giving it victory'.

The subsidiary role of women in Nazi society

A significant feature of Nazi society in the 1930s was its reactionary view of the place of women. The duties of women were defined by the party's propaganda in the slogan 'Children, Church, Kitchen' (*Kinder, Kirche, Küche*). Every effort was made to eliminate them from leading roles in political and economic life. To an extent this was an ideological aim, based upon the mystical Nazi regard for the breeding and rearing of a pure race. As Richard Grunberger also observes, 'women basked in Nazi esteem between marriage and menopause'. The policy also had a practical purpose, in that the removal of women from the competition for jobs made the full employment of the male population easier. Thus by 1936 only 37 of Germany's 7,000 university teachers were women, while married women were banned by law from the legal and medical professions, from the civil service, and from higher office in the Nazi party. Interest-free loans were made available to newlyweds who undertook that the wife would not seek employment outside the home.

The birth rate did indeed rise, from 1,200,000 births in 1934, to 1,410,000 in 1939. While the Nazis claimed this as a success for their methods, however, it remains quite likely that the increase may simply have arisen from the improving economic circumstances in contemporary Germany. In the Nazi attitude to women, as in other areas of Nazi policy, the necessities of politics came eventually to triumph over ideology. The industrial expansion of the Four-Year Plan once more made female employment unavoidable. Although professional posts remained closed to them, women once more constituted 33% of the total German workforce by 1939.

The rejection of Weimar culture

With the advent of the Nazis to power, one of the most exciting, experimental periods in Germany's cultural history gave way to one of the most stagnant. The 1920s had witnessed a period of unparalleled innovation and experiment in German art. In the aftermath of the collapse of the 'old' Germany, many of the cultural values of that 'old' society were challenged and re-interpreted. The dramatic work and production of Bertholt Brecht, the music of Kurt Weill, and the architecture of the Bauhaus movement are some examples of the inventiveness of 'Weimar' culture. It was immediately evident that artistic freedom played little part in Nazi philosophy and that cultural activity, like all other social and economic functions, was to be 'co-ordinated' to the needs of the regime. This view was summarised by Goebbels (December 1934), with the judgement that art 'remains free within its own laws of development but it is bound to the moral, social and national principles of the state'.

As in all other areas of activity, the Nazis quickly devised complex machinery to implement this 'co-ordination'. The Reich Chamber of Culture (*Reichskulturkammer* – September 1933), under the presidency of Goebbels, was the central body outside which no 'maker of culture' could legally practise his or her craft. Political undesirables and non-Aryans were automatically excluded. Cruder tactics were necessary to deal with the works of art already executed. 'Exhibitions of Shameful Art' (*Schandausstellungen*) were held, notably in Karlsruhe (1933) and in Munich (1937), with the works of **expressionists**, **cubists** and other modern movements prominent. The destruction of rejected books and paintings by fire was widespread. In Berlin in 1939, over 1,000 paintings and 3,700 drawings by modern artists were destroyed. The result of this was to rip the heart out of German art, literature and music. The list of those who abandoned their country to work abroad includes novelists and playwrights such as Thomas and Heinrich Mann, Stefan Zweig and Bertholt Brecht, the painter Oskar Kokoschka, and masters of the new art of cinema, Josef Sternberg and Fritz Lang.

The characteristics of Nazi art

Official taste in the Third Reich had three main distinguishing features.

1. The first was the rejection of **internationalism**.

---

1. In what ways were German workers affected by Nazi economic and social policies in the 1930s?

2. Is it justifiable to claim that the Nazi policies improved the living standards of many Germans in the 1930s?

Expressionists: Artists who use a style known as 'expressionism', in which reality is distorted in order to express their own emotions or inner visions.

Cubists: Artists who use the first abstract style of the 20th century in which objects, landscapes and people are represented as many-sided solids.

Internationalism: The response to cultural stimuli from abroad that had characterised the art of the Weimar period.

Philistinism: The act of being a 'Philistine', a person who has no feeling for art, or whose artistic taste is vulgar.

2. In its place, it demanded a stress upon, and a glorification of, those values that Nazism preached in other areas of policy.

3. It was frequently dominated by a conservatism, often a **philistinism**, that reflected the intellectual mediocrity of many of Germany's new leaders.

As historian Gordon Craig puts it, most of the products of this cultural 'revolution' were 'of a quality so inferior as to be embarrassing. What passed for Nazi art, when it was not a mere disguise for propaganda, was a reflection of the aesthetic ideals of a culturally retarded lower middle class, full of moral attitudinising and mock heroics and sentimentality and emphasis upon the German soul and the sacredness of the soil.' In literature one might refer to the books of Werner Beumelburg, a specialist in glorifying the spiritual experience of war, or of Hans Blunck, with his emphasis upon Nordic legend. In sculpture, Arno Breker's gigantic evocations of Teutonic manhood found particular favour with the *Führer* himself. Musical taste was dominated by the German 'giants' of the classical past, Ludwig van Beethoven and Amadeus Mozart, and by the German epics of Richard Wagner.

Propaganda and the cinema

In one discipline alone the products of the Third Reich rose above mediocrity. Although the film industry constituted in Goebbels' view 'one of the most modern and scientific methods of influencing the masses', he used it sparingly and intelligently. The most famous films of the era, such as *Hitler Youth Quex* (1933), *Jud Süss* (1940), and *Ohm Krüger* (1941), an exposé of British atrocities during the Boer War, all had clear political points to make. Yet these were subtly conveyed, and the films did have artistic merit. The most famous of contemporary German directors, Leni Riefenstahl, showed in her major works, *The Triumph of the Will* (1935), portraying the 1934 Nazi party rally at Nuremberg, and *Olympia* (1937), on the Berlin Olympic Games, that an obvious propaganda message could be conveyed with flair and originality.

Nazism and education

The theme of mediocrity is evident once more in German education under Nazism. The creation of a centralised Reich Education Ministry (May 1934) involved no major change in the structure of the educational system, but led to a radical revision of syllabuses. Great stress was now laid upon history, biology and German as the media by which the philosophy of Nazism could best be put across, while the stress upon physical fitness and development raised the gym teacher to a higher level of prestige than he or she had ever previously enjoyed.

University teaching, too, was subject to adjustments, such as the dismissal of 'unreliable' teachers, and the banning of such 'Jewish' theses as Einstein's Theory of Relativity. Between 1933 and 1938 45% of all university posts changed hands. As Nazi agencies competed with established bodies in other spheres, so too in education. Youth organisations sought to ensure the indoctrination of the young, to the great detriment of academic standards. From December 1936 it was compulsory for boys to serve in the *Jungvolk* organisation, paralleled by the *Jungmädel* organisation for girls, between the ages of 10–14. Thereafter, the boys graduated to the 'Hitler Youth' (*Hitlerjugend*) and the girls to the 'German Girls' League' (*Bund Deutscher Mädel*) until the age of 18.

1. What features were the Nazis most eager to introduce into German art and culture in the 1930s?

2. What purposes were art and education supposed to serve in Nazi society?

6.13 How did Nazi racial politics turn into genocide?

Nazi Germany was not the first or only racist state. Although Nazi racial policies were not rooted in a background of slavery, initially they bore some similarities to policies of apartheid in South Africa and segregation in the USA. Yet when Nazi policies developed into mass murder they were ultimately far more severe. Nazi policies of genocide have been compared with the mass killings perpetrated by Stalin in the USSR and Pol Pot in Cambodia, provoking considerable controversy over possible 'relativisation' of the Holocaust.

'Kristalnacht': Jewish shops damaged and plundered, November 1938

The word 'Holocaust' is something of a misnomer for the organised murder of millions of human beings by the Nazi regime. 'Holocaust', or the Jewish term *Shoah*, means literally a 'burnt sacrifice'. Yet despite being an ill-fitting term the word 'Holocaust' has come to stick. Genocide was linked to the wider attempt to create a racially pure 'folk community' (*Volksgemeinschaft*). The majority of victims of the Holocaust were murdered on grounds of race: most notably the Jews, and also almost the entire European population of Sinti and Roma (gypsies). But other groups were also targets, including homosexuals, Jehovah's Witnesses, communists, socialists, individual Christians and any others who stood up to Hitler. It is estimated that perhaps six million people – women and men, young and old – lost their lives in this systematic, bureaucratically organised or **'industrial' genocide**.

'Industrial' genocide: organised mass murder of large numbers of people by 'efficient', technologically advanced means in specially designed and constructed extermination centres or 'factories of death'

How important were Hitler's intentions within the context of the Nazi state structures?

Until the early 1960s, the Holocaust played little role in historiography. It came to prominence with the Adolf Eichmann trial in Jerusalem and the

Adolf Eichmann (1906–62)
Eichmann was in charge of Nazi emigration, evacuation and eventually extermination policies. He joined the Austrian Nazi party in 1932, and in 1934 he found a job in Himmler's SD, where by 1935 he was in charge of 'Jewish questions'. Following the *Anschluss* in 1938, Eichmann returned to Austria and ran the 'Office for Jewish Emigration' in Vienna, organising the forced exit of 150 000 Jews within eighteen months. In 1939, Eichmann was moved to the RSHA to deal with Jewish 'evacuations', and from 1941 the 'resettlement' policies that were ultimately to end in the extermination camps. Following the Wannsee Conference, Eichmann had the task of bureaucratic implementation of the 'Final Solution'. After the war, he managed to escape to Argentina; he was only finally discovered in 1960 and removed to Israel, where he stood trial in Jerusalem in 1961. He was found guilty and executed in 1962.

Auschwitz trial in Frankfurt, when the centrality of 'Hitler and his henchmen' remained more or less taken for granted. But with the rise of wider debates over Hitler's role in the structures of power, new twists developed. In the 1970s and 1980s a debate arose between the so-called intentionalists and the structuralists (functionalists).

The intentionalists emphasise Hitler's 'programme' (as in the works of Hildebrand, Hillgruber and Jaeckel): Hitler's murderous aims were translated into policies and practice as opportunities arose; there was a direct line from the anti-Semitism of *Mein Kampf* to the gas chambers of Auschwitz. In *The War against the Jews* (1975), Lucy Dawidowicz argues that the Holocaust resulted from Hitler's 'fundamental beliefs and ideological conviction'; the link 'between idea and act has seldom been as evident in human history with such manifest consistency'. Gerald Fleming claims that there was a 'single, unbroken and fatal continuum' between Hitler's early anti-Semitic outpourings and 'the liquidation orders that Hitler personally issued during the war' (*Hitler and the Final Solution*, 1985).

There is no doubt about Hitler's anti-Semitism. He shared the view, widespread among right-wing circles (and not only in Germany), that the Jews were not merely a religious group but also were racially distinct. Religious and cultural anti-Semitism had been prevalent for centuries. The racial version of anti-Semitism, a product of the new scientific theories of the nineteenth century, added a whole new dimension to the question. It meant that the Jewish Question could not be solved by conversion or assimilation: even if Jews renounced Judaism and converted to Christianity, they would still be irredeemably 'Jewish'. Hitler believed that this constituted a danger to the health of the *Volksgemeinschaft*, and compared Jews with a physical disease which had to be removed.

Hitler made numerous statements to this effect. Raging against 'Jewish Bolsheviks' and 'International Jewry' had been part of his stock-in-trade with the party faithful from the early 1920s, and repeated frequently, most notably in the hideous 'prophecy' made in a speech to the Reichstag on 30 January 1939. In subsequent references to his Reichstag 'prophecy', Hitler himself wrongly dated it to the outbreak of war in September 1939. The connection between war and the 'Jewish question' was of great significance.

But do Hitler's anti-Semitic utterances constitute evidence of a clear 'programme' that intrinsically meant, and had to mean, mass murder? And are Hitler's views a sufficient explanation of the transition from racial policies into genocide?

The functionalists argue that there was not a direct connection between Hitler's intentions and murderous outcome, but rather that there was a 'twisted road' (Karl Schleunes' phrase) to Auschwitz. Only the curious structures of power in the polycratic state explain how the crazy ideas of one man became mass murder by many.

Far from being a streamlined totalitarian state, in which Hitler's orders were simply turned into realities, functionalists argue that there were multiple, overlapping centres of power. Hans Mommsen and Martin Broszat argue that, while Hitler set the broad agenda, the 'cumulative radicalisation' of racial policy can be explained in terms of competition among underlings in ever more difficult circumstances. Genocide was the result of improvisation, of a continued search for new solutions, as the self-made problem of the 'Jewish question' became ever more acute. While not downplaying the role of Hitler, greater emphasis is given here to decision-making at the local level. In the wider context of Hitler's aim of making German-occupied Europe 'free of Jews' (*Judenfrei*, or *Judenrein*), ever more radical local initiatives were taken to 'cleanse' particular areas of Jews. Mass murder was a relatively late solution to an ever-growing

Hans Globke (1898–1973)
A civil servant in the Reich Ministry of the Interior, Globke wrote, along with Wilhelm Stuckart, the official commentary on the Nuremberg Race Laws which excluded German Jews from full citizenship rights. He was also involved in further 'legal' aspects of the persecution of Jews and the 'Germanisation' of occupied territories. Globke retained his position as a civil servant in the new post-war Federal Republic of Germany, employed in the capacity of State Secretary of the Chancellory as the chief aide to Konrad Adenauer, the first West German Chancellor, until his retirement in 1963.

'problem', rather than planned from the outset and instigated by an order from on high once conditions were right.

Theoretical interpretations have shifted somewhat in recent years. Moderate approaches have combined a focus on Hitler's intentions with an awareness of the importance of local initiatives and improvisation on the ground (examples, which disagree over detail, include the works of Philippe Burrin and Christopher Browning). Ian Kershaw has picked up on a phrase uttered by a contemporary, '**working towards the *Führer***', to combine recognition of the polycratic structures of the regime with the centrality of Hitler's role. New debates have opened up on questions such as the extent to which Nazi racial policies were the product of 'modernity', social engineering, and 'scientific' **eugenic theories**. The roles of the **planning intelligentsia** and other technocrats have been emphasised, as has the role of the Army alongside the SS.

How can we explain the 'cumulative radicalisation' of racial policies from 1933 to 1941?

While very few individuals (apart from extreme right-wing Holocaust deniers) dispute the established facts, controversies over interpretation continue to rage: revisiting the chronology is essential to explore these debates further.

Discrimination and stigmatisation in a 'racial state', 1933–7

In the early 1930s, German Jews were simply Germans who were Jewish. Many had married Christian or non-religious Germans, producing children whom Nazis categorised as '*Mischlinge*' ('those of mixed descent'). As Victor Klemperer, a Jewish German married to a non-Jewish German, noted in his diary in January 1939: 'Until 1933 and for at least a good century before that, the German Jews were entirely German and nothing else. Proof: the thousands and thousands of half- and quarter-Jews etc.' The identification of German Jews as distinctively different required a phase of stigmatisation, in the context of the wider policies of a racial state.

A boycott of Jewish shops and businesses took place at the beginning of April 1933, largely as a result of pressures on the part of Nazi party radicals. Finding that this met with popular disapproval, Hitler rapidly called off the action. Yet within days came a more legalistic approach to discrimination, in the form of the 'Law for the Restitution of the Professional Civil Service'. This excluded Jews, communists, socialists, and other 'undesirables' from a broad range of professional jobs. The legalisation of discrimination appears to have been met with widespread acquiescence and a lack of protest. In the following months, further measures to redesign German society along racial lines were taken. Compulsory sterilisation of those considered unsuitable to reproduce on grounds of supposedly hereditary diseases, disabilities and other conditions (including chronic alcoholism and 'asocial' behaviour) were introduced. Racism began to enter all areas of everyday life: hideous images of Jews represented as extremely greedy, sexually menacing, hook-nosed and untrustworthy, or metaphorically akin to dangerous germs or vermin were present not only in obvious propaganda outlets, but also in encyclopaedias, medical dictionaries, books on art or literature, and children's schoolbooks.

The Nuremberg Race Laws of 1935 illustrate the relative significance of the various pressures from party radicals, popular opinion, civil servants, and Hitler's role within a particular structure of power. By the summer of 1935 Nazi party radicals were becoming restless, while law-abiding Germans disapproved of random acts of violence. Concerned both to maintain personal popularity and to appease party radicals, Hitler resorted

'Working towards the Führer': A phrase used by contemporaries: carrying out Hitler's assumed will without being given an explicit order.

Eugenic theories: theories about the genetic or hereditary characteristics of a population, often accompanied by policies designed to 'improve' the 'stock'.

Planning intelligentsia: a term used by some historians to denote the groups involved in technical planning in relation to matters such as population policy and 'living space'.

'Mischlinge': the Nazi racist term for people of 'mixed' parentage, for example children of 'mixed marriages' where perhaps two of their four grandparents were Jewish.

to further legalisation of discrimination. At the Nuremberg party rally in September 1935, he announced the so-called Nuremberg Laws, which were hastily drafted by civil servants flown in from Berlin. With the Reich Citizenship Law, Jewish Germans were reduced to second-class citizenship. Mixed marriages were forbidden under the Law for the Protection of German Blood and German Honour, as was the employment of German women under the age of 45 in Jewish households. It then took several weeks for civil servants in Berlin to fight out among themselves the details of who precisely was to count as a Jew. Hitler typically sided with the emergent winner. The slightly more lenient definition of Jewishness won out, conforming neither to a strictly religious nor a strictly racial definition. Individuals with three or four Jewish grandparents were held to be Jews, while '*Mischlinge*' with two Jewish grandparents were considered Jewish if they practised Judaism or married a Jew, and not Jewish if they did not. Under this definition, there were approximately 502,000 full Jews and around 200,000 *Mischlinge* in Germany at this time, making up slightly over one per cent of the population (although Nazi guesses put it at just over double this figure).

In 1936, with the eyes of the world on Berlin during the Olympics, anti-Semitic polices were toned down. Foreign opinion during peace-time was very important to Hitler at this time, a factor which disappeared from the equation during war-time. Many Jews felt that perhaps the worst was over and things might revert to normal.

Radicalisation and physical degradation, 1938–9

Anti-Semitic policies soon shifted into a far more radical phase, however, with the marginalisation of conservative elites from late 1937 and the Nazification of foreign policy. The *Anschluss* of Austria in spring 1938 added a further 190,000 Jews, who found themselves at the receiving end of far more brutal treatment than German Jews had experienced; and in the expanded Reich, all Jews were now subjected to new measures of discrimination.

Passports were called in. New identification papers were marked with the letter 'J' for '*Jude*' (Jew), as well as new middle names – Israel for males, Sarah for females – to indicate Jewish identity. The Aryanisation of Jewish property – confiscation of Jewish possessions, shops and businesses – was dramatically accelerated, and Jews were reduced to an increasingly insecure existence. By the end of the year Jews were no longer able to practise law and medicine; Jewish children were excluded from German schools; Jews were banned from concert halls, museums, swimming pools, theatres, cinemas, walking in certain areas or sitting on park benches which had not been specially designated to them.

On 9 November 1938 (coincidentally the anniversary of the Beer Hall Putsch) Ernst vom Rath, who worked in the German Embassy in Paris, died as a result of an attack by a young Polish Jew called Herschel Grynszpan two days earlier. This was used as a pretext to unleash an orgy of violence against Jews, which Hitler discussed with Goebbels. Goebbels then coordinated the operation while Hitler distanced himself in public from what was represented as the people's 'spontaneous' revenge. Arson attacks on synagogues and looting of Jewish-owned department stores accompanied physical attacks on Jews in the *Kristallnacht* ('night of crystal') named after the heaps of broken glass from smashed windows. Official figures suggested that 91 Jews were killed; many more died during arrest and incarceration and hundreds committed suicide; 267 synagogues were destroyed and 7500 businesses vandalised. Jews were ordered to pay for the wanton destruction, while the proceeds of their insurance claims were confiscated by the state.

Ordinary members of the public appear to have been shocked by the violence and destruction of property.

Despite Hitler's Reichstag 'prophecy' a few weeks later, there is little evidence that a coherent policy of mass murder was on the programme at this time. In a discussion at a meeting shortly after *Kristallnacht*, Goering, Goebbels and Heydrich squabbled and failed to agree on whether Jews should be forced to wear some form of identification, whether they should have to use separate compartments in trains, and whether they should be constrained to live in separate quarters – or encouraged to emigrate.

Emigration was in fact being actively encouraged, most energetically by Eichmann's office in Vienna. However, having been made destitute by Nazi policies, few Jews could find ways of meeting the financial costs and paying the 'emigration tax'. In the Evian conference convened by US President Roosevelt in July 1938, it also became clear that while other countries were willing to express their sympathy, few were willing to accept unlimited numbers of Jews. It was thus becoming impossible for Jews to continue to live within Germany; but it was also becoming increasingly impossible for them to leave.

The search for 'solutions', 1939–41

With the outbreak of the Second World War, the situation changed. With killing going on all around, and the country in a state of war, there was a brutalisation of mentalities and a lower threshold of inhibitions to be crossed. Public opinion also mattered far less, at a time when the 'problem' appeared far greater. With the absorption of parts of Czechoslovakia in 1938–9, another 118,000 Jews had come under German jurisdiction; but the number of Polish Jews was on an altogether larger scale – nearly two million (of the more than three million Polish Jews) lived in the area occupied by Germany. Many of the *Ostjuden* ('Eastern Jews') were not at all like the assimilated or integrated Jews of Germany, but were highly distinctive in customs, dress and habits.

While mass killings of Jews did take place following the invasion of Poland, organised murder was not directed primarily against Jews: the educated Polish and political elites were the major targets. In Germany itself, the principal targets of the racial state at this time were the mentally ill and 'hereditarily diseased', who became victims of the euthanasia programme. This was authorised explicitly by Hitler in a written order of October 1939 and backdated to the outbreak of the war at the start of September; notably, it officially came to a halt in August 1941 as a result of popular protest in Germany.

By contrast, there was at this time an active search for alternative 'solutions' to the Jewish Question. The main focus was on the possibility of 'resettlement', with detailed plans for a Jewish reservation around Lublin, in Poland. Following the defeat of France in May 1940, plans were also actively considered for a Jewish reservation on the island of Madagascar, off the coast of Africa, although this foundered with the German failure to defeat Britain rapidly.

Meanwhile, Polish Jews were being herded into ever more crowded ghettoes. Starvation, illness and consequent high mortality rates served merely to exacerbate the Nazis' self-imposed 'problem', in which the Nazi metaphor of Jews as a germ or source of disease became an all-too ghastly reality. The search for 'solutions' was accompanied by rising frustration among those charged with dealing with the Jewish problem. This new climate brought about an even more radical shift.

The transition to mass extermination, 1941–2

The period following the invasion of the Soviet Union was crucial in the transition from a search for a variety of 'solutions' to the Final Solution in the form of mass murder. With the decision to launch 'Operation Barbarossa' and invade the long-term ideological enemy, the war entered a qualitatively new phase. This was not merely to be a military campaign, but also a racial and political war against 'Jewish Bolsheviks' and so-called inferior peoples. The conventional rules of warfare were abandoned. Definitive evidence such as a written 'Hitler order' unleashing the Final Solution is unlikely ever to be found, if indeed such a directive ever existed – which seems unlikely, given Hitler's awareness of the sensitivity of the issue and his experience with the euthanasia programme. On the basis of current knowledge, a number of different interpretations can be constructed, all relying to some extent on speculation and surmise.

According to the Commissary Order of June 1941, anyone considered to be even a potential enemy was to be killed outright; thus civilians could be summarily shot as potential Bolsheviks and subversives. Close behind the invading army came the special killing squads, or *Einsatzgruppen*, who had already committed atrocities in late June in Kovno, Bialystok, Lvov, and elsewhere. Contrary to the long-held myth of the honourable German Army, it is now clear that the Army also provided invaluable logistical and practical support to the work of the killing squads, and in some cases actively assisted them in their murderous tasks. Within weeks, the target had broadened: Jewish women and children as well as potential military opponents of the Nazis were being killed. On 31 July, Heydrich received a directive from Goering ordering him to prepare a 'Final Solution for the Jewish question in Europe', although the character of this directive is ambiguous – it speaks explicitly of 'emigration or evacuation' as the 'solutions' to be considered – and hence its interpretation is the subject of considerable debate. Christopher Browning argues however that Hitler probably first mooted a decision in favour of mass murder in July 1941, which was then firmed up in the autumn of 1941.

In August 1941, there was a rapid escalation of the numbers involved in killing, and in the numbers murdered in mass shootings (for example, at Riga); and both Eichmann and Himmler came to witness killings. Ian Kershaw points out that the notable variations in the numbers killed by different *Einsatzgruppen* suggest a considerable degree of leeway for local initiatives to be taken by different killing squads. He also argues that the fact that reinforcements had to be sent in suggests that the scale of the killing had neither been anticipated nor planned for in advance.

Mass murder had now begun, and a crucial threshold had been crossed. The invasion of Russia had also again dramatically increased the numbers of Jews under German domination, and hence the scale of the 'problem'.

Experience soon showed that shooting people into mass graves was less than efficient. It was relatively public and witnesses reported back what they had seen. It was also difficult to gain the compliance of those having to shoot naked women and children in cold blood, unless they had first been plied with copious quantities of alcohol. Experts from the now terminated euthanasia or 'T4' programme were brought in to give their advice. On 3 September, **Zyklon B gas** was first tested on Soviet prisoners held at Auschwitz.

Zyklon B gas: a highly poisonous gas used in the gas chambers of extermination camps such as Auschwitz. Other methods of killing, such as shooting people into mass graves, or gassing with carbon monoxide exhaust fumes in vans which had been specially designed for this purpose, were found to be less 'efficient'.

Philippe Burrin dates the decision to engage in the systematic mass murder of European Jews to the early autumn. The decision that Jews should be deported from the German Reich and the Protectorate of Bohemia and Moravia to the East was taken in mid-September, following the decision a month earlier that German Jews should be forced to wear the Jewish badge from September onwards. In October, emigration – which had in any event been very difficult – was completely prohibited. But it was not clear where Jews would be 'resettled', given problems with the Russian campaign. Already overcrowded ghettos, such as that in Lódz, began to receive ever larger numbers. Death rates from disease and starvation continued to rise, and the notion of selecting weaker Jews to be disposed of quickly no longer seemed so outrageous. On 8 December the first mass killing took place at Chelmno. Those selected from the Lódz ghetto were gassed to death.

Christian Gerlach claims the turning point was only reached in early December 1941. He distinguishes between the killings of Soviet and other Jews within the occupied territories, and the decision to deport Jews from across Europe. It was only as the war turned into a *world* war with the Japanese attack on Pearl Harbor and Germany's declaration of war on the USA, that Hitler took the ultimate decision to turn his 'prophecy' of January 1939 into murderous reality. On 12 December 1941, Hitler announced to party leaders that the Final Solution now meant genocide.

The meeting at the lakeside villa near Berlin in January 1942, known as the Wannsee conference, had originally been scheduled for early December and then postponed. It initially grew out of Heydrich's directive from Goering of the previous summer to draft a programme for the final solution, and also revisited the question of the definition of *Mischlinge*. Separate initiatives were now coordinated, and the Final Solution as a programme of mass murder moved into an altogether more terrifying phase.

A series of extermination centres were developed (Sobibor, Treblinka, Belzec, Majdanek, as well as the notorious Auschwitz II at Birkenau). Alongside their technological refinement, the Nazis also used psychological means in their implementation of mass murder. Gas chambers were disguised as shower rooms, and posters warning of the alleged dangers of lice were instrumental in calming those walking unwittingly to their death. At this stage, very large numbers were involved in the system of extermination: bureaucrats organising the deportation of Jews or constructing the train timetables; doctors involved in 'medical' experiments and 'selections'; industrialists benefiting from slave labour; technocrats dealing with population policy; SS thugs at the sadistic front line, as well as those prisoners forced to assist them. Although there were isolated uprisings, as in Warsaw, affected Jewish communities, facing almost certain defeat in face of intolerable odds, often resorted to traditions of 'anticipatory compliance' and attempts at 'alleviation'. As Raul Hilberg points out, these methods had worked tolerably well for centuries; but, in the face of this unprecedented evil, were now met by unprecedented disaster.

Every reconstruction of these events relies to a large extent on piecing

Female prisoners in barracks at Auschwitz, 1945.

Rudolf Vrba (1925–2006)
Born in Slovakia, Vrba was deported to Auschwitz in 1942. Vrba and a fellow inmate, Wetzler, miraculously succeeded in escaping in April 1944, and produced the *Vrba-Wetzler Report* with detailed information on the Holocaust. Through reports such as this and from other survivors, and news and rumour from soldiers, engineers, and other eye-witnesses at the front, the fact that 'resettlement' actually meant organised murder was widespread knowledge both among foreign governments and within Nazi Germany itself. But reports of such unthinkable atrocities were widely met with sheer disbelief. One of the minority of lucky survivors, after the war Vrba emigrated first to Israel, and subsequently to Canada, where he became a university professor.

together different fragments of evidence in the light of wider knowledge of Hitler's psychology, and that of those around him, with alternative interpretations possible for many ambiguous sources. It is also notable that all the historians mentioned here to a greater or lesser extent abandon the simple dichotomy between intentionalist and functionalist explanations. They focus rather on the constant interaction between Hitler's radical ideological goals (and fluctuating moods), on the one hand, and the wider field of forces and changing pressures in which he operated, on the other. Constant improvisation in the face of mounting problems and a narrowing of possible alternative 'solutions' provides little evidence of careful prior planning with only one possible 'programme' in mind; yet, varied initiatives did not suddenly come out of the blue, but were constantly given sanction, impetus and direction from the highest level.

To what extent were 'ordinary Germans' responsible for the Holocaust?

Immediately after the war was over, the Americans – briefly – held a notion of 'collective guilt', assuming that all Germans were bad Germans. At the same time, many Germans professed that they had 'known nothing about it', and that the post-war revelations of the atrocities 'committed in their name' came as a terrible shock. Neither of these positions is an accurate representation.

A nation of perpetrators?

Considerable controversy was occasioned by the publication in 1995 of Daniel Jonah Goldhagen's thesis, *Hitler's Willing Executioners: Ordinary Germans and the Holocaust,* which resurrected the notion of collective guilt. Making a strong distinction between 'Germans' and 'Jews', Goldhagen suggests that the explanation of the Holocaust is basically very simple: Germans killed Jews because they wanted to kill Jews. German political culture was deeply flawed by a long-standing and peculiarly virulent form of 'eliminationist anti-Semitism'.

There are all manner of theoretical, methodological and historical flaws in this highly emotive and persuasively written text. Goldhagen generalises, citing a small sample of people drawn from a cross-section of German society as 'all Germans'. He fails to explore the ways in which these 'ordinary men' – also studied by Christopher Browning, with rather different conclusions – might have been radicalised under conditions of extreme brutality and warfare. The work fails to compare them with similar perpetrators from other nationalities, such as Ukrainians, Romanians, and collaborators from the Baltic states. It reifies the 'collective mentality' of 'eliminationist anti-Semitism', suggesting that it somehow hibernated across decades of the eighteenth century when it remained 'latent' rather than empirically visible in the historical record. The highly 'culturalist' explanation in terms of a collective mentality allegedly persisting across centuries is suddenly abandoned in favour of an institutional explanation; after 1945, with the introduction of democratic political structures, Germans apparently suddenly ceased to have this anti-Semitic mentality.

It could in contrast be argued that 'ordinary Germans' were in fact radicalised by the conditions of warfare. The situational explanation suggests that ordinary people of any background can be driven to commit otherwise unthinkable atrocities under extraordinary circumstances. The 'ordinary men' of police battalions and those drafted to the front were not the ideologically committed anti-Semites of the SS units or the killing squads. It also seems, from the work of Omer Bartov, that 'ordinary Germans' had been to some degree affected by Nazi indoctrination and the pervasive ideology of anti-Semitism to which they had been exposed in preceding years. This difference between their attitudes and those of fellow killers from other backgrounds was the product of recent socialisation, not evidence of a centuries-old difference in 'collective mentality'.

Violence, legality and apathy

Saul Friedländer characterises Hitler's brand of anti-Semitism as one of 'redemptive anti-Semitism': a 'synthesis of a murderous rage and an "idealistic" goal', namely the total eradication of the Jewish race. This was common among members of the party elite, in the SS and SD, and among party radicals, but was not shared by the wider population, where 'anti-Jewish attitudes were more in the realm of tacit acquiescence or varying degrees of compliance'. (Saul Friedländer, *Nazi Germany and the Jews: Vol. 1: The Years of Persecution, 1933–39*, HarperCollins, 1997, pp. 3–4.)

During the 1930s, popular attitudes covered a wide spectrum. Hitler himself was well aware of this when he toned down his own virulent anti-Semitism in electoral campaigns before 1933. Once in power, while party radicals repeatedly demanded more violent actions, Hitler was unwilling to jeopardise his personal popularity and he called off the Jewish boycott of April 1933. He also reverted to legal measures in the Nuremberg Laws and he distanced himself from the *Kristallnacht* of 1938. The party radicals who engaged with glee on the rampages of looting, beating up and murdering of Jews were a small minority. Their criminal actions were both unleashed and sanctioned by the Nazi government, but many other Germans reacted with shame and horror to these events.

Germans had generally fewer scruples about the legalisation of discrimination. Jews could thus be stigmatised, removed from their status as German citizens with equal rights in German society, and ultimately removed from living in Germany and indeed from life itself, with only minimal protest on the part of bystanders and onlookers. News leaking out about the Holocaust was reacted to with apathy and disbelief. This stood in stark contrast to the public outcry supported by the Catholic Bishop von Galen against the euthanasia programme. Had a similar outcry been unleashed against the systematic vilification, violent maltreatment and sporadic killing of German Jews in the 1930s, the fate of European Jews might have been very different.

Kershaw points out that the persecution of the Jews 'would not have been possible without the apathy and widespread indifference which was the common response to the propaganda of hate'. It would also not have been possible 'without the silence of church hierarchies … and without the consent ranging to active complicity of other prominent sections of the German elites – the civil service bureaucracy, the armed forces, and not least leading sectors of industry' (Ian Kershaw, *Popular Opinion*, p. 372).

Hitler's own ideological goals and obsessive character were clearly central to the dynamics of the Holocaust. However, Hitler's views could only have had the impact they did within the extraordinary, quasi-feudal system of power, repression, hatred and aggression that had been constructed over the space of a very few years. This system had the active consent or compliance of the key elites, while the vast majority of 'ordinary Germans' retreated into their private spheres, primarily concerned with personal survival and matters of self-interest.

There can be no single or simple explanation for the Holocaust: neither Hitler's intentions, nor the curious structures of power, nor the alleged character of Germany's collective mentalities, can stand as easy scapegoats for this virtually incomprehensible crime.

Primo Levi (1919–87)
Born in Turin, Italy, Levi was trained as a chemist. A member of the anti-Fascist resistance in Italy, he was arrested and deported to Auschwitz in 1944. He wrote numerous books and poetry after the war, including *If this is a Man* and *The Periodic Table*. Unable finally to live with the guilt and pain of survival, he committed suicide in 1987.

6.14 To what extent was Nazi authority resisted within Germany?

NSDAP: *Nationalsozialistische Deutsche Arbeiterpartei* ('National Socialist German Workers' Party').

Sicherheitsdienst, SD ('Security Service'): the intelligence branch of the SS, under Reinhard Heydrich

**Joseph Goebbels
(1897–1945)**
Joseph Goebbels poured his intellectual energy into propaganda for the Nazi party. He joined in 1926 and took over the Berlin section of the NSDAP. In 1929 he became 'Reich Propaganda Leader', and was instrumental in the NSDAP's subsequent election successes. In March 1933 Goebbels became 'Reich Minister for Public Enlightenment and Propaganda', with total control over the press, radio and film. He played a key role in anti-Semitic events. He stayed with Hitler in the bunker to the last, and then, after poisoning his children, committed suicide alongside his wife, Magda.

Hitler was not brought to power in January 1933 on a tidal wave of popular support; nor did he 'seize power'. Rather, in the context of political stalemate and constitutional crisis, Hitler was appointed Chancellor in a mixed cabinet, by the ageing President Hindenburg. Prior to 1933, the Nazi vote had been volatile: climbing within five years from a mere 2.6 per cent in 1928 to more than one in three of the voters (37.8 per cent) at the height of economic depression and political crisis in July 1932. It then declined again to 33.1 per cent in November 1932. In January 1933, Hitler was still leader of the largest party; but even in the General Election of March 1933, the **NSDAP** failed to score more than 44 per cent of the vote.

In the following twelve years, Hitler's popularity first soared, with economic recovery and foreign policy successes, and then, with a reversal of Germany's fortunes in war, declined. Throughout the period, too, an increasingly formidable apparatus of repression and terror accompanied Nazi attempts to produce ideological conformity, and while a minority of Germans opposed Hitler in a variety of ways, none were ultimately successful.

How important were propaganda and indoctrination in producing consent?

There are difficulties with ascertaining levels of popular support in a dictatorship. While the results of rigged elections and direct votes by the controlling party in a one-party state can indicate high levels of support at certain times (as Robert Gellately argues in *Backing Hitler*), such results nevertheless have to be treated with a considerable degree of scepticism. While the regime's own reports from the security service or *Sicherheitsdienst (SD)* tended pessimistically to underestimate popular support, the reports of the Social Democratic Party in exile (SOPADE) tended, equally pessimistically but from the opposite perspective, to overestimate support. Historians have also used other types of evidence – diaries, letters, even the wording used in newspaper death notices (as in Ian Kershaw's *The Hitler Myth*) – to gauge popular opinion. Widespread voluntary cooperation in the implementation of policies and in the *Gleichschaltung* ('co-ordination') of organisations is also indicative of general agreement.

Overt propaganda
Control and manipulation of the news was of considerable importance. Joseph Goebbels, appointed Minister of Propaganda and Public Enlightenment in March 1933, rapidly sought to bring the highly diverse regional press of Germany under increasing Nazi control, through central control of editors and journalists under Max Amann's Reich Press Chamber. The Nazi newspaper, the *Völkische Beobachter*, increased in circulation and more Germans felt they needed to pay attention to it. Radio ownership expanded rapidly: by the outbreak of war, between two-thirds and three-quarters of Germans had access to a radio. Goebbels ensured not only that Nazi speeches and bombastic news bulletins were broadcast, but that there was no escape from exposure: radio broadcasts were boomed out in public places – cafés, squares – to Germans who did not possess a radio in their own homes or who might not want to listen to such bulletins.

Sophisticated visual representations were crucial. The architect Albert Speer was employed to design the buildings and townscapes of the 'master race', while 'German art' was celebrated and 'degenerate art' (by Jews, socialists and other 'undesirables') was banned and denigrated. A talented

Joseph Goebbels giving a speech in the Berlin Sports Palace on 18 February 1943, calling for a 'total war'.

young film-maker, Leni Riefenstahl, produced two famous 'documentaries': *Triumph of the Will* depicted Hitler in the context of the 1934 Nuremberg party rally, while *Olympia* deployed new cinematographic techniques to create powerful images of strength at the Berlin Olympics of 1936. The German film industry went into the mass production of light entertainment films, which far out-numbered obvious propaganda films, seeking to build up a sense of well-being. But Goebbels also knew when it was important to strike terror into people's hearts. As the devastating effects of 'total war' became all too obvious, Goebbels – most notably in his speech of February 1943 at the Berlin Sports Palace – turned to a more 'realistic' depiction of the situation and the 'Bolshevik threat' in an attempt to goad Germans into making the ultimate sacrifice for their country.

Racism was a major theme. Overt attempts at anti-Semitic propaganda were evident in films such as *Jud Süss*, about an eighteenth-century court Jew in the Duchy of Württemberg, and even more so in *Der ewige Jude* ('The eternal Jew'), with accompanying posters, and in Julius Streicher's rabidly racist magazine *Der Stürmer*. In stark contrast, there were more 'positive' images of the *Volksgemeinschaft* ('people's community') with members of the '**Aryan**' or '**master race**' in posters advertising, for example, the benefits of the *Kraft durch Freude* ('Strength through Joy') programme, or the Nazi youth organisations (*HJ* and *BdM*). Even the theme of 'sacrifice' could be made the subject of a compelling poster, as in advertisements to participate in the *Eintopf* ('One Pot') meals in support of the national economic effort.

'**Aryan**' or '**master race**': terms for an allegedly genetically superior 'race' in the Nazis' racist world view.

Thus propaganda was all around, and unavoidable. But two further elements appear to have been equally, if not more, important in producing consent.

The 'Hitler Myth' and the 'congruence of aims'
The first element is the 'Hitler myth'. As Ian Kershaw has brilliantly demonstrated, Hitler's role as charismatic *Führer* functioned as a major mechanism for cohesion. The *Führer* was projected as the saviour figure, above the fray, leading Germany onwards and upwards to a glorious future. If people were irritated by the squabbles and corruption of local NSDAP big-wigs, or annoyed by policies which adversely affected their own material interests, they could still take consolation in the belief that 'if only the *Führer* knew', all would be set to rights. The myth was carefully nurtured by Hitler, who stayed clear of day-to-day

policy-making and spats between his subordinates, and instead paid close attention not merely to the contents of his speeches but also to body language and the ways in which power was 'enacted' in rallies and other public representations.

The second element is the question of the similarities between Nazi policies and the aims of different social groups, plus the ways in which the government of the Third Reich actually succeeded in achieving widely shared aims. Popular support required more than propaganda, it was also dependent on improvements in the economic sphere and successes in foreign policy. Very few Germans shared Hitler's desire for war, although many were relieved and indeed elated by the rapid victories in the first two years of war. However, as the war progressed, the difference between ideology and reality became ever more apparent.

Defeat of the German army at Stalingrad dealt a death blow, not merely to the German military effort, but also to the Hitler myth. No amount of propaganda could disguise the truth. Hitler's personal popularity, and with it popular support for the regime began to wane well before the final defeat.

What was the role of terror and coercion?

The Nazi system of terror was the other side of the coin. Popular conceptions of the Third Reich are filled not only with images of adoring admirers of the Führer, but also of the brutality of jack-booted SS officers and horror scenes of corpses in concentration camps. After 1945, fear of Nazi repression was a convenient excuse for many Germans. But the picture is more complex.

The changing balance of forces of repression

Violence was an integral part of Hitler's rise to power: the brown-shirted SA ('*Sturmabteilung*') was effectively a private army, beating up political opponents on the streets and contributing greatly to the chaos of the closing months of the Weimar Republic – a chaos which Hitler ironically promised to solve. The immediate 'solution' to political violence was simply to outlaw political opponents and to 'legalise' only the Nazi use of force. Within weeks of Hitler's appointment as Chancellor, a system of informal prisons and labour camps was set up, with political opponents – mainly communists and socialists – being rounded up and incarcerated. The first more permanent concentration camp was opened in March 1933, at Dachau, a small town just north-west of the Bavarian capital Munich. Its opening was accompanied by much publicity, and generally favourable public reactions.

There were a number of key shifts in the balance of forces of repression in the Third Reich. The first came in 1934. The SA, under the leadership of Ernst Röhm , had grown massively in size and aspirations, and presented a growing challenge. In the uncertain conditions of 1934, with top priority being given by Hitler to rearmament, it appeared essential to retain the backing of the professional Army. In the so-called '**Night of the Long Knives**' – actually stretching over three days at the end of June and beginning of July – Ernst Röhm and other SA leaders were assassinated, along with other individuals with whom Hitler wanted to settle old scores (see pages 144–5). The mass murder was retroactively sanctioned by a law in early July. When President Hindenburg died in August, the Army, now restored to what they saw as their rightful place, swore a personal oath of allegiance to Hitler. This military sense of honour and being bound by one's oath was later used to justify obedience to Hitler. Curiously, even conservatives with such a strong belief in 'honour' had managed to swallow their scruples and had failed to protest against the blatant resort to murder.

Night of the Long Knives: the murders on 30 June 1934 (continuing until 2 July) of senior members of the SA, including its leader Ernst Röhm, and other political targets.

Heinrich Himmler with SS leaders, 1933.

In the course of the 1930s, another new power rose rapidly to prominence: the SS ('*Schutzstaffel*'). Originating as Hitler's personal bodyguard, its leader from 1929 was Heinrich Himmler, an effective empire builder who had first joined the SS in 1925 when it was but a small component of the SA. Under Himmler, the SS grew rapidly, and acquired a dedicated intelligence branch, the Security Service or SD (*Sicherheitsdienst*) led by Reinhard Heydrich.

Himmler also soon began to gain control of the regular and secret police forces, becoming police commander for Bavaria in April 1933, and Inspector of the Gestapo (*Geheime Staatspolizei*, or secret state police) in the powerful state of Prussia in April 1934. Having played a key role in the Night of the Long Knives, in July 1934 Himmler secured the independence of the SS from the SA and gained sole responsibility for running the concentration camps. In 1936, Himmler officially added the control of the conventional police forces across Germany to his empire, now boasting the title of 'Reichsführer-SS and Chief of the German Police in the Reich Ministry of the Interior'. In 1939, alongside the SS, Himmler coordinated the Gestapo, the SD, the criminal and the ordinary police forces under the umbrella of the **Reich Security Main Office (RSHA)**, headed by Heydrich. The internal organisation of the expanded SS was also increasingly specialised, with different units in charge of concentration camps, economic enterprises, educational and reproductive centres, as well as elite military units and *Einsatzgruppen* ('extermination squads').

RSHA *Reichssicherheits-hauptamt* (**Reich Security Head Office**): umbrella organisation from 1939 designed to coordinate the work of the Gestapo, the SD, and the criminal and ordinary police forces alongside the SS.

Einsatzgruppen: extermination squads following the Army behind the lines and rounding up and murdering those who were ideologically designated targets of the Nazi regime (Jews, gypsies and other 'undesirables').

Reinhard Heydrich (1904–42)

In July 1931, Heydrich joined the NSDAP and then the SS. Tall, blond and blue-eyed, he soon became Himmler's right-hand man, and from 1936 controlled the security police in the Reich. He became head of the RSHA in 1939, thus controlling the Gestapo, the criminal police and the SD. Heydrich played a major role in the 'Final Solution of the Jewish Question', directing the *Einsatzgruppen* who carried out mass killings in the Soviet Union in 1941, and convening the 'Wannsee Conference' of January 1942 to coordinate the implementation of genocide. He became Deputy Reich Protector of Bohemia and Moravia in September 1941, and died on 4th June 1942 following an attack by two members of the Czech Resistance. His assassination was hideously avenged by complete destruction of the village of Lidice where it occurred and estimates of perhaps 1300 to 4000 related murders.

Once the SS had taken control of the camp system, smaller, 'wild' camps were closed, and further camps were established. While Dachau had mainly held political prisoners, the new camps of the 1930s also took in 'asocials': not merely 'habitual criminals', but also people who simply refused to conform to Nazi societal norms, despite breaking none of the new laws. These people included Jehovah's Witnesses and homosexuals, as well as the allegedly 'work-shy' and people identified as gypsies, beggars and tramps, who could now be forced into slave labour. Ultimately, along-side these victims, the major targets of the extermination camps which were set up under the control of the SS from 1941 were Jews.

Ordinary Germans and the system of terror

Ordinary Germans were well aware of the brutal treatment received by opponents of the regime. Given the dread that this system of terror struck in the hearts of those opposed to the regime, it seems remarkable that many otherwise apolitical Germans actually welcomed the tough new line on 'criminals', the 'work-shy' and other 'asocials'. Also welcomed was the radical approach to Bolshevism, fear of which had played a large role in pre-1933 support for Hitler. Many initially felt that the wave of terror was essential to the restoration of stability. They believed that, despite the real growth in the apparatus of terror, by the mid-1930s a 'return to normality' was occurring.

Nazi terror, as Eric Johnson has shown in *The Nazi Terror: Gestapo, Jews and Ordinary Germans* (1999), was 'a selective terror' and it came in waves. Political and other opponents of the regime were among the first to be targeted and a variety of groups deemed in some way inferior or even 'unworthy of life' were to follow. A constant and vital target for the regime were the Jews. Those Germans who fell into none of these groups were largely able to ignore the repression. In *The Gestapo and German Society* (1990), Robert Gellately has shown how a relatively small Gestapo staff was even able to rely on voluntary denunciations by neighbours and colleagues. Overall, the German population was characterised by a degree of apathy.

Who opposed Hitler and why were they not more successful?

The question of dissent and opposition in Nazi Germany has been the subject not merely of historical but also political controversy. In East Germany, the allegedly leading role of communist resistance was cele-brated, with some recognition being given to socialists, Christians and others who had fought alongside the communists. In West Germany, by contrast, the role of the conservative nationalist resistance to Hitler, and in particular the July Plot of 1944, was awarded great prominence. In the course of the 1960s, however, western historians began to explore a wider range of dissent, resistance and opposition, as traditional approaches to political history were increasingly challenged. Such challenges were complemented by new developments in social history and the history of everyday life, or 'history from below'. (See M. Fulbrook, *German National Identity after the Holocaust*, 1999.)

More recent debates are rooted partly in disagreements over definition. Attempts to assassinate Hitler clearly constitute opposition in a strong sense; this is often termed 'resistance' by English-speaking historians. 'Dissent' may be disagreement with the regime, and 'non-conformity' is behaviour defined by the regime as unacceptable or illegal. But what of more mundane acts of 'refusal', such as refusal to give the 'Heil Hitler' salute, or to hang out a swastika flag? This is rather different from trying to overthrow the regime and its leader.

The German historian Martin Broszat widened debates over definition when he used the German word '*Resistenz*', or 'resistance' in the medical sense of 'immunity to infection', as in the case of Catholics or certain young people who were simply impervious to the Nazi message. His approach provoked controversy over whether it is actual behaviour and its effects, or rather motives and intentions, that are crucial to the definition of resistance. These debates stimulated a wide range of research into areas such as the varieties of grumbling and disaffection in everyday life.

Dissent and nonconformity in everyday life

Much of the low-level grumbling that went on was in defence of personal material interests (see Ian Kershaw, *Popular Opinion and Political Dissent in the Third Reich*). Peasants grumbled about the Entailed Farm Law (which sought to tie peasants to ancestral land by ensuring that farms were not sub-divided but inherited whole) and tried to get around policies controlling the sale of agricultural produce. Workers sometimes engaged in unofficial strikes and go-slows; but there was a lack of consistent opposition among the German working class, despite the best efforts of Marxist historians such as Tim Mason to find it. The existence instead of a patchy record of partial compliance and non-compliance has been explored by Alf Lüdtke and others. Periodic grumbling was perfectly compatible with support for other developments, such as foreign policy successes, and enthusiasm for the *Führer*.

Other people engaged in more explicit acts of non-conformity (see Detlev Peukert, *Inside Nazi Germany*, 1987). In towns across Germany there were small groups of generally working class young people who refused to go along with the official Hitler Youth movement: the 'Edelweiss Pirates', the 'mobs' (*Meuten*) in Leipzig and Dresden, the '*Blasen*' (a slang word for 'mob') in Munich, and the 'Deathshead gang' and 'Bismarck gang' in Hamburg. Among middle class young people there were groups who insisted on listening to and playing jazz music. Many Germans of all ages refused to give up listening to or reading the works of 'Jewish' composers and authors, or enjoying 'decadent' art; and many continued to listen to foreign radio broadcasts, make political jokes, or speak realistically – which was seen to be engaging in 'defeatism' – about the progress of the war.

These kinds of dissent were essentially demonstrative rather than effective, allowing many Germans to hibernate through the regime in a state of 'inner emigration', and illustrating the Nazi state's failure to achieve its total claims.

Organised groups and political parties

Gleichschaltung: Literally, 'putting into the same gear', or 'co-ordinating'; a term used to describe the ways in which organisations were 'brought into line' with Nazi aims and policies (or either forced to disband or outlawed).

Following the early period of *Gleichschaltung*, there were no independent institutional bases for organised opposition. The Communist Party (KPD) was first to be outlawed, followed by the Social Democratic Party (SPD), whose leaders had spoken out against the Enabling Act of 23 March. With the Concordat between Hitler and Pope, the Catholic Church received guarantees protecting religious practice, and the Catholic Centre Party dissolved itself. Similar fates befell the other political parties, and, with the 'Law against the Formation of New Parties' of 14 July 1933, the Third Reich became a one-party state.

Thousands of left-wing opponents of the regime found they were among its first targets, and were arrested and imprisoned in the early wave of terror. In the new conditions of underground organisation within the dictatorship, and following a change of line in Moscow in 1934, many left-wingers sought to transcend ideological hostilities and work together against the common enemy, but conditions were now far more difficult. Groups such as *Neubeginnen* ('New Beginning') met under extremely difficult circumstances, and were able to achieve little by way of visible effects. At a higher level, the members of the 'Red Orchestra' group working within the government, including Harro Schulze-Boysen and Arvid Harnack, sought to pass military intelligence to the Soviet Union, again with little practical effect. There was very much less that ordinary workers could do, far as they were from the levers of power: sabotaging munitions production or circulating underground leaflets served to maintain some morale. But by no means did all workers have left-wing sympathies, and denunciation and betrayal were not uncommon. It took only a few years of Nazi terror and torture to break the back of ordinary socialists and communists.

The Christian Churches

One might have thought that the institutional and moral power of the Christian Churches could have provided a strong base for principled opposition. But such opposition was in fact patchy: a few key campaigns, a few outstanding and courageous individuals, stand out against a more ambivalent picture of compromise and conformity.

Hitler sought at first to 'co-ordinate' the Churches under the Nazi umbrella, or at least render them neutral. The attempt to incorporate Protestants in the Nazi fold, as pro-Nazi *Deutsche Christen* ('German Christians') under a Reich Bishop was unsuccessful. Those pastors who found themselves in trouble with the new regime soon formed the nucleus of an anti-Nazi group, which became known as the *Bekennende Kirche* ('Confessing Church') associated with Dietrich Bonhoeffer and Martin Niemöller. Many individuals spoke out against Hitler and took up contacts with others opposed to the regime, such as those involved in the July Plot. Many, like Bonhoeffer, paid with their lives, while others suffered long periods of imprisonment. But prior to 1933 Protestants had generally been more likely to vote for the NSDAP than had Catholics (who remained loyal to the Centre Party), and after 1933 either made their peace with or even supported the regime. German Protestantism was thus deeply divided.

With some individual exceptions, Catholics were neutralised to a considerable extent by the Concordat of July 1933 between the Pope and Hitler. After this, Catholic resistance was, on the whole, defensive: for example, an energetic campaign was mounted against the Nazi proposal to remove crucifixes from schools. Perhaps the major example of at least partially successful resistance came from Bishop Count von Galen of Münster, who in August 1941 preached an outspoken sermon against Hitler's 'euthanasia' programme. Hitler, alarmed by this adverse publicity and always unwilling to risk loss of popularity, put an end to the formal programme of 'euthanasia', although killings continued on a less organised basis.

Active resistance by smaller sects, including notably Quakers, could involve little more than isolated acts of moral courage and witness. Such acts may have saved many individual lives, but were not capable of being effective against the regime in any wider sense. Jehovah's Witnesses were among the targeted victims of the regime.

Dietrich Bonhoeffer (1906–45)

A Protestant theologian and active participant in the 'Confessing Church' (*Bekennende Kirche*), Bonhoeffer put his spiritual and political energies into trying to assist all those who were persecuted by the Nazi regime. In 1939 in Britain, and again in 1942 in Sweden, Bonhoeffer sought unsuccessfully to act as an agent with foreign governments on behalf of high-placed conspirators against Hitler (including Beck and Oster). He was arrested by the Gestapo and imprisoned in 1943. Following the failure of the July Plot of 1944, Bonhoeffer was sent to Buchenwald concentration camp, and then to Flossenburg, where he was executed in April 1945. To this day, his theology has remained highly influential amongst Protestants, especially in Britain and the USA.

Groups and individuals against the state

The activities of some individuals and small groups particularly stand out. Among those who took a courageous moral stand were the Munich students, Hans and Sophie Scholl, who, along with one of their professors and a small group of friends, formed the *Weisse Rose* group ('White Rose'). They produced and distributed leaflets against the regime, and sought to make contacts with other resistance groups across Germany, but were ultimately caught, arrested, and executed in 1943.

One of the most notable individuals to act entirely on his own (the efforts of both Hitler and subsequently historians to find evidence of wider backing have drawn a blank) was the Swabian carpenter Georg Elser. Elser single-mindedly devised a plan to plant a bomb in the Munich Beer Hall, timed to go off when Hitler was positioned right next to it, delivering his annual speech commemorating the failed Beer Hall Putsch of 1923. Elser worked away, night after night, at hollowing out a pillar next to which Hitler would stand. Unfortunately, on the November night in 1939 when the bomb went off, Hitler had one of his famous lucky escapes: the weather being foggy, he had left earlier to take a train back to Berlin rather than going back by plane as originally planned. Elser, who had in the meantime attempted to escape over the border to Switzerland, was caught, imprisoned, and eventually executed in April 1945.

Many individuals assisted in hiding Jews, or seeking to reduce the burden of suffering in some way. They were generally isolated, working under difficult conditions, and easily betrayed. The activities of Oskar Schindler, a highly placed entrepreneur who was initially far from motivated by moral outrage, have been widely publicised in Spielberg's film *Schindler's List*. The apparently successful demonstrations in Berlin's Rosenstrasse by Aryan spouses against the deportation of their Jewish partners have recently been the subject of controversy among historians. Some Jews in mixed marriages were able to survive the genocide, and not only as a result of this particular protest.

Opposition in high places

In theory, those closest to Hitler were best placed to challenge his clearly murderous regime. Here, despite widespread praise, some historians point out that the record is faltering. The late emergence of opposition by leading Army members and those in government circles, among them those who had for some years supported the Nazi regime, along with their generally conservative, anti-democratic ideas of what should replace a Nazi regime, have been criticised by historians such as Hans Mommsen.

For a long time national conservatives went along with Hitler. It was only as Hitler's extreme aims began to differ more openly from those of the traditional elites, in the winter of 1937–8, that well-placed individuals in government, intelligence and Army circles – including Ludwig Beck, Hans Oster, Wilhelm Canaris, Franz Halder and Carl Goerdeler – began to think seriously about the possibility of challenging Hitler. Attempts were made to make contact with foreign governments, who tended to remain sceptical, and to discuss ways of removing Hitler from power, or even assassinating him. Following the Munich Conference of 1938, Hitler's domestic popularity was such that ideas for a **coup** were abandoned; and the dramatic military successes of the first two years of the War, alongside the problem of effectively committing treason while the Fatherland was at war, provided further obstacles to nationalist resistance. It was only when the option of an 'honourable' but inevitable defeat seemed preferable to a catastrophic defeat later, that active plans for a coup were resurrected.

Georg Elser (1903–45)

A Swabian carpenter, by late 1938 Elser single-handedly came to the view that Hitler was a dangerous man who must be removed from power. In November 1939, had it not been for Hitler's early departure following his anniversary speech at the Munich Beer Hall, Elser's assassination attempt might well have totally altered the course of history. As it was, however, Elser was arrested, imprisoned in Sachsenhausen concentration camp, and ultimately executed in Dachau in April 1945.

Ludwig Beck (1889–1944)

A professional soldier, Beck joined the Army in 1911 and served during the First World War, thereafter rising steadily in the Army hierarchy. From 1935–8 he was Chief of the Army General Staff. He became increasingly worried about Hitler's opportunist tactics and aggressive policies of wars of conquest, and about the growing influence of the Nazi Party over military affairs. Beck resigned his post in August 1938 over Hitler's plans to invade Czechoslovakia, and thereafter was highly active in the German resistance. Had the July Plot succeeded, Beck would have replaced Hitler as Head of State. Instead, however, Beck committed suicide on 20th July 1944.

Coup: A sudden violent or illegal seizure of government.

Claus Graf Schenk von Stauffenberg (1907–1944)
A devout Catholic, Stauffenberg was increasingly disturbed by the immoral character of the Nazi regime, particularly after witnessing the atrocities committed by the SS on the Eastern front. Developing an interest in socialist ideas, Stauffenberg became very active in resistance circles, comparing the ideas for a post-Hitler government of the conservative military resistance (Goerdeler, Beck) with those of the socialist and trade unionist Julius Leber. Stauffenberg devoted himself to the attempt to assassinate Hitler and if possible to replace the Nazis with an alternative government. It was Stauffenberg who unsuccessfully planted the bomb in Hitler's East Prussian headquarters on 20th July 1944. On his return to Berlin (initially unaware that the explosion had not killed Hitler), Stauffenberg was arrested and shot.

The most celebrated plot to topple Hitler, with clear plans for a post-Hitler alternative government, was the so-called 'July Plot' of 1944. Graf Schenk von Stauffenberg, sufficiently senior to have close access to Hitler, planted a bomb in a briefcase timed to go off when Hitler was meeting with military planners in his Wolf's Lair retreat in East Prussia. Despite technical problems, Stauffenberg embarked on his return to Berlin with the news of a successful explosion. Unfortunately, however, only half the explosives had detonated, and the briefcase had been moved under the protective cover of a very solid table; Hitler came away with little more than minor injuries and a ruined pair of trousers. The plotters, meanwhile, having been activated by Stauffenberg's mistaken message, were readily rounded up, along with many others who had been involved in some way with oppositional activities, and were put to death in a final wave of terror in 1944–5.

Evaluation
For long periods of time, there were common aims between the Nazi leadership and key elite groups in the economy, the Army, the civil service and among national conservatives. This only began to break down as the regime became more radical in the later 1930s. There was also much popular support for certain aspects of the regime. These were strengthened by the Hitler cult, particularly in the 'good times' of economic recovery. There was also widespread complicity in, and approval of, the regime's treatment of those seen to be potentially 'dangerous'. Outright political opposition was suppressed in a brutal manner very early on. Thereafter, dissent and resistance were isolated. Also important was the increasing fragmentation of society, with the destruction of institutional bases for resistance, and significant numbers of people concerned primarily with matters of self-interest, remaining apathetic about the fate of others.

From a 'fundamentalist' perspective, it is clear that the Nazi regime was defeated only by war. The 'societal' interpretation, by contrast, suggests that dissent and nonconformity set limits to the success of the regime's 'total claims'. Moreover, there were some important, if limited, successes in specific areas: the euthanasia programme was at least officially stopped; and, although percentages were small, significant numbers managed to survive persecution in hiding, or to escape through the assistance of courageous opponents of the regime.

6.15 Was Hitler responsible for the Second World War?

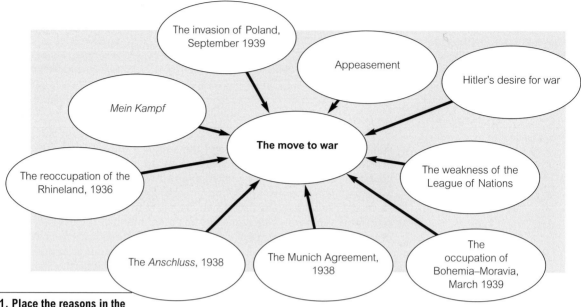

1. Place the reasons in the mind map into long-term and short-term reasons.

2. Which do you regard as the most important reason why war broke out, apart from 'Hitler's desire for war'? Explain your answer.

3. At what point in the period 1933 to 1939 do you think that war became inevitable? Give reasons for your answer.

IT takes more than a single person, and indeed more than a single country, to wage a war. Yet for twenty years or so after the outbreak of the Second World War, the explanation of the War's origins seemed simple enough, and could be condensed into one word: Hitler. An aggressive war of expansion, infused with ideas of racial superiority and the exploitation of 'inferior' peoples appeared so obviously the outcome of the world view presented by Hitler in his 1924 book, *Mein Kampf*, and the war itself appeared to represent so clearly the battle of the forces of good against evil, that it hardly seemed worth looking for further explanation. As A. J. P. Taylor put it in *The Origins of the Second World War* (1961):

> '... an explanation existed which satisfied everybody and seemed to exhaust all dispute. This explanation was: Hitler. He planned the Second World War. His will alone caused it.'

In A. J. P. Taylor's interpretation, by contrast, this Hitler-centric explanation was turned on its head. Hitler – despite his modest social class background and Austrian origins – was recast as a traditional politician pursuing conventional German foreign policy aims. Hitler was however a highly effective opportunist; thus the real problem, according to Taylor, lay in the fact that during the 1930s Hitler was presented with so many opportunities for the revision of Germany's position in Europe. Taylor's account, published in the same year as the German historian Fritz Fischer's controversial reappraisal of the origins of the First World War, raised a storm of controversy. Whether or not Taylor was right in his assessment of earlier historical explanations – which were arguably more varied and complex than he suggested – it is certainly the case that, since the early 1960s, the field has broadened massively, with lively debates over a number of areas.

German foreign policy in international context: Revisionism, *Lebensraum*, world mastery?

The Second World War was a highly complex phenomenon. It consisted not of one single war, but of many separate conflicts, with different geographical arenas and periods of conflict across the world. It was preceded by phases of aggression involving many powers, such as the Spanish Civil War in Europe and conflicts involving Japan in the Far East. Many states were also interested in some revision of the European order which had emerged from the Treaty of Versailles. Hitler's role within this broader context of international instability is the subject of some disagreement.

Was a Second World War inevitable? The legacies of the Great War

Thirty Years War thesis: The argument that the Second World War was in some respects a continuation of the First World War, with continued flashpoints and unresolved conflicts across Europe in the period 1914–45.

On the one hand, there is what has been dubbed the **Thirty Years War thesis**, a comparison with the period of sporadic warfare which raged across central Europe in the period 1618–48. According to this view, the 1919 Versailles settlement at the end of the 'Great War' of 1914–18 was problematic in so many respects that a further war appeared to be inevitable sooner or later. There had been fundamental alterations to the international balance of power, which resulted in a multiplicity of local conflicts and disputes, alongside a lack of genuinely 'national' solutions for territorial borders, as well as instabilities of the European economy. As Marshal Foch, who had been in charge of Allied armies in France in 1918, said of the Treaty of Versailles: 'This is not peace. It is an armistice for twenty years.'

There were major shifts in the wider international context and in the character and strengths of the European powers. The USA, following its late entry into the war, soon retreated into **isolationism**; it signalled dissatisfaction with the Treaty of Versailles as early as November 1919. But the Europe it abandoned was very different from that of the pre-war era. The Great War had wreaked havoc on the economies and politics of the European states most directly affected. The newly created communist Soviet Union was economically weak, internally unstable, and politically suspect as far as other powers were concerned. Italy's post-war instability eventuated in the rise of the fascist leader Mussolini, who played on a widespread feeling among Italians that in the Versailles settlement they had not received their just rewards for assisting in the defeat of Germany. Britain had both domestic social unrest and colonial concerns to worry about. Despite heightened awareness of the horrors of modern warfare after the experience of the trenches and shell-shock on the western front, Britain favoured a degree of revision to the Treaty of Versailles and resumption of friendly relations with Germany. France, also economically weakened and devastated by the loss of so many lives, shared a border with Germany. France was thus most directly concerned about enforcement of the provisions of the Treaty of Versailles, and most worried about future German capacity for aggression. With the disappearance of the Empires of Tsarist Russia, Imperial Germany, and Austria-Hungary, a raft of new 'nation states' were created in central Europe, none of which entirely conformed with notions of national boundaries. Thus there were countless disputed borders and potential flashpoints, from Vilna and Memel through Silesia and the Sudetenland to the Rhineland and South Tyrol.

Isolationism: A view prevalent in the USA that it should concern itself solely with its own domestic affairs and not be involved in European conflicts.

Finally, to this catalogue should be added the economic consequences of the war. Some were unavoidable, others (notably in the case of the German inflation of 1923), were made very much worse by deliberate government policies of exacerbating pre-existing trends. Widespread unwillingness to accept the territorial, military, political and economic provisions of the Treaty of Versailles, as well as the 'national humiliation' it allegedly entailed, was also highly visible in Germany.

If this view of general international instability is correct, Hitler was merely the person who happened to be in charge of Germany when the inevitable eruption happened. He might have added colour and detail to the shape of events, but could not be held to be the primary or sole cause

The Locarno Treaty, 1925: A treaty between Germany, France, Belgium, Italy and Britain, guaranteeing the western frontiers of Germany with France and Belgium. Although Germany concluded separate agreements with Czechoslovakia and Poland, the 1926 Berlin Treaty between Germany and Russia left Poland in a vulnerable position and the question of Germany's eastern frontiers remained open.

The League of Nations: based on US President Wilson's 'fourteen points' of 1918, this was set up in 1919 as part of the Versailles settlement 'to create mutual guarantees of the political independence and territorial integrity of States, large and small equally'. Germany was admitted in 1926, and withdrew in 1933.

Dawes Plan/Young Plan: the Dawes Plan of 1924 regularised Germany's reparations payments in the short term. The Young Plan of 1929 was designed to be a final settlement of a much reduced reparations bill, to be paid over 59 years.

Wall Street Crash of 1929: following years of rising investment on the American stock market in New York's Wall Street, a sudden loss of confidence precipitated a spiral of selling and dramatic losses in share prices in October 1929. The resulting bankruptcies occasioned massive unemployment and inaugurated years of economic depression in the USA, with reverberations across Europe, most marked in Germany, which had been dependent on short-term loans from the USA.

Revisionism: the view that the Treaty of Versailles was in need of revision.

Hitler's programme: the notion among some historians that Hitler had clearly formulated aims and plans to achieve his goals, which he then pursued single-mindedly.

Congruence of aims: specific areas over which different groups agreed with Hitler about desired ends, without necessarily accepting much, if any, of the wider ideological baggage of Nazism.

of war. Without the First World War, there would, as Kershaw has cogently argued, have been no Hitler. The logic of those adhering to the 'Thirty Years' War thesis' is to suggest that even without Hitler, there would have been a Second World War.

Against this view, many historians argue that there were in fact successful measures for stabilisation of the international system in the 1920s. The **Locarno Treaty** of 1925 regularised and recognised Germany's western borders, providing a degree of German assent to the 'Diktat' of Versailles in this area. **The League of Nations**, and Germany's entry into it in 1926, appeared to provide an international framework for the peaceful resolution of disputes. Finally, the **Dawes Plan** of 1924, and the **Young Plan** of 1929 which replaced it, seemed to offer realistic measures for dealing with reparations. Revision of the Treaty of Versailles was thus on the international agenda and peaceful adjustments were not impossible in principle. From this perspective, the international situation might well have stabilised with peaceful resolution of disputed issues, had it not been for the **Wall Street Crash of 1929**, the consequent plunge into Depression and the related rise of ideological movements, of which the most virulently aggressive was Nazism in Germany.

What did the rise of Hitler add to this unstable situation?
Revisionism now came to play an important role in a rather different way. In the context of economic crisis after 1929, widespread resentment at Germany's 'national humiliation' after Versailles could be linked with the hatred whipped up by Nazi propaganda of the so-called 'November criminals'. The Nazis claimed that the 'Bolsheviks' and 'Jews' had conspired to 'stab Germany in the back', resulting in the loss of the war.

To the traditional revisionist demands were now added Hitler's views on the 'master race' and its alleged need for *Lebensraum* ('living space'). Thus began a policy not merely of revision but also of aggressive expansion, colonisation of new territories in eastern Europe, and ultimately perhaps even world domination. In his political tract *Mein Kampf*, written while in Landsberg prison in 1924 and published in 1925, and in his unpublished *Second Book* of 1928, Hitler presented foreign policy aims which, linked intrinsically to his rabid racism, seemed to go way beyond those of traditional revisionism.

Whichever view is held of international instability, Hitler's aims did seem to add new ingredients to the equation. Yet even the role of **Hitler's programme** is disputed.

Hitler's role: master plan or effective opportunism?

If Taylor was reacting against an undue emphasis on Hitler as the primary cause, then soon there was in turn a reaction, with Hitler's intentions brought right back into centre stage. Revisionism was clearly a key element in the so-called **congruence of aims** between the Nazi leadership and conservative nationalist elites in Germany – without which Hitler would not have come to power. According to some historians, however, Hitler had clearly defined more radical goals, or a 'master plan', which continually guided his actions and informed his strategies as events unfolded.

Hitler's Programme?
The notion that Hitler was operating according to a master plan or pre-conceived programme, rooted in a consistent and strongly held *Weltanschauung* ('world view') was argued most fully by a number of German historians in the late 1960s and early 1970s.

Andreas Hillgruber argued in *Germany and the Two World Wars* (1967) that during the 1920s Hitler developed 'a firm program, to which he then single-mindedly adhered until his suicide in the Reich Chancellery on April 30, 1945.' This programme entailed a 'stage plan': first, Germany would gain control of continental Europe and colonise Russia in order to gain *Lebensraum*. Germany would then become a world power with African colonies and a strong navy (on a par with Britain, Japan and the USA). Finally, probably after Hitler's own lifetime, Germany would engage in a 'battle of the continents', fighting the USA for world domination. The scheme was further infused with racist ideology, linking Bolshevism and **'international Jewry'**, both of which were targets for destruction.

'International Jewry': Hitler's vague and ideologically loaded term for an assumed international network of Jews, who were allegedly behind both 'Bolshevism' and 'international finance capitalism'.

According to Eberhard Jaeckel in *Hitler's World View: A Blueprint for Power* (1969), by the time of writing his secret *Second Book* of 1928, Hitler had developed a 'grand design' which then remained his guiding plan. Jaeckel claims: 'Few statesmen have ever pursued their goals with greater obstinacy or tenacity' Klaus Hildebrand in *The Foreign Policy of the Third Reich* (1973), agrees that the ultimate aim of Hitler's 'Programme' (which he dignifies with a capital 'P') was and remained 'world domination based on race'.

Some historians, however, dispute the coherence of Hitler's views, pointing to the inconsistencies, gaps and poor judgements in his thinking. These historians doubt that Hitler's rag-bag of prejudices really amounted to a 'master plan', with any serious strategy for translating megalomaniac fantasies into actual practice. Nor is it easy to assess the evidence of Hitler's speeches and writings. A quotation can be found to support virtually every side of the argument; but the significance of such quotations is far more difficult to determine. A. J. P. Taylor was highly sceptical of using Hitler's words as evidence. In *The Origins of the Second World War* (1961) he claims:

> 'If his talk of peace was play-acting, so also was his talk of war. Which would become real depended on events, not on any resolution taken by Hitler beforehand.'

Moreover, Hitler did not operate in a vacuum. To identify a coherent plan from Hitler's utterances and writings is not necessarily to demonstrate that it was his own ideas that actually determined the course of German foreign policy in the 1930s.

Hitler was also to some extent a product of his time. The quest for *Lebensraum* within central and particularly eastern Europe was not unique to Nazism: concepts of some form of German domination of *Mitteleuropa* ('Central European Area') had been under active discussion among German nationalist circles for some time. Notions of access to *Lebensraum* in central Europe were built on the view that political boundaries were not natural frontiers fixed for eternity, but were rather the product of struggles for command over valuable land and resources. Similarly, a notion of racial superiority, although most virulent in Nazism, was shared by many European elites. The imperialist adventures of France and Britain were based on the view that it was entirely permissible to exploit other areas of the world, and to export the culture of the colonial power to native peoples whose own customs were held to be inferior.

Hitler's role must also be seen in the context of the changing character of government and the development of the Hitler state. There were multiple variants of foreign policy visions and views present throughout the 1930s, and to a greater or lesser extent these informed German policy-making at different moments during this time. However, there was a distinct shift (and radicalisation) of those in a position of power to translate views into policy from the mid-1930s onwards.

Mussolini welcomes Hitler to Italy during his state visit, May 1938.

'Congruence of aims'?

In the early years of the Third Reich, the Army, the Foreign Office and the Nazi Party were largely in agreement over the need for revision of the Treaty of Versailles. Plans for rearmament were discussed within the first weeks of Hitler's Chancellorship. In October 1933 Germany withdrew from the Disarmament Conference in Geneva and Hitler announced Germany's intention to withdraw from the League of Nations. By January 1934 a worried Poland concluded a ten-year non-aggression pact with Germany. But when in the summer of 1934 a crisis arose following the murder of Austrian Chancellor Dollfuss by Austrian Nazis, Mussolini's mobilisation of Italian troops at the Italian border with Austria was sufficient to diffuse the situation for the time being.

The German threat, however, continued to grow, prompting further jostling for what proved to be rather unstable alliances. On 9 March 1935, Goering revealed the existence of a German air force – which had been expressly forbidden under the Versailles Treaty – and a week later universal military conscription was announced. In April, representatives from Britain, France and Italy met at the Italian resort of Stresa and condemned German rearmament. The unanimity of the Stresa Front was, however, short-lived. Neither Britain nor Italy were happy about France concluding a treaty with communist Russia in May 1935; and the British naval agreement with Germany, concluded in June 1935, was a clear signal that Britain was prepared to condone breaches of the Treaty if this seemed in Britain's interests. In the autumn of 1935, somewhat inconsistent and vacillating responses on the part of both France and Britain to the Italian invasion of Abyssinia led ultimately to economic sanctions against Italy. These sanctions signalled the break-up of the Stresa front and, curiously, a degree of rapprochement between Germany and Italy.

The radicalisation of foreign policy

Radicalisation can be observed from 1936 onwards, with increasing Nazi control of the economy, foreign policy and military planning. Hitler gained a pivotal role in the determining of both the aims and methods of foreign policy, apparently providing clear evidence of putting a 'programme' into practice. Yet Hitler's plans were not all achieved, and his methods were often highly opportunistic, seizing favourable moments and exploiting sudden turns in events to his own advantage.

In early 1936, Hitler chose to act on the question of the Rhineland, a demilitarised zone under the provisions of the Treaty of Versailles. The remilitarisation of the Rhineland had long been on the general revisionist agenda, although traditionalists would have preferred this to be negotiated through normal diplomatic channels. Hitler, however, unsettled by loss of popular support within Germany, and concerned to maintain his image as the charismatic *Führer*, wanted a more spectacular achievement. Hitler saw a brief window of opportunity offered by Italy's invasion of Abyssinia (a war he managed to assist in prolonging by sending arms to the Abyssinian resistance to Mussolini's troops). Choosing a more high profile approach, Hitler, in March 1936 sent in German troops, confident that the French would offer little resistance. Events proved this strategy correct: the French failed to meet the fairly minimal German display of force with any

Germany's expansion, 1933–39.

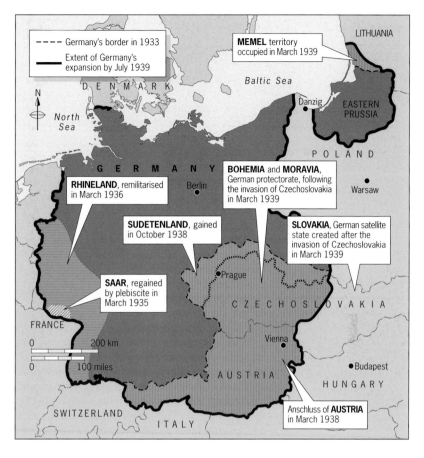

serious counter-force, and the British treated the Germans' action as little more than re-entering their 'own back garden'. Hitler scored a major propaganda coup and his domestic popularity soared.

In spring 1936, there were shortages of meat, butter, raw materials and foreign exchange in Germany. Despite these shortages, Hitler announced that he wanted to be ready for war 'within four years', with no adverse effects on domestic consumption. Against the advice of the Ministry of Economics under Hjalmar Schacht, Hitler abandoned liberal economic doctrines and authorised Goering to increase armaments production under the auspices of the new Four-Year-Plan Office, set up in August 1936. Schacht was forced to resign in November 1937.

The outbreak of the Spanish Civil War in 1936 increasingly polarised opinion in Europe. Nazi Germany and fascist Italy intervened on behalf of the nationalist rebels under Spain's General Franco, who had risen against the left-wing Spanish Republican government coalition in Spain, while

Hjalmar Schacht (1877–1970)
An economics graduate and financial expert, Schacht was in charge of stabilising the German currency in the inflationary crisis of 1923, and was involved in negotiating the Dawes Plan of 1924 and the Young Plan of 1929.

Increasingly disillusioned by Weimar politics, Schacht helped to gain support for Hitler among financial and industrial circles in 1932–3. He became Minister of Economics in 1934, contributing greatly to Germany's economic recovery and early rearmament. Disagreeing

with Goering's policies of autarchy under the Four Year Plan, Schacht resigned as Minister of Economics in 1937. In his capacity as President of the Reichsbank in 1938–9, Schacht sought to organise a plan for the emigration of German Jews. Increasing disaffection with Hitler led

to contacts with resistance circles, and following the failure of the 1944 July Plot Schacht was imprisoned. Acquitted at the Nuremberg trials, Schacht was able to enjoy a long and lucrative retirement in the Federal Republic of Germany.

Russia and Communists across Europe supported the Republicans. In the course of 1936–7, Germany and Italy became closer in the Rome-Berlin Axis, while the attempts of Hitler's Nazi agent in London, Joachim von Ribbentrop, to gain an alliance with Britain seemed to be leading nowhere. Japan now began to look like a more suitable ally.

By 1937, the German re-armament programme was causing tensions between the conflicting priorities of the Army, Navy and Air Force. Army leaders were concerned about potential social unrest; and they were rattled by Hitler's increasingly strident tone with respect to foreign policy, captured in the 'Hossbach memorandum' of November 1937. In the spring of 1938 the Army leadership was purged. War Minister Werner von Blomberg was dismissed, and the War Ministry was replaced by a new High Command of the Armed Forces (OKW) under Wilhelm Keitel a unique arrangement in a peacetime state. The Commander-in-Chief of the Army, Werner von Fritsch was ousted and replaced by General Walther von Brauchitsch. Hitler himself assumed a more prominent military role as Commander-in-Chief of the Armed Forces. The Foreign Ministry was also 'Nazified', with Foreign Minister Konstantin von Neurath replaced by Joachim von Ribbentrop.

In 1938–9 foreign policy moved into a radically new gear, with Hitler both creating and manipulating new opportunities in a rapid escalation of diplomatic and military action. Austrian Chancellor von Schnuschnigg was summoned to Hitler's Alpine retreat at Berchtesgaden in March 1938, and forced into giving the post of Austrian Minister of the Interior to a Nazi. When von Schuschnigg nevertheless called a plebiscite on whether or not to maintain Austrian independence, Hitler mobilised the German army. With no moves on the part of Italy, France or Britain to defend Austria, on 12 March 1938 German troops were able to march into Austria unopposed. Hitler returned triumphant to his home town of Linz, and announced the *Anschluss* ('union') of Germany and Austria.

Having encountered no serious international opposition to revision of German borders, Hitler next turned his attentions to the Sudetenland area of Czechoslovakia, where unrest among ethnic Germans had been stirred up by the local Nazi leader. With Hitler designating 1 October 1938 as a date for military invasion, the Army Chief of Staff, General Beck, and others in government and intelligence circles began to feel uneasy, and plans for a possible coup were seriously discussed at high levels for the first time.

Fate now intervened in the form of British Prime Minister Neville Chamberlain, whose policies of 'appeasement' have occasioned much historical controversy. Braving the rigours of modern travel by aeroplane, Chamberlain met Hitler at Berchtesgaden and again in the rapidly convened Munich Conference in September 1938. Britain, France and Italy and Germany – in the absence of representatives from both Russia and Czechoslovakia (the country directly affected) – tried to avert war by conceding to German demands. Hitler, infuriated that he had been cheated of his planned war, was nevertheless emboldened. In March 1939 German troops invaded the now militarily weakened state of Czechoslovakia and a week later they seized the Lithuanian port of Memel.

In the meantime, however, Britain had been rapidly rearming, and according to some views the time for effective rearmament had been bought by the policy of appeasement. On 31 March 1939, Britain offered a guarantee to Poland that it would come to Poland's defence if there were any further German moves of aggression. Hitler, who had failed to obtain his desired alliance with Britain, concluded a **Pact of Steel** with Mussolini in May. Russia was wooed both by the western powers (who needed Russian help to prevent German expansion eastwards), and by Hitler, who had no desire to fight a war on two fronts. In the event, in late August 1939

Wilhelm Keitel (1882–1946)
A professional soldier, Keitel took on the post of Chief of Staff of the High Command of the Armed Forces following the purge of the Army leadership in February 1938. An adulating supporter of Hitler, Keitel played a major role in ensuring that the Army assisted the SS, and justified the implementation of terror and mass murder in the occupied territories on the eastern front. He was found guilty by the Nuremberg Tribunal and executed in October 1946.

Pact of Steel: Signed on 22 May 1939, this created a military alliance between Germany and Italy in the event of war, and confirmed Italy's break with France and Britain.

the German-Soviet non-aggression pact, arranged by Joachim von Ribbentrop, with its provisions for a carve-up of Poland between Russia and Germany, gave Germany the green light for the invasion of Poland on 1 September 1939. Honouring its guarantee, on 3 September the British government announced that it was now at war with Germany.

Hitler's strategies shaped not only the outbreak but also the course of the war. His most fateful interventions were the ideologically loaded invasion of 'Bolshevik' Russia in the summer of 1941, and the declaration of war on the mighty USA following the Japanese attack on the American base at Pearl Harbor in December 1941. It is these acts that transformed a European War into a World War.

In what ways were social and economic developments and foreign policy related?

The Third Reich was inherently unstable, built on a policy of drive and dynamism. From its inception, the Third Reich was geared to prepare for war – and rearmament carried major implications for economic and social developments. These, in turn, arguably conditioned the character of foreign policy and the nature of the war which resulted. Hitler's own popularity was also closely related to developments in foreign policy.

Popular opinion and foreign policy

Hitler constantly had an eye on his personal standing with the German people: as we have seen, much of his support was rooted in the 'Hitler myth'. To remain a national saviour figure above the strains and strife of daily life required him to deliver the goods, and do so in a way that did not upset significant sections of the population. Such considerations, while never entirely deflecting Hitler from his principal aims, certainly played a role in foreign policy developments. Conversely, the developments in foreign policy affected Hitler's own standing in the popularity stakes.

Public opinion was less directly relevant to a dictatorial government than to a democratic government, as in the cases of France and Britain, whose economic policies in relation to rearmament had to have a constant eye on potential social unrest. Fear of consumer dissatisfaction nevertheless played a major role in Hitler's thinking with respect to economic policy. Domestic considerations also affected the timing and character of some foreign policy developments, as in the case of the re-militarisation of the Rhineland.

On the occasion of the Munich Conference in 1938, Hitler himself felt cheated of a planned war, but German public opinion appeared mightily relieved that imminent war had been averted and that Germany had made a significant foreign policy gain by peaceful means.

The economy and foreign policy

The German economy was deeply affected both by the drive for rearmament and the demands of war. It was further complicated by Hitler's concern not to compromise standards of living and hence his own popularity. Economic recovery had set in already in late 1932, although from 1933 it was enhanced by rearmament-related initiatives. Work creation schemes and prestige projects such as the building of the German **autobahn system** were designed not merely to tackle unemployment, but to raise a sense of national pride in the *Volksgemeinschaft*. In addition, they were important in developing a basic preparedness for war. Rearmament was not a major concern at this time, accounting for perhaps only 18 per cent of expenditure in work creation schemes in the period 1932–4; but from the mid-1930s onwards it became increasingly important.

Autobahn system: the network of motorways across Germany.

Volksgemeinschaft: the supposedly harmonious and racially defined 'people's community' or 'folk community', which Hitler claimed to be constructing in Germany in place of a modern society riven by class conflicts.

By 1936 there was a growing economic crisis, causing political tensions. The Minister of Economics, Hjalmar Schacht, wanted to scale down the escalating costs; but Hitler was unwilling either to abandon plans for rapid rearmament or to risk consumer dissatisfaction. This led directly to the break with orthodox economic planning, and the creation of Goering's new Four-Year-Plan office. This was a typical illustration of the polycratic character of the regime, where if Hitler was not satisfied with one quarter, he simply empowered someone else to deal with the issue. It also meant radically increased state intervention in the economy. From 1936 onwards, preparation for 'war within four years' meant attempting to square the economic circle: to combine a high standard of living with the demands of rapid arms production.

By 1938–9, rearmament expenditure had risen by 70 per cent above the level of the previous two years. The focus was now on autarky (self-sufficiency) rather than reliance on imports from abroad. In part this required the enhanced production of synthetics, or substitutes for raw materials which could no longer be obtained from elsewhere. In part it also entailed a shift to exploitation of the resources of other countries, including Austria after the Anschluss, and Czechoslovakia following the invasion, as well as bilateral agreements with other countries such as Romania, an important supplier of oil. Consumption as a percentage of national income declined from 71 per cent in 1928 to 59 per cent in 1938, although domestic unrest was not as great as might have been expected under a democratic regime. Certain sections of business were adversely affected by the shift to autarky and increased state intervention, although it operated to the advantage of sectors engaged in the production of synthetics, such as I. G. Farben.

Economic developments had implications for the timing and character of the war. According to the opinions of some historians, from 1936 onwards the economy became increasingly 'unhinged'. They argue that it entailed going to war sooner rather than later, and shaped the nature of the war that could be fought. In principle, the economy could in future only be sustained by a successful war of conquest, acquiring and exploiting further territories as the need arose, as Hitler himself believed. However, because of the speed and type of rearmament, Germany would not be ready for major war until the mid-1940s. Until then, all Germany could prepare for were 'lightning strikes' or a *Blitzkrieg* style of warfare evident in the early months of the war. By contrast, both Britain and France would be militarily prepared for war by 1939.

These developments also had major implications for German society. Germans in the concentration camps were deployed as slave labour, working in appalling conditions such as in the quarries of Mauthausen, or in the growing empire of SS industrial enterprises. Despite Nazi ideology on the role of women, who supposedly belonged in the spheres of 'children, kitchen, church', by 1939 52 per cent of women of working age were in employment. Increasingly, foreign labour was brought into Germany to assist in production. All these trends developed massively during the war itself.

What difference, then, did Hitler make?

Many foreign policy developments of the 1930s might have come about under any conservative nationalist and revisionist government. Rearmament and the revision of Germany's boundaries as defined in the Treaty of Versailles were shared very widely. Yet it was Hitler's interference in, and radicalisation of, foreign policy which made a crucial difference in several respects.

Hitler's foreign policy goals were a top priority for him, driving alterations to the domestic power structure. His determination to press on with rearmament at all costs, altered the balance between the Nazi party, the state and the Army. It also greatly increased state intervention in a changing economy. The rearmament programme affected the timing and character of the war which Germany ultimately fought. It hence conditioned, although it did not necessarily predetermine, the outcome of the war.

In terms of the involvement of particular combatants, Hitler failed to gain an alliance with Britain. He turned a war against Russia into one of extraordinary ideological aggression and racial hatred. He also brought the previously isolationist USA into European affairs in a way which was to be of major long-term significance for twentieth-century European and world history. Finally, it was in the midst of this conflagration that the Holocaust was unleashed.

6.16 Historical interpretation: Was Hitler a weak dictator?

The question of whether Hitler was a 'weak dictator' matters massively. Answers to this question have not been purely academic, but have been of enormous personal and political significance. The debates have taken many forms over the last sixty years, but underlying all the twists and turns of the historical controversies lies a common moral thread. A 'strong dictator' capable of realising his intentions and imposing his own will would leave little space for alternatives. On the other hand, if Hitler were a 'weak dictator', far wider circles would be implicated in questions of guilt and complicity. Debates over whether Hitler was a 'weak dictator' are thus tangled up with wider debates over collaboration and opposition, racial policy and foreign policy. In short, the question of how to evaluate Hitler's role as dictator is central to understanding the Third Reich.

Some historical controversies concern specific hypotheses which can be resolved by further empirical research and new evidence. Other historical controversies are harder to resolve because they hinge on completely different interpretations of what is essentially the same evidence. This is the case in relation to many aspects of the debates over Hitler's role in the Nazi state.

The development of the historical debates

Debates over Hitler's role began already during the Third Reich. Much of Nazi propaganda was devoted to portraying the regime as a streamlined state, with a pyramid of power culminating in the figure of the *Führer* at its peak. Yet some contemporary observers recognised that the structures of power in the Third Reich were not quite this simple, and the 'duality' of the old state structures which continued to operate alongside new Party organisations led Ernst Fraenkel, for example, to develop notions of a '*Dual State*' (1941), while Franz Neumann presented the image of a many-headed monster in his *Behemoth* (1942).

Totalitarian theories in the 1950s and 1960s
In the immediate post-war period, however, the focus on Hitler himself remained predominant. Presented as a positive image while Hitler was in power, Hitler's supremacy was simply given a negative shading after 1945. For many Germans agonising over their recent past, condemnation of Hitler as a kind of magician who had blinded the masses with his charisma and led innocent Germans astray was highly appealing. It seemed both to exonerate them from blame, and to account for Hitler's undoubted mass

Monopoly capitalism: A phrase used by Marxists for a particular stage of advanced capitalism, in which capital is increasingly concentrated in fewer and fewer hands.

Auschwitz: The largest of the Nazi concentration camps, including the infamous extermination centre at Auschwitz-Birkenau, as well as Auschwitz I, where Josef Mengele carried out his notorious 'medical' experiments, and subsidiary camps where slave labourers were worked to death for major German industrial enterprises. At the height of the killings in the summer of 1944, over 9000 people could be killed within 24 hours in the gas chambers of Auschwitz.

appeal. So too did a focus on power and oppression, and the notion that there was no alternative to carrying out *Führer-Befehl* ('Hitler's orders').

The older notion of totalitarianism was revived in the 1950s and 1960s. In Hannah Arendt's use of this term in her seminal analysis of *The Origins of Totalitarianism* (1951), the emphasis was on the dynamism of the movement, and on the mobilisation of the masses by a demonic leader, drawing attention to dictatorships of left and right, Nazism and Stalinism. The similarities between fascist and Communist dictatorships were identified rather differently in the work of Friedrich and Brzezinski (1956), who defined totalitarianism in terms of a formal list of attributes: a state with one party and one official ideology, capable of dominating the population through a monopoly of the means of propaganda (the media) and coercion (police and army) as well as control of the economy. Later critics of the concept were quick to note that these definitions were very different from one another, leading to quite different conclusions about whether Nazism or Stalinism was 'more' or 'less' totalitarian; but as a label of political critique, making a sharp distinction between democracy and dictatorship, the term had its uses.

The effective equation of Nazism and Communism under the more general concept of totalitarianism was politically convenient as a 'bridging' ideology in the West in the Cold War. (Meanwhile, in Communist East Germany a rather different notion of Nazism as a form of fascism rooted in **monopoly capitalism** was being developed; this too, by shifting blame to the 'capitalist-imperialists' and large land-owning classes, managed conveniently to exonerate the allegedly innocent German 'workers and peasants' from any blame.) According to widely held views in West Germany, many crimes had been perpetrated 'in the name of the Germans' – who allegedly had 'known nothing about it' – by 'Hitler and his henchmen'. A focus on Hitler as the almost archetypal 'strong dictator' has pervaded images of Hitler ever since, present in innumerable popular films and documentaries, as well as presenting a continuing thread in the historiography.

The emergence of notions of Hitler as 'weak dictator'
Yet, particularly from the later 1960s onwards, Western historians began to register increasing unease about this representation of Hitler's role. Historians providing evidence for the war crimes trials of the 1960s, including the famous **Auschwitz** trial, began to realise that the system of terror was not sustained by 'Hitler's orders' alone (Buchheim et al., *Anatomy of the SS – State* (1967)). A number of studies began to demonstrate that the structures of power in the Third Reich were far more complex than had previously been realised.

The notion of Hitler as strong dictator was explicitly challenged by Edward N. Peterson in his path-breaking book, *The Limits of Hitler's Power* (1969). In this detailed exploration of central and regional government, Peterson painted a picture of confusion, competition and rivalry. There were rivalries not merely between the old state apparatus and the new party institutions, but also splits and tensions within each of these, and cross-cutting tensions with and within other groups such as the Army and different sections of big business. In effect, Peterson's work amounted to a revolution in conceptions of Hitler: far from being the strong dictator of official imagery and popular imagination, Hitler was in fact a weak dictator.

The debate between structuralists (functionalists) and intentionalists
Hans Mommsen, who first started developing the notion of weak dictator in his 1960s work on civil servants in the Third Reich, also emphasised Hitler's personal insecurity, his unwillingness to take decisions, his over-dependence on popularity and willingness to agree with the last powerful

person who had talked to him. Historians such as Martin Broszat began to explore the complex, ever more chaotic structures of power, in what they termed a 'polycratic state' – a state with multiple, competing and overlapping, centres of power. This became known as the 'structuralist' approach, in which the explanatory focus was shifted to the ways the institutional structure functioned; hence, it is also sometimes termed a 'functionalist' interpretation.

Such an approach contrasts strongly with the interpretation presented by those who emphasise Hitler's intentions and 'world view' (as explored by Eberhard Jaeckel in his book *Hitler's Weltanschauung: A Blueprint for Power*, 1972). In Karl Dietrich Bracher's detailed analysis (*The German Dictatorship*, 1969) Hitler's 'programme' and ultimate goals presented the driving force in what – despite Bracher's recognition of conflicts among different power groups – remained for Bracher essentially a 'totalitarian' state. For 'Hitler-centric' historians such as Andreas Hillgruber or Klaus Hildebrand (*The Third Reich*, 1984), the policies of world conquest and racial extermination must be explained primarily in terms of Hitler's intentions. For intentionalist historians, then, Hitler remains a strong dictator.

These controversies between structuralists and intentionalists were analysed in a key contribution by Tim Mason at a conference in 1979, where the political and moral implications of different historical interpretations gave rise to a particularly heated debate. This controversy exploded in the 1980s into an extended debate on the origins of the Holocaust. There are a number of ways of evaluating these conflicting interpretations, including: changing structures of power; Hitler's leadership style; and the implementation of policies.

How did political structures develop in the process of 'cumulative radicalisation'?

The real 'seizure of power'? Gleichschaltung or co-ordination (1933–4)
The first 18 months of Hitler's rule saw the ruthless establishment of a dictatorial one-party state. This involved the systematic dismantling of the liberal-democratic constitution, the destruction of federalism and the imposition of Nazi rule in the localities, and the destruction of the organisational bases for political opposition, independent association and freedom of speech. The real *Machtergreifung* ('seizure of power') after his constitutional appointment as Chancellor does indeed initially seem to lend support to the view of Hitler as strong dictator.

Despite the political capital the Nazis made out of the Reichstag Fire of 27 February, using it to declare a state of emergency and to persecute Communists and socialists, the NSDAP failed to gain an absolute majority in the Election of 5 March 1933, polling just under 44 per cent of the vote. Nevertheless, the Enabling Act of March 1933 (the necessary two-thirds majority having been cobbled together by a combination of coercion and persuasion) allowed Hitler to change the constitution at will and to pass any legislation he wanted.

The first concentration camp for political opponents, Dachau, was opened in March. The 'Law for the Restoration of a Professional Civil Service' of April 1933 purged the professions of Jews, socialists and other potential opponents of the regime. The dismantling of local government autonomy also began with the imposition of *Reichsstatthalter* ('Reich Governors') in the *Länder* ('provinces') in the spring of 1933, and was finalised with a 'Law for the Reconstruction of the Reich' abolishing their constitutional role in January 1934. After the celebration of the traditional day of labour on 1 May 1933, on 2 May independent trade unions were abolished and labour was rapidly incorporated in Robert Ley's 'German Labour Front' (DAF). Following the ban on the Social Democratic Party in June, the other political parties dissolved themselves, and the role of the NSDAP as the only legally permitted party was enshrined in the 'Law against the Formation of New Parties' of 14 July 1933. Within six months of coming to power, Hitler appeared to have control not only over the political system and the means of coercion, but also over many aspects of social and cultural life.

The first stage of the construction of the dictatorship culminated in August 1934. Following President Hindenburg's death on 2 August, Hitler combined the roles of President and Chancellor into that of *Führer*, thus uniting the roles of head of state and head of government. In light of the beheading of the SA, including its leader, Ernst Röhm, in the Night of the Long Knives a month earlier, the Army swore a personal oath of allegiance to Hitler.

All of this makes it look like a simple case of a single-party state in which the leader of the party, Adolf Hitler, held absolute power – although, it should be noted, power sustained by compromising some of his own party's more radical interests with those of traditional authorities such as the Army. Yet – as just indicated – the realities were rather more complex. Since Hitler had come to power entirely by legal, constitutional means, he inherited the structures of a modern bureaucratic state. There was, moreover, much in this system which was essential for the running of an advanced industrial economy, and most importantly, for the preparation for war. Thus Hitler had to reach certain compromises with key traditional elites – particularly conservative nationalists in the civil service and the Army – and with powerful economic interests in order to pursue his ultimate, overriding objectives.

An unstable 'congruence of aims'? The 'dual state' (1934–7)

In the apparently 'stable' middle years, such compromises worked – but only up to a point. While the Army and the conservative nationalists had a real interest in rearmament and revision of the Treaty of Versailles, and industrialists had an interest in the suppression of the rights of labour and the return to a stable economy, there were other elements in this rather volatile equation.

On the one hand, there was repeated pressure from party activists for radical change, dynamism, continual revolution – an echo, particularly among older party members, of the pre-1933 dynamism of the party as a mobilising force. There was at the same time the continual concern of Hitler himself with his own image and popularity among the majority of the German people, requiring him to keep a constant eye on public opinion. He had no wish to be associated with the less popular actions of, for example, the Nazi *Gauleiter* in the provinces, or with unpopular policy decisions on particular issues which affected people's day-to-day lives. Hitler's key policies remained vague and essentially negative: to rid Germany of a range of 'community aliens' (defined in racist and biological terms), to attack socialists and Communists, to acquire 'living space' and make Germany great again on the international stage. He had little interest in the nitty-gritty of the day-to-day details of running a modern state and economy. Such a combination was hardly likely to produce stability for long.

In the event, what developed was a curious hybrid: an ever-changing set of Nazi party institutions and practices was superimposed on old bureaucratic administrative structures, creating growing complexity and rivalry between party and state organisations. There were personal rivalries within the party, with its essentially feudal structures, personal loyalties and individual fiefdoms. Similar rivalries were increasingly characteristic of civil service organisations too. Given Hitler's distrust of ministers meeting to confer informally with one another – the only way they could even seek to coordinate policies, as normal practices of cabinet government were discontinued – there was a lack of cooperation among the state ministries, and a lack of coordination of policy. Competition and rivalry was further exacerbated by the creation of new, hybrid institutions, and by Hitler's habit of appointing 'plenipotentiaries' (people with an almost unlimited and ill-defined brief) for particular purposes. All this seemed to lead to 'government without administration', in many respects without direction, apparently out of control.

Often Nazi institutions competed with state institutions over the same ground: for example, Goebbels' empire controlling 'Propaganda and Enlightenment' challenged the state's responsibility for Science, Education and Popular Education; while Robert Ley's German Labour Front (DAF) sought to outweigh the Ministry of Labour. In other cases, aspects of pre-1933 Nazi ideology were abandoned in favour of other goals, as with conflicting demands for social revolution and the economic needs of rearmament, creating further rivalries. Powerful personal empires could be built up through combinations of party and state offices, as in 1936 when Heinrich Himmler was appointed '*Reichsführer* SS and Chief of the German Police in the Ministry of the Interior', controlling both the regular police force and the security police (under Reinhard Heydrich).

'Cumulative radicalisation'? 1938–45

This essentially unstable situation tipped over into a more radical phase in the winter of 1937–8. Following Hitler's lengthy speech in November 1937 to the Army leadership outlining megalomaniac plans for eventual world domination – a speech captured in the 'memorandum' penned by one of those present, Hossbach – increasing disquiet was registered by military leaders. In the spring of 1938, control over military matters and foreign affairs was distinctly 'Nazified': the War Minister, Werner von Blomberg, and the Commander-in-Chief of the Army, Werner von Fritsch, were dismissed (involving personal scandals and smears on the private lives of each). Following some institutional reorganisation, they were replaced by Generals Wilhelm Keitel and Walther von Brauchitsch; Foreign Minister Konstantin von Neurath resigned and was replaced by Joachim von Ribbentrop; and Hitler himself took over general command of the Army. In 1938–9 the regime entered a distinctly more radical phase in both foreign and racial policies, including: the annexation of Austria in the *Anschluss* of March 1938; the Sudeten crisis culminating in the Munich Agreement of September 1938; and the stepping-up of discrimination and violence against Jews, the seizure of Jewish property and businesses, pressures for emigration, and the pogrom known as the **Reichskristallnacht** of 9 November 1938.

The process of radicalisation became ever more apparent after the German invasion of Poland in September 1939 provoked war in Europe. Hitler's personal control of military strategy could, with luck, produce breathtaking successes, as in the *Blitzkrieg* of the early months; but in the longer term his ideologically driven decisions were suicidal. The unprecedented brutality following the invasion of the Soviet Union in June 1941, the hubris of declaration of war on the USA following the Japanese attack on Pearl Harbor in December 1941, the unleashing of the murderous **Final Solution of the Jewish Question** – all these raise fundamental questions as to the role of Hitler's own intentions in what has variously been described as the 'twisted road to Auschwitz' and the 'German catastrophe'.

Reichskristallnacht: Literally, 'crystal night': a night of organised violence against Jewish property, including arson attacks on synagogues and the smashing of windows in Jewish department stores, followed by the arrests and imprisonment of many Jews and the demand that they foot the bill for the damage caused.

'Final solution of the Jewish question': The Nazi euphemism for the Holocaust: the fact that, in order to 'remove' Jews from Europe, Jews were being systematically murdered in very large numbers.

Does Hitler's leadership style provide evidence of strength or weakness?

Images of power

What then was Hitler's own role in this changing situation? At first glance, Hitler's style of leadership appears almost self-evidently to be that of a strong dictator. His own position within the party was unique, even in the 1920s: from his re-entry into politics in 1925 onwards, he embodied the **Movement**, and his 'Will' was frequently decisive. Once in power, the appearance of strength was massively reinforced. The presentation of Hitler's image in Nazi propaganda, such as **Leni Riefenstahl's** film of the 1934 Nuremberg Party Rally, *Triumph of the Will*, is that of the supreme dictator, capable of uniting the *Volk*, attracting the adulation of the masses, and confidently leading the German people towards their glorious destiny as 'master race'. Hitler appeared personally to embody the slogan *'Ein Volk, ein Reich, ein Führer!'* ('One People, one Empire, one Leader!').

The orchestration of ceremonial displays of power – serried ranks of the SA or the SS, the Hitler Youth organisation (*Hitlerjugend*) or the League of German Maidens (*Bund Deutscher Mädel*) – added to the image of a well-organised, stream-lined state with Hitler at its head. So too, in a very different way, did state-sponsored terror and violence right from the outset in 1933: the rounding-up and incarceration of Communists and socialists, the exclusion of Jews and political opponents from professional occupations, the enforced sterilisation of those thought to carry hereditary diseases, the suppression of independent organisations and civil rights. It is little wonder that an image of Hitler as 'strong dictator' was readily associated with a murderous regime in which, in the six peace-time years alone, as many as 12 000 Germans were convicted of high treason.

Hitler's lifestyle and the practice of government

Yet on closer inspection, the realities appear more complex. Hitler had little interest in or patience with the details of policy or the bureaucratic processes of modern government. Once the Enabling Act was passed in March 1933, there was no longer any need either for parliamentary support in the Reichstag or a presidential decree for any legislation to be approved. While Hindenburg was still alive, Hitler made some effort to go through the motions of 'normal government'; he held as many as 72 formal meetings of the cabinet in 1933. But by 1937 the number of cabinet meet-

Movement: Emphasised the dynamism of the Nazi party in contrast to other parties at this time; Hitler's image was projected as that of the saviour who would lift Germany out of the abyss.

Leni Riefenstahl (1902–2003): Film-maker, photographer and actress. Best known for her propaganda films.

Nuremberg Nazi Party rally, September 1936. These formal displays of power created an image of a powerful and well-ordered state with Hitler at its head.

ings had declined to a mere six; in 1938 there was only one such meeting, which turned out to be its last.

Hitler's own lifestyle added to the problems of efficient government: he tended to rise late, and enjoyed watching films, talking with friends, indulging in architectural planning and dreaming. He disliked the German capital, Berlin, and preferred to spend as much time as possible in his Bavarian mountain retreat at Obersalzburg, with its spectacular views across the breathtaking Alpine landscape above Berchtesgaden. Thus the routine business of government was left largely to others, often having to operate without much clear guidance on specifics.

Hitler had a contempt for the life of minor officials and civil servants (harking right back to his contempt for his own father's aspirations for him which he had rejected as a young man); he had a low regard for the law, and preferred giving oral rather than written commands. He tended to side with the last person he had spoken to, and also greatly disliked taking decisions on particular policy issues. These habits often gave rise to considerable confusion, and well-founded debates between those charged with the formation and execution of contradictory policies. Hitler then often left his underlings to fight it out among themselves, taking the view – perhaps rooted in social Darwinist notions of the 'survival of the fittest' – that the strongest would inevitably win. Routine access to Hitler became ever less possible, such that eventually whoever was fortunate enough to be able to 'catch his ear' – particularly if Hitler happened to be in a good mood at the time – and could gain Hitler's personal approval for a particular proposal was able to come out claiming it was 'Hitler's will'.

Interpretations of Hitler's leadership style in political context

How then is one to interpret this leadership style? Those who argue that Hitler was a strong dictator suggest that rivalry among underlings is evidence of a policy of divide and rule. People were ultimately dependent on Hitler's personal approval for realising their plans; they had no independent institutional basis for authority, other than Hitler's will. Thus Hitler's intentions alone were decisive. When he did not get what he wanted from one quarter, he would simply instruct someone else to carry out his orders.

Those who see Hitler rather as a weak dictator have a different interpretation. They agree that, if Hitler failed to get his way by one institutional channel, he had a tendency simply to set up a rival organisation, or appoint an ad hoc 'plenipotentiary' to deal with that particular area of policy. But in Hans Mommsen's view, this meant that Hitler was ultimately a weak dictator, at the mercy of those below. Some individuals, such as Hermann Goering or Heinrich Himmler, were able to build up immense personal power bases; others argued their corners far less successfully, but were engaged in a constant struggle for position. Hitler's hesitance in reaching decisions, and his tendency to wait to side with whoever was emerging as a winner, meant – on this view – that he was often more of a final rubber stamp than the person in the driving seat.

Recently historians have sought to combine a renewed focus on Hitler's own power with a recognition of the complexity of power structures which the structuralists rightly identified. Ian Kershaw, in a series of seminal works, suggests that Hitler's position as 'charismatic leader' was, paradoxically, in large part a product of the increasingly chaotic structures of power. With the competing, overlapping centres of power there was simply no other ultimate source of decision-making, and the 'Hitler order' was the only final authority that could be cited. Moreover, Hitler had a constant eye on his popularity with the population at large, and thus consciously sought to distance himself from day-to-day decision-making processes. At the

---

Hermann Goering (1893–1946)

At ease in high society and fond of a luxurious life-style replete with traditional hunting pastimes and costumes to match, Goering – who had joined the NSDAP and the SA in 1922, and had taken part in the Beer Hall Putsch of 1923 – facilitated Hitler's acceptance by conservative and business elites in the later Weimar years. Alongside other offices, Goering became Prussian Minister of the Interior following Hitler's appointment as Chancellor in 1933. He collaborated with Himmler and Heydrich in setting up the network of concentration camps and terror in the Third Reich, playing a key role in exploiting the Reichstag Fire of February 1933, the Night of the Long Knives against the SA in June 1934, and the maltreatment of Jews after *Kristallnacht* in 1938. In 1936, Goering was appointed to take charge of the 'Four Year Plan Office' preparing Germany for war within four years. His increasingly powerful industrial empire brought him personally large profits. In control of the *Luftwaffe* (Air Force) during the Second World War, Goering mismanaged the attack on Britain, and began to lose Hitler's favour. Sentenced to death by hanging following the Nuremberg trial, Goering managed to commit suicide by taking a poison capsule.

same time, the notion of 'working towards the *Führer*' (a phrase taken from a contemporary source) encapsulates the way in which Hitler's undoubted personal power and extraordinary hold over his close followers stimulated actions 'from below' that did not always require specific orders from above. Thus, in Kershaw's interpretation, Hitler's own prejudices set the tone and ultimate aims of the regime, while underlings competed for his favour. It is possible in this way to synthesise the notion of the polycratic state, riddled by internal rivalries, with that of Hitler's supreme role at the centre, shaping the parameters and ultimate goals of the regime.

How far can policies be explained in terms of Hitler's 'programme'?

It is easy enough to write the history of the Third Reich in terms of Hitler's 'world view', expounded in virulent form as early as *Mein Kampf*. On the intentionalist view, once in power Hitler's prejudices could simply be translated into hideous reality once conditions were right. Yet on closer inspection this seems an oversimplification. While Hitler's ultimate goals mattered more than some of the more radical proponents of the 'weak dictator' thesis might like to concede, Hitler's own intentions are merely a necessary but not a sufficient explanation of the way in which policies were actually formed and effected in the Third Reich.

Policy outcomes were always a result of a combination of different pressures and forces, the balance of which constantly changed. Pressures on Hitler from party radicals and activists; restraints proposed by party moderates, conservative nationalists, or civil servants; the aspirations of different economic interest groups or sections of the Army; wider public opinion, including in the peace-time years reactions abroad as well as at home – all these played a significant role in processes of policy formation. Such pressures might affect timing or details of policy – but not, where it mattered to Hitler, the overall direction and ultimate goals.

When the areas which were closest to Hitler's heart – expansionist foreign policy goals and aggressive racial policies – are examined, it is clear that Hitler never compromised in the pursuit of his ultimate aims, however much he trimmed the details of the route according to circumstances and constraints. Yet at the same time, the circles of those implicated in the realisation of these policies must be spread far wider than the intentionalist case would suggest.

Conclusion: a strong leader in a polycratic state?

The realities are more complex than either side of what has been a very polarised debate would suggest. But it now seems possible in some respects to combine aspects of both sides of the earlier debates. It seems ever more clear that the structure of the Nazi state was indeed polycratic, with many competing centres of power, and not the streamlined dictatorship suggested by the notion of totalitarianism. Yet this very complexity was in part a product of the way in which Hitler operated – appointing people to new positions, creating ad hoc posts with ill-defined powers, constantly changing the structure of the system. And, almost paradoxically, Hitler's own role as a 'charismatic leader' was itself in part a product of this increasingly chaotic power structure, since his 'will' alone remained the only decisive factor. Moreover, his undoubted wider popularity remained a key integrative factor for the regime.

Through this complex structure Hitler was in large measure able to have his own way as far as his ultimate 'negative' goals with respect to racial and foreign policy were concerned – though a devastating war of total destruction and absolute defeat hardly corresponded to Hitler's dreams of a Thousand-year Reich. To explain how such a situation developed thus implicates far wider circles, not only in the Nazi party (as in the 'Hitler and his henchmen' focus) but also in the civil service, the Army, and among the economic elites; in other words, among those who not merely helped Hitler into power in 1933 but who also thought that they could continue to negotiate compromises with Nazism in the pursuit of their own interests.

6.17 What was the impact of the Second World War upon civilian life in Germany?

How was Germany governed during the war years?

In general, the Second World War served to aggravate the divisions and confusions that existed before 1939 in the government of the Third Reich. One of the most striking features of wartime government was the steady withdrawal of Adolf Hitler, for so long the public inspiration of the Nazi movement, from the public eye. From November 1941 he assumed direct responsibility for all military operations, and was only rarely seen in public after that date. Such important matters as war production and law and order were left in the hands of the various agencies that competed for influence in Nazi Germany.

In particular, the SS under Heinrich Himmler and the Party Chancellery under Martin Bormann extended their influence, at the expense of the traditional ministries of the state. The SS played an increasingly important role in the economic organisation of the state, largely through the creation of an extensive group of companies involved in war production (*Deutsche Wirtschaftsbetriebe*). It also became involved in a complex range of strategic economic activities, including mining, armament manufacture and the production of foodstuff. In addition, the SS had at its disposal the enormous slave-labour resources of the concentration camps. It has been suggested by Alan Milward, a leading expert on the economic history of the war, that in building this economic 'empire' Himmler envisaged such a degree of control over the German economy as would ultimately undermine conventional German capitalism. At the same time, control over the Gestapo and the security service (SD) gave Himmler an unrivalled degree of influence within German society. The rapid expansion of the *Waffen SS* also extended this influence into the heart of the German army.

Although Martin Bormann could not seriously rival so extensive an 'empire', he had the advantage of working in close proximity to the *Führer* himself. Between 1943, when he was appointed as Hitler's personal secretary, and 1945, he was able to ensure that the Party Chancellery steadily eliminated the influence of the Reichs Chancellery, the body by which government business had traditionally been forwarded to the head of state. The influence of traditional administrative bodies was steadily eroded. Local administration, for instance, came increasingly under the control of the Party as the powers of the *Gauleiters* were extended. Appointed Reich Defence Commissioners (September 1939), they assumed responsibility for military matters within their *Gau*, and in 1943 were given overall control of all local civil administration. From September 1944, the *Gauleiters* were also responsible for the activities of the **Volkssturm**. Similarly, education, the judiciary and the civil service came under even tighter Party control. Wartime measures provided for the removal of teachers who were considered to be insufficiently loyal to the party (September 1941) and for a purge of leading officials in the Ministry of Justice (April 1942).

Volkssturm: A party militia established to form a last line of resistance against invading allied forces.

How effective was the German economy during the war years?

Traditionally, historians have assumed that in 1939 the Nazi state envisaged a war made up of short, sharp conflicts, interspersed with periods of temporary peace in which the economy could recover and consolidate. Only in 1942, when it became clear that the Reich was locked into a more profound conflict, did this 'Blitzkrieg mentality' give way to a state of 'total war', in which the economic resources of the state were exploited to the full. Such an interpretation was challenged by Richard Overy, in *War and the German Economy: a Reinterpretation* (1982). In his view, Germany's leaders had been anticipating a prolonged state of 'total war' since the mid-1930s, and the German economy had been geared to meet such demands since the establishment of the Four-Year Plan in 1936. The German economy was better prepared for the pressure of prolonged warfare than historians have usually imagined. Nevertheless, the government was taken by surprise by the Franco–British declaration of war in 1939, and became involved in an extensive conflict earlier than expected.

It was for this reason, Richard Overy argues, that the German war economy quickly encountered serious difficulties. Also, its organisation was confused and inefficient. Gordon Craig adds, in *Germany 1866–1945* (1978), that the Nazi government remembered very clearly the collapse of civilian morale in the last years of the First World War, and did not wish to risk a similar collapse by mobilising the economy too rigorously in 1940. Overy's reinterpretation identified a range of problems that included shortage of raw materials, shortage of manpower, and characteristic disputes about the control and the priorities of production. The provision of more workers was one of the major achievements of the German war economy. It was brought about by three distinct strategies.

- One was the comprehensive redeployment of the existing German workforce, which meant that by 1943 61% of all German labour was employed in war production, compared with 21% in 1939.

- The second was an enormous increase in the female workforce, amounting to half the female population by the beginning of 1944.

- Lastly, the Nazi authorities in occupied territories were able to recruit or to conscript enormous numbers of foreign workers (a total of 8 million by 1944) to aid war production in the Reich.

Greater problems existed over the co-ordination of resources and production. These were addressed by Hitler's 'Rationalisation Decree' (December 1941), which sought to streamline war production and to restructure control of the economy. The architects of this restructuring were Fritz Todt, who was appointed Minister for Armaments and Munitions in March 1940, and Albert Speer who succeeded him upon his death in February 1942. Its main institution was the Central Planning Board set up in April 1942. Speer's memoirs (*Inside the Third Reich*, 1970) make it clear that, while his personal friendship with Hitler was of great value, and endowed the minister with considerable authority, his efforts were still liable to be resisted at every turn by other vested interests, such as those of the *Gauleiters* or of the SS.

How much did Todt and Speer achieve?

It could be argued that Todt and Speer were remarkably successful in maintaining high levels of war production under the most difficult circumstances. The statistics for military production between 1942 and 1944 are impressive, with weapon production trebled despite the fact that the funds allocated to such production only increased by 50%. Even so, statistics suggest that the German economy was under enormous stress from 1943 onwards. In that year allied bombing forced the diversion of two million men and 50,000 pieces of artillery into anti-aircraft service. By the following year, according to Speer himself, aircraft production was 31% below target, and tank production 35% below. In the final year of the war, it has been estimated, absenteeism in German factories ran at a daily average of 25%, due to illness, stress and the dislocation caused by enemy action.

What was the impact of war upon the civilian population?

The war placed a considerable strain upon the German population from the outset. Strict rationing came into force at the start of the war, and between 1939 and 1941 German workers were considerably less well fed than their British counterparts. Consumption declined by 25%, compared with only 12% in Britain. Research suggests that German civilians derived little benefit from the additional food resources that were made available by German military victories, the vast bulk of them being directed towards military consumption. Other commodities, such as clothing, also became more difficult to obtain as production was geared increasingly towards the requirements of the war effort. As early as 1941, 40% of all textile output and 44% of all manufactured clothing was earmarked for use by the armed forces.

The civilian population within the Reich remained relatively sheltered from enemy action until 1942. In that year, the British and American air forces abandoned their policy of avoiding areas of heavy civilian population. The first of a series of 'thousand bomber raids' was launched against Cologne in May 1942, and in August of the following year another such raid killed 40,000 civilians in Hamburg. From mid-1944, Germany's enemies enjoyed almost total aerial superiority, and the vulnerability of German towns to devastating aerial attack became ever greater. The final official statistics for the damage caused to Germany by aerial bombardment alone are staggering. In the years immediately after the war, the Federal Statistical Office in Wiesbaden established that 593,000 German civilians had been killed by this means, and that 3,370,000 buildings had been destroyed, including 600,000 in Berlin alone.

There is much evidence to suggest that Nazi propaganda had been so effective that public confidence in Hitler's leadership remained high, even when Germany was on the verge of defeat. Historians have agreed no explanation of this, but have drawn attention to a range of factors. Goebbels worked incessantly in the Ministry of Propaganda. He pursued clever tactics in stressing to Germans what the consequences of defeat might be: pillage and rape at the hands of vengeful and barbaric Russians, for instance; or the destruction of the nation's industrial wealth by the terms of the **Morgenthau Plan**. Public faith in Hitler's personal infallibility also remained high until the very last stages of the war. Albert Speer's anecdote from the last weeks of the war probably captured a mood that was relatively familiar.

Morgenthau Plan: A plan devised between 1943 and 1945 by Henry Morgenthau, Secretary to the US Treasury, for the organisation of the German economy at the end of the war. His intention was that defeated Germany should be divided once more into a number of minor states, that the industrial bases of these states should be dismantled, and that their economies should be primarily agricultural.

1. In what different ways did the Nazi Party further extend its influence over German political and economic life in the years 1939–45?

2. By what means did the German economy meet the demands of 'total war'?

3. How much justification is there for the claim that 'the Nazi government organised its war effort efficiently and met the demands of total war with considerable success'?

'In Westphalia, in March 1945, I stood unrecognised in a farmyard talking to the farmers. The faith in Hitler that had been hammered into their minds all these years was still strong. Hitler could never lose the war, they declared. Even among members of the government I still encountered this naïve faith in deliberately withheld secret weapons that at the last moment would annihilate an enemy recklessly advancing into the country.'

Source-based questions: Conformity and resistance in Nazi Germany

SOURCE 1

From Joachim Fest, Hitler, published in 1974

The peculiar babble of voices presumably speaking for the German opposition, should make it clear that it was not a bloc. To treat it as if it were a single concept is inaccurate; it was a loose assemblage of many groups objectively and personally antagonistic and united only in antipathy for the regime. Three of these groups emerge with somewhat sharper contours. (1) The Kreisau Circle, called after Count Helmut James von Moltke's Silesian estate. This was chiefly a discussion group of high-minded friends imbued with ideas both of Christianity and socialist reform. (2) Then there was the group of conservative and nationalist notables gathered around Carl Goerdeler, the former mayor of Leipzig, and General Ludwig Beck, the former army chief of staff. These men, not yet understanding the meaning of Hitler's policies, were still claiming a leading role for a Greater Germany within Europe. So strong was their leaning towards an authoritarian state, that they have been called a continuation of the anti-democratic opposition in the Weimar Republic. (3) Finally, there was a group of younger military men such as von Stauffenberg, with no pronounced ideological affiliations, although for the most part they sought ties with the Left.

In terms of background, a strikingly large number of the conspirators belonged to the Old Prussian nobility. There were also members of the clergy, the academic professions, and high-ranking civil servants. On the whole, those oppositionists who were now beginning to urge action were people originally from the conservative or liberal camp, with a sprinkling of Social Democrats. The Left was still suffering from the effects of the persecution, but it too, with characteristic ideological rigidity, feared any alliance with army officers as a 'pact with the devil'. Among the many participants in the opposition there was, significantly, not a single representative of the Weimar Republic; that republic did not survive even in the Resistance. But members of the lower middle class were also conspicuously absent, and also businessmen. The latter remained fixated upon the traditional German alliance between industrial interests and power politics. Business always came to heel when the state whistled.

SOURCE 2

From T.W. Mason, Worker Opposition in National Socialist Germany, published in 1981

I would like to start by drawing a distinction between the political resistance of the working class under National Socialism and that which I want to call Worker opposition.

To political resistance belong only the politically conscious actions of members of persecuted organisations, which strove to weaken or overthrow the dictatorship in the name of social democracy, communism or trade unionism. That is to say, political activity which was characterised by a rejection and challenging of National Socialism based on political principle. But this heroic, tragic battle in the underground in no way exhausts the role of the working class in the Third Reich. Alongside the dogged propaganda work of the illegal groups, from 1936 onwards, economic class conflict was revived once more in industry on a broad front. What is more this battle about the fundamental economic interests of the working class does not even seem to have been organised in any way. It expressed itself in spontaneous walkouts, in collective pressure on employers and on National Socialist institutions, in go-slows, staying off work, taking sick leave, etc.

This refusal of the working classes to subordinate itself fully to the National Socialist system of dictatorship can be called opposition: it made use of the contradictions within the capitalist economic order and of the dictatorship, and sharpened these contradictions. This distinction between 'Opposition' and 'Resistance' is based upon the actual historical experiences of the working class, which are of central importance for an analysis of this entire theme, for the factual separation of the illegal resistance groups from their class was a decisive success of the state-political terror in the Third Reich.

SOURCE 3

From Ian Kershaw, The Nazi Dictatorship, published in 1993

As institutions the Churches offered something less than fundamental resistance to Nazism. Their considerable efforts and energies in opposing Nazi interference with traditional practices were not matched by equally vigorous denunciation of Nazi inhumanity and barbarism – with the notable exception of [Cardinal] Galen's open attack on the 'euthanasia' programme in August 1941. In defence of humanitarian rights and civil liberties, the response of both churches was muted.

The detestation of Nazism was overwhelming within the Catholic Church and grew more extensive within the Evangelical Church. But defiant opposition in the sphere of the 'Church struggle' was compatible in both major denominations with approval of key areas of the regime's policies, above all where Nazism blended into 'mainstream' national aspirations: support for 'patriotic' foreign policy and war aims; obedience towards state authority (except where it was regarded as contravening divine law); approval for the destruction of 'atheistic' Marxism; and readiness to accept discrimination against Jews. In all of these areas the Churches as institutions felt on uncertain ground – a reflection of the fact that popular backing could not be guaranteed, and that such issues fell outside what was regarded as the legitimate sphere of Church opposition, which was correspondingly limited, fragmented and largely individual.

SOURCE 4

Statement issued by Catholic Bishops in Bavaria, December 1936

After the deplorable fight carried on by Communists, Free Thinkers and Freemasons against Christianity, we welcomed with gratitude the National Socialist profession of positive Christianity. Our *Führer* in a most impressive speech acknowledged the importance to the state of the two Christian Churches and promised them his protection.

Notwithstanding the Concordat of July 1933, there has developed an ever-growing struggle against the Papacy. Catholic organisations and societies were promised protection for their continued existence. In reality, their continuation has gradually become impossible. The clergy are regularly insulted in speeches, writings, broadcasts and cartoons, yet the perpetrators go unpunished. It is not our intention to renounce the present form of government or its policy. The *Führer* can be certain that we will give all our moral support to his struggle against Bolshevism, but we do ask that our Church is permitted to enjoy her God-given rights and freedoms.

SOURCE 5

Part of a report secretly compiled by the underground organisation of the SPD, Autumn 1936

Although the anti-Bolshevik agitation is making a deep and powerful impact, the National Socialist mood has not penetrated very deeply. However, Hitler has understood how to appeal to nationalist instincts and emotional needs, which were already there. He stands outside the line of fire and criticism of the Government, whereas Goebbels is almost universally loathed, even among Nazis. The reduction in unemployment, and the drive it shows in its foreign policy are the big points in favour of Hitler's policy. He knows how to handle the popular mood and continually to win over the masses. No previous Reich Chancellor had understood anything of that.

Answer both questions (a) and (b).

(a) Using your own knowledge and the evidence of Sources 1, 3 and 4, what do you consider to have been the main reasons for which German conservatives entered into opposition to the Nazi regime in the period 1933–45? [10 marks]

(b) Using your own knowledge and the evidence of all five sources, how far do you agree with the judgement that 'Nazism failed to convince many Germans of its ideology, yet was never seriously threatened after 1933 by political or social opposition from within Germany'? [20 marks]

Source-based questions: The condition of the workers in the Third Reich

Study the four sources and then answer ALL of the sub-questions.

(a) Study Source C.

From the Source and your own knowledge, explain the reference to 'the time of inflation'. [20 marks]

(b) Study Sources A and B.

Compare the judgements expressed in these Sources on the social projects launched by the Nazi state. [40 marks]

(c) Study all of the Sources.

Using all of these Sources and your own knowledge, explain how far you agree with the judgement that the German working classes derived no genuine benefits from Nazi rule in Germany between 1933 and 1939. [60 marks]

SOURCE A

A Nazi writer explains how the 'Strength Through Joy' movement represents the beginnings of a new society

The comradely experience of work and the equally comradely experience of leisure time belong together. In them lies the idea of social life itself. The 'Strength Through Joy' land and sea trips mean far more than social travel in the normal sense: their value lies neither in the type of transport nor in the destination of the journey, but solely in the community experience. It is the great experience of nature which provides the best prerequisite for comradeship, so that one can say that these trips undertaken together represent the beginnings of a transformation of social life. A new type of culture is in the process of being born.

Willi Müller, Social Life in the New Germany, published in Berlin in 1938

SOURCE B

Opponents of the Nazis argue that their social projects have hidden motives

For a large number of Germans the announcement of the People's Car came as a pleasant surprise. For a long time the Volkswagen was a big talking point among all classes of the population. With the Volkswagen the leadership of the Third Reich has killed several birds with one stone. In the first place, it removes for a period of several years money from the German consumer which he would otherwise spend on goods that cannot be supplied. Secondly, and this is the most important thing, they have achieved a clever diversionary tactic in the sphere of domestic politics. This car obsession, which has been cleverly induced by the Propaganda Ministry, keeps the masses from becoming preoccupied with a depressing situation.

A report by underground SPD agents from the Rhineland, April 1939

SOURCE C

The Deputy Führer explains why German workers should accept wage-restraint

The *Führer* has repeatedly stated that under the present circumstances wage increases must lead to price increases. This in turn will lead to the endless vicious circle familiar to the German people from the time of inflation. Wage increases, therefore, can only be damaging rather than beneficial to the general public and to the individual, and so must be avoided at all costs. The fact that the economic position of large sections of our people is not what we would want it to be is the fault of the political, economic and trade union leadership of the post-war years. One must not overlook the importance of the fact that the virtual elimination of unemployment at the present time is due solely to the *Führer* and his movement.

A speech by Rudolf Hess, October 1937

SOURCE D

An official Nazi report gives details of working conditions in the revitalised German economy

The discrepancy between the available labour force and the number of orders has in general led to a considerable increase in the number of hours worked. Fifty-eight to 65 hours a week are no longer exceptional. And some factories continue overtime, even when there is a reduction in orders, because they are afraid of losing workers. The extraordinary demands made upon the German workers, particularly during the period of tension [caused by the crisis over Czechoslovakia], have on the whole been met without any difficulties. Thus the Reich Trustee of Labour for the Saar–Palatinate region reports that it is not uncommon for railway workers, for example, to work up to 16 hours a day.

Report of the Reich Trustees of Labour, Autumn 1938

Further Reading

Texts designed for AS and A2 Level students

The Weimar Republic by John Hiden (Longman, Seminar Studies series, 1974)
The Third Reich by David Williamson (Longman, Seminar Studies series, 1995)
From Bismarck to Hitler: Germany 1890–1933 by Geoff Layton (Hodder & Stoughton, Access to History series, 1996)
Germany: the Third Reich, 1933–45 by Geoff Layton (Hodder & Stoughton, Access to History series, 2000)
Hitler and Nazism by Jane Jenkins (Longman, History in Depth series, 1998)

More advanced reading

A vast literature exists on the history of Nazi Germany, and new works appear constantly. What follows can only be a selection of lasting, classic works.
The German Dictatorship by K.D. Bracher (Penguin, 1978)
The Hitler State by Martin Broszat (Longman, 1981)
A Social History of the Third Reich by R. Grunberger (Penguin, 1974)
The War against the Jews, 1933–45 by Lucy Dawidowicz (Pelican, 1975)
The Nazi Dictatorship: Problems and Perspectives of Interpretation by Ian Kershaw (Arnold, 1993) and
Modern Germany Reconsidered, 1870–1945 edited by Gordon Martel (Routledge, 1992) both provide good surveys of recent research and debate on Nazi Germany.
Weimar Germany by Paul Bookbinder (Manchester University Press, 1996)
The Rise of the Nazis by Conan Fischer (Manchester University Press, 1995)
    Many biographies of Hitler have been published, of which the best are probably:
Hitler: A Study in Tyranny by Alan Bullock (Penguin, 1962)
Hitler and Stalin: Parallel Lives by Alan Bullock (HarperCollins, 1991)
Hitler by Joachim Fest (Penguin, 1973)
Hitler by Ian Kershaw (Arnold, 1991)
Himmler, Reichsführer SS by Peter Padfield (Macmillan, 1990) provides the same service for another prominent member of the Nazi leadership.
Nazism 1919–1945: a Documentary Reader edited by J. Noakes and G. Pridham (Exeter University, 1983) provides an excellent range of contemporary documents on Nazi Germany.

7 Germany divided and reunited, 1945–1991

Key Issues

- Why, and with what consequences, was Germany divided following the Second World War?

- How did West Germany become a successful European state in the period 1949–1989?

- How far did East and West Germany become completely different states in the period 1949–1989?

- Why was Germany reunited in the years 1989–1991?

7.1 How and why was Germany divided into two states in the period 1945–1949?

7.2 The founder of modern Germany: Konrad Adenauer?

7.3 Historical interpretation: The West German economic miracle – myth or reality?

7.4 How and why did East Germany develop differently from West Germany in the years 1949–1989?

7.5 What were the main issues in foreign policy affecting East and West Germany in the years 1949–1989?

7.6 How significant was Helmut Kohl in bringing about German reunification in the years 1989–1991?

Framework of Events

1945	May: Germany surrenders. End of Second World War
	July/Aug: Potsdam Conference on future of Germany
1946	Apr: SED formed in Soviet Zone
1947	Jan: Bizonia created in US and British zones
	Jun: Marshall Plan announced in US
1948	Jun: Berlin Blockade crisis begins. Lasts until May 1949
1949	May: Basic Law creates West German State
	Jun: First Bundestag elections give victory to Adenauer and CDU/CSU
	Oct: Creation of German Democratic Republic (East Germany) in Soviet zone
1952	May: West Germany allowed its own armed forces; GDR closes border with West Germany except in Berlin
1953	Mar: Death of Soviet leader Stalin
	Jun: Riots in East Berlin (GDR)
1955	May: West Germany joins NATO; GDR joins newly formed Warsaw Pact
1957	Jan: Saarland joins West Germany
1958	Mar: Beginning of crisis over future of Berlin between USSR and the West
1961	Aug: Berlin Wall crisis
1963	Oct: Adenauer retires as West German Chancellor
1969	Oct: First Socialist Chancellor of West German, Willy Brandt, forms coalition government
1970	Mar: Beginning of *Ostpolitik*
1971	May: Erich Hoenecker becomes leader of GDR
1980	Jan: National Green Party formed
1982	Sept: Kohl become West German Chancellor
1985	Mar: Gorbachev becomes Soviet leader.

1989	Aug: Thousands of East Germans attempt to leave for the West, via Hungary
	Oct: Large demonstrations in Leipzig (GDR) against GDR government
	Nov: GDR opens Berlin Wall
1990	Mar: First free elections in GDR
	July: West German currency (Deutschmark) introduced in GDR
	Dec: First all-Germany election returns Kohl as Chancellor
1991	Mar: Reunification of Germany
	June: Berlin replaces Bonn as new capital of united Germany.

The leaders 1949–1991

West Germany's Chancellors
1949–1963: Konrad Adenauer (Christian Democrat)
1963–1966: Ludwig Erhard (Christian Democrat)
1966–1969: Kurt Kiesinger (Christian Democrat)
1969–1974: Willy Brandt (Social Democrat)
1974–1982: Helmut Schmidt (Social Democrat)
1982–1998: Helmut Kohl (Christian Democrat)

East Germany's leaders
1946–1950: Wilhelm Pieck and Otto Grotewohl (SED and PDS)
1950–1971: Walter Ulbricht (Socialist Unity Party [SED])
1971–1989: Erich Honecker (SED)
1989–1989: Egon Krenz (SED)
1989–1990: Hans Modrow (SED)
1990–1991: Lothar de Mazière (Christian Democrat)

Elections to the West German national parliament (Bundestag) 1949–1990

Germany operated a 'proportional representation' electoral system, where the number of seats won reflected, proportionately, the number of votes cast.

CDU – Christian Democratic Union
CSU – Christian Social Union
SDP – Social Democrat Party
FDP – Free Democrat Party

Year	CDU/CSU		SDP		FDP		Greens	
	% of vote	Seats	% of vote	Seats	% of vote	Seats	% of vote	Seats
1949	31	139	29.2	131	11.9	52		
1953	45.2	243	28.8	151	9.5	48		
1957	50.2	270	31.8	169	7.7	41		
1961	45.4	242	36.2	190	12.8	67		
1965	47.6	245	39.3	202	9.5	49		
1969	46.1	242	42.7	224	5.8	30		
1972	44.9	165	45.8	230	8.4	41		
1976	48.6	243	42.6	214	7.9	39		
1980	44.5	237	42.9	228	10.6	54	1.5	0
1983	48.8	255	38.2	202	7.0	35	5.6	28
1987	44.3	234	37.0	193	9.1	48	8.3	44
1990	43.8	319	33.5	239	11.0	79	5.1	8

Overview

Federal: A form of government where political power is shared between a central government and state governments. In Germany, state (*Land*) governments had responsibility for internal law and order, education and welfare.

NATO: The North Atlantic Treaty Organisation, founded by a military treaty signed in 1949, and still in existence. It was created to protect western Europe from Soviet military aggression. Its most important member was the USA.

THE history of Germany between 1945 and 1991 is linked directly to the history of the Cold War in Europe. The division of Germany, in the years 1945 to 1949, was the result of growing tension between the USA and its Western allies and the USSR. None of the Allied powers, in 1945, had planned to divide Germany into two states. However, from 1949 the division of Germany between the **Federal** German Republic (FRG), also known as 'West Germany', and the German Democratic Republic (GDR), also known as 'East Germany', was a symbol for the division of Europe into non-communist and communist areas. By the 1960s the border between the FRG and the GDR was the most heavily defended in the world.

The creation of the FRG may have been the product of the Cold War but it owes its early development to one man, Konrad Adenauer. He can justly be regarded as the father of the West German state. Under his leadership, from 1949 to 1963, West Germany became a major state in non-communist Europe. It became an independent state and was admitted to **NATO** in 1955.

If Adenauer was the father of West Germany, Walter Ulbricht can be regarded as the key figure in the development of East Germany. As political leader from 1949 to 1971 Ulbricht brought about a political and economic revolution in the GDR. He established a communist dictatorship, dominated by the Socialist Unity Party (SED), the East German communist party.

Although Adenauer and Ulbricht were important in the domestic history of Germany, it was the USA and the USSR that ultimately determined their political and international positions. As long as the USSR was willing to defend communism with armed force the GDR would remain a communist state. When this guarantee was removed, in 1989, the GDR quickly collapsed.

However, this does not mean that German politicians were unable to influence events. It was mainly under East German pressure that the USSR accepted the building of the Berlin Wall in 1961. It was also on the initiative of the West German Chancellor, Willy Brandt, that relations between the FRG and the GDR improved in the early 1970s through his policy of *Ostpolitik* (eastern policy).

The reunification of Germany in 1991 was a product of the Cold War. The rapid decline of the USSR in the 1980s led to the weakening of Soviet control over eastern Europe. In 1989 communist governments fell all across eastern Europe, and the GDR was no exception. On the fortieth anniversary of the founding of the

---

Willy Brandt (1913–1992)
West Germany's foremost Social politician. He was mayor of West Berlin during the Berlin Wall crisis of 1961. He became head of the SDP from 1964 to 1987. He was Chancellor of the FRG from 1969 to 1974.

He was born Herbert Frahm. However, he changed his name during the Nazi period when he fled Germany to avoid persecution. He settled in Norway and became a Norwegian citizen. He joined the SDP in 1948 following his return.His major contribution to post-war Germany was his policy of *Ostpolitik* (Eastern policy) which greatly improved FRG relations with the GDR, Poland and the USSR. For his efforts he won the Nobel Peace Prize in 1971. At home he introduced major social reforms. In 1974 he was forced to resign when it was announced that one of his close advisers was a member of the GDR secret police (Stasi).

GDR, demonstrations against the GDR government paved the way for rapid political change. The USSR's failure to support the GDR government resulted, first, in the fall of its leader, Erich Honecker, then the communist government itself. One of the most symbolic photographs of the end of the Cold War was the sight of ordinary Germans pulling down parts of the Berlin Wall on the night of 9/10 November.

Although communism collapsed in the GDR, by early 1990 it took the actions of FRG Chancellor Helmut Kohl to bring rapid reunification in 1990. He was able to win support for reunification in his own state, and he also was able to persuade his NATO allies and the USSR that a reunified Germany would not destabilise Europe. By early 1991, Germany was reunited. It wasn't an equal merger of two states. Instead, the former GDR was 'merged' into the FRG.

1. In what ways did German politicians influence the development of Germany between 1945 and 1991?

2. Assess the view that the history of Germany in the years 1945 to 1991 was a history of the Cold War in Europe.

7.1 How and why was Germany divided into two states in the period 1945–1949?

Which additional reasons can you add to this mind map to explain why Germany was divided by 1949?

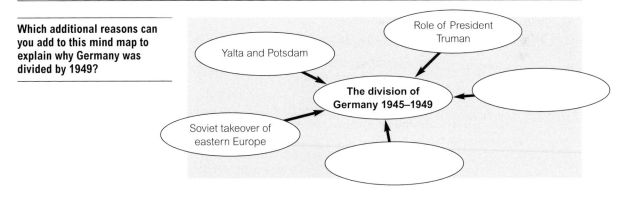

'Point Zero', May 1945

In May 1945 Germany had reached 'point zero' (*Nullpunkt*). Hitler had committed suicide on 30 April. Most other senior Nazi leaders had been captured. On 8 May Germany had unconditionally surrendered to the Allied powers. Following the surrender, all Germany was under military occupation. Virtually every city in Germany had suffered extensive devastation as a result of Allied aerial bombing. Over 4 million Germans had died in the war. Between 6 and 7 million Germans were prisoners of war. By the end of 1945 a further 10 million ethnic Germans had been expelled from their homes in eastern Europe and forced to live in the military occupation zones of the Allied powers.

The German state had ceased to exist. What would take its place?

Allied plans for post-war Germany

During the war, the Allies had developed a variety of plans about what to do with Germany after the war. At the Tehran Conference of November/December 1943 the USSR, the USA and Britain had decided to divide Germany into five areas. The Ruhr and Saar industrial regions were to be placed under international control and the Kiel Canal and the city of Hamburg would be controlled by a new organization, the United Nations.

In 1944, following a conference in Quebec (Canada), Britain and the USA supported the Morgenthau Plan, named after the US Treasury

Secretary. It planned to destroy German industry and turn Germany into an agricultural country. This idea was dropped in the spring of 1945. The main meetings which decided Germany's future were held in Yalta (on the Crimean Peninsula), in February 1945 and at Potsdam (in Germany) in July/August 1945. On both occasions the main decision makers were the USSR, the USA and Britain.

What was agreed at the Yalta Conference, 4–11 February 1945?

At Yalta it was agreed to divide Germany into four military zones – one each for the USSR, Britain, the USA and France. France was included because the USA was committed to withdrawing its troops from Germany by 1947. This would have left Britain alone facing the USSR. The Occupation Zones would be administered by each Allied power but were overseen by an Allied Control Council representing all four Powers. A similar situation was planned for Austria.

A source of potential tension was the future eastern border of the German occupation zones. Stalin, the Soviet leader, insisted that Poland be given large areas of former eastern Germany – up to the Oder and western Neisse rivers. This would compensate Poland for the loss of large areas of eastern Poland which Stalin wanted incorporated in the USSR.

Tension at Potsdam, July/August 1945

The second Allied Power meeting was on the outskirts of Berlin. At this conference US President Harry S. Truman had replaced Roosevelt (who had died in April). In August 1945 the British Prime Minister, Winston Churchill, had been replaced by the Labour leader, Clement Attlee, following a general election. Stalin remained Soviet leader until his death in 1953.

It was agreed to set up the Allied Control Council. This would oversee the four military zones of occupation. It would have representatives of the USSR, Britain, USA and France. It was also agreed to enforce four policies: denazification, demilitarisation, decartelisation and democratisation.

The first part of this policy began with the Nuremburg War Crimes Trials of leading Nazis in 1945–1946. However a full denazification process was not implemented in the Western zones. The US commander, Lucius Clay, decided by 1947 that to encourage rapid German economic recovery, former Nazi administrators and civil servants had to be employed.

The most successful policy was demilitarisation, where the entire armed forces of Germany were dismantled. It was only after 1955 that East and West Germany were allowed armed forces.

Decartelisation aimed to destroy the large companies of Germany which had provided the economic base for the Nazi regime. This was only temporarily introduced in the West but completed in the Soviet zone with the state takeover of all industry. Finally, democratisation eventually was introduced in the Western zones in 1949. In the Soviet zone a strict communist regime was created.

It was also decided that Germany should pay large amounts of **reparations** to the Allies. However, there was some disagreement about how this would take place. As the USSR had lost 25 million dead and had been devastated economically, Stalin wanted a large amount of reparations ($20 billion). In the end it was agreed that each Allied power take reparations from their own zones. However, Britain and the USA would give the USSR 10% of the industrial machinery from their zones and a further 15% in exchange for food and raw materials from the Soviet zone. However, no overall agreement was reached over reparations.

A large area of disagreement was over the future borders of the Soviet

Josef Stalin (1879–1953)
Soviet leader from 1924 to 1953.

Reparations: Payments made by a defeated state to compensate the victorious state(s) for damage or expenses caused by the war.

Zone and Poland. Britain and the USA wanted the border to be the eastern Neisse river. However, by the time of the conference the Poles were expelling ethnic Germans from east of the Oder and western Neisse river area.

Despite all the tension between the USSR on one side and Britain, USA and France on the other, there was no attempt at this stage to divide Germany. This was shown by the Soviet agreement to have four-power control of Berlin and Vienna. Both these capital cities (of former Germany and Austria) were deep within the Soviet military zones. Stalin hoped to see a neutral, demilitarised Germany and Austria. (Austria, in fact, became a neutral state in 1955.) The situation in Germany, however, was to change with the development of the Cold War in Europe.

The Cold War and the division of Germany

Between 1945 and 1949 Germany was divided in two. On one side was the Soviet zone, which became the German Democratic Republic – 'East Germany'. On the other side would emerge the German Federal Republic. – 'West Germany'.

This development cannot be understood without reference to the Cold War. In the years following Germany's defeat the former Allies, the USSR, USA and Britain began to fall out. So much so, that by 1949, Europe had been firmly divided into a Western area and a pro-Soviet area. As British Prime Minister, Winston Churchill had stated in 1946, an 'Iron Curtain'

Occupied Germany and Austria 1945–48

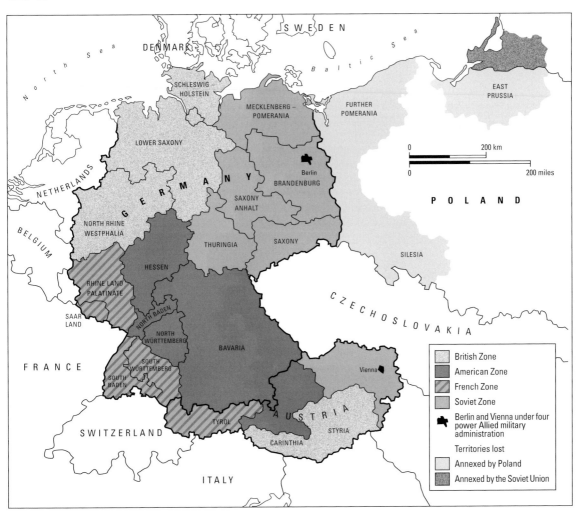

had descended on Europe, dividing it in two. Caught in the middle of this divided Europe were Germany and Austria.

There are a variety of differing historical interpretations about why the Cold War began. The traditional differences between communism and non-communist states, which dated back to the **Bolshevik Revolution** in Russia in 1917, is mentioned as the root cause. However, following Germany's defeat, Stalin began establishing Soviet-style communist governments in areas occupied by the Soviet (Red) army. These included Poland, Romania, Hungary, Bulgaria, Czechoslovakia and eastern Germany. By 1947 the USA became so alarmed that they issued the Truman Doctrine (March 1947) which offered support to all governments facing communist subversion. Later in the same year the USA offered Marshall Aid to all countries in Europe. This was economic aid to help recover from the war. However, Stalin saw it as an attempt to undermine communist control in eastern Europe. Eventually, one key event in Germany led to a complete breakdown in Western–Soviet relations – the 1948 Berlin Blockade crisis.

Bolshevik Revolution: The communist takeover of power in Russia in October 1917.

The Berlin Blockade crisis and the creation of two German states

The immediate cause of this crisis was the creation of 'Bizonia'. In order to encourage German economic recovery, Britain and the USA had decided to merge their two zones of occupation into one economic unit. It took effect on 1 January 1947. Stalin saw this as an attempt to create a united, anti-Soviet German political entity in the western zones. This fear was confirmed when the French zone decided to join Bizonia, and then an administrative headquarters was established in Frankfurt-am-Main to administer the enlarged zone.

All the signs of crisis emerged at a meeting of the Foreign Ministers of the occupying powers, which took place in London in November and December 1947. The conference ended in a deep division between the USSR and the West. The USSR had claimed that Bizonia had broken the Potsdam Agreement of 1945. The USA and Britain refused to accept a Soviet proposal for a central German government, which they thought might become communist.

The immediate cause of the crisis was the Western decision to introduce a new currency – the Deutschmark – into their three zones. This would take effect on 20 June 1948. The Soviet reaction was to block off road, rail and waterway links between the Western zones and their occupation areas in Berlin.

Lasting almost a year, the Berlin Blockade crisis was the most serious crisis between the USSR and the West since the end of the Second World War. Stalin believed the blockade would force the Western Allies to abandon their areas of Berlin. This was a serious miscalculation. The blockade forced the West, under American leadership, to stand up to Soviet threats. When it was proved that the West could provision their areas of Berlin by air, Stalin abandoned the blockade – on 11 May 1949.

The impact of the crisis was enormous. It divided Germany in two. In the West the immediate response was to create NATO (The North Atlantic Treaty Organisation). This was a defensive military alliance aimed against the USSR.

The blockade also speeded up the economic and administrative reorganisation of the Western occupation zones into one unit.

The biggest impact of the crisis was to divide Germany into two political units. In the west, the British, French and American zones would be formed into the Federal Republic of Germany (FRG) – 'West Germany'. In the Soviet zone, an alternative German government would be formed, the German Democratic Republic (GDR) – 'East Germany'.

The creation of an independent West German state

1. List the major events which led to the division of Germany in the years 1945 to 1949. What do you regard as the most important reason for this division? Explain your answer.

2. To what extent was the USSR responsible for the division of Germany in the years 1945 to 1949?

1949	Basic Law creates West Germany
1951	West Germany gains control over its foreign policy
	West Germany joins European Parliament
	West Germany joins the European Coal and Steel Community
1954	High Commission abolished
1955	West Germany becomes an independent state. It joins NATO and is allowed its own armed forces, as long as they are commanded by NATO
1957	Creation of EEC – the 'Common Market'. West Germany is one of six original members, along with France, Italy, Holland, Belgium and Luxembourg
1972	West Germany is admitted to the United Nations.

The Basic Law (Grundegesetz) May 1949

This law established the Federal Republic of Germany (West Germany) in 1949.

- West Germany was to be a federal state.
- Political power was split between a central (federal) government based in Bonn and the governments of each individual state (*Land*; plural *Länder*)
- The Head of State was a president.
- Real political power was in the hands of the Chancellor, who controlled the majority of seats in the Bundestag.
- The National Parliament would have two chambers:
- The Bundestag (Lower House) was directly elected by the German people.
- The Bundesrat (Upper House) represented the governments of the individual German states (*Länder*)
- Unlike the Weimar Republic (1919–33) the Bundestag could not remove a Chancellor or individual minister.

- They only had power to remove the entire government and then only if a replacement Chancellor had already been nominated.
- The president was a figurehead position with no political power. The president was chosen by members of the Bundestag and the Bundesrat, not directly elected by the people.
- Small extremist parties were prevented from entering the Bundestag because of the rule that parties had to receive 5% of the vote to win any seats.
- A Federal Constitutional Court was created to ensure that the Federal and *Land* governments followed the Basic Law.
- A High Commission replaced the commanders-in-chief of the four Allied Powers. This had considerable power. It could veto laws passed by the Bundestag and change the Basic Law. It lasted until 23 October 1954 when it was abolished.
- West Germany had no army and no foreign minister (until 1951).

7.2 The founder of modern Germany: Konrad Adenauer?

Which of these achievements do you regard as the most important? Explain your answer.

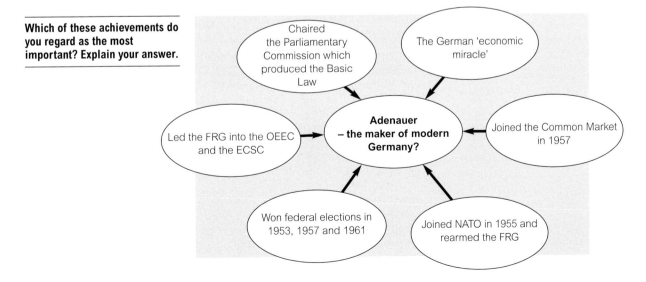

**Konrad Adenauer
(1876–1967)**
The first Chancellor of the
Federal German Republic.
Founder of the Christian
Democratic Union (CDU)
in 1946. Chancellor from
1949 to 1963.

Born on 5 January 1876 to a middle-class family in the Rhineland. Attended the universities of Munich, Bonn and Freiburg where he studied law and economics. In the First World War became member of Catholic Centre Party, and in 1917, was elected mayor of Cologne. In 1926 was asked to stand for position of Chancellor but declined. From 1933 to 1945 he opposed Hitler. He was forced out of position of mayor of Cologne and arrested twice during Nazi period.

On second occasion he was imprisoned for a short time in a concentration camp.

From 1945 to 1949 Adenauer returned to politics and became chair of the parliamentary commission which drafted the constitution for the FRG. In 1949 he became Chancellor. During his time as Chancellor the CDU dominated West German politics. Under his leadership, the FRG joined the Organisation for European Economic Co-operation, the European Coal and Steel

Community and the Common Market. In 1955 the FRG became an independent state and was admitted to NATO. Also in the period 1949 to 1963 the FRG achieved a spectacular economic recovery, becoming one of Europe's major economies. However, Adenauer was accused of being dictatorial in the way he ran the government. His fall was associated with the *Der Speigel* affair where attempts were made to censor the press.

'The greatest German'?

In 2003 the German Television station, ZDF, held a poll on who was the greatest German ever, and three million people took part. Konrad Adenauer came top of the poll, ahead of religious reformer Martin Luther and philosopher Karl Marx. What made Adenauer such an important figure in modern German history?

Born in 1876, in the Rhineland, Adenauer was already an experienced and elderly politician by the end of the Second World War. He had become Lord Mayor of Cologne (Köln) in 1917. He was an opponent of Hitler and the Nazis. In 1934 he was arrested by the Gestapo and imprisoned for two days. Later, in September 1934, he was arrested again and placed in a detention camp at Bauweiler. He was accused of taking part in the July Bomb Plot which attempted to assassinate Hitler.

Therefore, by the end of the war Adenauer had excellent anti-Nazi credentials and was one of the most experienced and senior politicians in western Germany.

Adenauer's rise to power, 1945–1949

As Germany had reached 'zero point' Adenauer helped create a new political party out of the ruins of defeat. Before the rise of Hitler he had been a member of the Centre Party (the German Catholic Party). In 1945 he was one of the key founder members of the Christian Democratic Union (CDU) a party for both Protestants and Catholics. It supported a capitalist-style economy with a strong welfare state – the 'social market economy'. Adenauer was the chairman of the CDU in the British zone.

The CDU joined with its Bavarian equivalent, the Christian Social Union, to form the CDU/CSU. This party dominated West German national politics from 1949 to 1969, and again in the 1980s.

Adenauer's administrative and political experience was also used by the Allied powers. In 1945 he again, briefly, was appointed Mayor of Cologne, by the British. However, of greater significance was his role as head of the Rhineland *Land*. This was the local government unit recreated by the Western Allies after the war. With the Allied powers in control of any

Land: The term for a state within Germany (plural: *Länder*)

central administration, minister-president of a Land was the highest post a German could hold.

Adenauer was one of the first German politicians to grasp the significance of the growing tensions between the Western Allies and the USSR. His main political opponent was Karl Schumacher, head of the Social Democratic Party (SDP). The SDP supported state control of the economy. This stood in marked contrast to the views of the Western Allies, especially the USA.

Schumacher also opposed Allied plans such as Bizonia.

At the beginning of the Berlin Blockade crisis, in July 1948, the minister-presidents of the Länder were asked, by the Western Allies, to form a 'Parliamentary Council'. Its purpose was to draw up a constitution for a west German state. Adenauer chaired the council. It drew up the Basic Law which created a federal, democratic state. In May 1949 this political entity became the Federal German Republic (FRG) – 'West Germany'. The capital of this new state was the small Rhineland town of Bonn, instead of the city of Frankfurt am Main. Bonn was where the Parliamentary Council had met. It was also close to Adenauer's hometown of Rhondorf.

In August 1949 democratic elections were held in the British, French and American zones. The CDU/CSU won 139 seats compared to 131 for the SDP and 52 for the Liberals (FDP). Adenauer was elected Chancellor by one vote, and took office on 21 September – at the age of 73.

No one expected a politician of his age to dominate West German politics for the next 14 years! Adenauer had risen to the position of Chancellor because of his anti-Nazi past. He was also seen as a strong anti-communist. He was also clever enough to understand the impact of the growing Cold War on East–West relations. His support for the ideas of the Western Allies meant that he out-thought his major political opponent, Karl Schumacher of the SDP.

The achievement of West German independence

In October 1945, Adenauer, in an interview with Western journalists, had stated that the Western Allies should create a Federal Republic from their three zones. In 1949 West Germany was created out of the three western military zones. However, it was far from a truly independent state. The Allied High Commission, under the Basic Law, had ultimate political power, with the power to veto legislation. The FRG had no control over its foreign policy. It had no armed forces and it was not recognised as a separate state by most of the world. But by 1955, Adenauer – more than any other person – had created an independent West Germany integrated into Western Europe and the Western world.

A turning point in this development was the Petersberger Agreement of November 1949. Under the agreement, the FRG could create diplomatic relations with other countries. In return, Adenauer said he would support international control of the Ruhr industrial region. This agreement caused fierce debate in the Bundestag. However, using the agreement, Adenauer was able to get West Germany membership of the Council of Europe and the Organisation for European Economic Co-operation (OEEC) in 1951. It also enabled the FRG to take a seat on the International Ruhr Authority. Later in 1951 West Germany was a founder member of the European Coal and Steel Community (ECSC), the forerunner of what eventually became the European Union (EU). The formation of the ECSC enabled the FRG to bring an end to the International Ruhr Authority.

Adenauer's greatest triumphs came in 1954. The Allied High Commission was abolished and, through the Paris and Bonn treaties, the

Warsaw Pact: A military treaty between the USSR and its European Allies. Created in 1955 as a response to the FRG entry into NATO.

FRG became a fully independent state. It was allowed to have full diplomatic relations with other countries, and to join NATO. It could now have its own armed forces but they could only operate under NATO command.

Following the achievement of independence, the FRG signed the Treaty of Rome in 1957. This created the European Economic Community (EEC), the 'Common Market'. In the same year, the Saarland voted to rejoin Germany and became a new *Land* of the FRG.

However, although Adenauer had won West German independence, it did come at a price. This development consolidated the split between the FRG and the GDR. In 1955, in response to the FRG admission to NATO the GDR joined its communist equivalent, the **Warsaw Pact**. The split was further reinforced by the 'Hallstein Doctrine'. In 1951 Professor Hallstein, the State-Secretary of the West German Foreign Office, had negotiated the end of the Allied High Commission, which took effect in 1954. However, the Hallstein Doctrine declared that the FRG would not have diplomatic relations with any country which recognised the GDR. This policy helped to poison relations between East Germany and West Germany until the beginning of *Ostpolitik* in the early 1970s.

The master of domestic politics

In August 1949 Adenauer was elected Chancellor by just one vote. However, he went on to win the September 1953 election by an increased majority. The scale of the victory, with the CDU/CSU gaining 45 per cent of the vote, confirmed Adenauer as the dominant force in West German politics.

Part of Adenauer's success was the recovery of the West German economy. Marshall Aid, from 1948, had begun the economic recovery. This was also aided by the outbreak of the Korean war (1950–53) which led to an increased demand for German goods. It was also aided by Adenauer's handling of foreign affairs, joining the ECSC and signing the European Defence Community treaty with France, both in May 1952.

In addition, Adenauer cleverly won support from the right wing of German politics by allowing approximately 150, 000 officials to return to their posts after their initial dismissal by the Allied 'denazification programme'. He was also responsible for the Equalisation of Burden Law of 1952. This redistributed wealth, in the form of a tax on the rich, to help those Germans who were casualties of the war and the 9.5 million ethnic Germans who had been expelled from eastern Europe. In the subsequent twenty years 90 million Deutschmarks were redistributed.

However, Adenauer dominance was also aided by the actions of the main opposition leader, Karl Schumacher of the SDP. Schumacher believed that the social market economy would collapse. He was also fearful that the extreme right in German politics would exploit its support for German nationalism. As a result, Schumacher opposed improved economic links with other western European states – especially France. He also vehemently opposed West German rearmament. When Schumacher died, in August 1952, the SDP had failed to make an impact on the German electorate.

Adenauer exploited the situation very effectively. He made a state visit to the USA in April 1953. In June, an uprising took place in East Berlin against communist rule. Both events helped to increase anti-communist feeling in the FRG and reinforced the need to rely more heavily on the USA and NATO. During the 1953 election campaign, Erich Ollenhauer, Schumacher's successor as head of the SDP, was no political match for Adenauer.

Franz Josef Strauss (1915–1988)
Leading member of the Christian Social Union, the Bavarian equivalent of the Christian Democratic Union (CDU). Born in Munich, the son of a butcher. He studied history and economics at Munich University. In the Second World War he served in the German army. He was hospitalised on the Eastern Front through frostbite.

He became an MP in the first FRG parliament in 1949. In 1953 he was made Minister for Special Affairs and then Minister of Nuclear Energy in 1955.

His most important post in the Adenauer government was as Minister of Defence from 1956 to 1962. He was forced to resign because of the *Der Speigel* scandal. He returned to national politics from 1966 to 1969 as Treasury Minister. From 1976 until his retirement from politics Strauss was a great rival to Kohl for leadership of the CDU/CSU. From 1978 to his death in 1988 Strauss was Minister-President of Bavaria.

From zenith to nadir

From 1953 to 1957 Adenauer consolidated his position as the 'strong man' of German politics. In 1955 the FRG had become a sovereign state. The West German armed forces had been created. In 1957 West Germany joined the Common Market and the Saarland was returned to the FRG.

In the build-up to the 1957 election Adenauer showed his authority over the CDU/CSU by promoting Franz Josef Strauss of the CSU to the post of Defence Minister and sacking several economic ministers who had supported an interest rate rise. To thwart the SDP opposition he introduced index-linked state pensions, in January 1957, which included a one-off rise of approx 70%. This could be seen as a massive bribe for the electorate. However, it did consolidate Adenauer's view of a social market economy.

With the opposition in disarray, Adenauer won 50.2% of the vote, the biggest electoral win in post-war German history.

In his final term as Chancellor, foreign policy predominated. Khrushchev, the Soviet leader, began a major diplomatic offensive to change the status of Berlin, which was still under four-power military control. Beginning in November 1958 the crisis soured East–West relations. It came to a head with the building of the Berlin Wall, in August 1961. The Berlin Wall crisis increased the national and international profile of the SDP mayor of West Berlin, Willy Brandt.

In the same period, Adenauer faced defeat in his attempt to introduce commercial television to the FRG. It was a *Länder* responsibility to provide unbiased public broadcasting. In trying to introduce commercial television Adenauer was disregarding the Basic Law. He was defeated on the proposal in the Federal Constitutional Court in February 1961. He was also defeated in the Bundestag in an attempt to reform the health system.

Finally, in 1959, Adenauer tried to block the rise of his main rival for CDU/CSU leadership, Ludwig Erhard. Erhard had been seen as the architect of Germany's rapid economic recovery. Adenauer tried to get himself chosen as the next West German president, with control over foreign affairs. This was unconstitutional under the Basic Law. As a result, Adenauer withdrew his proposal and Heinrich Lubke became president in his place.

Adenauer's fall: the *Der Spiegel* affair, 1962–63

Der Spiegel is a widely respected magazine. On 10 October 1962 it published an article which claimed that, in the recent NATO manoeuvres,

Ludwig Erhard (1897–1977)
Born in Furth, Bavaria. He joined the German Army in 1916 during the First World War. He was seriously wounded in 1918. After the war he studied economics, receiving a doctorate in 1925. During the Second World War he wrote extensively on economics. In 1945 he became economics consultant to the US occupation forces. He then became Economics Minister in Bavaria. In 1947 he became a central figure in the creation of Bizonia, the currency union of the British and US zones. In 1949 he was elected to the *Land* parliament of Baden-Württemberg, in SW Germany. At this stage he joined the CDU. In the same year he became Adenauer's Economics Minister. He is widely credited with organising the economic conditions which led to the FRG's 'economic miracle' in the 1950s. In 1963 he succeeded Adenauer as Chancellor. Although re-elected in 1965, he resigned in 1966 when the CDU–FDP coalition collapsed.

the German forces had performed poorly. It was clear that the information had been leaked from classified NATO documents. Not only was this a serious breach of security it occurred at the height of the Cuban Missile Crisis, one of the most serious crises of the Cold War.

The affair reached national prominence because the Defence Minister, Franz Josef Strauss – an Adenauer appointee – ordered the arrest of the journalist responsible for the article, along with several editors of the magazine. This was done on the grounds of treason against West Germany.

The action of the government caused a furore. It was another example of how the Adenauer government had tried to bend constitutional rules. The affair led directly to Adenauer's downfall. His government held power only because of the support of the Liberals (FDP). As a result of the affair they threatened to withdraw from the coalition with the CDU/CSU if Adenauer did not resign in 1963. At the age of 87, in October 1963, Adenauer resigned in favour of his rival, Ludwig Erhard.

Adenauer: the verdict

The 73-year-old Konrad Adenauer seemed an unlikely founder of modern Germany when he became Chancellor by only one vote, in 1949. However, by the time of his fall from power West Germany had become the most powerful economic state in Europe. West Germany had been readmitted to the international community and was a leading figure in the EEC (Common Market).

During his period of power, political stability had been maintained through the dominance of the CDU/CSU. During his Chancellorship, West Germany experienced an economic miracle. By 1963 the vast majority of West Germans had accepted his idea of a social market economy. Following their third successive defeat in the 1957 election, Adenauer's leading opponents, the SDP, abandoned their support for a state-controlled economy. In the Bad Godesberg Declaration of 1959 the SDP accepted Adenauer's version of German economic development.

Adenauer was also extremely shrewd in interpreting the views and intentions of the Western Allies. As a known anti-Nazi he was able to climb rapidly within the political structure of the British zone. As a noted anti-communist his views fitted nicely into the Cold War climate of post-war Europe. In the early 1950s he was called the 'Chancellor of the Allies' by his political opponents.

However, he developed a reputation for getting things done – although he also developed a reputation for trying to force his own views on the government and the Bundestag. His attempts to subvert the Basic Law led to accusations of authoritarian behaviour. In the end, it was a high-handed act by his Defence Secretary that led to his downfall. His desire to stay in politics meant that following his resignation as Chancellor he stayed on as Chairman of the CDU until 1966 – one year before his death.

1. From the information contained above, identify four ways in which Adenauer was able to make the FRG an important European state in the years 1949 to 1963.

2. How far does Adenauer deserve the title 'the creator of post-war Germany'?

7.3 The West German 'economic miracle' – myth or reality?
A CASE STUDY IN HISTORICAL INTERPRETATION

Which of the reasons in the mind map can be linked to the work of Ludwig Erhard? In order of priority, list the reasons which led to an 'economic miracle'. Are any of the reasons you mention linked in any way? If so, which ones?

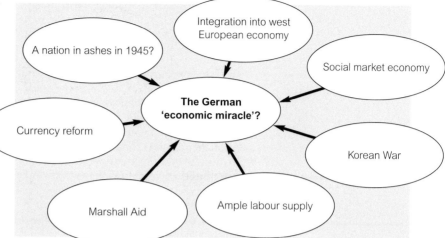

In 1945 Germany had reached 'zero point'. The whole country had been occupied by foreign troops, and most German cities had been devastated by Allied bombing. However, by the 1960s it had experienced rapid economic recovery. In 1970 West Germany was the world's third largest economy, after the USA and the USSR.

Real economic growth from 1951 to 1960 averaged 8% per year. Inflation was kept low at an average of 1.1%. Unemployment fell from 11% in 1950 to just 1.3% in 1960. As a result, West Germany outperformed all its rivals in western Europe.

Was this an 'economic miracle'?

Germany in 1945: a nation in ashes?

It seemed that Germany had risen in a spectacular way from the ashes of military defeat in a remarkably short period of time. However, although many German cities were devastated, this was not the case with much of German industry. It was only in 1944 that damage from aerial bombardment had surpassed industrial production. In fact, in May 1945 Germany had industrial plant which was 20% above 1936 levels. According to the US Strategic Bombing Survey, by David McIsaac, published in 1976, Germany's machine tool industry had increased by 75% since 1938. This was an important sector of the post-war West German economy.

An ample labour supply

Although most of its cities suffered extensive damage, Germany still possessed an educated, skilled work force – what economists call 'human capital'. Even though Germany lost millions killed and captured during the war, they were replaced by millions of German refugees who had been expelled from eastern Europe in 1944–46. Approximately 9.5 million of them settled in West Germany. Also between 1949 and the building of the Berlin Wall in 1961, 3.8 million Eastern Germans fled the GDR for West Germany – most of them young, skilled workers.

Finally, from the late 1950s, West Germany introduced the 'guest-worker' (*Gastarbeiter*) scheme. In 1959, foreign workers numbered just 150,000. By 1966 this had expanded to 1.2 million. The FRG actively recruited specific types of worker, mainly from Turkey and Greece. These workers made up for labour shortages in industries such as mechanical and electrical engineering. They also provided cheap labour in declining industries such as textiles and shipbuilding. This helped maintain German economic competitiveness against its international rivals.

As a result of these developments West Germany had both an ample and relatively cheap labour force on which to base its economic recovery and growth.

The social market economy

Considerable weight is placed on the West German idea of a 'social market economy' – a middle way between unregulated private enterprise and a state-controlled economy. The aim was to allow private enterprise but also to allow the government the power to 'police' the market. This would involve preventing monopolies forming, allowing fair competition and ensuring that Germany had a strong currency .This idea dated back to the 1930s, when the Freiburg School of economists, known as 'Ordoliberal economists', such as Franz Böhm and Walter Eucken, had a major impact on the economic thinking of leading members of the CDU, especially Ludwig Erhard.

In 1947 the CDU produced the anti-private enterprise Ahlen Programme. However, by 1949, under Erhard's influence the party had adopted the Düsseldorf Principles. These principles, which evolved into the 'social market economy', were the basis for CDU/CSU economic policy from 1949 to the 1970s. This policy allowed the German economy to develop rapidly without causing major conflicts between trade unions and industrialists.

Currency reform

A major factor behind economic recovery was the introduction of the Deutschmark (DM) to replace the Reichsmark (RM). The currency reform was introduced into the three Western zones of occupation on 20 June 1948. As well as the replacement of one currency by another, it also involved giving the banks large deposits of the new DM to give to industry to invest in economic recovery. This stimulated the development of industry.

Of greater significance was the creation of an independent central bank, the German Central Bank – the Bundesbank. This bank had the responsibility to manage the currency – including the power to raise and lower interest rates – without direct political interference. In 1992 David Marsh produced a book entitled *The Bundesbank: The Bank that Rules Europe*. This reflected the bank's importance in both the West German and European economies.

The immediate impact of the currency reform was to cause deflation. However, it also removed most of the commercial debt of German industry. In doing so it gave Germany the vital benefit of currency stability through the 1950s and 1960s.

Marshall Aid

In 1947 the US Secretary of State, George Marshall, announced the European Recovery Plan, which became known as the 'Marshall Plan'. Between 1947 and 1952 it provided western European states with $13 billion of aid – 'Marshall Aid' – for economic reconstruction. In December 1948 alone the western area of Germany received $99 million. In 1950 Marshall Aid accounted for 37% of western German imports. Clearly, this Aid helped stimulate the growth of the economy. Much of the Aid money was used to improve railways and the electrical and steel industries.

However, its importance has been overstated. Although western Germany received $1.6 billion between 1948 and 1952, this was equivalent to the 'Government and Relief in Occupied Areas' money provided by the Germans themselves to aid German refugees moving to western Germany ($1.6 billion between 1946 and 1952). Also, West Germany's rivals received more from Marshall Aid. Britain received $3.4 billion and France $2.8 billion.

The Korean War, 1950–1953

At the time when Marshall Aid was beginning to cease, the West German economy received another boost, because of the Korean War. The rapid rearmament of the USA and Britain meant that German exports, such as machine tools and motor vehicles, were in demand, giving another impetus to economic growth. Also, unlike the USA, Britain and France, West Germany did not have to expend any money on armaments until the mid-1950s.

Ludwig Erhard: the father of the economic miracle?

Erhard had made his name as Economic Director of the Bizone Council in March 1948. He was responsible for the economic merger of the British and American zones of occupation.

In 1948 Bizonia was controlled by the military governors appointed by Britain and the USA. The economy was strictly regulated, with price controls and rationing. This led to a large black market and the hoarding of goods and materials. On 20 June, when the new DM currency was introduced, Erhard announced the end of price controls. This was made without the knowledge of the military governors and, overnight, it brought the black market to an end.

The combined effect of currency reform and deregulation led to a big increase in industrial production, up 30% between March and August 1948. The fact that the French and Soviet zones did not experience such spectacular economic growth helped to strengthen the case for Erhard's reforms. But the increase in consumer demand led to an increase in inflation, and on 12 November 1948 a general strike was organized against price increases. The German Central Bank (Bundesbank), however, increased interest rates which led to a fall in inflation by the end of the year.

Having weathered the storm of deregulation the West German economy was now in a perfect position to exploit the upturn in demand for its exports during the Korean War. In December 1951 Erhard aided economic development further through the Investment Aid Law. This involved a Federal Government subsidy to manufacturing industry of 3.2 billion DM. As a result, the investment level of the West German economy rose from 19% in 1950 to 24% by 1960, far ahead of Britain and France.

As Adenauer's Economics Minister, Ludwig Erhard provided the foundations of economic prosperity which underpinned the CDU/CSU dominance of German politics in the years 1949 to 1969. Following Adenauer's resignation in 1963, Erhard became Chancellor from 1963 to 1966.

As the historian D.G. Williamson (2001) noted in *Germany from Defeat to Partition, 1945–1963*, 'Erhard had engineered a brilliant capitalist restoration. He had encouraged free enterprise and nearly halved the FRG's protective tariffs.'

However, Erhard's period as Economics Minister was not one of unlimited success. His economic policies of the late 1940s led to a steep rise in unemployment, reaching 3 million in 1950. He was fortunate that the Korean War helped stimulate the West German economy – in the second half of 1950 German industrial production rose by one third.

Also Erhard failed to limit the power of big business. In 1957 his Anti-Trust Law (Law on Restraints on Competition) proved ineffective at curbing its economic power. As a result, firms such as Krupp and Thyssen in steel production and Bayer (chemicals) epitomised the economic miracle (*Wirtschaftwunder*). Also, while Erhard freed industry to more open competition, farming remained heavily subsidised, a fact sustained by West German entry into the Common Market in 1957. Finally, the 1957 Pension Act and the development of a welfare state increased state expenditure, storing up problems for future FRG governments in the 1980s and 1990s.

Erhard eventually replaced Adenauer as Chancellor in October 1963. Although he won the 1965 Federal Election, the economic condition of the FRG was changing. The economic growth fell from 6.2% per year in 1954 to 4.5% in 1965. Unemployment rose from 100,000 to 200,000 and inflation rose by 4%. Erhard hoped to raise taxes to meet a budget deficit, but the four FDP (Liberal) ministers in his government resigned. As a result, a new coalition government of CDU/CSU and the SDP under Kurt Keisinger was created in October 1966. Having been Economics Minister for fourteen years, Erhard lasted a mere three years as Chancellor.

Germany's integration into the western European and world economies

While Erhard may have been seen as the father of the so-called economic miracle, his work was greatly helped by Adenauer's policy of integrating West Germany back into Europe. West Germany joined the Organisation of European Economic Co-operation and the European Payment Union in 1950. In the following year it joined the General Agreement on Tariffs and Trade (GATT). Also in 1951 it joined the European Coal and Steel Community. In 1952 it joined the International Monetary Fund, and in 1957 it was a founder member of the Common Market (EEC).

Membership of these organisations allowed West Germany to take full advantage of the liberalised global economy. This was aided by an under-valued Deutschmark which made West German exports very price-competitive. For instance, in the early 1950s West German coal sold for $10.50 per tonne against the world price of $30 per tonne.

Summary

In 1939 Germany was the world's second largest economy, after the USA. By the 1960s West Germany had become the third largest economy after the USA and USSR. It could be argued that following the devastation and destruction caused by the Second World War West Germany had merely re-established itself as a leading economic power. It would fall to fourth largest economy by 1980, following the rise of Japan.

So, was the economic miracle just a myth? Certainly, parts of the myth were overstated – the 'zero point' of 1945, the idea that the currency reform of 1948 and Marshall Aid were the turning point in West German economic development and the undying wisdom of Erhard's policies.

However, by any economic measure, West German economic growth in the 1950s and 1960s was spectacular. Was this due more to changing world economic conditions – or was it due more to German ingenuity?

1. Identify three reasons why the FRG experienced rapid economic development in the 1950s. What do you regard as the most important reason? Explain your answer.

2. What evidence is there for and against the view that the FRG experienced an 'economic miracle'?

7.4 How and why did East Germany develop differently from West Germany in the years 1949–1989?

Which of these reasons was the most important in making the GDR a communist state? (You may wish to look at Section 7.6 on the collapse of the GDR.)

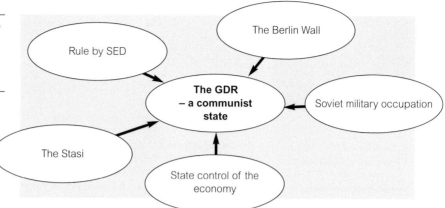

There is strong evidence to suggest that the USSR was against the division of Germany into two states. This will explain why Stalin, the Soviet leader, was willing to allow three western occupation zones in west Berlin. These were deep within the Soviet occupation zone (see map on page 201).

Throughout the period from 1945 until his death in 1953 Stalin hoped to create a united but neutral German state. This would offer a buffer between the communist controlled eastern Europe and the West.

It also explains why, throughout the process of division, the USSR reacted to developments initiated by the West. The creation of the German Democratic Republic (GDR) followed the creation of West Germany, in 1949. The USSR only recognized the GDR as a separate state, in 1955, after West Germany joined NATO.

The creation of the GDR in 1949

The creation of a communist state in Germany came from two interlinked sources. The first was the tradition of German communism which existed before the rise of Hitler. In 1932 the KPD (German Communist Party) had won 100 seats in the Reichstag. In 1945, those German communists who had suffered imprisonment under the Nazis were released, and many of those who had fled to the USSR returned. The other source came from the USSR. Like the rest of Soviet-occupied Europe, East Germany had a Soviet-style administration established from 1945.

In the Soviet zone a communist party was created from this background. It was the Socialist Unity Party (SED). As early as November 1946 the SED drew up plans for a German Democratic Republic. However, it wasn't until after the creation of the FRG that the GDR was formed. This took place on 30 May 1949.

In 1949 the constitution of the GDR was not unlike the Basic Law of the FRG. In contrast to the situation in Nazi Germany, more than one political party was allowed to exist in the GDR. On 10 June 1945 an anti-Nazi group of parties was created under the Soviet Administration of Germany (SMAD). This group included the CDU and Liberals (LDPD). In 1948 two further parties were created. These were the German Democratic Farmers' Party (DBD) and the National Democratic Party of Germany (NDPD).

In *Stalin's Unwanted Child: The Founding of the GDR*, historian W. Loth regarded the events of 1949 to 1952 in the GDR as a *coup d'état*. The creation of a communist dictatorship in the GDR was not unlike developments in other **Eastern Bloc** Soviet satellite states.

Eastern Bloc: The area of eastern Europe with communist governments which were allied to the USSR. They were Poland, Romania, Bulgaria, Hungary, Czechoslovakia and the GDR.

**Walter Ulbricht
(1893–1973)**
Born in Leipzig, Ulbricht can be regarded as the founder of the GDR. He was leader of the GDR from its creation until 1971. Before the First World War he was a tailor

and member of the SDP. He fought in the First World War from 1915 to 1917 but then deserted because he opposed the war. He was caught and imprisoned until the end of the war.
In 1917 he joined the far-left group, the Independent SDP, and in 1920 joined the German Communist Party (KDP). He was elected to the national parliament (Reichstag) from 1928 to 1933. After the Nazi takeover in 1933 he lived in exile in France and Czechoslovakia until 1937. From 1937 to 1945 he

lived in the USSR. On the day of Hitler's suicide, Ulbricht and other German communists arrived in Eastern Germany with the aim of creating a communist regime. He became the leader of the GDR following its creation. He narrowly survived overthrow in the June 1953 uprising.
Ulbricht from 1950 onwards rapidly established a communist state in the GDR. Virtually all businesses became state owned and the SED (communists) dominated all aspects of political life.

The Berlin Wall was built in 1961 to stop the mass emigration of people from the GDR to the FRG. Ulbricht developed a reputation for being a hard-line anti-reform communist. He supported the suppression of liberal communists in Czechoslovakia in 1968. His approach made him increasingly unpopular in the SED. On 3 May 1971 he was forced to resign for 'reasons of poor health'. In fact he had been ousted by his successor Honecker, who had the support of the USSR.

The SED dominated the GDR. In the 1949 elections to the GDR parliament (*Volkskammer*) the SED list of candidates won 99% of the votes! Voters were asked: 'Do you support German unity and peace?' If so, they had to vote for the SED list. Within the party, the policy of democratic centralism was introduced. Decisions made by the SED ruling committee, the Politiburo, had to be followed by all elements of the SED. During the first half of 1951 the SED purged its own membership. Those seen as unreliable –150,000 people – were expelled.

In December 1949 the Supreme Court and the Department of Public Prosecutions were established under strict SED control. By April 1950 over half the judges and 86% of public prosecutors were SED members. In 1950 the Ministry of State Security was created. Its members, the Stasi, eventually dominated GDR life. By the 1980s about a quarter of the GDR population were informants for the Stasi.

As in other communist states, significant emphasis was placed on educating youth. The school curriculum was changed radically to reflect Marxist-Leninist principles. A youth movement, the FDJ (Free German Youth Movement), was formed which was effectively controlled by the SED.

In 1952, at the Third Congress of the SED, local government was reorganized. The five *Länder* were abolished and replaced by 14 Districts (*Bezirke*). Unlike the FRG, the GDR became a centralised police state under the strict control of the SED.

In July 1952, the first ruler of the GDR, Walter Ulbricht, unveiled his plans to 'build socialism' in the GDR. This would involve a programme of rapid industrialisation and the 'collectivisation' of agriculture. These were to be achieved through Soviet-style central economic planning, initially through a Two-Year Plan, followed by a Five-Year Plan and then, following Soviet procedures, a Seven-Year Plan.

By introducing a Soviet-style dictatorship, Ulbricht must take as much blame for the division of Germany as any other German politician. By 1952, the FRG and GDR were clearly on radically divergent paths of development.

How different were the FRG and GDR?

By the 1960s the citizens of the FRG regarded themselves as superior to their fellow Germans in the GDR. The FRG had experienced spectacular economic growth during the 1950s. It was a democracy with very strong local government in the form of the *Länder*. The GDR was a centralised communist dictatorship where the government controlled the courts, police and press. Standards of living and quality of life were clearly better in the West. Why did this occur?

Part of the answer is in the industrial base of both states. The FRG inherited the main German industrial region, the Ruhr. From 1957 it also contained the important industrial area of Saarland. The FRG had abundant coalfields to fuel industrial growth. It also had a large and expanding population – 40 million in 1949, rising to 51 million by 1961.

In contrast, the GDR was mainly agricultural. The great eastern industrial area, Upper Silesia, had been seized by Poland in 1945. Also, the USSR took much of whatever industrial plant it had possessed as part of wartime reparations in 1945. It also had a smaller – and declining – population. With only 19 million in 1949, the GDR had lost 3.8 million of its best workers to the FRG by 1961.

Although the GDR experienced annual growth rates of 8% in the 1950s this slowed down to 2.3% between 1960 and 1962. Also collectivisation of agriculture proved to be both extremely unpopular and economically disastrous.

However, these differences are not the whole story. The FRG became integrated into the Western and global economies. As an export-led economy the FRG benefited greatly from membership of GATT, the European Coal and Steel Community and then the Common Market.

In contrast, the GDR suffered from central planning and membership of the Soviet Bloc. In fact, it was the most prosperous of the Eastern Bloc countries that comprised COMECON, but its growth rate was no match for the FRG. In motor vehicle manufacture, for example, by 1970 the FRG had a worldwide reputation for its Volkswagen, BMW and Mercedes Benz cars. The GDR, in contrast, produced the fibreglass-bodied Trabant!

These contrasts do not mean that the development of the FRG was without tensions and crises. In 1968, student riots and demonstrations occurred across western Europe. Initially these were linked to opposition to US involvement in the Vietnam War, but they soon became general demonstrations against West German society. In the 1970s more radical opposition occurred. A group of extreme left-wing students formed the Baader–Meinhof Group. This group took part in terrorist attacks across West Germany. Their attacks coincided with the problems caused by the 1973 oil crisis which had led to a fourfold increase in oil prices and a rise in inflation and unemployment.

The GDR developed into a 'niche' society. This was a term used by the FRG's first representative in the GDR, Gunter Gaus. He suggested that most East Germans had come to accept communism and they managed to live life as best they could. In the GDR citizens had a high standard of welfare provision and near full employment. They also prided themselves on having the highest living standards in the Soviet Bloc. As a result, they began to dissociate themselves from the worst aspects of communist rule, such as lack of press freedom and political repression. However, as the events of 1988–1989 showed, the idea of a 'niche' society came apart very rapidly when the prospect of moving to the FRG became a possibility.

The June 1953 uprising: revolution or Western plot?

The most important event in the history of the GDR before 1989 was the uprising on 15⁻17 June 1953. It began in East Berlin. In all, 500,000 East Germans demonstrated against the GDR government in 350 places. It was suppressed by the Soviet (Red) Army, and 50 demonstrators were killed in the process.

The immediate cause of the uprising was the government's decision to increase workloads by 10%, whilst keeping the same wage rate. This had to be done to help pay for the first Two-Year Plan. But before this proposal came into effect, Stalin died, in March 1953. The new Soviet leadership wanted a less harsh approach in the GDR in order to gain popularity. This 'New Course' was reluctantly accepted by Walter Ulbricht. However, the 10% workload increase remained. This led to the demonstrations in East Berlin. At 2.00 p.m. on 17 June the GDR government gave way on the 10% workload issue. However, demonstrators now changed their demands to free elections, free trade unions and price reductions.

In the GDR the uprising was portrayed as a Western attempt to undermine communism. In *Contemporary Germany* (2000), the historian Mark Allinson claimed the importance of June 1953 had been overstated – 'the rebellion was not general, but concentrated in a number of districts. The vast majority of the GDR population went about its business normally, and many defended the SED cause'. However, in 1993 two East German historians, Armin Mitte and Stefan Wolle claimed that the uprising was a virtual revolution. They based their views on evidence uncovered in the former GDR archives. They concluded that 'without the intervention of Soviet troops the GDR would have collapsed in June 1953 within a few days'.

The GDR did survive for another thirty-five years, but it was always dependent upon Soviet military support. When this was withdrawn it did collapse, in 1989.

1. Identify four ways in which the GDR was made a communist dictatorship in the years from 1949.

2. 'Compared to the FRG, the GDR was a failed state.' How far do you agree?

The building of the Berlin Wall, 1961

The GDR may have survived the 1953 uprising, but it was a state in crisis. Forced collectivisation and the creation of a Soviet-style regime forced hundreds of thousands to flee to the West. Before the uprising, 447,000 people had fled between January 1951 and April 1953. To stem the flow, the GDR sealed off the border with the FRG, except for Berlin, in early 1952. In 1957 westward migration was denounced and was punishable by up to three years in prison for those caught. But migration continued at an ever-increasing rate, primarily through Berlin. In 1960, 190,000 fled. In the first six months of 1961 a further 103,000 left. The GDR was on the verge of economic collapse. It was losing its young, skilled workforce.

The GDR problems coincided with a showdown between the USSR and the West. The Soviet leader, Nikita Khrushchev, demanded a renegotiation of Allied control of Berlin in November 1958. US–USSR relations deteriorated rapidly following 'the U2 incident' of 1959. In August 1961 Khrushchev was willing to accept GDR demands to close the last border between the GDR and the West. Ulbricht's Security Minister, Erich Honecker, planned the operation. On 13 August, East Germans began building the Berlin Wall. Known in the GDR as the 'Anti-Fascist Defence Wall' it completely sealed off East from West Germany. From 1961 to 1989 the border between the two Germanies was the most heavily defended in the world.

Berlin Wall, 7 September 1962

Although the construction of the Wall provoked a major international crisis, it saved the GDR from collapse.

The stable years, 1961–1989?

In 1963 the GDR launched the 'New Economic System'. Its aim was to decentralise economic decision-making. Instead of concentrating only on output, making profits and improving quality now became legitimate targets.

Although the GDR had living standards below the FRG, it did experience the best standard of living in the eastern Bloc. Between 1965 and 1970 the percentage of GDR workers owning fridges, for example, rose from 26% to 36% and those who owned TV sets rose from 28% to 54%.

In 1971 Ulbricht stepped down to be replaced by Honecker as leader of the GDR. Honecker reversed the policy of economic decentralisation, but he did embark on a major housing programme to tackle the acute housing shortage. Under his leadership, relations improved with the FRG during the period of détente and *Ostpolitik*, and the GDR was admitted to the UN. The GDR also began to develop as a major Olympic sporting nation, excelling in athletics and swimming. It was only after the fall of the GDR, in 1989, that the widespread use of illegal drugs to enhance their performance was admitted. In the interim, the GDR had performed well at the 1976, 1980 and 1988 Olympics. In the 1974 Football World Cup they even beat the holding nation, West Germany, 1–0, in the only competitive match between the two Germanies.

In 1978 Honecker even allowed a degree of religious toleration, making an agreement with the Protestant church leadership. The Stasi still watched over every aspect of GDR life. Now, however, most of the GDR could pick up West German television and many GDR citizens could witness the huge difference in life between East and West Germany.

However, in a totalitarian dictatorship, like the GDR, it was difficult to assess the degree of support for the regime. The USA and the West claimed that the GDR was a mere puppet of the USSR and only existed because of Soviet military force. The GDR claimed it was building a socialist society which had support from most of the population.

In 1985, when the new Soviet leader, Gorbachev, announced a radical new liberal course for the USSR and the eastern Bloc it was possible to test which of these views was closer to the truth.

1. Produce a timeline of the Cold War in Europe, as it applied to Germany.

Identify two periods of crisis. Identify a period of improving relations.

Who, or what, do you think was most responsible for the periods of crisis?

2. Assess the view that Erich Honecker was mainly responsible for the improvement of relations between the FRG and GDR in the years from 1969.

Erich Honecker (1912–1994)
Leader of the GDR from 1971 to October 1989. Born in the Saarland, in western Germany. Saarland was separated from Germany from 1920 to 1935 and became a separate area outside Germany from 1945 to 1955.

The son of a coal miner, he joined the Young Communist League in 1926 and the German Communist Party (KPD) in 1929. He worked as a roofer but was then sent to Moscow for training as a full-time organiser for the KPD. He was arrested by the Nazis in 1935 and was imprisoned until the end of the Second World War. In 1946 he joined the SED (new German communist party). In 1958 he became a member of the Central Committee of the SED. He rose to fame as the person who was in charge of building the Berlin Wall in 1961.

He was able to oust Ulbricht in 1971, and with Soviet support he became leader. Under his leadership he made sure that the GDR had the highest standard of living amongst the communist countries of Europe. In 1978 he made an agreement with the Protestant churches granting them more freedom. However, he would not tolerate any political opposition and the Secret Police (Stasi) maintained a tight surveillance of GDR society.

He opposed Gorbachev's reforms from 1985. His downfall was linked to the collapse of Soviet power across eastern Europe in 1989. Without Soviet support, he was ousted by Egon Krenz.

7.5 What were the main issues in foreign policy affecting East and West Germany in the years 1949–1989?

The impact of the Cold War

The foreign policy of the two Germanies was linked directly to the Cold War which developed from 1945. Germany became the battleground in the increasing tension between the USSR and the USA and its Western allies.

The two Potsdam conferences of 1945 decided the future of Germany immediately after the Nazi surrender. Germany was divided into four military zones of occupation. The USSR, USA, Britain and France each controlled one zone. In addition, a large part of pre-war Germany was handed over to Poland. This area contained approximately half of East Prussia and the whole of Silesia, which was a major industrial area. Half of East Prussia was given to the USSR. Also, Berlin, deep inside the Soviet zone, was divided into four occupation zones.

With the increase in tension between the West and the USSR, Germany became the centre of the first major post-war crisis – the Berlin Blockade of 1948–1949. In an attempt to prevent the Western Allies creating a pro-Western German state in their zones the USSR attempted to force the Western Allies out of their occupation zones in Berlin. The resultant crisis led directly to the creation of two German states. The three western zones comprised the Federal Republic of Germany (FRG). The German Democratic Republic (GDR) was created from the Soviet Zone.

West German rearmament in the early 1950s

During the first half of the 1950s West German rearmament became the central issue in the Cold War in Europe. By 1953 the US armed forces were stretched across the world and, in particular, in Korea. The US president, Eisenhower, planned to reduce US forces in Europe. To replace them it was suggested that West Germany be rearmed. This suggestion was treated with suspicion by both the USSR and France. The French, under the Pleven Plan of 1951, wanted any German armed force to be part of a western European army. But by 1954 the Pleven Plan was dead. In the following year the US persuaded France and the rest of NATO to accept West German rearmament, and West Germany was admitted to NATO. In retaliation, the USSR recognized the GDR as a sovereign state and also created the 'Warsaw Pact' – the Soviet equivalent of NATO – admitting the GDR as a member.

The Berlin Wall crisis of 1961

The most serious Cold War crisis involving Germany, since 1949, came in 1961 when the GDR and USSR built the Berlin Wall. To the GDR this development was a success. It stopped large-scale migration from the GDR to the FRG. However, it confirmed the idea that the FRG and GDR were completely separate states. At the height of the Cold War in 1961 the idea of German reunification was further away than at any time since 1945.

Willy Brandt and Ostpolitik

From 1963 the USSR and USA decided to lessen the tension in the Cold War. This led to a policy of détente by 1969. This coincided with the election of Social Democrat Willy Brandt as Chancellor. Brandt brought about a revolution in relations between the FRG and GDR. Until 1969 the main policy of the FRG towards the GDR was contained in the Hallstein Doctrine. This declared that the FRG would not have diplomatic relations with any country which had similar relations with the GDR. As many countries wished to trade with the FRG, this meant that the GDR was isolated internationally, except for support from communist states.

Brandt's policy was termed '*Ostpolitik*' (eastern policy). It took place at the same time as détente but was a distinct process. The high point of *Ostpolitik* was the Basic Treaty of December 1972, which accepted the division of Germany into two states but allowed for closer economic links. The FRG and GDR now recognised each other as independent states. The Basic Treaty had been preceded by other agreements with eastern European states:

- The Moscow Treaty (August 1970, with USSR) in which the FRG recognised the western borders of Poland. The treaty also supported the entry of the FRG and GDR to the United Nations.

- The Warsaw Treaty (December 1970, with Poland) which recognized the Oder–Neisse line as the western border of Poland. It also allowed Germans remaining in Poland to emigrate to the FRG.

- The Berlin Agreement (September 1971, with the USSR). The USSR recognised West Berlin's links with the FRG and agreed to better communication links between them.

The impact internationally was significant. In 1973 both the FRG and GDR became members of the United Nations. In 1975 the FRG and GDR signed the Helsinki Accords, which guaranteed human rights across Europe. It was the high water mark of détente.

Why did Germany become the centre of the 'Second Cold War', 1979–1985?

In 1979 détente came to an abrupt end with the Soviet invasion of Afghanistan. In 1980 the US boycotted the Moscow Olympics. In 1980 a free trade union movement, called 'Solidarity', developed in Poland. In 1981 martial law was introduced in Poland, and Solidarity was suppressed. A Second Cold War had begun.

Germany became the centre of the Second Cold War in 1983 when the USA placed Pershing II and Cruise missiles in western Europe. In the same year, NATO launched operation Able Archer, a major exercise. Historian John Lewis Gaddis regards this event as the most serious crisis in the whole Cold War, more serious than the Cuban Missile Crisis. If war had developed, Germany would have been the initial battleground.

However, in 1985 the USSR chose a new leader, Mikhail Gorbachev. Not only did Gorbachev lessen Cold War tensions, he created the climate for the eventual reunification of Germany in 1989–1991.

Mikhail Gorbachev (1931–)
Soviet leader from 1985 to 1991. Nobel Peace Prize winner in 1990.

Summary

Between 1945 and 1989 the two German states were products of the Cold War. The two states were the centre of periodic crises: 1948/49; 1961 and 1983. The border between the FRG and the GDR became the symbol of the division of Europe between East and West. However, even in the tense atmosphere of the Cold War, relations between the FRG and GDR did improve. The main contributor to this change had been West German Chancellor Willy Brandt. In 1983/84 the FRG loaned the GDR 1.95 billion Deutschmarks. This caused many commentators to suggest that the GDR was now financially dependent on its German neighbour. Yet in 1985 the division between FRG and GDR seemed to be as great as at any time since 1945. Everything had changed by 1989. In November of that year the Berlin Wall fell, and the rapid process for reunification had begun.

7.6 How significant was Helmut Kohl in bringing about German reunification in the years 1989–1991?

Can you link together the different factors mentioned in the mind map? Draw lines between them. Which do you think were more important for the fall of the GDR – the external reasons or the internal reasons?

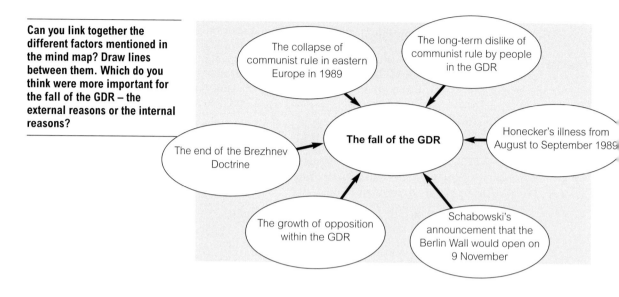

The period 1989 to 1990 is known as *Die Wende*. This literally means 'the change', and it refers to the reunification process. The process consisted of two separate but linked developments: the collapse of communist rule in the GDR in 1989 and the rapid process of reunification in 1990.

Why did communist rule collapse in the GDR in 1989?

1989 began as a year of promise for the GDR. It marked the fortieth anniversary of the founding of the state. It would be the crowning glory for East German leader Erich Honecker. In 1987 he had made an historic visit to the FRG and his home in Saarland. However, by the end of 1989 Erich Honecker had been removed from power and the GDR was on the point of collapse. How did such a revolutionary change take place?

The decline in Soviet power in eastern Europe

The SED government prided itself that the GDR was the most economically advanced country in the eastern Bloc. It also had the highest standard of living. In the world of sport the GDR had an international reputation in athletics and swimming. Honecker announced in January 1989 that the Berlin Wall would last for fifty – perhaps a hundred – years.

Yet the signs of its downfall were already apparent. In 1985, Soviet leader Mikhail Gorbachev had overseen major reforms in the USSR. The policies of perestroika (restructuring) and glasnost (openness) aimed to reverse the increasing economic decline of the USSR. These moves towards major political and economic reform were met with suspicion by Erich Honecker.

He feared the whole process of reform would undermine, not strengthen, communist rule in the GDR. The memoirs of Gunther Mittag, head of the GDR's economy, reveals how desperate things had become by 1983/84.

As the German historian Lother Kettenacker noted in 1997, once Gorbachev's reforms were introduced the GDR began to crumble.

Therefore, the collapse of the GDR cannot be separated from the collapse of Soviet power across eastern Europe. By the end of 1989, communist rule had collapsed in Poland, Hungary, Czechoslovakia, Romania and Bulgaria as well.

The Revolution of 1989

Leonid Brezhnev (1906–1982)
Soviet leader from 1964 to 1982. Responsible for the Brezhnev Doctrine of 1968 which declared that the USSR had the right to intervene militarily in Eastern Europe.

The beginning of the end began in Hungary. In April 1989 Mikhail Gorbachev visited Hungary. He made the momentous decision to abandon the Brezhnev Doctrine. First put forward in 1968 by Soviet leader Leonid Brezhnev, it claimed that the USSR had the right to intervene militarily across eastern Europe in order to defend communism. Without Soviet military power to support them, all communist regimes in the eastern Bloc were now vulnerable.

Within the GDR, opposition groups had already begun to form in 1986–1989. The two most important groups were the Protestant Church and New Forum.

In *The Unification of Germany 1989–1990*, historian Richard Leiby (1999) stated that the Protestant clergy were 'the real revolutionaries'. On 13 February 1986, Church leaders called a meeting for 'Justice, Peace and the Preservation of Creation'. Although suppressed by the Stasi, this meeting was the start of growing Church opposition to the SED. From 1986 to 1989 the Church provided leadership for the disillusioned – and their churches provided a base for opposition. New Forum was registered as a group with the GDR authorities on 19 September 1989. Organised by Barbel Bohley and Jutta Seidel, it claimed that communication between the SED government and GDR population had broken down. Its aim was to open up dialogue between government and people.

The beginning of open protest came following local elections in the GDR on 7 May 1989. The election results showed widespread support for the SED, but many believed that the elections had been manipulated by the government. The Church and New Forum led protests. Beginning with evening prayers, protestors took to the streets, most notably in Leipzig.

The turning point: 9 October

Politburo: The committee of ministers who ruled the GDR.

Tiananmen Square: Site of demonstrations in Beijing in June 1989 which demanded greater political freedom. Brutally suppressed by the Chinese army.

October was the month for the celebration of the creation of the GDR, and the Soviet leader, Mikhail Gorbachev, was the main guest. However, signs of the future collapse were already in place. In June, **Politburo** member and future GDR leader, Egon Krenz, congratulated the Communist Chinese leadership for suppressing the **Tiananmen Square** protestors. This showed that the GDR was unwilling to reform. On 10 September Hungary allowed GDR holidaymakers to leave the Eastern Bloc via Hungary to Austria, and thousands took the opportunity to leave.

At this critical point, Erich Honecker was ill – from 21 August to the end of September – with gall bladder problems.

On 9 October, Soviet leader Gorbachev arrived in the GDR. He informed the GDR leadership that 'life punishes those who come too late', suggesting that the GDR must reform itself. This lack of Soviet support was central to the collapse of the GDR.

A demonstration of 70,000 took place in Leipzig. The demonstrators demanded political change and supported non-violence. Another demonstration the same night occurred in Dresden. And this time the State Police did not disperse the demonstrators. This was the beginning of the end.

On the same day, FRG Chancellor, Helmut Kohl, warned the GDR leader that 'internal peace and stability cannot be guaranteed by force and by denying the people a voice.'

On 18 October Honecker was forced to resign, and he was replaced by

Helmut Kohl (1930–)
Pictured here right with Erich Honecker (see profile page 217) during a meeting in Bonn, West Germany, September 1978. Kohl was born in Ludwigshafen in SW Germany. A Catholic, his father was a civil servant. Leading CDU politician who was Chancellor of the FRG from 1982 to 1990, and then the first Chancellor of a reunited Germany, 1990–1998.

He joined the CDU in 1946. He studied at the universities of Frankfurt and Heidelberg, where he studied history and politics. He entered politics as a local councillor in Ludwigshafen in 1960. In 1963 he was elected to the state parliament of Rhineland-Palatinate. In 1969 he was elected Minister-President for the Rhineland-Palatinate. He rose to national prominence in 1973 when he became Federal Chairman of the CDU. In 1976 he was the CDU/CSU's choice as candidate for Chancellor. However, the SDP won the election. From 1976 to 1982 Kohl became leader of the CDU/CSU opposition in the federal parliament (Bundestag). In 1982 the coalition of the SDP and FDP collapsed and Kohl became Chancellor of a CDU/FDP coalition. In the 1983 federal elections Kohl won a major victory.

For much of the 1980s he worked closely with French President Mitterrand to strengthen the European Union. He also worked closely with the USA. He allowed the USA to place Cruise missiles on FRG soil in 1983. In 1987 he won another federal election.

His greatest hour came in 1989 to 1990 when he helped organise the peaceful reunification of Germany. He retired as Chancellor in 1998 and then retired from the federal parliament in 2002.

Krenz. Demonstrations across the GDR grew – 300,000 demonstrated in Leipzig on 23 October. On 1 November Krenz asked Gorbachev for support. But he received none – the USSR had abandoned the GDR to its fate. On 8 November, apart from Krenz, the entire Politburo was forced to resign by the senior SED membership. On 9 November, the new GDR leadership decided to open the Berlin Wall the following day. However, a gaffe by Günter Schabowski, first Secretary of the SED, at a press conference implied that the Wall would open that evening. Crowds from both East Berlin and West Berlin then met at the Wall and forced the opening up of the border crossings.

On 6 December Krenz was forced to resign, along with most of the SED leadership. Hans Modrow – a reformer – became prime minister. On 5

Egon Krenz (1937–)
Leader of the GDR for the last two months of 1989. Born in Kolberg, which is now in Poland but was in Germany then. His family were expelled by the Poles at the end of the Second World War. He joined the SED in 1955, becoming a member of the Politburo in 1963.

He replaced Honecker on 18 October 1989, following extensive demonstrations across the GDR demanding reform and freedom. In a desperate attempt to prevent the collapse of SED rule he fired the Prime Minister, Willi Stoph and two thirds of the Politburo on 7 November. On 9 November the Berlin Wall was opened and on 18 November Krenz formed a coalition government with other parties. This led to the resignation of the entire SED leadership. Krenz was forced to resign on 7 December 1989.

Hans Modrow (1928–)
The last Communist leader of the GDR. Took over from Egon Krenz on 7 December 1989. Born in Jasenitz, now in Poland. He served in the Volsturm (German Home Guard) at the end of the Second World War. Held as a POW by the USSR until 1949. Became senior SED official in Dresden in 1953 and became a member of the GDR parliament (*Volkskammer*).

Rose to national prominence on 13 November 1989 when he replaced Willi Stoph as prime minister. On 7 December he replaced Krenz as leader. He lost power in the first democratic elections to be held in the GDR in March 1990. Following reunification, he became an MP in the Federal parliament and an MEP.

February he formed a government including opposition representatives, and declared himself in favour of German reunification.

1989's political revolution

11 January	Hungary legalises independent political parties.
11 April	Soviet troops leave Hungary.
24 August	Communist rule ends in Poland.
10 September	Hungary allows thousands of GDR holidaymakers to cross the border into Austria.
1 October	Thousands of GDR citizens allowed to leave for FRG from FRG embassies in Poland and Czechoslovakia.
9 October	Leipzig demonstrations. These were not suppressed by the State Police.
18 October	GDR leader Honecker resigns.
9 November	Berlin Wall opened.

Celebrations at the Berlin Wall after unification, 1989

1. What message does this photograph give of the Berlin Wall?

2. What message does the photograph on page 215 give?

Summary

In the end, the GDR collapsed for a variety of reasons:

- Gorbachev's decision to abandon the Brezhnev Doctrine removed Soviet military support for the GDR.

- The rapid political change in the rest of the Eastern Bloc, in 1989, undermined the GDR leadership. The decision by Hungary to allow GDR citizens to leave for the West was the beginning of a major migration.

- Honecker refused to support political and economic change.

- His absence from power from 21 August to the end of September left the government leaderless.

- The growth of opposition within the GDR through the Protestant churches and groups such as New Forum.

- Krenz's decision not to use force to confront demonstrators from 9 October.

- The opening of the Berlin Wall on 9 November.

Even though communism collapsed in the GDR, by the end of 1989 there was no evidence to suggest this development would lead quickly to the reunification of Germany. It took the actions of the FRG Chancellor to achieve this change.

Helmut Kohl: the man who reunited Germany?

There were a number of obstacles in the way of German reunification at the start of 1990:

- First, the FRG and GDR were completely different societies. The FRG was a capitalist democracy with a strong economy. The GDR had been a communist dictatorship with a centrally planned economy. Even though the GDR had been the most prosperous Eastern Bloc state its economy was on the verge of collapse by 1989. There was no precedent in modern European history of uniting two states which were so different.

- Secondly, Germany had been the centre of the Cold War in Europe. Any attempt to unite Germany would have to get agreement between the USA and NATO on the one hand, and the USSR on the other.

- Thirdly, the leader of the main opposition party in the FRG, Oskar Lafontaine of the SDP, was against any rapid move to reunification.

Kohl's bombshell

The first significant act by Kohl came on 28 November 1989. He announced his '10 Point' plan to reunify Germany. He had done so without first notifying his NATO allies. The most significant policy was Point 5:

> We are ready to take a decisive step, that is, to develop confederational structures between both states of Germany with the aim of creating a federal state.

Kohl immediately appeared as 'the Chancellor of unity'. With a general election in 1990, this move gave Kohl considerable support in the FRG. In the FRG the dominant party was the CDU. In the GDR, the CDU was an important opposition party. However, Mrs Thatcher, British Prime Minister, and President Mitterrand of France both expressed concerns about Kohl's plan. It was also rejected by Krenz, the GDR leader.

The roles of the USA and the USSR

President George Herbert Bush was a key figure in supporting Kohl. The FRG was seen as the US's most dependable European ally. On 29 November the US gave cautious support to the idea of reunification, as long as it met four points:

- The form of unification should not be decided beforehand.

- Unity had to take place within NATO.

- Unity should be the result of a peaceful gradual process.

- The boundaries of the 'new' Germany should be the FRG and GDR.

The turning point for the rapid reunification of Germany came from Gorbachev. Having met Bush on 2/3 December 1989, Gorbachev announced that the USSR would not interfere with the wishes of the German people. This position was confirmed following a visit by Kohl to Moscow on 10 February 1990.

The key international support required for reunification came from the

Mrs Thatcher (1925–)
British prime minister from 1979 to 1990. Known as the 'Iron Lady'. She was a strident anti-communist and a strong supporter of US Presidents Reagan (1981–1989) and Bush.

Francois Mitterrand (1916–1996)
French president from 1981 to 1995.

George Herbert Bush (1924–)
US president from 1989 to 1993.

'Two plus Four Talks'. These involved the two German states (FRG and GDR) and the four Powers (USA, USSR, Britain and France). They began on 5 May and ended on 12 September. On 2 October the former wartime allies renounced all their former rights over Germany.

President Bush of the US was able to persuade the USSR, Britain and France to leave German reunification to the German people. They agreed that:

- The new Germany would be part of NATO.

- No foreign troops would be stationed in the former GDR.

- The USSR agreed to remove its troops by 1994.

- Germany renounced the right to make or use nuclear, chemical or biological weapons.

- The new German army would be 370,000 – far less than the old FRG armed forces.

The Cold War in Europe had begun in Germany and, in 1990, it ended there.

Kohl unites Germany

As a result of the actions of the USA and the USSR, it now all hinged on the first democratic election in the GDR, which was held on 18 March 1990. From December to March Kohl made several promises which speeded up the unification process. He promised a currency union where the GDR Ostmark would be equal to the FRG Deutschmark. He also promised that if the CDU-led 'Alliance for Germany' won the election, the GDR would be admitted to the FRG as five new *Länder*. As a result, the CDU-led alliance won a landslide victory with 48% of the votes. The first democratically elected leader of the GDR was de Mezière of the CDU.

The reunification process took place in two major parts. First, on 1 July 1990 a currency union was created with parity between the FRG and GDR currencies. The old GDR became part of the Deutschmark zone.

Then the FRG parliament, the Bundestag, admitted the GDR as five new *Länder* to the FRG, using Article 23 of the Basic Law, the FRG Constitution. On 31 August 1990 German unity was formally declared and came into effect on 3 October 1990.

1. Give three reasons why you think the GDR collapsed by the end of 1989.

What do you regard as the most important reason? Give reasons for your answer.

2. Does Helmut Kohl deserve to be regarded as the creator of German reunification in the years 1989 to 1990?

Summary

The reunification (*Die Wende*) occurred at exceptional speed. No one could foresee how quickly communist rule in Eastern Europe would collapse in the second half of 1989. When it did, FRG Chancellor Kohl acted quickly to create a united Germany. In the end, the FRG absorbed the former GDR. It was not a merger of equals. Also, *Die Wende* occurred at a unique time when the USSR was very weak internationally. By August 1991 Gorbachev was gone. In November 1992 Bush was defeated in the US presidential elections. Both these leaders had paved the way for Kohl to reunite Germany.

Source-based questions: The reunification of Germany 1989–1990

SOURCE A

(From a speech by FRG Chancellor, Helmut Kohl in Dresden, in the GDR, 19 December 1989)

The first thing I want to pass on to you is a warm greeting from all your fellow citizens in the Federal Republic of Germany.

The second thing I would like to communicate to you is my recognition and admiration for this peaceful revolution in the GDR. We are experiencing for the first time in German history a non-violent revolution that is taking place with such seriousness and in a spirit of solidarity. I thank you all very much for that. It is a demonstration for democracy, for peace, for freedom, and for the self-determination for our nation. And self-determination means for us in the FRG that we respect your opinion.

In my first discussion with the GDR leader, Hans Modrow, we agreed to work intensely in the next few weeks so that as early as spring we will be able to agree a treaty about cooperation between the FRG and GDR. We seek close cooperation in all areas: in economics, transportation, environmental protection and in culture. Above all, we seek in economics the closest possible cooperation, with the clear aim of improving living conditions in the GDR as quickly as possible. It is decisive for the future that the people of Germany be able to come together.

SOURCE B

(From an article by East German novelist, Gunther Grass, published in 1990. He was a holder of the Nobel Prize for Literature.)

I fear a Germany simplified from two states into one. I reject this move and would be relieved if it didn't come about. I fear I am already a traitor to the fatherland. Any fatherland of mine must be more diverse. It must be a fatherland that has grown through suffering to be more open to Europe. It comes down to a choice between a nightmare and a dream. Why can't we help the GDR to achieve enough stability to allow its citizens not to migrate to the FRG? Why do we not support German confederation rather than reunification? Do we want a super Federal Republic? Economic power would be concentrated in the old FRG. Isn't this more than we had ever dared hope for? Isn't closer links between the two German states what we should pursue?

SOURCE C

(From *Germany in 1989* written by German historian Klaus Larres, published in 2001)

While the first German revolution for over a century was brought to a successful end in October 1990, most of the revolutionary events occurred in 1989. The mass demonstrations on the streets of east German cities, the flight of thousands of people to the West via Hungary, and most importantly, the opening of the Berlin Wall and the downfall of Honecker all happened in 1989. In particular, the last two events meant there was no way back. It would however be wrong to claim that these changes would lead to eventual reunification. In early 1990 there was still serious talk within the GDR and the FRG of a democratic 'third way' for East Germany, maintaining it as an alternative and independent state to the FRG.

However, the successes of 1989 gave the vast majority of the East German people the motivation to continue their own agenda. They wanted better living conditions and democratic freedoms. These could be best achieved by unification with West Germany. The first serious calls for unification could be heard on the streets of Leipzig as early as 19 November 1989.

SOURCE D

(From *The Fall of the GDR* by British historian David Childs, published in 2001)

Hans Modrow, the GDR leader, kept in close contact with Moscow, but he found his influence was in steep decline with the Soviet leadership. It was Gorbachev who met him on 30 January 1990. He told Modrow, 'The majority of people in the GDR no longer support the idea of two German states and it seems impossible to preserve the GDR.' According to a West German magazine, *New Germany*, on 31 January 1990, Modrow was told by Gorbachev that there was an agreement between Germans in the East and in the West and the Four Powers that the unity of Germany was not in doubt.

This sealed the fate of the GDR. Two days later Modrow released his idea for 'Germany, united Fatherland'. This looked like a surrender, even treason, to some GDR leaders. There were more resignations from the government.

In February Modrow made a last ditch attempt to save his proposal for 'Germany, united

Fatherland'. This would involve confederation of the two German states, not reunification as such. This was rejected by Kohl, who insisted that he would wait until the outcome of the GDR March elections before going into talks on unity. The French newspaper, *Le Monde*, on 3 February rightly described the sudden conversion of Modrow to German unity as a reaction to the rising demands for unification from the masses and the continuing exodus of thousands of East Germans to the West.

SOURCE E

(From *Dividing and Uniting Germany* by two British historians, J.K. Thomanek and Bill Niven, published in 2001)

The leaders of the four countries which had been allies in World War II were equally overtaken by events in the GDR. By the time they came together for the first time on 5 May 1990 for talks with GDR and FRG leaders, they were aware that unification was totally unavoidable and that the timetable was now a matter of months. However, it was outside the Two Plus Four negotiations that the stumbling blocks to unification were removed. These were the question of a united Germany's membership of NATO and the removal of Soviet troops from the GDR. These questions were resolved at a historic meeting between Gorbachev and Kohl on 16 July 1990. Gorbachev conceded the membership of NATO and agreed to the removal of Soviet troops. On 12 September, the Two Plus Four negotiations were concluded in Moscow. This concluded in the end of the post-war period.

1. Study the sources and, using information contained in this chapter, explain the meaning of the following words and phrases (which have been highlighted):

(a) Federal Republic of Germany (Source A)

(b) The Berlin Wall (Source C)

(c) The Four Powers (Source D)

(d) NATO (Source E).

2. Study Source A. How does Helmut Kohl, by his use of language and style, try to persuade East Germans to support reunification?

3. Study Sources B and E. In what ways do these sources agree and disagree on the future of the GDR?

4. Study Sources A, C and D and information from the chapter. How far did the move to German reunification come from the people of the GDR?

5. Study sources A–E and information from this chapter. To what extent was the reunification of Germany due to Helmut Kohl's ability to exploit the desire for unity from the people of the GDR?

Further Reading

Texts designed for AS and A2 Level students

Germany from Defeat to Partition by D.G. Williamson in Seminar Studies in History series, Longman, 2001, covers the 1945 to 1963 period in both FRG and GDR. Contains sources in the final quarter of the book.

Dividing and Uniting Germany by J.K. Tomancek and Bill Niven, in Making of the Contemporary World series, Routledge, 2001.

More advanced reading

The Fall of the GDR by David Childs, Longman, 2001.

The Unification of Germany 1989–1990 by Richard A. Leiby, Greenwood Press,1999.

A History of Germany 1815–1990 by William Carr, Arnold,1991. Final two chapters cover the period 1945 to 1991.

Germany since 1945 by Pol O'Dochartaigh, in the Studies in Contemporary History series, Palgrave, 2003.

Germany since 1946 by Lothar Kettenacker, Opus, 1997.

Adenauer, Profiles in Power, by Ronald Irving, Longman, 2002.

The Longman Companion for Germany since 1945 by Adrian Webb in the Longman Companion to History series,1998.

Germany since World War II (Short Oxford History of Germany) by Klaus Larres, to be published in 2009.

Index

Glossary terms